P9-BTY-045

Stanley Cavell and the Claim of Literature

STANLEY CAVELL
AND THE CLAIM OF LITERATURE

David Rudrum

The Johns Hopkins University Press
Baltimore

Printed in the United States of America on acid-free paper
2 4 6 8 9 7 5 3 1

The Johns Hopkins University Press
2715 North Charles Street
Baltimore, Maryland 21218-4363
www.press.jhu.edu

Library of Congress Cataloging-in-Publication Data

Rudrum, David, 1974–
Stanley Cavell and the claim of literature / David Rudrum.
pages cm
Includes bibliographical references and index.
ISBN 978-1-4214-1048-7 (hardcover : alk. paper) — ISBN 978-1-4214-1049-4 (electronic) — ISBN 1-4214-1048-6 (hardcover : alk. paper) — ISBN 1-4214-1049-4 (electronic)
1. Literature—Philosophy. 2. Literature—History and criticism—Theory, etc. 3. Cavell, Stanley, 1926—Criticism and interpretation. I. Title.
PN49.R775 2013
801—dc23 2012048653

A catalog record for this book is available from the British Library.

Special discounts are available for bulk purchases of this book. For more information, please contact Special Sales at 410-516-6936 or specialsales@press.jhu.edu.

The Johns Hopkins University Press uses environmentally friendly book materials, including recycled text paper that is composed of at least 30 percent post-consumer waste, whenever possible.

For my son,
Cedric.
Daddy misses you.

Contents

Acknowledgments

First and foremost, let me begin by thanking everyone at the Johns Hopkins University Press, in particular Matt McAdam for taking an interest in this project and for his invaluable support.

It is equally important to thank my colleagues and my students at the University of Huddersfield. The full extent of my gratitude to them is, in fact, easily quantified: they afforded me the priceless opportunity of a semester of sabbatical leave, during which the introduction, chapters 2 and 7, and most of the conclusion were written. Without it, if I have done my sums right, about two-thirds of the pages in this book would yet be unwritten.

Intellectual debts, however, are harder to measure, and harder still to repay. My balance sheet in this project resembles that of most of today's Western governments: what I owe to my creditors far outstrips the value of my own output. For discussions of Beckett, I am immensely grateful to Stanley Cavell, Marjorie Perloff, James Conant, Paola Marrati, James Noggle, Anselm Haverkamp, Christoph Menke, Katrin Trüstedt, Hent de Vries, and Christopher Johnson. For the chapter on Wordsworth, I am similarly indebted to Richard Eldridge, Kim Evans, Asja Szafraniec, James Loxley, and Andrew Taylor. Thanks to Jami Bartlett and her colleagues at the University of California, Irvine, for inviting me to talk about tragedy, and to Jan Balakian and Joshua Polster for the opportunity to air my views on Miller—both were immensely rewarding experiences. Ralph Berry, Garry Hagberg, and Lawrence Rhu formed a phenomenal triumvirate of brains to pick. My colleague Merrick Burrow made some helpful suggestions about finding a publisher for this project, and my friend Tim Shaw has helped me develop some fun ways of teaching the ideas herein. The oldest of these debts, however, is to Josh Cohen, who about ten years ago handed me a syllabus to teach that steered me away from my fixation on Wittgenstein and Beckett and toward Thoreau's *Walden* and Poe's "The Imp of the Perverse," thereby—unbeknownst to us both—sketching out the perimeter of this project for me.

An earlier version of chapter 3 appeared as "From the Sublime to the Ordinary: Stanley Cavell's Beckett" in *Textual Practice* 23, no. 4 (August 2009): 543–58, and chapter 5 was published in an earlier form as "What Did Cavell Want of Poe?" in *Angelaki* 10, no. 3 (December 2005): 91–99. Both are used here by permission of the publisher, Routledge (Taylor & Francis Ltd., http://www.tandf.co.uk/journals). An earlier version of chapter 4 appeared, under the same title, as chapter 11 in *Stanley Cavell: Philosophy, Literature, and Criticism*, edited by Andrew Taylor and James Loxley (Manchester: Manchester University Press, 2012), pp. 166–80. I am grateful to Manchester University Press for permission to use this material here.

In the final analysis, I am most heavily indebted to Alice, to my sister Julia, and to my parents, Malcolm and Helga. They helped me see the funny side of debating the politics of marriage whilst my own was in free fall. Writing about the link between the idea of America and a tragic father-son relationship was not easy at a time when, tragically, my own son was being taken from me to live there. So it is finally to him that I dedicate this volume. Cedric, I only wish I could have spent the time it took to write this book with you instead.

Abbreviated Titles

The following abbreviations are used to refer to Stanley Cavell's works:

CHU	*Conditions Handsome and Unhandsome: The Constitution of Emersonian Perfectionism*. Chicago: University of Chicago Press, 1991.
CoR	*The Claim of Reason: Wittgenstein, Skepticism, Morality, and Tragedy*. New ed. Oxford: Oxford University Press, 1999.
CoW	*Cities of Words: Pedagogical Letters on a Register of the Moral Life*. Cambridge, MA: Belknap Press of Harvard University Press, 2004.
CT	*Contesting Tears: The Hollywood Melodrama of the Unknown Woman*. Chicago: University of Chicago Press, 1990.
DK	*Disowning Knowledge in Seven Plays of Shakespeare*. Updated ed. Cambridge: Cambridge University Press, 2003.
IQO	*In Quest of the Ordinary: Lines of Skepticism and Romanticism*. Chicago: University of Chicago Press, 1988.
MWM	*Must We Mean What We Say? A Book of Essays*. New ed. Cambridge: Cambridge University Press, 2001.
PDAT	*Philosophy the Day after Tomorrow*. Cambridge, MA: Belknap Press of Harvard University Press, 2005.
PoH	*Pursuits of Happiness: The Hollywood Comedy of Remarriage*. Cambridge, MA: Harvard University Press, 1981.
PoP	*A Pitch of Philosophy: Autobiographical Exercises*. Cambridge, MA: Harvard University Press, 1994.
PP	*Philosophical Passages: Wittgenstein, Emerson, Austin, Derrida*. Oxford: Blackwell, 1995.
SoW	*The Senses of Walden*. Expanded ed. Chicago: University of Chicago Press, 1992.
TNYUA	*This New Yet Unapproachable America: Lectures after Emerson after Wittgenstein*. Albuquerque, NM: Living Batch, 1989.
TOS	*Themes Out of School: Effects and Causes*. Chicago: University of Chicago Press, 1984.

Stanley Cavell and the Claim of Literature

INTRODUCTION

Approaching the Unapproachable

Stanley Cavell is among the most influential and significant of contemporary philosophers. His works have achieved a level of eclecticism unparalleled in Anglo-American thought. Not only does Cavell's philosophy succeed in accommodating the "ordinary language" tradition of J. L. Austin and Ludwig Wittgenstein with the "continental" tradition from Kant to Derrida and the American tradition of thought represented by Emerson and Thoreau, but his writings more generally seek to reconcile the discipline of traditional academic philosophy with a range of other humanistic disciplines, including psychoanalysis, film, music, the arts, and, above all, literature.

This eclecticism has made Cavell as many enemies as it has friends, particularly in Anglo-American philosophy departments, where the rigorously logical procedures of analytic philosophy are deeply entrenched in the very conception of what philosophy is taken to be. Coming to the philosophical scene at a time when logical positivism, with its relegation of statements about ethics or aesthetics to the condition of nonsense, was still a recent memory (and sometimes still a driving force), Cavell began what he has called "a lifelong quarrel with the profession of philosophy" (*TOS*, p. 31) by championing the innovative view of language put forward by J. L. Austin in his (then) brand-new William James lectures, which would later become famous as the groundbreaking text *How To Do Things With Words*. Challenging philosophy's very conception of itself—and particularly the conception of philosophy on offer in the model of analytic philosophy he had inherited—Cavell has from the very outset of his career confronted the limits of his discipline, winning him both admirers among those discontented with the formation of contemporary philosophy and critics among those hostile to changing it.

An integral part of Cavell's strategy has been to complement his challenges to philosophy's conception of itself by highlighting moments of intersection and possibilities of rapprochement between philosophy and other disciplines that, when philosophers are not snubbing with oblivious indifference, they have regarded as competitors. The discipline toward which Cavell has repeatedly turned, from his very first book, *Must We Mean What We Say?*, right up to his most recent work, and with which he has engaged in more depth and more variety than any other discipline, is the study of literature. Through extensive, provocative, and rigorous engagements with authors ranging from Shakespeare to Ibsen, from the romantics to Beckett, his writings avowedly seek to explore "the participation of philosophy and literature in one another" (*IQO*, p. 12).

This aspect of Cavell's philosophical project soon brought it to the attention of a small number of literary critics and theorists, who took a keen interest in its interdisciplinarity. "In Cavell's work," said an early commentator, "literature is always bringing to mind philosophy, and philosophy is always opening itself to literature, generating a dialogue that transforms each one."[1] It is important to emphasize the mutual reciprocity of this process: Cavell is not to be understood, as some hostile literary critics would have it, as imposing or foisting the concepts and methodologies of philosophy onto poetic and literary texts, whose creativity is thereby sidelined or even shackled. As Cavell himself has put it, "The burden of my story in spinning the interplay of philosophy with literature is not that of applying philosophy to literature, where so-called literary works would become kinds of illustrations of matters already independently known" (*DK*, p. 179). Instead, his works call for, and put into practice, what Cavell has dubbed "a new literary-philosophical criticism" (*MWM*, p. 110). But here too there is the possibility for misunderstanding. Cavell, much as he is committed to questioning the divide between literature and philosophy, is scrupulously careful not to efface it. His own writings fit neatly a description he gives of Wittgenstein's as "challenging any given distinction between supposed genres of philosophy and literature that I am aware of. . . . Notwithstanding, it does not follow that the distinction between philosophy and literature is thereby meant to be levelled, but rather that the genres occur simultaneously, and perhaps work to deepen their differences, even to bring them to a crisis."[2]

Thus, Cavell's take on the interdisciplinary relationship between literature and philosophy differs in several crucial ways from those of his contemporaries. He does not take the rather hierarchical or, if you will, imperialistic view that sees the role of philosophical aesthetics as legislating for critical practice. Nor does he take the pragmatist view epitomized by Richard Rorty, according to which the difference between a philosophical text and a literary one is essentially institutional, and one that both philosophers and literary critics would do better to leave to university administrators and librarians rather than see it as threatening the intellectual integrity of their disciplines. Nor does he take the classic deconstructive view—though he does, to an extent, share its emphasis on the textuality of philosophy and its concomitant exposure to the same widespread ambiguity and paradox in expressing itself that literature is heir to. The fact is that Cavell constantly resists the urge to provide any neat formulation of the relationship between philosophy and literature as he sees it.

I will have more to say about this in due course, but the sheer openness of Cavell's position on this question can be gauged from his statement that "I do not deny that there are differences . . . between philosophy and literature or between philosophy and literary criticism; I am suggesting that we do not understand these differences. At various moments I am led to *emphasize* distinctions between philosophy and various of its competitors" (*MWM*, p. xxxii), while at other moments he is equally concerned to minimize these differences, as when he declares that "the literary is essential to the power of philosophy; at some stage the philosophical becomes, or turns into, the literary" (*IQO*, p. 109). For some, this would no doubt be a classic instance of Cavell's flatly contradicting himself. But there is, in reality, no contradiction here; rather, if philosophical and literary texts and disciplines appear to merge into one another at times and to segregate themselves at others, then this points toward incoherencies in the way each discipline is conceived, practiced, and taught rather than toward incoherencies in Cavell's thinking. Put this way, the very idea that there can be *a* relationship between literature and philosophy is itself incoherent, given the vastly broad variety of texts subsumed under each term. Cavell's refusal to formulate a neat account of this relationship is thus a good deal more coherent than an attempt from either discipline to impose an artificial unity upon it.[3]

And yet the absence of such a neat account has itself proved troublesome for the reception of Cavell's thought, especially on the literature side of the divide. Literary theorists, particularly those of the period from the late 1960s to the late 1980s, when Cavell's central texts were published, all too often felt that it was the task of literary theory to "translate" or "adapt" the work of a particular thinker—say Derrida, or Foucault, or Lacan, or Bakhtin—into a particular method or, perhaps, technology for the reading, evaluation, and criticism of literary texts. In short, it was necessary to construct a Derridean—or Foucauldian, or Lacanian, or Bakhtinian—literary theory. In all these constructs, the thinkers' key terms needed to be extracted from their works, and a set of procedures extrapolated for applying them to novels, poems, and plays. Happily, Stanley Cavell's work presents such literary theorists with the starkly obvious hopelessness, not to mention philosophical emptiness, of proceeding this way. As Michael Fischer, the author of the first book on Cavell, put it:

> A bibliography on Cavell seems disappointingly short and well-worn . . . (who hasn't already read *Walden* or the "Intimations Ode"?) and a Cavell glossary seems as superfluous as defining "ordinary" and "acknowledgment," to mention only two of his key terms. Appreciating Cavell means not just valuing everyday life and ordinary language but trying to hold onto their considerable insights. For an academic reader Cavell is thus difficult in a disconcerting way.[4]

In a nutshell, if Cavell's writings on literature show us anything, it is that no serious student of either literature or philosophy can rest on the laurels of a predefined theoretical or methodological approach to his or her subject. Insights into texts from either field are not to be gained by bringing ready-made answers to them. In this respect, Cavell is emphatically *not* a literary theorist, and if readers of this book hope or anticipate that its task is to expound some kind of "Cavellian theory of literature" or "Cavellian literary theory," they will be—and quite possibly deserve to be—disappointed: such terms are vapid oxymorons. This disappointment will, I hope, be compensated for by their discovering instead a thinker whose writings shed fresh light on such crucially important literary topics as the act of reading; the role of the author; the relationship between ordinary language, literary language, and performative language; the status of literary characters; and the nature of ethics and politics in literary study—and yet who does so in ways that cannot be reduced to, or subsumed under, a pat, simplistic theoretical rubric. Each of Cavell's essays on a literary text derives its import from its specificity and sensitivity to that particular text and to the philosophical concerns he regards that text as raising. For this reason, constructing an artificial mode of Cavellian theory from his work is as impossible as it is ultimately undesirable.

Indeed, Cavell has, for most of his career, been gloriously at odds with the principal trends in late twentieth-century literary theory, such as New Historicism or deconstruction. Speaking of the latter in particular, and of what he has called "my, let's say, ambivalence toward deconstruction" (*PoP*, p. 84), he has often acknowledged his common ground with it—for example, how "at one stroke" it seemingly provides a simultaneous solution to the exclusion of the literary from philosophy's attention, to the exclusion of continental philosophy from American philosophy departments, and to the problem of "philosophy's indifference to the literary conditions of its own existence," all of which Cavell lists as among his principal quarrels with philosophy as practiced in America (see *TOS*, pp. 31–32). Yet his resistance to endorsing too strongly the many obvious similarities of concern between his own work and deconstruction has to do largely with the way that the claims deconstruction makes—claims of subjecting itself and the texts it studies to ongoing and potentially endless textual and philosophical examination—are belied by the way this supposedly iconoclastic, interrogative, antifoundational enquiry has been reduced by the academy to a stable methodology that contains, rather than multiplies, the very questions it seeks to ask. Cavell's ambivalence toward deconstruction, then, hinges precisely on the way it has been appropriated and transformed into a systematic literary theory:

> The very success of deconstruction in American literary theory should give one to think that the idea of deconstruction as an incessant questioning of itself is an illusion, an ideological pitch; to think that precisely what deconstruction provides is a mechanism of answer, a set of routines that makes unendingness, questionability, instability, undecidability, into a safe, lilting doctrine, with answers prepared for every objection, and a prepared, confined place and shape for every apparent lack of answer. And it provides the great reassurance of having plenty of company while yet maintaining the air of subversion.[5]

By contrast with the way that so many rigorous and challenging thinkers and philosophers have found their insights tamed and harnessed by the systematizing process of constructing a literary theory from them, Cavell's work has thus far remained—thankfully—impervious to this process. Perhaps the most and the best that can be said of any "method" in his tremendously varied interpretations of literary and philosophical texts is this: "My aim in reading is to follow out in each case the complete tuition for a given intuition (tuition comes to an end somewhere)" (*DK*, p. 5). This constant and ceaseless refusal, throughout the length of his forty-year career, to nail his colors to a procedural, methodological, or theoretical mast is perhaps the most refreshing, original, and worthwhile aspect of his work, since he thereby liberates himself from the confines of a particular and specific approach to his subject. This is why there can be no such thing as a "Cavellian theory" or a "Cavellian approach" to literature—and it's a good thing too.

II

Let us pause for a moment to ask what is meant by having, or taking, a particular "approach" to literature. In both of the last two universities where it has been my privilege to teach, the introductory course on literary theory was renamed "Approaches to Literature" on the basis that the word *theory* in the title "Introduction to Literary Theory" might seem daunting, or just plain boring, to students in their first year of university study. Why should it be any less intimidating, or any more exciting, to have an "approach" to literature than to have a "theory" of it? What, indeed, does it *mean* to "approach" a text?

Cavell sets himself this very question in the introduction to his study of a text by Ludwig Wittgenstein:

> I was supposed to be saying something more . . . first, by way of introducing myself, and concerning how we should approach Wittgenstein's text. Accordingly, I will say, second, that there is no approach to it, anyway I have none. Approach suggests moving nearer, getting closer; hence it suggests that we are not already near or close enough; hence suggests we know some orderly direction to it not already taken within it; that we sense some distance between us and it which useful criticism could close. (*CoR*, p. 6)

Looking at it this way, one wonders what gives us so much as the very idea that we *can* "approach" literature, as if somehow it lay too far off from our present coordinates and we needed either to move it from its present position toward ours or else to pack our critical baggage together and move to within commutable distance of it.

Cavell takes up this question of "approaching" in a book that takes its title from a quotation from Emerson. When Emerson refers to what he calls "this new yet unapproachable America," Cavell asks, not unreasonably, "Why is this new America said to be yet unapproachable?" (*TNYUA*, p. 91). His answer is that Emerson finds America unapproachable precisely because he "is already there" (*TNYUA*, p. 91), and so "its presence to us is unapproachable . . . because there is nowhere *else* to go to find it" (*TNYUA*, p. 92). The trouble with this answer, of course, is that it appears anticlimactic, banal, and so downright obvious as to be utterly empty. Once we have realised that, for someone in Emerson's predicament, "there is no nearer for him to get since he is already there," we can scarcely avoid the feeling that "somehow that itself is what is disappointing, that this is what there is" (*TNYUA*, p. 108).

I want to suggest that the readers and students of literary texts, and perhaps of many philosophical ones too, stand in a relation to their subject that is precisely Emerson's predicament vis-à-vis his new America. Literary theory—and literary studies as a discipline—has all too often fostered in its students the assumption that a specific method, theory, or approach can get us closer to literature, or can get literature closer to us. Such an assumption is not so much either true or false as it is unquestioned, unexamined, and hence potentially spurious. It is not that the various theories of literature and their claims are simply wrong or unable to withstand scrutiny—one could hardly argue that of such a broad and complex field without descending to oversimplification or obscurantism—but rather that they inculcate, at the same time as they profess that their procedures furnish us with an *approach* to literature, the very sense of critical distance from it that approaching it aright ought to efface. No theory of literature that I am aware of is altogether exempt from the paradoxical tendency to regard its object from a position of scholarly detachment or even remoteness while simultaneously promising to yield a fresh, heightened degree of proximity or even intimacy with the selfsame object of study. Perhaps the starkest example of this paradox can be dated right back to one of the discipline's defining moments: I. A. Richards's commitment to maintaining a critical, scientific distance from the text, while arguing that this distance is essential to an approach he calls "close" reading.

Stanley Cavell, in his writings on literature, does not feel the need to spell out an "approach." For example, when writing on Shakespeare, as we shall see in chapter 2, he prefers each play to set before us its own conception of the key philosophical issues behind it. Shakespeare's plays turn out to offer us critical insights into such crucial themes as history, philosophy, and even theatricality itself. Similarly, Wordsworth's poetry is said to articulate its own understanding of poetic language and how it works, while Poe's story "The Imp of the Perverse" also turns out to meditate on the theme of writing, and Thoreau's *Walden* on the theme of reading *Walden*. Rather than approach these texts from afar, viewing them through the lens of a theory that constructs the critical difference we perceive between ourselves and it, Cavell prefers that literature itself teach us how to approach it and, indeed, whether any closer proximity to it—so often a wistful fantasy of intimacy—is necessary or even desirable. Perhaps this is a roundabout way of saying that instead of needing a set of theoretical terms with which to approach literature, we must learn to read it on its own terms.

If I am right that a reader's relationship to literature is analogous to Emerson's relationship to his new America—and particularly that there is no approach that would get us closer to it—then sooner or later any reflective reader of any text is liable to feel, like Cavell's Emerson, that "*I* cannot get 'it' nearer . . . ; if it is to become nearer *it* must come nearer, draw closer" (*TNYUA*, p. 108). But for this to happen, "we have to turn toward it" (*TNYUA*, p. 92). For Cavell, then, there is an important sense in which, rather than *our* "approaching" literature, it is *literature* that approaches *us*: " 'I cannot get it nearer' . . . is, precisely, the direction of reception, or being approached," he says (*TNYUA*, p. 109). The question becomes, then, whether we are up to the task of being receptive to literature once it approaches us. And unlike the approachability peddled by the various theories of literature, there is no predictably theorized, prescribed, mapped out direction from which this kind of approach may come. Cavell's reorientation of the question of approaching the unapproachable thus becomes a matter of fostering our openness and receptivity as readers, our openness to whichever direction literature approaches us from. As Cavell says of Emerson, "In specifying his inability to get it nearer he is leaving a direction open," a direction Cavell goes on to name "indirection" (*TNYUA*, pp. 108–9).

Reformulating the issue of the "approach" as something texts do to readers as much as readers do to texts is, at least potentially, a revolutionary move. It is perhaps related to Heidegger's description of the work of art as "letting truth happen," a description that, as Cavell has observed, applies equally well to philosophy (see *TNYUA*, p. 3). If we are to accept this reorientation, then straightaway it becomes clear why it is important to Cavell that we allow literary texts to teach us the terms and concepts by which to understand them. Doing so is the very opposite of mastering an independent set of theoretical terms and concepts with which we (imagine we) "approach" them. And yet, I can imagine, just as the untested assumption that we can "approach" a text is potentially spurious, so too the idea that we can let a text approach us and teach us an understanding of itself is equally questionable. For some philosophers, the very idea of understanding a thing "in its own terms" would be nonsensical, while for others, it would have to involve a paradox no less self-contradictory than that of the distance/proximity paradox of an "approach" to literature. That is, if the terms and concepts by which we are to understand a text are to be learned from the text itself, how could we ever reach a position whereby we understood it well enough to grasp its key terms and concepts? Surely we would have to understand a text solidly before we could master its terms and concepts, yet on this account it is the terms and concepts that teach us the understanding of the text. Stephen Mulhall, one of Cavell's earliest exponents and expositors, helpfully demonstrates how this paradox is itself a confusion arising from the false picture foisted upon us by the idea of approaching literature:

> Our paradox was: if the terms needed to approach a book can only be learned from the book itself, how can we ever begin to learn from it, this or anything? It can now be seen that the misunderstanding here arises from our having recourse to the idea of there being an approach to the text—for that places us entirely outside the text, and makes the text entirely opaque to us. The reality is that anyone capable of opening its covers is already close enough to learn from it—in part because no reader can begin a text entirely without a range of relevant capacities and experiences, or a basic orientation toward it; in part because to begin to read it is to begin to learn from it, which includes beginning to learn how to read it.[6]

This is why Cavell's writings on literature are so distinctive and so refreshingly different from most contemporary literary theory: he recognizes the risks and accepts the challenges of "leaving myself . . . without an approach" (*CoR*, p. 6), embracing it as a means of refreshing our understandings of literature and how we read it.

The lack, or, better, the refusal to set out any prescripted "approach" and the related impossibility of formulating a Cavellian theory of literature go some way toward explaining why many commentators on the subject feel that Cavell's writings on literature have been neglected, or at any rate underappreciated, by literary critics and theorists. As Garrett Stewart has observed, while Cavell has written "some of the most passionate and commanding essays on literary aesthetics and literary value to be found anywhere in the postwar critical canon," the uptake of his work in literary circles has until very recently been slight, leading Stewart to ask, "Why has this work been to a discernible extent overlooked in the discussions that stand most to gain from engaging it?"[7] The question, as Stewart is aware, is a complex and frequently asked one:

> My essay lines up behind several others of the last decade on the regrettable undercirculation of Cavell's ideas. This alone may give pause. How many books and articles on the disciplinary nonassimilation of Stanley Cavell's thinking would begin to count as redress? But then that is not exactly the right question. The point is not to decide how much Cavell is appreciated, or not, or how widely, or even how deeply—and then to fill the gap. The point is to wonder (and so to ask out loud) why there persists a particular *kind* of "hesitancy"—or resistance—wherever the work is quarantined from serious consideration.[8]

Michael Fischer, the first to address Cavell's "neglect by American literary theorists,"[9] put it down to the fraught relationship between Cavell's work and America's then dominant penchant for deconstruction. Richard Wheeler, on whose work Stewart builds, pointed out that many of Cavell's concerns, such as the autonomy of the artwork or the intentions of the author, are apt to strike poststructuralist theory as those of an unfashionably liberal humanist: from Althusser's Marxism to Lyotard's postmodernism, the "human" has all but vanished from the discourse of continental literary theory, while in America the success of New Historicism has laid down an emphasis on historical context that is very different from Cavell's. Accordingly, his writings on literature, when they are not distancing themselves from deconstruction and its allies, may very well strike literary theorists as simply out of touch.

A better explanation may well be needed, however, because in recent years Cavell has written sympathetically about such key figures in literary theory as Maurice Blanchot, Walter Benjamin, and Emmanuel Levinas, and yet these essays have done comparatively little to establish diplomatic links between his philosophy and literary theory. That is not to say that Cavell remains a marginal figure; on the contrary, his work is attracting more interest in literary studies than ever before, and a steady stream of published work on the relationship between the two has recently gathered pace. However, this work is not theoretical, or, more precisely, it does not seek to establish or employ some kind of Cavellian literary theory. Rather, Cavell is becoming a crucially important thinker precisely because his work does *not* involve what I have elsewhere described as the "detour" through literary theory: it practices instead a face-to-face dialogue between the literary and the philosophical.[10] Cavell's new-found recognition as an important and influential model for interdisciplinary readings of literary and philosophical texts derives, then, from the encouraging development that, in his own words, "the time is passing in which the onslaught of literary theory in these decades served mostly to exacerbate the mutual distrust of philosophical and literary studies."[11]

And so Cavell's writings on literature provide us with what we might call an alternative to literary theory. It is an alternative in which philosophical and literary texts are able to interact and take the measure of each other in ways that can generate new insights into both: "Why philosophy and literature do not know this about one another—and to that extent remain unknown to themselves—has been my theme it seems to me forever," he says (*IQO*, p. 155). Yet the nature of this interaction, and of the insights it produces, is unstable and unpredictable and hence rather like the way in which literature approaches us, something that is open and to be left open, or, better, kept open. Cavell's rather experimental manner of keeping the interaction between philosophy and literature open forms the subject of the next section.

III

"But can philosophy become literature and still know itself?" With these words, Stanley Cavell concludes his masterpiece *The Claim of Reason* and thereby poses a question for his readers that he leaves unanswered. This is a strategy that Cavell has drawn on throughout his long and distinguished philosophical career. During the course of this book, several other examples will arise, such as "Must We Mean What We Say?," "What Did Derrida Want of Austin?," "Who Does the Wolf Love?," and "Politics As Opposed to What?" Clear answers to these questions are something of a rarity.[12] For Mulhall, this is because "his words should be acknowledged as genuine rather than a rhetorical question—one that his work is designed also to pose with respect to philosophy and psychoanalysis and to philosophy and cinema, and to which he does *not* claim to know the answer."[13] For a traditional philosopher, this would be a problematic stance to take up: philosophers, surely, ought to know, or rather *discover* or at the very least *suggest*, the answers to the questions they ask. Put simply, philosophers are supposed to be in the answers business.

That Cavell does not see it as incumbent upon him to answer so many of the questions he poses to literature[14] and its all-too-often troubled relationship with philosophy results in a discursive strategy that is not only apt to frustrate his first-time readers but also liable to call into question the very basis of his claim to philosophy. In a moment of conversational candor he confessed to "a guilty philosophical conscience," pondering whether "I may be asking something of the literary that the philosophical should scrupulously deny itself, something that plays with truth."[15] This would be a dangerous admission indeed for a philosopher who has accused certain of his contemporaries in literary theory of "literary softness posing as philosophical hardness" (*IQO*, p. 133) and gone on to insist, in his critiques of deconstructive literary critics in particular, that "I can recognize no expression of mine to be philosophical which simply thinks to escape my profession's paradigms of comprehensibility; so that the invocations of the name of philosophy in current literary debate are frequently not comprehensible to me as calls upon philosophy" (*TOS*, p. 32). After all, if the answers certain literary critics provide to their questions strike Cavell as incomprehensible—answers, predictably, that often turn out "always already" to involve "undecidability," "aporia," or other deconstructive clichés—then is it more comprehensible, from the point of view of philosophy, to provide no answers at all? Surely this strategy takes Wittgenstein's conclusion in the *Tractatus* rather too far.

And yet, that said, there are circumstances in which withholding an answer is indeed the best answer one can give. Cavell, in his defense, has a fine nose for such occasions. As Mulhall puts it, "The form taken by his acknowledgement as a philosopher of the otherness of the disciplines that abut his own is that of posing or asking questions about them; on his view, giving answers to those questions (whatever they may be) would amount to severing rather than maintaining those relationships, and so failing to acknowledge them."[16] That is, no philosopher can truly be said to take an interest in literary criticism, and no literary critic can truly be said to take an interest in philosophy, if they come to their work with a ready-made notion of what kind of interdisciplinary link they are trying to forge. Cavell, to his credit, and to the immeasurable benefit of both literature and philosophy, prefers simply to keep the precise nature of the connection open. He states that his "primary business" with both subjects is "the reading of a set of texts . . . placing them in a loosely woven net of concepts. The point of the loose weave is to register that I am as interested in the weaving together of these texts as I am in their individual textures, and that I wish to leave open, or keep open usefully, how it is one gets from one to another of them" (*IQO*, pp. 3–4). This strategy of leaving questions unanswered then becomes a crucial tactic in the keeping open of the central question of interdisciplinary communication between literature and philosophy:

> Is the issue of communication between philosophy and literature itself a philosophical or a literary issue? Something mannerly and no doubt something unmannerly in my prose is caused by my acceptance of such a question and by my refusal to decide it prematurely, to decide it judiciously ("It is both"), or to decide that it is undecidable ("It is neither quite") before closing with it, keeping it open, enacting it, experimenting. (*DK*, p. 3)

Thus, the lack of answers to questions pertaining to literature and philosophy is neither a defect nor yet a withholding: it is a form of experimentation with concepts and ideas, embodied in the experiment of Cavell's unique style of writing.

To call Cavell's prose "experimental" is, I trust, to do it more justice than did the first readers of *The Claim of Reason*, whose reviewers—Anthony Kenny, for example—found its idiosyncratic style all but impenetrable.[17] The fact is that he is asking questions of philosophy that are asked in different contexts of literature—"What is philosophy? How is it to be written?" (*MWM*, p. xxxvii)—and seeking answers in the process of writing and discussing the topic. That is what is "experimental" about his prose. Many philosophers choose to call it "literary," though there is a degree of dissensus as to what is meant by this. Most of the first philosophers to read his books considered it in some way a bad thing; most of the first literary critics considered it importantly heuristic. As Michael Fischer put it, "Cavell thus does not simply cite literature, but in his own prose—for better or for worse—draws on the resources of literature in responding to philosophical skepticism."[18] Another early literary commentator observed of *The Claim of Reason* that it is:

> written in a literary spirit. It is a text of philosophical parables, allegories, myths, and metaphors; it invites us to understand philosophy from a literary perspective. But is it so written simply to challenge us to compare and contrast philosophical and literary contexts? Why is the text constructed and written as it is, and why is it enveloped with a literary spirit? What is the value of a literary context? It seems that for Cavell the literary context is one which encourages, allows, and exhibits many-voices, many-perspectives, self-reflection, and self-criticism; it encourages what we might call a philosophical pluralism. . . . Just as the spirit of Wittgenstein's *Philosophical Investigations* is presented by Cavell as one of self-criticism, multiple-perspectives, and many-voices, i.e., as literary, so Cavell's own text . . . is self-reflective, self-critical, and spoken with many-voices.[19]

While I do not wish to disagree with this description of the self-reflective, self-critical pluralism—or, to put it more succinctly, experiment—in Cavell's work, the trouble with the diagnosis is that it sets up an opposition between philosophical and literary writing that Cavell is at considerable pains to avoid. In the new preface to *Must We Mean What We Say?* he is quite clear on this point:

> It will be said that two of [the essays in this book]—those on *Endgame* and on *King Lear*—are pieces of literary criticism, or at best applications of philosophy, while the remainder are (at least closer to being) straight philosophy. I wish to deny this, but to deny it I would have to use the notions of philosophy and of literature and of criticism, and the denial would be empty so far as those notions are themselves unexamined and so far as the impulse to assert such distinctions, which in certain moods I share, remains unaccounted for. (*MWM*, pp. xxxi–xxxii)

Accordingly, when Garrett Stewart observes that "if Cavell writes neither exactly philosophy nor exactly literary criticism, maybe what he writes is in fact literature," he instantly, and very sensibly, clarifies this with, "And not, of course, literature as opposed to philosophy."[20]

The best way to read Cavell, I find, is to leave as open as he does the issue whether he writes "philosophy" or writes "literature" and, instead of fixating on the grandiose proper names of academic disciplines—each so ill-defined as to require scare quotes—to attend to the term that is thereby overlooked: *writing.* In the same preface, Cavell observes "that *writing* plays differing roles in different enterprises, even that 'writing' means something different, or has a different inflection, in contexts like 'writing a novel,' 'writing a fugue,' 'writing a report,' 'writing (up) an experiment,' 'writing (down) a proof'" (*MWM*, p. xxxv). That the status or nature of writing is itself something open to question is partly what makes Cavell such an important thinker for those interested in literature. But philosophers have arguably even more to learn from this question than do literary critics. Cavell continues his observation with the remark that "the writing of philosophy is *difficult* in a new way. It is the difficulty modern philosophy shares with the modern arts (and, for that matter, with modern theology; and, for all I know, with modern physics), a difficulty broached, or reflected, in the nineteenth-century's radical breaking of tradition within the several arts" (*MWM*, p. xxxvi).

We have already called Cavell's writing "experimental," and it is this quality that is central to the predicament of modernist art and literature that Cavell has described. In his view, asking of a modernist artwork, Is it art? or of a modernist text, Is it literature? is to miss the point entirely because this question is itself what modernist artists and writers are already asking in their works.[21] It is hardly difficult to see that Cavell's experimental writing qualifies as modernist according to this criterion, or hence to see how those philosophers who berate his style by asking, Is it philosophy? are wasting their breath, not to mention their ink and paper. But an important question arises here. If, as Cavell suggests, a modernist sculpture that fails to attain the status of artwork becomes a mere object or thing, if a play that fails to aspire to the condition of tragedy becomes a melodrama as a result of this failure, if a modernist symphony that fails as a piece of music becomes simply noise—then what does failed philosophy become? What is the "other" of philosophy?

The responses to Cavell's writing suggest that many philosophers think their discipline's polar twin is literature. Whether commending Cavell for his literary style or taking him to task for it, commentators from both camps follow the lead established in ancient times by Plato in setting literature up as the stalking horse of philosophy, threatening its claims to reason. It has been an ongoing feature of Cavell's entire life's work to act as a peacemaker in the quarrel between these disciplines set out in the *Republic*,[22] and so, I contend, *both* these camps are equally in the wrong: whether Cavell's writing is to be commended or condemned, it is not to be identified with the writing of literature. Nor is it by any means the case that writing that fails as philosophy is thereby to be considered literature. The idea of modernism helps us out again here, because if experimental writing fails to aspire to the condition of literature, it thereby becomes at best mere words, at worst just nonsense—and this gives us to see that modernist literature is in some sense *about* words, about the language it is made of, just as modernist painting is often said to be *about* painting and even paint itself. And so modernist literature shares the criterion for its success with modernist philosophy of language: both are experiments with words. It is not that the disciplines are polar twins. It is rather that there are different ways of taking these experiments, and different ways of taking up their results, than that the failure of an experiment in philosophy is cause to brand it *literature*, regardless of whether the term is used in praise or in castigation. The modernist streak in Cavell's experimental writing can indeed make it seem "as if to overthrow the reign of reason, the reason that philosophy was born to establish, is not alone the task of, let us say, poetry but is now openly the genius or mission of philosophy itself" (*IQO*, p. 121). But it would scarcely be an experiment at all if it were not openly prepared to confront, to test, and if necessary to modify or reject the very founding assumptions behind it.

IV

But how are we to know if experiments are successful? It is one thing to leave open where and how we draw the line between literature and philosophy but quite another to embark on analyses and arguments based on the perceived failure or success of works of art, literature, and philosophy. At the risk of sounding like Cavell's nemesis, the skeptic—a risk, I think, worth taking here—how are we ever to know whether they succeed or fail? How are we to know what results such experiments have produced?

Unlike experiments in science, experiments in philosophy do not always have a ground from which to assess their outcomes. In this respect, they resemble experiments in literature and art. If, as I have suggested, Cavell's experiments have something of the character of modernism about them, then a useful way of understanding them is pointed to by J. M. Bernstein's observation that, according to Cavell's account, "modernist works are sites of transcendental claiming."[23] What is meant by this? What is a claim, and what is the importance of claiming?

To stake a claim is metaphorically to stick one's neck on the block: it is to make a statement in the public domain that asserts something one believes to be the case and about which one presumably feels strongly enough to declare it openly and publicly. Whether or not it contains, explicitly or implicitly, an appeal to the grounds that would justify, defend, or otherwise argue for its content *qua* claim, it is nevertheless a provisional kind of utterance, but one whose provisionality awaits ratification in the form of uptake in and from the public domain to which it was addressed. To put it another way, "*claim* designates my pretension to speak in the name of the community."[24] Thus, a philosopher is one who is in the business of making claims of reason. As Richard Eldridge has it:

> To undertake the task of philosophy is then to attempt . . . making what Cavell calls a claim of reason, a claim about what our criteria are. One will find oneself saying what we would say when: "this is what we call an accident as opposed to a mistake, or this is what we call justice, or love, or knowledge." Such claims of reason are lodged as reminders and vehicles of reorientation—to and on behalf of both others and oneself—when the applications of the concepts expressed by these words are somehow both dimly available and yet attenuated or disputed. . . . Such utterances are claims all at once to self knowledge (of what one would say when), to community (to what we would say when), and to reason (to what it makes sense to say when).[25]

There are, however, different kinds of claims and claiming, even within philosophy. Some claims, for instance, will be made in the name of, and will come to rest upon, grounds that are scientific, or empirical, or logical: agreement with these claims can thus be "postulated," to use a term Cavell borrows from Kant's third *Critique*.

These are not, though, the kinds of claims that are made in discussing works of art or aesthetics, and not the kinds of claims that are made in literary criticism. Rather, "the judgment I make in discussing" works of art and literature, Cavell says, "expresses my pleasure and sense of value in it and awaits your agreement upon this" (*PDAT*, p. 21). There is nothing besides this validation—in its various forms of agreement, acceptance, and uptake—that can ground the kinds of claims that we make in literary criticism and in aesthetic debate more generally. That is because all our attempts to ground our claims, regardless of whether we appeal to historical context, to authorial intention, to "the words on the page," or to anything else, are themselves claims about how to proceed in the business of literary criticism, which claims are themselves dependent in their turn upon agreement, acceptance, and uptake in order to stand. Claims made in literary criticism and in any discussion of aesthetics are thus in an important sense groundless; in fact, they seek to secure their own grounding.

Cavell, in "investigating the act of criticism" (*MWM*, p. 311), breaks down Kant's model of aesthetic judgment in order to describe what exactly is involved in the act of entering a claim about something aesthetic, such as a literary text: "One person, risking exposure to rebuff, singles out another, through the expression of an emotion and a claim of value, to respond in kind, that is, with appropriate emotion and action (if mainly of speech), here and now" (*PDAT*, p. 26). Rightly thought of, then, the claims of literary criticism are—to use a term that came up earlier in discussing whether Cavell has an approach to literature and the question of its relation to philosophy—essentially and importantly *open*: "The logic of my claim is that the claim is open to rebuke, perhaps from myself. Certainly I am asking myself, in entering such a judgment, from whom I must fear and bear rebuke" (*PDAT*, p. 82). And so it is an important feature of the claims we make in literary criticism, and in any talk of art, that these claims may fail. They are, to reiterate, provisional. Cavell goes on to suggest that any claim in aesthetics or criticism is "tinged with an anxiety that the claim stands to be rebuked. It is a condition of, or threat to, that relation to things called aesthetic, that something I know and cannot make intelligible stands to be lost to me" (*PDAT*, p. 9). And if this is so, then this description of the fragile status of the claims made in literary criticism, in art and aesthetics, is equally applicable to the claims that are made in the very kind of philosophy central to Cavell's thought: the philosophy of ordinary language.

Cavell's perceptive diagnosis of a "connection between the arrogation of the right to speak for others about the language we share *and* about works of art" (*PDAT*, p. 9) is a vastly important insight: it helps us, I think, to understand the depth and the strength of the alliance between literature and philosophy that so much of his work is built upon. Viewed in a certain way, both these aspects of his thought can come to seem like similar endeavors. This is because of a basic similarity in the nature of the kinds of claims that underpin them:

> Kant's characterization of the aesthetic judgment models the relevant philosophical claim to voice what we should ordinarily say when, and what we should mean in saying it. The moral is that while general agreement with these claims can be "imputed" or "demanded" by philosophers, they cannot, as in the case of

> more straightforward empirical judgments, "postulate" this agreement (using Kant's terms). (*PDAT*, p. 9)

Ordinary language philosophy, then—which, as we have seen Richard Eldridge observe, makes claims to reason, self-knowledge, and community on the basis of what we ordinarily say—is as wide open to rebuke and disagreement as claims about literature and art. We ought not, perhaps, say of this philosophy that it is straightforwardly "groundless," but rather that its grounds are precisely what it is searching for—searching by making claims that are open, provisional, and fragile. An ordinary language philosopher like Austin or Wittgenstein makes claims about, and in a sense on behalf of, a linguistic community. Some of its classic claims could be paraphrased as "This is what we ordinarily call 'knowing how to go on'" (Wittgenstein) or "We would not ordinarily say this was an excuse" (Austin),[26] where *we* designates simultaneously the people of whom the claim is being made and the people whose assent is necessary to ground the claim. Clearly, this is not the same thing as making a claim about a literary text. Nevertheless, the similarities behind how making a claim is structured in each field are enough to suggest to Cavell some ways in which the claims of literary criticism can exemplify for philosophers the dangers and perils besetting their own claims to reason. This, perhaps, is why Cavell feels that ordinary language philosophers should pay careful attention to literature.

In an essay entitled "Aesthetic Problems of Modern Philosophy"—the site of probably his best discussion of claims and claiming—Cavell observes that all too often, claims in aesthetics take two basic forms: either "a critical position will finally rest upon calling a claim *obvious*" and/or "a critical discovery will present itself as the *whole* truth of a work, a provision of its total meaning" (*MWM*, p. 311). Philosophers or not, many of us could be forgiven for finding such claims "a little idiotic," because, in the latter case, a "claim to total meaning" will *always* leave something out and, in the former case, a "claim [to] be obvious" will *always* encounter someone who doesn't find it obvious—"maybe the critic himself won't tomorrow," Cavell wryly remarks (*MWM*, p. 311).

Philosophy's historical shunning of literature might not be hard to understand if this were all that its critical claims amounted to. But Cavell asks us to reserve judgment here: instead of dismissing literary criticism, "we have to ask: How could serious men habitually make such *vulnerable* claims? (Meaning, perhaps, claims so *obviously* false?)" (*MWM*, pp. 311–12). While it is no doubt true that "criticism is inherently immodest and melodramatic" (*MWM*, p. 311), that is not to say that, from the standpoint of philosophy, its claims are to be automatically discounted. Instead, "our familiar ways of taking them are what make them seem a bit simple" because we "take a claim to obviousness as a claim to certainty, and [we] take the claim to totality as a claim to exhaustiveness" (*MWM*, p. 312). Philosophers who smugly dismiss the claims made in literary criticism therefore do so at their peril, because their own discipline's handling of similar kinds of claims has often been just as fraught and no less incoherent. For example, most philosophers will sooner or later encounter some form of "claim to total meaning": their response has typically been "to attempt exhaustiveness rather than to investigate the concept of totality" (*MWM*, p. 312), which is, in effect, to construct a vicious circle. Similarly, by taking claims to obviousness as claims to certainty—a basic error of epistemology—philosophy's response "has been to distrust conviction rather than to investigate the concept of the obvious" (*MWM*, p. 312), a mistake it took Wittgenstein, and his philosophy of ordinary language as "investigations of obviousness" (*MWM*, p. 312), to correct.

In summary, then, literary criticism is instructive for philosophy because its claims are *so* vulnerable and *so* fragile that they exhibit for students of "ordinary language" the risks at stake in making claims about things so essentially groundless as literary texts, and, perhaps more importantly, the ways in which such quintessentially groundless claims can be entered, understood, and debated—and then validated, rebuked, or modified—in spite of, and no doubt because of, their extreme vulnerability and fragility. Cavell's own writings on literature, eschewing systematic theories or approaches and remaining consistently "open," are among the best possible examples of such exploratory claims: that is what it means to call them "experimental." This, no doubt, is why literature is so very central to his work, and to his conception of philosophy: literature teaches ordinary language philosophers the importance of being open.

For it to do so, we, like Emerson before his new yet unapproachable America, must be able to open ourselves to literature, and this is where Cavell's writings have much to teach literary critics too. If critics are in the business of making claims about literary works, then Cavell's example teaches them the equally important lesson that literary works make claims upon us. Earlier, we saw J. M. Bernstein describe Cavell's characterization of modernist artworks as "sites of transcendental claiming," which is to say that a painting by Jackson Pollock, which appears to consist of spilled paint, is in effect awaiting our affirmation to its question, Is this a painting? Similarly, a poem by, say, Gertrude Stein, which appears to be made up of haphazard words, is making a claim upon us: it asks that we consider it as poetry, and its status as literature awaits our agreement to do so. But Cavell's writings on literature make clear that it is not just modernist works that make claims upon us. Rather, "the sort of emphasis I place on the criticism, or reading, of individual works of art" consists, he says, first and foremost in "letting a work of art have a voice in what philosophy says about it, and I regard that attention as a way of testing whether the time is past in which taking seriously the philosophical bearing of a particular work of art can be a measure of the seriousness of philosophy" (*PDAT*, p. 10).

The claim of literature, then, is a phrase that designates the power of literary texts to unsettle both our critical understanding of literature and our philosophical understanding of the world. That this phrase gives my book its title is meant to draw attention to Stanley Cavell's unerring ability to allow the texts he reads to enter claims into his discussions of them on their own terms. Accordingly, questions such as What is reading? or What is an author? or What is a character? or What is a historical context? are to be viewed as questions asked not just in Cavell's essays but by the writings of Shakespeare, Beckett, Thoreau, and the other authors studied in those essays. His response to these claims of literature is to test them against other claims, partly other claims of literature but also philosophy's claims to reason. This explains why, as I observed earlier, so many of the questions asked in his essays remain unanswered: this is an essentially two-sided, dialogical process in which the validation or rebuke of the claims of literature does not, or not solely, come from the voice of the individual but, like the claims of ordinary language philosophy, constitutes a further claim on behalf of a collective. In ordinary language philosophy, this collective is the linguistic community; in aesthetics and literary criticism, this collective is better termed a *culture*. The neatest description Cavell gives of this process is simultaneously a description "that warrants the name of philosophy" and also the name of "education": he says that his task is "to confront the culture with itself along the lines in which it meets in me" (*CoR*, p. 125). This amounts to a reorientation of our stance—both individual and collective—toward literature. It is a stance in which literature and criticism, culture and individual voice, can approach and make claims upon each other. This, and not the methodological construct of traditional literary theory, is what it means to do "philosophical criticism" (*MWM*, p. 313).

V

The aim of this book is to explore, as fully as possible, the significance of literature and literary texts to Stanley Cavell's thought. In an important sense, even a central one, its aim is radically at odds with that of Cavell's writings. This is because his essays are renowned for their interdisciplinary knit, in which discussions not only of literature and philosophy but also of film, psychoanalysis, music, and sculpture interilluminate and cross-fertilize one another. Hence, singling literature out and extracting it from the rich discussions in these writings may well appear wrongheaded, counterproductive, and perhaps even a betrayal of Cavell's entire intellectual enterprise. Repudiating this possibility would require so much effort as to undercut its own denials by protesting too much; instead, the chapters that follow are the claims on which to judge whether what is ultimately an artificial segregation has been worthwhile.

Presented below are detailed and thorough engagements with Cavell's readings of each of the major writers that occupy his essays: Thoreau, Shakespeare, Beckett, Wordsworth, Poe, and Ibsen. These are followed by a chapter on tragedy, which, because of the central importance of the tragic to Cavell's thought and the range of his engagement with it (from Greek tragedy to Shakespeare to *Faust*) is perforce genre- rather than author-oriented. The chapters demonstrate how Cavell's work on each topic brings to light a new perspective on a crucially important theme in literary study: more or less, each chapter begins by engaging with Cavell's own writings on a particular author and proceeds, by discussing those writings and the literary texts themselves, to address broader issues underpinning criticism and theory. Thus, chapter 1, on Thoreau, explores the very bedrock of the study of literature—the nature of reading and textual interpretation. It is followed by a chapter on Shakespeare, which fleshes out the previous chapter's emphasis on the reader by exploring, among other things, the complementary significance of the author in questions of literature. Next, we turn to Beckett to explore the relationship between ordinary language and literary language; to Wordsworth to explore the relationship between literary language and performative language; and then to Poe to deconstruct the assumptions behind both these linguistic relationships. The chapters deepen in complexity as the book progresses, raising issues to do with the relationships between politics and literature (via Cavell's discussion of Ibsen) and the ethical dimensions of literature (via Cavell's discussions of tragedy). Along the way, through Cavell's readings of literary texts and the philosophical issues they raise, I also hope to demonstrate how Cavell's thought critiques, and is in its turn critiqued by, the work of other recent philosophers and theorists of literature, including Jacques Rancière, Paul de Man, Emmanuel Levinas, and Giorgio Agamben.

My hope is that these individual chapters will demonstrate what I have argued throughout this introduction: that Cavell's thought, because of its sensitivity to the particularities of individual texts, be they literary or philosophical, resists those who would construct a Cavellian literary theory. That is not to say, however, that I conclude that Cavell's thought lacks wider application to texts besides those he himself studies: on the contrary, in the conclusion I seek to demonstrate the very opposite by showing how such key Cavellian terms as *tragedy*, the *ordinary*, and *America* intersect in exactly the ways Cavell describes in a modern literary classic—Arthur Miller's *Death of a Salesman*—which Cavell himself has never written about. I thus conclude by meditating on the further applicability of Cavell's ideas across the field of contemporary literary studies.

Serious readers of Cavell will no doubt take me to task for a glaring omission from the list of literary authors I propose to study here. As Simon Critchley rightly says, "The name 'Emerson' has a privileged status in Cavell's discourse,"[27] and so my contents page and index are likely to strike some Cavellians as hopelessly incomplete. In an important sense this is true, yet in another sense it is false. What is true is the sheer centrality of Emerson to Cavell's thought: if, in the Cavellian order of things, Emerson did not exist, then it would no doubt be necessary for Cavell to invent him. What is false—and what, after much reflection, keeps Emerson out of this book—is the idea that for Cavell the name of Emerson names a writer of literature. That is the very claim that generations of American philosophers, who neglected the philosophical import of Emerson's essays by branding them (merely) *literature*, used to exclude Emerson from the discipline of philosophy. It was precisely to disinter Emerson's work from its unkempt grave in philosophy departments, and precisely to exorcise his reputation as a writer of not-very-belletristic essays that could scarcely withstand the scrutiny of a contemporary analytic philosopher, that Cavell began his engagement with—one could almost say his engagement *to*—Emerson. Accordingly, at a time when, thanks in large measure to Cavell's intervention, Emerson is once again respected in American philosophy departments, a chapter on Emerson in a book on Cavell's writings about literature would be as counterproductive in certain respects as it would appear to be necessary in others. I am aware, of course, that much the same could be said of Thoreau and *Walden*, but Thoreau, by contrast, is and always has been as widely taught in literature departments as he is undertaught in philosophy departments, and in any case, to borrow a phrase from Emerson, we cannot spend the day in explanation.

Such, then, is the shape of things to come, and, in keeping with the idea that the claims I shall have to make, insofar as they are claims, will be fragile, open, and provisional, I can think of no better directions for reading this book than the words Cavell uses to describe his: "While such limited forays as I have reported will hardly count as answers to questions concerning the bearing of philosophy and literature on one another, I expect them to count as preparations for such answers" (*IQO*, p. 145).

CHAPTER ONE

Making Sense(s) of *Walden*

Just a few pages ago I promised to deliver a book that would discuss Stanley Cavell's readings of literary texts and that might even venture to offer the occasional Cavellian reading of its own. Given a book of this nature, and especially one entitled *Stanley Cavell and the Claim of Literature*, there would be good grounds for a reader to expect me to begin by setting out what it is that makes Cavell's readings so distinctive and insightful, or, in other words, to spell out what makes a reading Cavellian. What are the distinguishing features, the strengths and weaknesses, the advantages and disadvantages, of a Cavellian reading? Pressing though these questions are, they overlook, and perhaps thereby beg, a more fundamental question raised by the idea of a "Cavellian reading"—not the question What is Cavellian? but the question What is a reading? and, relatedly, What is reading? These questions seem to me to be the more urgent in a book examining the study of literature.

In other words, a book about the relation of Stanley Cavell's work to the study of literature should logically begin by analyzing the idea of reading. There are two good reasons for this. Firstly, since the study of literature is predicated on an activity we call reading, it makes good sense to start an investigation from there. And secondly, Cavell is virtually unique among philosophers in the importance he assigns to the activity of reading. Indeed, he begins his masterpiece by giving voice to "the thought, as I express it at the opening of *The Claim of Reason*, that philosophy may be inherited . . . as a set of texts to be read" (*IQO*, pp. 14–15).

Perhaps it is dangerously easy for those versed in contemporary literary theory to underestimate how controversial this idea is for traditional philosophy. The idea that, as Espen Hammer summarizes it, "philosophy, rather than a set of given problems to be solved, should be understood as a set of texts to be *read*"[1] is apt to underwhelm those who, trained to disregard the notion of anything *hors-texte*, have come to see the world and all that is in it as textual and thus reconfigure our relationship to the world by replacing epistemology with reading. This position is as in need of Cavell's intervention as that of the traditional philosopher, for whom the textuality of philosophical concepts and problems is at best irrelevant, perhaps even a distraction.

The error of the traditional philosopher—that is, of the academic philosopher, typically a professor or student—is "an idea that philosophy begins only when there are no further texts to read, when the truth you seek has already been missed, as if it lies behind you" (*IQO*, p. 15). Because they regard what they read merely as a vehicle for ideas and concepts, such readers find the *expression* of those ideas and concepts of no interest, and the journey of reading thereby becomes a necessary evil to be plodded through in order to attain a position of mastery from which they can finally begin to philosophize. For readers like these, the moment of philosophy will always come too late. It is postponed—one might also say repressed, or suppressed—in the interest of arriving at an authoritative or definitive purview, which is never actually achieved because nothing would count as achieving it. Reading, which was supposed to provide the laborious path to this viewpoint, turns out to do no such thing. That is because the activity of reading has been misconceived: it is not a process of *acquiring* new ideas and concepts but one of *generating* them through a more interactive philosophical engagement with the texts one reads. It is therefore worth asking whether philosophers who avoid this engagement with their texts can really be said to "read" them.

As opposed to the indifference toward reading manifested in traditional philosophy, certain literary theorists stop only fractionally short of declaring that it's *all* reading, that is, that, since knowledge and understanding are "always already" filtered or even constructed through language, it is impossible to conceptualize a form of human activity that does not in some way partake of, hence amount to, the condition of reading. Decoding and interpretation simply become our mode of being in the world. What such a position misses is the *specificity* of the idea of reading, which, as the term is used in ordinary language, seems to imply an activity that is not quite the same as, not entirely reducible to, and certainly not synonymous with the idea of interpretation. Cavell demonstrates this in his attempt to paraphrase the following metaphor:

> If I said "The human body is a text," then I would feel quite sympathetic to the claim that this is a metaphor and to the request for a paraphrase. But I might have

> been using that remark as a simile, and I could exhaust its content by saying, "I mean, it can be read." . . . Suppose I say, "I mean, it can be interpreted, understood." But this could have been the *first* explanation for my simile of the text. And it seems to me not to exhaust the meaning either of "text" or of "read." On the contrary, the idea of reading seems to tell me what *kind* of understanding or interpretation I might aspire to. Then what I need is not a paraphrase or translation of the word "read," but an account of why it is that *that* word is the one I want—after which I may move away from it or move on from it. (*CoR*, p. 363)

What this suggests is that nothing is gained, philosophically, from taking up a position of the kind that claims that it's *all* reading unless we have sought first to clarify the specific complexities and nuances of the word *reading* itself and what it is taken to mean in its ordinary (as well as its extended) sense. Which is not to say that Cavell seeks to restrict, or constrict, the way the word *reading* is used either in philosophy or in literary studies. For Cavell, rather, what is understood by (or as) reading is not something that can be entirely given independently of any act of reading. It is something to be learned in the process of reading—something, in short, to be taught by the text that is the object of our reading.

This amounts to the dizzying suggestion that every text contains the terms for its own reading, or, more ambitiously, that each text proffers its own theory of what reading is. Nowhere does Cavell make this point more clearly than in his bold study of Henry David Thoreau's text *Walden*, whose purpose lies primarily "in determining why *Walden* is itself about . . . its own writing and reading" (*SoW*, p. xiii). For Cavell, "the task of *Walden* as a whole . . . for us who are reading, is epitomized in discovering what reading in a high sense is and, in particular, . . . what reading *Walden* is" (*SoW*, p. 5). But this turns out to be no easy task, for the following reason:

> Every major term I have used or will use in describing *Walden* is a term that is itself in play within the book, part of its subject—e.g., migration, settling, distance, neighborhood, improvement, departure, news, obscurity, clearing, writing, reading, etc. And the next terms we will need in order to explain the first ones will in turn be found subjected to examination in Thoreau's experiment. . . . Once in it, there seems no end; as soon as you have one word to cling to, it fractions or expands into others. (*SoW*, p. 13)

Tracing the pattern of Walden's self-reflexive theory of reading, then, could all too easily result in a drawing of a Möbius strip.

As I mentioned in the introduction, Cavell's insight leads, seemingly, straight to a chicken-and-egg type of conundrum: if we are to learn from a text how to read that text, how can we ever be in a position to begin? We would have to learn the process of reading from the process of reading, which seems paradoxical. Cavell, indeed, calls it "the (apparent) paradox of reading" (*IQO*, p. 115). Granted, Thoreau may well propose a theory of how to read *Walden* in *Walden*. But then, asks Cavell, "How can we read his theory of reading in order to learn how to read him? We would already have to understand it in order to understand it" (*IQO*, p. 115).[2] So, if the mode of reading employed by traditional philosophers results in their arriving at the moment of philosophy belatedly, a philosopher employing Cavell's mode of reading appears to be in danger of never getting there at all.

This is a danger to which Cavell is highly alert. It is also one that he feels besets Thoreau, and consequently one that Thoreau is, as it were, modeling in order to demonstrate that it also besets his readers. Cavell diagnoses a particular "myth of the reader" (*SoW*, p. 68) in *Walden*, and it is one that is easily missed. When Thoreau tells us of borrowing an axe in March 1845 and taking it to the woods to fell timber for his house, he adds, "I usually carried my dinner of bread and butter, and read the newspaper in which it was wrapped."[3] Shortly afterwards, as Cavell points out, Thoreau confides: "In those days, when my hands were much employed, I read but little, but the least scraps of paper which lay on the ground, my holder, or tablecloth, afforded me as much entertainment, in fact answered the same purpose as the Iliad" (*W*, p. 42). Cavell wants us to take this last turn of phrase literally: Thoreau really does mean to say that a scrap of newspaper is as useful to him as epic poetry. If we do not see that reading a newspaper can bestow epic significance upon the everyday events it reports and, conversely, that Homer can make the heroic deeds of an ancient and forgotten civilization speak to our ordinary daily lives, then we have missed the point of reading, and with it the point of reading *Walden*.

Thoreau, as Cavell reads him, is suggesting: "If you do not know what reading can be, you might as well use the pages of the *Iliad* for the purpose for which newspaper is used after a meal in the woods. If, however, you are prepared to read, then a fragment of newspaper, discovered words, are sufficient promptings" (*SoW*, p. 68). As for the *Iliad*, Thoreau finds himself apparently too busy for it once again in the summer that follows his spring days in the woods. He tells us: "I kept Homer's Iliad on my table through the summer, though I looked at his page only now and then. Incessant labor with my hands, at first, for I had my house to finish and my beans to hoe at the same time, made more study impossible" (*W*, p. 91). Cavell asks of this passage:

> More study than what? More than looking at Homer's page now and then or more than hoeing his beans? ("I did not read books the first summer; I hoed beans" [*W*, p. 102]). From his description, I picture the book lying open on the table. Could looking at a page now and then, under any circumstances, constitute study? If not, how would turning the pages help? (*SoW*, p. 69)

So Thoreau's *Walden*, in passages like these, seems to instantiate Cavell's "paradox of reading." Or, more accurately, it refines the problem by turning the paradox into a tautology: if you don't know what reading is, you will be unable to read, Cavell seems to be saying.

II

Perhaps there is something rather familiar about Cavell's strategy thus far, at any rate to those readers versed in the American version of deconstruction. Surely what Cavell has done in reading *Walden* this way is to locate within it various "allegories of reading," which demonstrate how reading, both as it is conceived in these allegories and as it is practiced by readers, generates an alternation of blindness and insight, culminating in aporetic paradoxes that reveal, in the final analysis, that reading *Walden* and reading in general are simultaneously necessary and impossible. So might Paul de Man have put it. His colleague J. Hillis Miller might have preferred to say that the experience of reading a text culminates in the experience of its unreadability. Either way, the reading of *Walden* sketched above appears closely to resemble the textual strategies already on offer in the Yale school of deconstruction. Cavell has, of course, been vociferously critical of such readings, especially those of de Man.[4] So what, then, is the difference between these deconstructive positions and the way Cavell himself goes about the business of reading?

The principal distinction, perhaps, is that Cavell conceives of reading as "letting ourselves be instructed by texts we care about" (*IQO*, p. 53), and he finds it telling that the etymology of the word "has something to do with being advised" (*CoR*, p. 363), so that to read a text is to have it teach us something and to learn something from it, such as how to read it. "So the sense of paradox expresses our not understanding how such learning happens," he suggests (*IQO*, p. 116). Whereas deconstruction is content to come to a rest on this paradox, even to fixate on it, Cavell sees it as standing in the way of the learning process he regards as at stake in reading. That does not mean we can simply disregard or ignore the paradox. Rather, it is a paradox to be worked through, and Cavell does so as follows:

> I was just saying in effect that you cannot understand a text before you know what the text says about itself; but obviously you cannot understand what the text says about itself before you understand the text. One way of investigating this is to ask whether "before" bears meaning in this formulation, and if not, whether there is a paradox here. Another is to say that what you really want to know is what a text knows about itself, because you cannot know more than it does about this. (*IQO*, p. 53)

So the paradox of reading dissipates somewhat if it is reframed such that what takes place in reading a text is not that we learn how to read that text but that we learn something new about reading, something we did not know before. That texts are by definition scenes of instruction means that the key question Cavell sees a reading as setting out to answer is not the question of traditional hermeneutics—"What does a text mean?"—but rather the more elusive question, "What does a text know?" (*IQO*, p. 117). And so Cavell's conception of reading is subtly but crucially distinct from the concept of interpretation.

The distinction, however subtle, is nevertheless worth insisting upon because of the way Cavell reverses the polarities of the verbs *to read* and *to interpret*. In the Cavellian order of things, it is the text that interprets the reader rather than the reader that interprets the text. This reorientation is perhaps somewhat counterintuitive, at least at first blush. It amounts to a wholesale revision of the very idea of reading, and one that literary studies as well as philosophy would do well to take seriously. To the best of my knowledge, it is a reorientation with few, if any, direct precedents or parallels in the body of literary theories of the act of reading. Its closest neighbor would probably be Harold Bloom, who observes in his later work that "Shakespeare reads you more fully than you can read him,"[5] though as I shall explain shortly, Bloom sees a rather different set of consequences arising from this insight than does Cavell. What, then, could be meant by Cavell's claim that it is the *text* that does the reading?

Once again, it is a process that Cavell sees modeled in Thoreau's *Walden*. If we wish to progress beyond the paradox of reading I have just outlined, we have to learn from *Walden* how to read it. And how do we do that? According to Cavell, "To read the text accurately is to . . . check its sentences against our convictions" (*SoW*, p. 65), which means that the text is, after a fashion, reading us. This is true of reading anything philosophical. Or rather, it is true of reading anything *philosophically*. Whether we are reading Socrates or Beckett, Derrida or Shakespeare, Kant or Jane Austen, we cannot claim that we are *either* reading *or* philosophizing unless we are submitting our own thoughts, beliefs, and values to the scrutiny of whatever text we find in front of us. That is why "there is no philosophy present until the philosopher is *being* read" (*IQO*, p. 19), which in turn explains why, for those philosophers with a traditional conception of what reading amounts to, the moment of philosophy seems to come too late. As Espen Hammer explains, "For me to read the other, I must simultaneously allow myself to *be read*: reading requires the readiness to open oneself to the other, to be singled out and thus read by the other."[6] Lawrence Rhu goes further still, discerning an "ethical principle of criticism" in this openness to the other that comes into being when "texts read us as much as we read them."[7]

This principle, as I see it, forms the condition of possibility for what, in the introduction, I termed *the claim of literature*. To read, in the Cavellian sense, is to pay careful and close attention to the claims literature makes on us—to recognize, in other words, that texts are awaiting acknowledgment, uptake, and agreement from us, not simply in regard to their content, or to their merit *qua* texts, but, more fundamentally, in regard to the cues or invitations they give us to reflect on the claims we use to order or to justify our own lives. The business of interpretation, then, is to get the interpreter to reinterpret him- or herself. (In this way it partially resembles the process of psychoanalysis, a point shortly to be enlarged upon.) If this does not take place, then we cannot claim to have read a text successfully. And the responsibility for failure in these matters lies squarely with the reader, not the text. As Stephen Melville correctly observes of Cavell's readings of Emerson (though he could make the very same point about Cavell's readings of Thoreau or Shakespeare or Beckett; or Kant or Heidegger or Austin): "Cavell does not take the measure of Emerson, but Emerson of him—as if we were to ask not 'Does Cavell read Emerson well?' but 'Does Emerson read Cavell well?' And if our answer is 'No,' then it would not be that Emerson reads badly but that Cavell is not, in Emerson's light, worth reading."[8]

Thus, the claims that literature makes on readers are structurally different from the claims literary criticism makes on them. A critic is a reader who makes claims about the texts he has read. The claims are addressed to other readers and may as probably be rebuked or repudiated as they may be accepted and agreed with. Any reader familiar with the same text can reject or rebuke a claim of literary criticism (though it helps if the reader has a counterclaim to advance and justify in his or her turn). But if a reader rejects a claim of *literature*, then it is the reader who stands rebuked. That is why, for example, it is a standing rebuke to F. R. Leavis and his posturings as a reader that he found only four novelists in the English language who were "great" enough to deserve his attention, and that he felt that most literature did not repay the trouble of reading it. Well might Thoreau object that "it is not all books that are as dull as their readers" (*W*, p. 98).

At this point, it is worth a brief aside to point out that Cavell and Harold Bloom, both of whom regard the process of reading as involving the reader being read by a text, nevertheless part company about the exact nature of this process. The two may seem to share very similar reading habits; for instance, they both express a reverence for Shakespeare, a deep enthusiasm for Emerson and Wordsworth, and a strong interest in Beckett and Ibsen. Both are anxious—at times, perhaps, *too* anxious—not to be too closely associated with the practitioners of deconstruction. Cavell even cites Bloom's work on romanticism in *In Quest of the Ordinary* (see *IQO*, p. 45). But, crucially, for Bloom, reading is "a solitary praxis."[9] As he sees it, "Real reading is a lonely activity" involving "the self, in its quest to be free and solitary."[10] Cavell uses the same word, *quest*, to describe reading, but he certainly would not concur with Bloom that reading entails a "relationship [that] is altogether solitary."[11] On the contrary, for Cavell, literary texts are "works of art we cannot bear not to share" (*PDAT*, p. 9). This difference is vastly important because for Bloom, reading does not, and, in his view, should not and *cannot* involve a moral or a political experience, whereas for Cavell, as we shall see in chapter 6, "the risk of aesthetic isolation [compares] with that of moral or political isolation" (*PDAT*, p. 9). Thoreau is, in fact, a good example to use when it comes to highlighting these two different conceptions. From a perspective like Bloom's, living a solitary life on Walden Pond is something Thoreau does for himself only, and for his own self-improvement. Like the act of reading, it is essentially something private. Cavell's grounding in the work of Wittgenstein, however, entails a suspicion of the idea of privacy, since the word *private* functions all too often as a synonym for the word *metaphysical*. So, according to *The Senses of Walden*, Thoreau's life on Walden Pond is indeed solitary, but it is *not* a private existence, and indeed his opting for a life of solitude amounts to a political claim by which he rebukes his society. The same might be said of the Cavellian view of reading.

Once again, Thoreau anticipates Cavell's conception of reading a text as being read by it. Thoreau, perhaps less sanguine than Cavell, states in the chapter "Reading" in *Walden* that "the best books are not even read by those who are called good readers" (*W*, p. 97). He unpacks this once more seemingly paradoxical assertion by explaining that most readers have learnt to read only "primers and class-books" by the time they leave school (*W*, p. 98) and that they do not seek to improve their powers of reading afterwards, so that "our reading, our conversation and thinking, are all on a very low level" (*W*, p. 98); indeed, "of reading as a noble intellectual exercise [most men] know little or nothing; yet this only is reading, in a high sense, not that which lulls us as a luxury and suffers the nobler faculties to sleep the while, but what we have to stand on tip-toe to read and devote our most alert and wakeful hours to" (*W*, p. 95).

Certainly, in passages like these, Thoreau anticipates Cavell's view that what is traditionally called reading fails to live up to what reading can be. But where in *Walden* does Thoreau describe reading as *being read*? Cavell locates the answer in a metaphor whereby Thoreau compares the reading of "the noblest written words" to the practice of stargazing: "*There* are the stars, and they who can may read them" (*W*, p. 93). Thoreau's gloss on this metaphor comes a page or two later: "The works of the great poets have never yet been read by mankind, for only great poets can read them. They have only been read as the multitude read the stars, at most astrologically, not astronomically" (*W*, p. 95). And yet, this repudiation of astrology notwithstanding, Cavell points out that to read the stars is precisely to interpret your own life in their light—which is what being read by a text consists in. Cavell says of Thoreau's metaphor:

> This is an interpretation of nature as a text, of course, but it is one of Thoreau's clearest interpretations of what reading itself is. It interprets reading (dangerously invoking, to revise, the idea of the astrological) as a process of *being read*, as finding your fate in your capacity for interpretation of yourself. "Will you be a reader, a student merely, or a seer? Read your fate, see what is before you, and walk on into futurity." What is before you is precisely not, if you catch Thoreau's tune, something in the future; what is before you, if you are, for example, reading, is a text. He asks his reader to see it, to become a seer with it. Only then can you walk beyond where you are. (*IQO*, p. 16)

And so, as Cavell sees it, Thoreau's metaphor of reading as stargazing is another instance of how *Walden* models the practice of reading *Walden* to its readers, which here turns out to be the same as being read by it.

Of course, for students of literary theory, this metaphor of reading as stargazing is once again liable to have a somewhat familiar ring to it. The very same image is famously used by Wolfgang Iser, the phenomenologist of literary reception and of reader response. In his celebrated and widely anthologized essay "The Reading Process: A Phenomenological Approach," Iser compares the way texts elicit different responses in different readers to the way in which "two people gazing at the night sky may both be looking at the same collection of stars, but one will see the image of a plough, and the other will make out a dipper. The 'stars' in a literary text are fixed; the lines that join them are variable."[12] This striking similarity between these two thinkers' metaphors for reading appears less coincidental after discovering in Cavell's acknowledgments to *The Senses of Walden* that "my emphasis on the topic of *Walden*'s reader was encouraged by the attention paid to the topic of the reader in the writings and conversations of Wolfgang Iser" (*SoW*, p. viii). When one bears in mind that Iser's essay and Cavell's book first appeared in the same year, one cannot help speculating as to who might have influenced whom.[13] But the speculation is immaterial, because Cavell uses the metaphor with an emphasis very different from Iser's. For Iser, stargazing is an image of reading in that it constitutes something of a join-the-dots puzzle: the reader is free to fill in the "gaps" between the pieces of information ("stars") drip-fed us by the text. Meaning is thus forged through an interaction or negotiation between text and reader (with which I do not imagine Cavell would disagree) in an alternating process of retrospecting and prospecting that "concretizes" the text's phenomenological "gestalt" (at which, perhaps, Cavell might demur). But for Cavell, the "stars" that need to be joined together so as to form an interpretation are not distributed solely in the "outer space" of the textual firmament; there are just as many stars to connect in our inner space, and (to extend the stargazing metaphor to the breaking point) some are not visible to the reader's naked eye: we need the lens of a powerful text to help us discern them.[14] Such a text, that is, as Thoreau's *Walden*.

Walden speaks directly of the power of texts to effect understanding, change, and philosophical growth in their readers. As Thoreau enthuses:

> There are probably words addressed to our condition exactly, which, if we could really hear and understand, would be more salutary than the morning or the spring to our lives, and possibly put a new aspect on the face of things for us. How many a man has dated a new era of his life from the reading of a book. The book exists for us perchance which will explain our miracles and reveal new ones. (*W*, p. 98)

Since, as Cavell points out (see *SoW*, p. 48), the words *morning* and *spring* are woven with the regularity of a repeat pattern into the fabric of *Walden*'s prose, it is not too big a jump to see in this passage a hint that perchance such a book does exist, right in front of us, right now, in the shape of *Walden* itself: "It is the first step in entertaining Thoreau's intentions and ambitions to understand that he is there describing the pages he has himself readied for our hands" (*SoW*, p. 4). And it is germane that Thoreau brings *Walden* to a close by returning to the idea of a text that might shed the light of morning on us. But since "only that day dawns to which we are awake," it is up to the reader to apprehend, or "realize," this morning: otherwise it will be a "morrow which mere lapse of time can never make to dawn" (*W*, pp. 296–97). And Thoreau ends by connecting this dawning of realization to the very act of stargazing we have just connected to textual interpretation: "The sun is but a morning star," reads the book's final sentence (*W*, p. 297).

III

If, however, Cavell's account of reading amounts to something along the lines of "You don't read *Walden*; *Walden* reads you," then a number of very sensible objections could be made to such a view. Perhaps the most obvious of these is that it threatens to turn the act of reading into something closer to navel-gazing than to stargazing—that is, a narcissistic exercise in self-contemplation not unlike gawking at oneself in a mirror, with the text acting as looking glass. For a philosopher whose writings on literature have identified narcissism as an inflection of skepticism, and whose principal philosophical objective has been to contest the powerful impulses toward skepticism in all its inflections, this is a serious charge.[15] Cavell acknowledges its importance: "The accusation that in one's extended interpretations one is turning a work of art into a Rorschach test is desperately wrong but precisely significant and deserving of careful response," he writes (*TOS*, p. 52). His response, suggested perhaps by the vocabulary of narcissism and Rorschach tests, is to draw upon the procedures of psychoanalysis by arguing that "access to the text is provided not by the mechanism of projection but by that of transference" (*TOS*, p. 52).

Whereas *projection* of one's own concerns onto the other—or, in our case, onto a text—is rooted in a need to deny that we have such concerns in the first place (Freud saw it as a defense mechanism), *transference* reroutes the buried and unconscious feelings and concerns we have toward a particular object and foists them onto a new one. More specifically, in the context of the practice of psychoanalysis, it arises when a patient transfers such internalizations onto the therapist. Since, according to Cavell, the "text takes up the position of analyst rather than analysand,"[16] it is not hard to see why psychoanalytic transference should be such a useful analogy for him: texts read us not because they mirror back to us whatever of ourselves we choose narcissistically to project onto them but because they bring to light our buried thoughts and feelings and help us to acknowledge them and analyze them. Fairly early on, Freud went from regarding transference as a hindrance to the psychotherapeutic process to regarding it as a help, in that it foregrounds precisely the issues in need of discussion and *durcharbeiten*. Texts do the same thing. That is how they read their readers. Understood this way, it is not the process of being read that is narcissistic but the refusal to submit oneself to its challenges.

As Stephen Mulhall has emphasized, there is thus an importantly therapeutic aspect to how Cavell reads reading.[17] Mulhall calls this "redemptive reading," and Thoreau's *Walden* once again provides Cavell an object lesson in it: "Cavell's Thoreau has therapeutic designs on his readers: . . . his writing . . . involves presenting himself in such a way as to elicit his readers' transferences and to encourage them to interpret those transferences (e.g. 'He is isolated, but then so am I'); from which activity his readers are supposed to learn how they might recover themselves."[18] For Cavell, as Mulhall points out, reading these texts of recovery in this way is not only about connecting ideas or concepts, thoughts or feelings: it is also a matter of attending to the words themselves so that they may interpret us. Mulhall summarizes Cavell thus:

> Such reading is a matter of waiting on words, allowing them to manifest their own independence to us—in short, being passive so that they may be active; but the life they thereby exhibit is their life in our common language—their life in the language of their readers. . . . By allowing words to draw us through their complexities of sense in this way, we allow them to make or recover connections and associations of meaning in ourselves. . . . Reading words in this way is thus a matter of allowing them to interpret aspects of our own life back to us in a way which reanimates it. . . . It does not seem unduly fanciful to think of such reading as a matter of allowing ourselves to be read.[19]

In *The Senses of Walden*, Cavell is forever allowing Thoreau's words to take on a life of their own in order for them to interrogate the assumptions of our own lives. Rather than explicate one of Cavell's examples, however, allow me to advance one of my own.

Shortly after Thoreau's oft-cited advice to "beware of all enterprises that require new clothes, and not rather a new wearer of clothes" (*W*, p. 23), we are treated to the following good-humored gripe against the dictates of the fashion industry:

> When I ask for a garment of a particular form, my tailoress tells me gravely, "They do not make them so now," not emphasizing the "They" at all, as if she quoted an authority as impersonal as the Fates, and I find it difficult to get made what I want, simply because she cannot believe that I mean what I say, that I am so rash. When I hear this oracular sentence, I am for a moment absorbed in thought, emphasizing to myself each word separately that I may come at the meaning of it, that I may find out by what degree of consanguinity *They* are related to *me*, and what authority they may have in an affair which affects me so nearly; and, finally, I am inclined to answer her with equal mystery, and without any more emphasis of the "they,"—"It is true, they did not make them so recently, but they do now." (*W*, p. 24)

This passage is ideally suited for our purposes, because in it Thoreau exhibits the very practice of "emphasizing to myself each word separately" that Cavell claims epitomizes how *Walden* is to be read: "it means in every word it says" (*SoW*, p. 4). Equally, Thoreau is a good Cavellian here: he appreciates that because words mean what they say, it follows that "I mean what I say" when I utter them. But what could "They do not make them so now" really mean, and how could it be meaningful to answer it in the way Thoreau does? That we need to ask this question of his "It is true . . . but they do now" demonstrates how effectively Thoreau puts his readers in the same condition he finds himself thrown into by his tailoress's gnomic pronouncement—finding themselves obliged to investigate their relationship to what seemed like ordinary language.

At one level, "they do now" is a self-fulfilling prophecy: by implying that a certain garment is back in vogue, Thoreau creates the conditions required for his tailoress to make such a garment, which will render the statement "they do now" literally, if belatedly, "true." But what, in this explanation, accounts for the force Thoreau attaches to the word *they*—the mysterious identity he dwells upon as if it were a stumbling block? The third-person plural is used three times in Thoreau's "they did not make them so recently, but they do now," both as subject of the sentence and as its object, and it occurs twice in the tailoress's utterance. Who are "*They*"? Thoreau's argument is based on a strategy not unlike a chiasmus: it should not be that men are made by their clothes, but that their clothes are made by men—or, in his case, by a woman.[20] Yet he finds that this is not so: his clothes will not be made, presumably because of what other men will make of him if he wears them. If we try this strategy of reversal on Thoreau's response, so that the subject of the sentence—*They*—is in fact the clothes, and the object—*them*—the wearers, then he is saying that recently clothes did not make their wearers "so" but now they do. But how are we to understand the word *so*? The only way Thoreau uses it here, apart from his echo of the tailoress's use (for whom it is a synonym for *thus* or, more literally, *in this fashion*, which tells us nothing, and that is surely Thoreau's point), is to suggest the extent of his feelings—he is "*so* rash" as to demand these unfashionable clothes. Why? When the clothes were fashionable, they were worn by conformists, who required neither Thoreau's persistence nor his bravery to wear them. Were Thoreau to wear them now, those same clothes would make him, in his own word, "rash." No doubt, for Thoreau that is reason enough to have them made and don them with satisfaction. And that same satisfaction is available to me, the reader, if I am prepared to allow the text to speak to my inner nonconformist in this way. It could even be argued that a reader who entertains such a seemingly far-fetched interpretation in the first place has already done so. This may not be entirely true, but it is nonetheless usefully false. For readers who are not prepared to weigh each word of what Thoreau says and means in his response to the tailoress are likely to find themselves sharing the bafflement she must no doubt have felt upon hearing this cryptic reply. And to be put in her position is, precisely, to be put in the position of a conformist, dictated to by fickle popular taste.

How much of this reading is attributable to Thoreau's self-interpretation, how much to Cavell's gloss on Thoreau, how much to Mulhall's gloss on Cavell, and how much to me is clearly unknowable. That a confluence of four readers has helped bring it about might, however, deflate the allegation that Cavell's model of reading is a species of self-centered narcissism. But what, in the above interpretation, would count as transference? I would be prepared to admit, in a confessional moment, that I happen to be one of those academics whose dress sense is regularly pilloried by colleagues and students alike. But it would trivialize Thoreau's point if that were the psychoanalytic backing to my interpretation, and anyway, that is not exactly an example of transference. More obviously, I have transferred my Cavellian sensibilities onto *Walden*. But since, for instance, Thoreau hints at Cavell's insistence that we do and must mean what we say, this transference seems openly invited by the text—as if an anachronistic intertextuality,[21] as it were—and self-indulgent though it may be, this transference is hardly narcissistic. Instead, the reading presents a challenge to me: it goads me out of a state of bewildered conformism.

I find it preferable to describe this challenge as self-indulgent rather than narcissistic, since reading encourages us to indulge thoughts and ideas that clearly we formed, yet they appear to have come to us from elsewhere—from the text. As Mulhall has it, "Cavell's readings inculcate a sense that the text under interpretation delivers up thoughts that are his, but that he did not know he had—thoughts hitherto unacknowledged as his own returning with an uncanny sense of familiarity."[22] This is entirely consonant with a short dictum of Emerson's, near the beginning of his essay "Self-Reliance," that Cavell takes as a sort of mission statement for the way both he and Emerson conceive the act of reading: "A man should learn to detect and watch that gleam of light which flashes across his mind from within, more than the lustre of the firmament of bards and sages. Yet he dismisses without notice his own thought, because it is his. In every work of genius we recognize our own rejected thoughts; they come back to us with a certain alienated majesty."[23] More or less the same could also be said to happen in a successful experience of psychotherapy:[24] the therapist helps us to drive ideas out into the open, but the equally pressing task is to get us to acknowledge them as our own. The text, then, is not a Rorschach test but the therapist administering it. The idea is to indulge ourselves in giving voice to thoughts we would otherwise have remained unaware of. As Garrett Stewart concludes: "It was in the same year as *Must We Mean What We Say?* one recalls, that Georges Poulet famously said of reading and its transfers of consciousness that I become 'the subject of thoughts other than my own.' Cavell would return those thoughts to us as our own after all."[25]

In light of this conclusion, however, another obvious criticism of Cavell's conception of reading would be that in likening the process to transference, it encourages readers to read their own concerns into a text, or at least that it cannot prevent them from so doing. In *Pursuits of Happiness* Cavell tackles this objection head-on, and his riposte to it is worth quoting at length:

> Naturally I do not deny that some readings are irresponsible in fairly straightforward ways. But "reading in," as a term of criticism, suggests something quite particular, like going too far even if on a real track. Then the question would be, as the question often is about philosophy, how to bring the reading to an end. And this should be seen as a problem internal to criticism, not a criticism of it from outside. In my experience people worried about reading in, or overinterpretation, or going too far, are, or were, typically afraid of getting started, or reading as such, as if afraid that texts—like people, like times and places—mean things and moreover mean more than you know. This is accordingly a fear of something real, and it may be a healthy fear, that is, a fear of something fearful. It strikes me as a more discerning reaction to texts than the cheerier opinion that the chase of meaning is just as much fun as man's favorite sport (also presumably a thing with

> no fear attached). Still, my experience is that most texts, like most lives, are underread, not overread. And the moral I urge is that this assessment be made the subject of arguments about particular texts. (*PoH*, p. 35)

This passage is cited by Colin Davis as a clear instance of when "Cavell's project contains a staunch and explicit defence of overreading."[26] It sets up an opposition between "underreading" and "overreading" and counsels against the dangers of the former rather than of the latter. Underreading according to this description is about curtailing the possibilities of reading by imposing an artificial limitation on it. Rather than letting a reading run its course and bring itself to an end on its own ("internal") terms, underreading involves placing an external demand for closure on the text. Overreading, on the other hand, may well entail some pretty "bizarre, disorienting interpretive leaps." But this, according to Davis, is no bad thing in itself, *provided* the intention is to "push the interpretation of literature and cinema beyond the limits of what we might readily expect or accept that a text or film might mean" so as "to test or to exceed the constraints which restrict the possibilities of meaning released by a work."[27] Thus, for Davis, overreading can be an activity as worthy of praise as censure.

To return to a point I made in the introduction, this explains why it makes little to no sense to speak of a Cavellian "approach to" or "theory of" literature. To the degree that "overreading is motivated by a fierce commitment to the singularity of the work of art and to its potential to transform our ways of thinking,"[28] it cannot be contained within a fairly predictable set of interpretive procedures and operations, inevitably highlighting the same more or less definable concepts and themes, such as is necessary to constitute a literary theory or approach. On the contrary, such theories and approaches are precisely what Cavellian overreadings are trying to contest, as prescriptive paradigms for the study of literature. So the desire to curtail overreading is a desire to curtail interpretation to within the boundaries of the familiar and the knowable. In this sense, as Davis rightly points out, it is akin to the desire to prevent or to abolish skepticism.[29] But since, according to Cavell's diagnosis, this desire is actually one of the most pernicious symptoms of skepticism itself—a desire that is literally self-destructive in that it yearns to bring its doubts to an end yet cannot—it follows that approaches and theories are apt to be tools that help the skeptic to curb overreading and supplant it with supposedly theoretical underreadings instead. To pursue this thought, what is suggested by it is that Cavell's picture of reading implies that the key to a successful reading is what his philosophy terms *acknowledgment*, entailing a willingness to relinquish the skeptic's insistence on, as it were, the knowability of knowledge. In this, it once again resembles the psychotherapeutic process, in that the process can reach its goal only with the recognition and acceptance of ideas, and not with any amount of insistence on the acquiring or proving of additional knowledge. So the outcome of a successful reading is, in part, a moment of acceptance—an acceptance of the claim of literature.

That is not to say that Cavell finds these outcomes easy to achieve. On the contrary, his actual practice as a reader, whether of literary or philosophical or filmic texts, exhibits the difficulty of such acceptance: "It is still in part myself whose conviction I seek" (*PoH*, p. 81), he says of certain claims he makes in his reading of the film *It Happened One Night*.[30] Some may see this as evidence of the tenuous, even preposterous nature of overreading: its claims cannot even secure the assent of those who assert them. And that is partly the point, because, as I clarified in the introduction, the defining feature of claims of criticism is that though they may attempt to speak with a universal voice, they cannot postulate the universal agreement that empirical or logical or scientific claims might aspire to. Instead of universal proofs, they trade in individual acceptance. It is eminently possible, says Cavell, that the critic who advances a claim as "obvious" today will find himself unconvinced by it tomorrow (*MWM*, p. 311). So Cavell's overreadings, like Thoreau's *Walden*, offer a picture of reading as an overcoming of skepticism in a therapeutic moment of acknowledgment in which the claims of the text on the reader are countertransferred as claims the reader may make for the text. In Davis's admirable formulation: "So the claim of reading is the text's claim on its readers, its claim to possess and therefore to dispossess us in the act of reading; and it is also the reader's repossession of a voice in the claim to speak for a text which speaks to and of its reader."[31]

Certainly, this is a sound description of a successful act of reading. But these acts are not always successful, and "you cannot always know when the fire will strike" (*CoR*, p. 338). There are different ways to handle the uncertainty that results from this. The underreader tackles it with readings that claim as little as possible, presumably on an understanding that the less that is claimed, the less there is to disagree with, and hence the less risk there is of rebuke. By contrast, Cavell could be said to take a leaf out of Thoreau's book. At the conclusion of *Walden*, Thoreau returns to the question of his readership, first broached on the book's opening pages, and asserts:

> It is a ridiculous demand which England and America make, that you shall speak so that they can understand you. . . . As if that were important, and there were not enough to understand you without them. . . . As if there were safety in stupidity alone. I fear chiefly lest my expression may not be *extra-vagant* enough, may not wander far enough beyond the narrow limits of my daily experience, so as to be adequate to the truth of which I have been convinced. (*W*, pp. 288–89)

Speaking like a true overreader, Thoreau reveals himself here to be more concerned about formulating his thoughts so as to give "adequate" voice to his thoughts—where "adequate" means adequate enough to convince *himself* rather than another. This quite neatly describes the stance Cavell takes in his readings. It also returns readers of *Walden* to an observation Thoreau makes about them at the very start of the book: "As for . . . my readers, they will accept such portions as apply to them. I trust that none will stretch the seams in putting on the coat, for it may do good service to him whom it fits" (*W*, p. 6). And this, it seems to me, not only sums up the nature of reading; it is also, as a result, a serviceable (if belated) epigraph to the reader of the chapters of this book.

CHAPTER TWO

The Avoidance of Shakespeare

William Shakespeare occupies a unique position in the writings of Stanley Cavell. No other writer of what we would readily identify as literature has preoccupied him to anything like the extent Shakespeare has.[1] Both his masterpieces *Must We Mean What We Say?* and *The Claim of Reason* conclude with an essay on Shakespearean tragedy, and this tradition has been continued in more recent works such as *Emerson's Transcendental Etudes* and *Cities of Words*. Even after the publication of *Disowning Knowledge*, the volume that brought together Cavell's writings on Shakespeare in earlier texts such as *Themes Out of School* and *In Quest of the Ordinary*, his engagement with Shakespeare has been extended and expanded in later works such as *Philosophy the Day after Tomorrow*. In sketching the background to Cavell's thought, then, Shakespeare's name needs to be ranked alongside those of such hugely influential figures as Austin and Wittgenstein, Emerson and Thoreau.

And yet Cavell's Shakespeare essays have until recently met with a mixed reception, and often with no reception at all, unless wholesale indifference among literary critics and philosophers alike may be considered a reception. Lawrence Rhu, in addressing this issue, observes that for some less than generous commentators, "Cavell seems to be simply drawing upon the cultural capital of the swan of Avon himself, the most bankable of bards. . . . Cavell strikes such critics as a name-dropper seeking to show off his familiarity with the canonical in-crowd."[2] Such criticisms are empty. For while Cavell freely confesses, "Of course I share the temptation to idolatry of Shakespeare" (*DK*, p. 30), he is just as keen to flaunt the limits of what he calls "my amateur forays into Shakespeare" (*DK*, p. 179) as he is to talk them up. Indeed, the preface to *Disowning Knowledge* is itself something of an exercise in disowning knowledge.[3]

If there are philosophers who suspect Cavell of trying to enliven philosophy with a smattering of literary window dressing, so too there are literary critics who accuse him of moving in the opposite direction: as an interdisciplinary imperialist trying to colonize literature by imposing ideas from philosophy onto it. In fact, nothing could be further from his stated aims:

> The misunderstanding of my attitude that most concerned me was to take my project as the application of some philosophically independent problematic of skepticism to a fragmentary parade of Shakespearean texts, impressing those texts into the service of illustrating philosophical conclusions known in advance. Sympathy with my project depends, on the contrary, on unsettling the matter of priority (as between philosophy and literature, say) implied in the concepts of illustration and application. The plays I take up form respective interpretations of skepticism as they yield to interpretation by skepticism. (*DK*, p. 1)

Michael Fischer, one of the earliest commentators on Cavell's thought in general and his literary concerns in particular, insisted that "in turning to Shakespeare . . . Cavell is not simply documenting ideas already gleaned from philosophy. . . . If anything, for him philosophical expressions of skepticism 'intellectualize' problems first worked out in literature."[4] But to put the matter this way is to emphasize the distinction between literature and philosophy in a way that is far removed from Cavell's practice in his Shakespeare essays. In fact, the question that hostile literary critics put to Cavell is a question he already asks of himself ("But what is it that calls for philosophy, Shakespeare's play or my manner of reading the play?" [*DK*, p. xiv]).[5] His riposte to it explains that rather than importing philosophy into his reading of Shakespeare, he is more than happy to move in the reverse direction and "count certain texts as philosophical that may not announce themselves so. I do not mean that Shakespeare's texts, for instance, are to count as philosophy, but if not, then the most responsive texts in the world, to the world, the ones accordingly most extreme in their manifestation of philosophy's first virtue, are not philosophy" (*DK*, p. xv). It is not that Cavell is trying to deny the distinction between literature and philosophy in his readings of Shakespeare, but rather that he is happy to leave open where to draw it. As he says of his Shakespeare essays, "I become perplexed in trying to determine whether it is to addicts of philosophy or to adepts of literature that I address myself" (*DK*, p. 2). It is unsurprising, then, that one early description of *Disowning Knowledge* calls it "a volume of writings on Shakespeare that not many will recognize as either philosophy or literary criticism."[6]

With this in mind, my primary object in this chapter is not to follow up, develop, challenge, or critique any of the philosophical insights or literary interpretations to be found in Cavell's Shakespeare essays. It is rather to pursue an answer to a question Cavell asks (in his essay on *Coriolanus*) and, characteristically, does not answer, namely, "What is a play of Shakespeare's?" (*DK*, p. 144). That is, in asking what kind of an object, entity, or thing a Shakespeare play is for Cavell, I am questioning whether it means the same thing there as what others might take it to mean and, indirectly, whether Cavell is talking about "Shakespeare"—in the sense other commentators might take this name—in the first place.

To start with, it is fairly clear that the name *Shakespeare* does not function for Cavell as the byword it sometimes serves as throughout Anglophone culture—a word to be splashed across film posters, T-shirts, mugs, and the names of theater companies for purposes primarily commercial. Cavell's engagements with Shakespeare are too many and too rigorous to be considered an academic equivalent of such name-dropping. (The allegations of Cavell's thirst for cultural capital and kudos are in this sense baseless.) Nor does he attach to it a Foucauldian "author function" in the sense of regarding Shakespeare as a "founder of discursivity."[7] Furthermore, in Cavell's works the name *Shakespeare* only rarely serves to designate a once actually existing, historically situated playwright of the Renaissance era. Insofar as it does function as the name of a writer, it is sometimes left open whether Cavell regards *Shakespeare* as naming a playwright or a philosopher. On the one hand, he insists that "Shakespeare could not be who he is—the burden of the name of the greatest writer in the language, the creature of the greatest ordering of English—unless his writing is engaging the depth of the philosophical preoccupations of his culture" (*DK*, p. 2), while also claiming that, when insisting this, "the name 'Shakespeare' meant, in the work I was doing, a challenge to any lingering fantasy of philosophy's cultural mastery" (*PDAT*, p. 29).

What is reasonably clear is that for Cavell *Shakespeare* is sometimes a proper name attached to a specific corpus of work and sometimes the name attributed to an intelligence that creates and organizes (and yet could hardly be said to "control") these works. But that only broaches the smallest part of the question, "What is a play of Shakespeare's?" In one of the first essays to review Cavell's work in this area, Richard Wheeler points out that a number of concepts taken from the vocabulary of fairly traditional aesthetics—the autonomy of the artwork, the unity of the artwork, the artwork as expression of the artist's inner thoughts and/or feelings, the artwork as product of the artist's intention, the artwork as an insight into human nature—all "[play] a role in Cavell's thought generally and in his criticism of Shakespeare in particular," while they are simultaneously often widely debunked "as a humanist illusion among new historicist and cultural materialist critics."[8] Garrett Stewart has claimed, quite convincingly, that this explains the relative neglect of Cavell's work on Shakespeare in literary studies, and indeed the gulf separating Cavell's approach from that of the New Historicism is vast enough to account for it.[9] While I shall return to this question in due course, what is of most interest to me here is that none of the concepts of traditional aesthetics cited above is used in anything like a traditional way in Cavell's approach to Shakespeare. All of them find themselves interrogated and modified as a result of their encounter with Shakespeare's plays.

To demonstrate this, I propose to outline six possible answers to the question "What is a play of Shakespeare's?" in order to see how Cavell exposes them as deficient or incoherent. I should make emphatically clear that none of these answers is entire of itself or mutually excludes any of the other answers: a play of Shakespeare's may be considered all six at once. Moreover, they are of my sketching rather than Cavell's, and the order in which I set them out here does not reflect that of their importance in Cavell's work or that of their cropping up in his essays. That I present six such answers is a function simply of my abandoning the search for more: there are doubtless other possible answers "out there." With such prefatory qualifications, it seems to me that Shakespeare plays can reasonably be thought of as

- *products of their time*, that is, contextually situated, historically conditioned artefacts;
- *plays to be performed in a theater*, that is, scripts produced for and following the conventions of a dramatic performance;
- *a set of philosophical ideas*, that is, debates or explorations of concepts or intellectual themes;
- *words on a page*, that is, texts comprised of words intricately arranged in suggestive ways;
- *the actions of their characters*, that is, complex chains of events or deeds involving (and mostly carried out by) the people in/of the play; and/or
- *embodiments of authorial intention*, that is, manifestations of the mind that shaped them, including any "message" it may have put there.

A Shakespeare play can, in principle, be thought of as any of these things, individually or in some combination with one another, including all six of them at once. But while Cavell invokes all of these ideas (albeit to varying extents), he rarely adopts them in straightforward or commonsensical ways, as we shall see.

II
Products of Their Time

At first blush, it would seem that Cavell makes little or no room for contextual or historical factors in his work on Shakespeare. But this is only superficially true. He says of *Antony and Cleopatra*: "If this play is Shakespearean history, then the events of its Rome must form some precedent and parable of the events of . . . Shakespeare's world" (*DK*, p. 20). There is in fact a keen historical sense of the intellectual backdrop to Shakespearean tragedy in most of Cavell's essays on Shakespeare, because the context of early modern thought can provide, at the very least, a great deal of circumstantial evidence for his claim that the "advent of skepticism" (*DK*, p. 20) is a key theme in these plays and that "this mode of tragedy is a response to the crisis of knowledge inspired by the crisis of the unfolding of the New Science in the late 16th and early 17th centuries" (*DK*, p. xiii).

Perhaps this intellectual backdrop is not quite what is usually meant by *historical context*, at least in undergraduate seminars and textbooks. But then what is? "Something about the succession or the passing of Elizabeth, or about her predecessors or her successor?" (*DK*, p. 20). This would be the more conventional answer. Controversially, though, Cavell argues that "These events seem, if not the wrong size, a poor shape" (*DK*, p. 20). Instead, he points us in another direction, toward the epistemological birth pangs of modern science and philosophy. "It is an inciting fact of our culture that Galileo was born the same year as Shakespeare," he points out (*DK*, p. 35), and elsewhere he suggests "that the advent of skepticism as manifested in Descartes's *Meditations* is already in full existence in Shakespeare" (*DK*, p. 3). As Michael Fischer explains:

> Cavell makes the historical point that replacing acknowledgment with knowledge in the (vain) hope that we can save our lives only by knowing them is also one legacy of modern epistemology, which begins in the writings of Galileo, Bacon, and Descartes, Shakespeare's contemporaries. These thinkers start to define knowledge in terms of certainty and sense experience, suggesting that all genuine connection with the world hinges on what is present to the senses—and that turns out, as Cavell says, "not to be the world." (*MWM*, p. 323)[10]

This Cavellian version of historicism is open to a number of challenges, even if one grants his point that characters like Othello, Lear, Leontes, and Hamlet comport themselves as skeptics.[11]

In the first place, a certain degree of anachronism is involved. Even accepting that skepticism is a prominent theme in Shakespeare[12] and that Shakespeare was sufficiently grounded in contemporary philosophy to have read Montaigne, there is no escaping the fact that Shakespeare belonged, as Cavell knows, to "the generation preceding that of Descartes" (*DK*, p. 3). Nevertheless, he claims:

> However strong the presence of Montaigne and Montaigne's skepticism is in various of Shakespeare's plays, the skeptical problematic I have in mind is given its philosophical refinement in Descartes's way of raising the questions of God's existence and of the immortality of the soul (I assume as, among other things, preparations for, or against, the credibility of the new science of the external world). (*DK*, p. 3)

As for the new science itself, there is scant evidence to suggest that Shakespeare himself had much familiarity with it to speak of. Once again, this does not deter Cavell: "I do not claim that Shakespeare had read the major texts presenting the new science, nor knew more about it than he could have picked up in conversation, given his capacity to listen" (*DK*, p. 36). To a historicist, then, it must surely be hard to recognize Cavell's Shakespeare scholarship as historicism at all: embracing anachronism and lacking evidence, surely what Cavell advances as historical context fails to amount to anything more than a vague appeal to a set of ideas that may or may not have been loosely "in the air" throughout Renaissance Europe.

Strikingly, however, Cavell seeks not so much to deny or refute a challenge to the historical aspects of his work on Shakespeare as to forestall it by turning on its very head what is customarily meant by historicism:

> I do not command the learning to argue seriously on historical evidence that the shaking of the ground of human existence in what philosophy calls skepticism, finds its way into Shakespeare's words . . . hence to argue that the unique endlessness of the Shakespearean order of words is a function of that shaking. My conviction, or evidence, is in something of the reverse state. Given my intuition of the occurrence of skepticism in Shakespeare, it is from him that I would have to learn, were I a historian, what to look for to give his history. (*DK*, p. 4)

To a straightforward empiricist historian—if there are still any left—this would be nonsense: how could we ever learn from Shakespeare what would and would not count as his historical context? Surely, even if that fantasy were possible, on grounds of objectivity he would be the last person we should ask. The point is that Cavell is challenging, perhaps in a somewhat counterintuitive manner, the way the relationship between literature and historical context is ordinarily conceptualized.

To explain by analogy: if it is not a legitimate move to impose a philosophical framework upon a literary text and call it an "interpretation," why would this not also be true of a historical framework? If it is often the case that the resistant literary text yields insights into the philosophical framework imposed upon it, why not also into the historical framework? Just as Cavell's Shakespeare essays refuse to get bogged down in interdisciplinary trench warfare between literature and philosophy, so too he wastes no time with a historicist perspective that sees Shakespeare's plays as simply embedded in context and conditioned by history, so that interpretations of them become saturated or even determined by the terms of another discipline. Alluding to E. M. W. Tillyard's classic textbook, Cavell argues: "If there is an Elizabethan world picture, Shakespeare questions it, so shatters it, as surely as the new science did. No 'source,' no received conception, survives its incorporation into Shakespeare without sea-change" (*DK*, p. 36).

New Historicist critics are likely to agree with Cavell that the view of historical context to be found in "old" historicism, as represented by Tillyard or perhaps by certain Marxist critics, is indeed overdetermined and crude: for a New Historicist, no text is ever merely or simply a product of its time. The trouble is that New Historicists are likely to object equally strongly to the view that Shakespeare—or anyone else—is capable of "shattering" his world picture: this suggests a view of unfettered human agency that goes right against the grain of New Historicist ideas, like those of Stephen Greenblatt or Michel Foucault. As both Richard Wheeler and Garrett Stewart have demonstrated, there are deep-seated methodological divergences between the way Cavell and the way the New Historicists conceptualize Shakespeare's plays. Cavell comments—rather too briefly—on this difference when surveying his reading of contemporary Shakespeare scholarship:

> In reading the feminist and/or the psychoanalytic critics I did not feel that I had *in advance* to answer the questions, What does Shakespeare think women are, or think psychology is? but that I could read these pieces as part of thinking

> about these questions; whereas I found myself, in reading the new historicist critics, somehow required to have an independent answer to the question, What does Shakespeare think history is? . . . Is it in the way science thinks, in the way magic thinks, or religion, or politics, or perhaps in the way works of art, for example, works of poetic drama think? It is not clear that these questions make good sense. (*DK*, p. 226)

Such comments are bound to strike some as unfair: surely the New Historicism conceives the lines between text and context as permeable and even fluid and thus as less rigidly dogmatic than many psychoanalytic critics do. This is no doubt true, and if it were indeed what Cavell meant, then the New Historicists would have a right to feel aggrieved. It is more likely, however, that *Shakespeare* is not functioning in this context as it would for a New Historicist, that is, as the name of a historically conditioned subject. Cavell speaks of Shakespeare's shattering of the Elizabethan world picture in terms of its "incorporation into Shakespeare." That is hardly how it would be described if *Shakespeare* meant simply the name of a playwright living in and through the Elizabethan era. Whatever term might more conventionally be substituted for *incorporation*—*appropriation*, *treatment*, *handling*, and *depiction*, while not equivalents, are certainly more common—if *Shakespeare* meant such a subject, then we would expect the preposition *by*, not *into*. The New Historicist criticism that Cavell's Shakespeare is conceived too straightforwardly as a "free agent" and not as a historically conditioned and situated subject thus turns out to have underestimated what that name stands for in his works, since *Shakespeare* is capable of incorporating and subsuming history itself. Clearly, this is a curious feat for the contextually situated subject of the New Historicism.

Stephen Mulhall attempts to clarify matters by explaining that

> when Cavell talks of "Shakespeare," "Freud," or "Cukor," those words are used primarily as names of the authors of a certain body of plays, books, or films rather than as the proper names of individuals—so that Cavell's Shakespeare, whilst not exactly not a creature of the Elizabethan era, is always capable of putting the defining assumptions of that era into question (e.g. his use of cultural stereotypes such as the Bastard and the Moor) and is anyway primarily identified by (and so with) his texts.[13]

Perhaps it will be objected that this conception confuses Shakespeare as a historically existing subject with Shakespeare as a fluctuating corpus of texts, some by but most about him. Strangely, though, these were some of the very criticisms first levelled against the New Historicism by humanists, "old" historicists, and Marxists alike. It might also be objected that Cavell is replicating the methodology of poststructuralism, reducing the author to an endless tissue of textualities à la Roland Barthes. But this is not wholly accurate, for Cavell's Shakespeare is no less meaningful, no less unique, for comprising a corpus of texts. Unlike much poststructuralist scholarship on this issue, Cavell emphasises his sense of "the wonder that just these orders of words can have been found, that these things can be said at all. . . . It is that sense of empirical uniqueness of the nests of instances called Shakespeare's that I do not want denied when iconoclasm comes to destroy its idolizations" (*PDAT*, p. 36).[14]

This kind of vocabulary, coupled with a desire to distance himself from New Historicism on the one hand and poststructuralism on the other, has perhaps made Cavell out to be a rather more conservative commentator on Shakespeare than he in fact is. It is certainly true that Cavell sometimes expresses himself in the same terms as an arch-traditional liberal humanist might: seeking to elevate Shakespeare's individuality and unique creative genius from being mired in a slough of history that might dilute or obscure it[15] and seeking to view the plays as completely autonomous artworks instead.[16] Perhaps this is regrettable, but not because these views are straightforwardly traditional and somehow thereby repugnant or perhaps even wrong. This would be so only if *Shakespeare* were operating here simply as the proper name of an artist embedded in history.[17] But Cavell's Shakespeare, rightly understood, is something better conceived as distributed *throughout* history. For Lawrence Rhu, Cavell sees Shakespeare's plays as "meeting places in an otherwise groundless world."[18] That is why they can incorporate other sources—philosophical, scientific, or historical—whether those sources are texts or contexts. Shakespeare's plays are historically situated, certainly, but primarily because their readers are too, including all the readers there have ever been of these plays.[19] Despite their historicity, they can speak to all men in all times and all places. Yet they do so not because they are "timeless" or "universal" in any liberal humanist sense but because men in all times and all places have spoken *to* them. However, they are not meeting places where consensus can readily be achieved, let alone assumed. Rather, "thus conceived, they also suggest images of our lost conviction in shared understandings; they show that our mutual participation in common cultures such as ⌊Shakespeare's⌋ words might constitute is always in jeopardy."[20]

A Shakespeare play, then, is located in history, not as a man in a particular society or an artifact in a particular period—products of their time no doubt—but rather as, like human history itself, a groundless ground in which the views of different people from different societies and periods are spoken and are spoken for:

> "To be or not to be." "A tale told by an idiot." "Are you fast married?" "Look down and see what death is doing." "Then you must find out new heaven, new earth." . . . Nothing but the ability to be spoken for by these words, to meet upon them will weigh in the balance against these visions of groundlessness. Nothing without, perhaps nothing within, Shakespeare's words could discover the power to withstand the power Shakespeare's words release. Is this, since then, the demand we place, to greater or lesser extents, on all writing we care about seriously? (*DK*, pp. 19–20)

This explains why Cavell's Shakespeare is as capable of incorporating history (or even of "shattering" it) as it is of being influenced by it; why it is untroubled by scholars' lack of historical evidence or anachronism; and, above all, why it is from Shakespeare that we must learn what historical context is, and what validity it has, in the first place. But it is also why Cavell's essays on Shakespeare are scarcely referring to what historicists, new or old, mean by *Shakespeare* at all.

III
Plays to Be Performed in a Theater

To regard a text as a play—as opposed, perhaps, to regarding a play as a text—is to regard it in the light of the conventions of drama, taking "drama" as a literary genre and, perhaps more importantly, as a social institution. It may seem, at first, that the latter set of conventions is not at issue here, because the social conventions for a dramatic performance are not peculiar to, and indeed have little to do with, the corpus of Shakespeare.[21] This, as we shall see, is only partially true; nevertheless, it makes sense to begin by exploring the question "What is a play of Shakespeare's?" in relation to literary genre, that is, the set of literary conventions of and for a play.

In his earlier work, Cavell makes it perfectly clear that Shakespeare's plays cannot be reduced to a set of conventions. That does not mean that they are not conventional, even formulaic; it is rather to say that conventions cannot, of themselves, provide a satisfactory answer to our question:

> Shakespeare's plays are conventional in the way that their language is grammatical, in a way that a football game satisfies the rules of football: one has to know

> them to understand what is happening, but consulting them will not tell you who plays or speaks well and who mechanically, nor why a given remark or a particular play was made *here*, nor who won and who lost. You have to know something more for that, and you have to look. (*DK*, p. 48)

There are several problems with trying to understand Shakespeare's plays in terms of the conventions of and the conventions for theater, and perhaps the most glaring of these is that Shakespeare's plays are often unconventional; hence, if we insist on a conventional account of them *qua* plays, they sometimes turn out to be bad plays: "When the well-made play shows us what drama is we say that Shakespeare is poor at plotting, and since we know he is great we excuse him, and then we cross our minds and say that the defects will not be noticed in the heat of performance" (*DK*, p. 82). In fact, viewing Shakespeare's plays in terms of a set of conventions is all too often either a means of or an occasion for providing excuses for them: if a Shakespeare play is seen as conventional, some critics will feel the need to exonerate Shakespeare's originality and genius by saying that he was bound by the conventions of his age; if it is unconventional, some critics will feel the need to exonerate the play by saying that Shakespeare had such originality and genius that he was bound to challenge the conventions of his age. In both cases, we have a poor picture of what the words *Shakespeare* and *conventions* mean.

Cavell views the matter like this:

> It is a particular man, call him Shakespeare, we are dealing with, and while it is doubtless true that a knowledge of the conventions he inherited is indispensable to the full understanding of his work, the idea that these conventions supply him with solutions to his artistic purposes, rather than problems or media within which those purposes are worked out, is as sensible as supposing that one has explained why a particular couple have decided to divorce by saying that divorce is a social form. (*DK*, p. 48)[22]

This is why it is no solution to avoid the debate, as some of Shakespeare's devotees have, by sidestepping into another genre and regarding Shakespeare's plays as *poems*—that is, as following a different set of conventions, conventions belonging to poetry rather than to plays. Firstly, that is not strictly true ("Sometimes Shakespeare's plays are said to be poems, but obviously they are not poems; they are made in a medium which knows how to use poetry dramatically" [*DK*, p. 91]). And secondly, it too can become a means of or occasion for ducking the question ("We say that Shakespeare's plays are poems and therefore structures of meaning, and in this way account for their densities, assuring ourselves that even if we do not or cannot perceive them in a given moment they nevertheless have their effect" [*DK*, p. 82]).

If conventions can only give us at best an incomplete picture of what plays and poems are, and a poorer picture still of what "a play of Shakespeare's" is, that is not simply because they frame the question in ways Cavell (rightly) finds unsatisfactory; it is rather because the conventions of Renaissance drama are, in Cavell's view, in large measure what these plays are themselves about. His essays "look in a Shakespearean play for something like an idea of theater, as it were for the play's concept of itself" (*DK*, p. 144). And so, to borrow a phrase from Wittgenstein, in a satisfactory investigation of Shakespeare's plays, these conventions ought to be "what is explained, not what does the explaining."[23] As Cavell puts it, "If this work does not work as theater it cannot work as anything else either, or as everything else. But here I am asking what 'working as theater' means in this theater, what the conditions for it are (were); asking it, needless to say, because I find that the play is asking it" (*DK*, p. 30). In other words, then, "What is a play of Shakespeare's?" is a question already asked by Shakespeare's plays themselves. And just as Cavell suggests that we should learn from the plays themselves what relationship they weave with their historical context, so too should we learn from them what they see as the theatrical or dramatic conventions in which they participate, and how they work.

Probably the most obvious place in which to do this is the play-within-a-play that Hamlet calls "The Mouse Trap,"[24] but Cavell cites other examples too: the tale of the belly and the body's members that Menenius tells the crowd of mutinous citizens in the opening scene of *Coriolanus*;[25] the scene in which Hermione is resurrected at the end of *The Winter's Tale*;[26] and, in the finale of *Antony and Cleopatra*, Cleopatra's prophetic fear that she "shall see / Some squeaking Cleopatra boy my greatness / In the posture of a whore" (5.2.218–20).[27] All of these are moments in which these plays, in providing figures of what they take the conventions for plays to be, thereby provide us with what Cavell calls "our literal business with the work I am calling Shakespeare's" (*DK*, p. 30). And that business turns out to be philosophical.

What is at stake in Shakespeare's theater's interrogation of itself, and of theater itself, by itself? Its principal work, as Cavell sees it, is to present "the theatricalization of the world," "the theatricalization of human life," and "the theatricalization of one's existence" (*DK*, p. 37). Nowhere does the philosophical import of these meditations on the conventions of drama assume a greater significance than in Hamlet's speech on the nature of acting itself, whose purpose and whose end is, he tells us, "to hold, as t'were, the mirror up to nature" (5.2.23):

> Why assume just that Hamlet's picture urges us players to imitate, that is, copy or reproduce, (human) nature? His concern over those who "imitated humanity so abominably" is not alone that we not imitate human beings badly, but that we not become imitation members of the human species, abominations, as if to imitate, or represent—that is, to participate in—the species well is a condition of being human. Such is Shakespearean theatre's stake in the acting, or playing, of humans. Then Hamlet's picture of the mirror held up to nature asks us to see if the mirror as it were clouds, to determine whether nature is breathing (still, again)—asks us to be things affected by the question. (*DK*, p. 221)

In this way, meditating on the conventions of acting in plays turns out to be an invitation not only to meditate on the relation in which those conventions stand to the conventions of our everyday lives but also an occasion to reflect on the relationship between theatricality and subjectivity itself.[28]

As should by now be clear, when Cavell uses Shakespeare's plays in order to investigate the dramatic conventions of those plays, he turns out not to be investigating what most critics would consider those dramatic conventions themselves to be but rather investigating what is philosophically suggestive about the way they are (conventionally) pictured. No doubt some will find this to be another instance of Cavell's avoidance of Shakespeare, that is, redefining the question so that its terms do not coincide with the normal understanding of the word *Shakespeare* at all. (Here, that would mean his reframing the idea that Shakespeare's plays are shaped by the conventions of Renaissance drama, that what makes a play of Shakespeare's is just those conventions.) One tempting riposte to this suggestion would be that considering Shakespeare's plays primarily in terms of the conventions surrounding them—or, for that matter, the historical context surrounding them—is itself an avoidance of Shakespeare, in that to do so is to import considerations that are extraneous factors, circumstantial to the plays themselves and to the playwright who wrote them. But that, as we have seen, is far from the case. These plays incorporate, and thus contest, the conventions that are said to facilitate them, albeit in a somewhat different way from that in which they incorporate and contest their history.

I want to suggest that because of this incorporation and contestation, a Shakespeare play can be read as providing, to borrow a phrase that Cavell has used elsewhere of another text that has influenced him immensely, an "aesthetics of itself."[29] When using this phrase as a way into Wittgenstein's *Philosophical*

Investigations, Cavell takes it to imply that no philosophical aesthetics can help us appreciate the literary quality of Wittgenstein's text, nor, crucially, the symbiotic relationship between this literariness and that text's philosophical work.[30] *Mutatis mutandis*, no literary aesthetics or conventions can help us appreciate the philosophical quality of a Shakespeare play, nor the symbiotic relationship between this philosophical quality and the play's unconventional use of literary conventions. And if I am right that Shakespeare's plays, like Wittgenstein's *Investigations*, provide their own aesthetics, then this, Cavell says, "may be seen as challenging any given distinction between supposed genres of philosophy and literature that I am aware of."[31] If so, what Cavell is avoiding in reframing the picture of Shakespeare's plays as a set of dramatic conventions is a view of those conventions as ("simply," "solely," "purely") literary. In their investigations of the conventions for theatricality itself, Shakespeare's plays investigate philosophically their relation to our everyday lives and the conventions that surround how we live them, and not simply the conventions that pertain to the Elizabethan and the Jacobean stage. And if, in reading them in this way, Cavell ends up avoiding a vision of those plays as mere functions of the dramatic conventions that drive them, then perhaps that is a vision of Shakespeare that is worth avoiding.

IV
A Set of Philosophical Ideas

If, like Wittgenstein's *Philosophical Investigations*, a play of Shakespeare's provides us with what Cavell calls an "aesthetics of itself," then this straightaway problematizes the idea that a Shakespeare play could be conceived as consisting purely of a philosophical debate, or as the working out of philosophical concepts in dramatic form. For if the function of this auto-aesthetic is as Cavell describes, then Shakespeare's plays are no more built from philosophical ideas than they are from literary conventions—because they do not belong unambiguously to either literature or philosophy.

This notwithstanding, there is nevertheless much in Cavell's readings of Shakespeare to suggest that one potential answer to the question "What is a play of Shakespeare's?" would involve conceiving of a play as a basically philosophical entity. But what does this mean? Cavell's Shakespeare essays often advance interpretations that call upon philosophical debates around psychoanalysis, politics, or ordinary language, to the point where the play itself, rather than "exemplifying," "illustrating," or "instantiating" a philosophical idea, becomes an invitation to or occasion for philosophy in its own right. This involves something of an alteration in what "a play of Shakespeare's" is normally understood to be, because it places Shakespeare in a dialogue with thinkers such as Descartes, Emerson, or Freud, which some may find problematic. For example, Cavell asks, "If you are struck by . . . the way Shakespeare can interpret Freud's speculation about the inheritance of fantasy as well as Freud can interpret Shakespeare's representation of fantasy—then from whom shall we say we learn of these things primarily?" (*DK*, p. 189).

Against the (obvious) objection that such a dialogue is predicated on anachronism, the (equally obvious) response would be that, as we have seen, Cavell takes the name *Shakespeare* to designate a presence distributed throughout our cultural history since the Renaissance. This, no doubt, will strike some literary critics as avoiding "Shakespeare" in the sense they understand it. For other critics, Cavell would be avoiding Shakespeare here in transforming, or even reducing, the rich suggestiveness of Shakespeare's texts to what they might call a set of philosophical thoughts. This is an argument he is aware of: "There are readers of literature who take the view . . . that to derive such thoughts from texts such as Shakespeare's is to evince a blindness to, even a denial of, the very literariness of those texts, the particular interaction of the specific words of which the texts are woven. I must, of course, insist that it is precisely those very words that inspire those derivations."[32] Cavell immediately qualifies this insistence by conceding that the onus is on his essays, as specific critical interventions, to demonstrate the validity of deriving philosophical thoughts from Shakespeare's words and that his readings will stand or fall as interpretations of Shakespeare according to their success or failure in doing so.

And yet if the critical validity of Cavell's Shakespeare essays is a factor of their specificity or sensitivity to the individual features and particularities of the plays they study, then surely it has to be asked why a similar philosophical theme turns out to underwrite them all. That all the Shakespeare plays studied by Cavell turn out to hinge, in his view, on some aspect of skepticism may well appear to give the lie to his appeal to the specificity of his interpretations to the individual texts themselves. For some critics, no doubt, a rat can be smelled here. It seems all too convenient that Cavell's first encounter with Shakespeare follows on directly from his first discussion of the relationship between acknowledgment and avoidance, which is disrupted by skepticism,[33] and all too systematic that each of his subsequent essays on Shakespeare employs just these terms. Cavell offers "a reading of *Othello* as a depiction of the murderous lengths to which narcissism must go in order to maintain its picture of itself as skepticism, in order to maintain its stand of ignorance, its fear or avoidance of knowing, under the color of a claim to certainty" (*DK*, pp. 143–44). Coriolanus, at first blush as much the narcissist as Othello, turns out to be as much the skeptic:

> That Coriolanus's disgust is, as I read it, directly and emblematically a disgust with language, with the vulgarity of the vulgar tongue, seems revelatory of something in skepticism that Descartes and Hume, for instance, were not quite able to thematize; so revelatory of philosophy, or of a major strain in philosophy, quite generally. Coriolanus is thus a particularly vivid portrait of (one form of) *living one's skepticism*, a matter that is brought forth as an issue by Descartes and by Hume. (*DK*, pp. 12–13)

And so on for Lear, Macbeth, Hamlet, Leontes, Antony, and Cleopatra: all turn out to present us, in some ways, with pictures or models of skepticism.[34] Why do interpretations that stake their validity on claims to be individual readings of individual texts turn out to uncover, again and again, the same underlying philosophical thematic, the same pattern of thought?

One answer would be that the underlying pattern of thought simply *is* Shakespeare's, but Cavell rarely does more than hint at this as a possibility. Another answer, which Cavell seems to endorse quite explicitly on many occasions, is that the pattern of thought that is skepticism is a prominent feature of tragedy itself, and perhaps a precondition of Shakespearean tragedy. Indeed, at times Cavell even defines tragedy itself in terms of its relation to skepticism: "Tragedy is the result, and the study, of a burden of knowledge, of an attempt to deny the all but undeniable . . . that a loving daughter loves you, that your imagination has elicited the desire of a beautiful young woman, that however exceptional you may be you are a member of human society, that your children are yours" (*DK*, p. 179).[35] As neat a solution as it may seem to claim that skepticism is fundamental to, even criterial for, Shakespearean tragedy, in fact this claim offers nothing of the kind, for reasons that bear on the discussions we have already had of the previous two putative ways of understanding what a play of Shakespeare's is.

On the one hand, we have seen that Shakespeare's plays, products of a golden age of theater in which drama was an established and popular genre with a recognizable set of conventions, are, for Cavell, quite capable of breaking free from that genre and challenging those conventions. On the other hand, we have seen that Shakespeare's plays—preceded by Montaigne, contemporary with Bacon and Galileo, succeeded by Descartes—are fellow midwives at the birth of modern skepticism. So why, if Shakespeare's plays are capable of circumventing the governing theatrical conventions of their day, are they incapable of circumventing the philosophical climate of their day? If the answer to this is that the Renaissance's philosophical climate of scientific and philosophical skepticism is built into the genre of Shakespearean tragedy, this merely begs the question, because we have seen that for Cavell, Shakespeare's plays are of interest for their challenging the generic conventions of drama and theater.

To be fair, as Cavell sees it, the plays *do* constitute such a challenge: each and every Shakespearean tragedy Cavell reads is to be seen precisely as a challenge to the problems of skepticism, rather than as a straightforward example or illustration of those problems. There is nothing conventional or formulaic about the way Shakespeare's plays engage the thematic of skepticism:

> If Shakespeare's plays interpret and reinterpret the skeptical problematic—the question whether I know with certainty of the existence of the external world and of myself and others in it—it follows that the plays find no stable solution to skepticism. . . . Being Shakespearean texts they test, as well as test themselves by, their sources, so that in incorporating, let us say, a philosophical problematic, they test, as well as test themselves by, philosophy. What interpretation a text finds of skepticism is, accordingly, not knowable apart from what interpretation the text finds of itself. (*DK*, pp. 3–4)

It should go without saying that if the plays of Shakespeare are read by Cavell as exploring the same skeptical thematic, that certainly does not mean that they arrive at the same solutions or conclusions, nor that they explore it in similar ways. In fact, there is something of a simplification involved in the conception that Cavell reads these plays in terms of their exploration of the same thematic, in that the territory staked out for skepticism in Cavellian philosophy is vast—much larger than its role in the epistemological branch of traditional philosophy. To claim, then, that Cavell reduces Shakespeare's plays to problems of philosophical skepticism is apt to mean nothing, because Cavell is more concerned to expand, or even explode, what traditionally counts as philosophical skepticism. The skepticisms that Cavell finds in Shakespeare extend beyond epistemology to questions of ethics, aesthetics, politics (especially in the readings of *Coriolanus* and *Antony and Cleopatra*), and even ordinary language philosophy. Indeed, to paraphrase Cavell's tidy formulation (in "Aesthetic Problems of Modern Philosophy") that "ordinary language philosophy is about whatever ordinary language is about" (*MWM*, p. 95), we might say, rather less tidily, that the skepticism of Shakespearean tragedy is about whatever Shakespearean tragedy is about.

This brush with ordinary language philosophy is useful, and we would do well to bear in mind Cavell's background and influence in this area. If Shakespeare's plays can be read as occasions for or invitations to philosophy, then that is not, perhaps, because their author—Shakespeare—can be read as a philosopher grappling with the dawning of modern thought, nor because their interpreter—Cavell—can be read, alongside Wittgenstein and Austin, as a successor to or inheritor of it. It is rather because Cavell, after Wittgenstein and Austin, enables us to see philosophy as parceled up with language and thus, as Cavell suggests at the start of *The Claim of Reason*, to see philosophical problems as texts. From this viewpoint, it is not too big a stretch to see texts as philosophical problems, and who better to turn to than Shakespeare for the thorniest texts in the English language? For A. J. Cascardi, this is precisely what underwrites Cavell's readings of Shakespeare's plays:

> Cavell portrays his engagements with Shakespeare as unavoidable because it is Shakespeare who, above all writers, explores the full range of the commitments that language entails. The power of Shakespeare's work rests on his ability to envision characters who live out the fate of their words relentlessly, without compromise or escape, or who suffer disastrously from their failure to do so. . . . Shakespearean tragedy . . . is a form of drama in which language is drawn to extremes, but the force of Cavell's work is to magnify the intensities that are present within Shakespeare's work rather than to submit them to anything like a "philosophical" point of view extraneous to it.[36]

And so Shakespearean tragedy, in taking us so far beyond the "ordinary," gives us the means to take skepticism to, and often beyond, its logical conclusions far better and more clearly than "ordinary" life or "ordinary" language can. Viewed this way, "a play of Shakespeare's" is a philosophical entity not because it offers us a debate, an enactment, or a critique or justification of some conceptual philosophical "content" but because in its loss of the ordinary, its language unsettles us to the point where philosophy cannot be avoided.[37] And so the way Cavell imagines a Shakespeare play to be a philosophical entity is precisely an avoidance of some traditional image of Shakespeare as philosopher-playwright investigating ideas and concepts by penning dialogues and debates not far removed from the texts of Socrates, Plato, and their followers in the groves of Academe. Such a content-driven conception of philosophy is partly what is critiqued in the idea of Shakespeare's plays, like Wittgenstein's *Investigations*, offering an aesthetics of themselves. To locate the relationship between Shakespeare's plays and philosophy aright, one has to avoid the temptation to regard the plays as philosophical problems and instead follow up Cavell's suggestion that we regard philosophical problems as *texts*.

V
Words on a Page

In much contemporary literary criticism, Shakespeare's plays are most commonly conceptualized as more or less intricate and suggestive arrangements of words, and hence as texts. If the transition from the previous section seems a little deft here, we should be wary. True, Shakespeare's plays have an unnerving ability to take language itself to extremes, but as words on a page they are often as apt to strike us with their everyday ordinariness. "What," Cavell asks,

> is the difference between Cleopatra's anticipation or memory of Antony's "kiss / Which is my heaven to have" (V, ii, 301–2) and words that one imagines would be about the same in what are called drugstore novels; and, for that matter, what is the similarity of both of these with Jerome Kern and Dorothy Fields's "Heaven, I'm in heaven . . . when we're out together dancing cheek to cheek"? (*DK*, p. 32)

The question, I take it, is a genuine one: Cavell is not indulging in a modish iconoclasm that seeks to locate the value of Shakespeare's plays merely in the status afforded by common convention to the name *Shakespeare* in our culture or that seeks to level all distinctions between high art and mass culture.[38] Rather, the question is better thought of as follows: if we are going to characterize a Shakespeare play as a text, then we have merely replaced the question "What is a play of Shakespeare's?" with the question "What is a text of Shakespeare's?" What makes it different from any other text?

Unlike with drugstore novels and Irving Berlin songs,[39] it is sometimes less than clear how the Shakespearean text is constituted, because, like biblical texts or ancient epics, a Shakespeare text has been *constructed*—constructed by generations of editors and commentators who have shaped not just our understanding of the text but the actual text itself. There have even been editors who "fall to wanting to mark Shakespeare as theirs in their possessive editing of him" (*PDAT*, p. 35). In his recent essay "The Interminable Shakespeare Text,"

Cavell addresses this problem directly, pointing out that in the Arden edition of *Lear*, which he used for his first essay on Shakespeare, the problems occasioned by the substantial differences between the folio and quarto versions of the play were tackled head-on by Kenneth Muir's editing:

> Muir, for example, repeatedly cites multiple proposals of interpretation for a disputed passage and then without exception (that I recall) declares his favor for one of them, sometimes saying that one is "preferable" (without saying why), or "probable" (without specifying how the probability is measured), and sometimes avowing (as in a case in which he reports four interesting proposals, equally plausible it would seem) that he is "inclined to the second" as if honesty or honor demanded the judgment, and sometimes just stating that one or another is "obviously correct," without saying how the unobvious have come about. (*PDAT*, pp. 45–46)

Muir's editing policy is, in some ways, curiously reminiscent of Ernest Bloch's teaching, to which Cavell recalls being exposed as a student. In *A Pitch of Philosophy*, he recollects:

> He would play something simple, at the piano, for instance a Bach four-part chorale, with one note altered by a half step from Bach's rendering; then he would play the Bach unaltered. Perhaps he would turn to us, fix us with a stare, then turn back to the piano and repeat, as if for himself, the two versions. The drama mounted, then broke open with a monologue . . . "You hear that? You hear the difference?" His voice was surprisingly unresonant and sounded pressed with the labor of excitement, an exotic effect increased by his accent, heavily French, but with an air of something else. He went on: "My version is perfectly correct; but the Bach, the Bach is perfect; late sunlight burning the edges of a cloud. Of course I do not say you must hear this. Not at all. No. But." The head lowered a little, the eyes looked up at us, the tempo slowed ominously: "If you do not hear it, do not say to yourself that you are a musician. There are many honorable trades. Shoe-making for example."[40]

What is striking about this anecdote is that unlike most contemporary critics and theorists of culture, Cavell does not challenge the assumption that there is a "perfect" rendition of the Bach, a standard that surpasses the (merely!) "perfectly correct." Can this standard be applied to Shakespeare?

"The Interminable Shakespeare Text" is, in large measure, Cavell's response to certain critics—particularly the "New Textualism" represented by Margreta de Grazia and Peter Stallybrass—and their claim "that the Shakespearean text . . . literally and simply as a material thing, does not exist" (*PDAT*, p. 29). This is, admittedly, something of an oversimplification of the New Textualist position, which is better characterized, Cavell says, as challenging "a metaphysics of the perfect text," itself underpinned by "a companion metaphysics of the autonomous, omnipotent author and perhaps another of a transparent, univocal work" (*PDAT*, p. 34). The New Textualism can therefore be understood as emphasizing "skepticism *about* the Shakespearean text," in place of Cavell's interpretations, which locate skepticism "*within* the Shakespearean text" (*PDAT*, p. 30). Thus, in jettisoning the very idea of a "perfect" Shakespeare text, they form a diametric opposite to Bloch's intuiting of Bach's score as "perfect."

It is important not to get sidetracked here into questions of how this "perfection" or "correctness" might relate to questions of value or taste in aesthetics and in culture more generally; the issue is, rather, "What is a text of Shakespeare's?" That Hamlet refers, in the quarto version, to his "too too sullied flesh" and in the folio to his "too too solid flesh" might be enough to convince one "that this difference alone determined two entirely different plays, one psychologically driven, the other metaphysically" (*PDAT*, p. 33). But on the other hand, "the sense that it is the same play under change is as strong as the sense that each change changes the play. (Surely 'the same play' does not mean 'the same text' . . .)" (*PDAT*, p. 36). Is it necessary to decide on one version as "correct," "perfect," or perhaps "perfectly correct"? Cavell suspects not: "Since [the two versions] are so plainly different, and nevertheless both can seem perfectly right, we may entertain a moment of paralysis before the necessity of discarding either—not because we are looking for the perfect text but because we want both open possibilities at the same time" (*PDAT*, p. 34).

The New Textualists liken the editorial quest for a "perfect" text to a wild-goose chase and compare it to the Kantian "thing in itself," to which we can ultimately have no access; hence, for them, the "perfect Shakespeare text" does not exist. But it is precisely this transition from the incompleteness or contradictoriness of empirical data to a wholesale skepticism about the *Ding an sich* that, for Cavell, misses the main thrust of Kantian philosophy:

> If someone had a belief in a metaphysically perfect Shakespearean text, should he and she allow themselves to be talked out of it by recitation of the facts of Renaissance conditions of text production and transmission? Should Kant be talked out of the thing-in-itself by a rehearsal of the facts of the production of tables and chairs (or, using Kant's examples, houses and drifting boats)? (*PDAT*, pp. 32–33)

Rightly understood, "The denial of the thing itself, the perfect instance, denies nothing, something Wittgenstein calls a house of cards" (*PDAT*, p. 36), and so "both the metaphysical search for the perfect text and the skeptical attempt to demonstrate that the search is hopeless" (*PDAT*, p. 53) are equally misguided. This is because "an assertion to the effect that *this* text is the original or perfect text—the perfect realization of the play—is at best ambiguous and at worst empty, in a word metaphysical, hence . . . the *denial* of such an assertion is precisely as ambiguous or empty as the assertion itself" (*PDAT*, p. 36). Thus, admirable though the rigorous editorial scholarship of the New Textualism may be, it shares the same erroneous metaphysical picture of editorial "perfection" as the Shakespeare editors and scholars it is trying to critique.

Responding to empiricism with wholesale skepticism was the path Hume trod, and it was precisely his stance that scandalized Kant into philosophy. If the New Textualism can be characterized along these lines—namely, as taking imperfect knowledge of an object as an opening to a Humean skepticism, or as interpreting "a metaphysical finitude as an intellectual lack" (*MWM*, p. 263)—then a suitable corrective would be to take a more recognizably Kantian approach to the "thing in itself" that is a text of Shakespeare's. For Kant, the inaccessibility of the *Ding an sich* is not an invitation to throw the baby of knowledge out with the bathwater of things themselves; rather, the question becomes one of how my relationship to things can constitute my knowledge of them. Hence, in the New Textualist account,

> the lack of finality or uniqueness of the Shakespearean text threatens to leave out, or pre-empt . . . the constitution of my relation to the existence of such knowable objects as ones that fall under, for example, the concept of a text, and that of a Shakespearean text, and that of a text of *King Lear*, however foul or editorially repossessed a particular text may be. (*PDAT*, p. 33)

So the question "What is a text of Shakespeare's?" is better understood as a question asking what kind of a relation I stand in toward a Shakespeare text. For Cavell, "What I understand as establishing my relation to a work I sometimes characterize as tracing a text's resistance to my reading of it. I am just Hegelian enough to welcome a struggle here with what may equally be seen as my resistance to the play's demands upon me" (*PDAT*, p. 54). In other words, a Shakespeare text will inevitably contain ambiguities and multiplicities of meaning, leaving it open to interpretation and reinterpretation, with no single, fixed meaning as ultimately correct. That is simply in its nature, or, a Wittgensteinian might say, its grammar—the kind of thing it is.

There will always be those for whom this ambiguity or multiplicity is not enough—those who want to fix a definitive interpretation. Cavell hypothesizes that

> it is an antipathy to this metaphysical compulsion to choose . . . a single, fixed meaning (in a context in which there is no risk, intellectual or practical, in maintaining overt ambiguity, or multiplicity)—that, displaced, fuels the quest for an original, fixed text, hence for the practice of conflating, for example, the *Lear* texts. I find that I share the antipathy to the compulsion to choose the single meaning, but that I do not share the contempt for what is called the conflation. (*PDAT*, p. 46)

So what Cavell shares with the New Textualists, and what differentiates both of them from, say, certain critics of Kenneth Muir's generation, is that they are happy to leave questions of interpretation and meaning open when it comes to the Shakespearean texts. (Cavell gives a neat example of this in a concise reading of sonnet 122.) Certain editors, like Muir, quest for a definitively edited text that will ground meanings unambiguously; the New Textualists see this as naively idealistic, because such a definitive edition does not exist, and so editors should stop looking for it (roughly, this is Rorty's position regarding philosophy's quest for truth). For Cavell, both are equally wrong, because it is just as idealistic a mistake to assume that any such definitive edition could ultimately ground or fix our interpretations of Shakespeare in the first place. If it could, it would have ceased to be a "text" in the way that concept is ordinarily understood. It would have become precisely the sort of metaphysical entity that the New Textualists (rightly) observe does not exist.

So if a Shakespeare text is, by definition, never "perfect," and if it is always open to reinterpretation and re-editing, then why did the young Cavell in Ernest Bloch's music class not feel the same way about a Bach chorale? *A Pitch of Philosophy* makes it clear that hearing the difference in the two versions of Bach is no more important than—and indeed is not altogether separable from—the *understanding* of which version is felt to be "perfect," and that is something for which each listener, conductor, and performer must take responsibility, just as "The Interminable Shakespeare Text" makes clear that ultimately each reader, director, and actor must take responsibility for his or her choice of version. The consequences for these choices are thus something they are "perpetually arriving at" (*PDAT*, p. 54). Put in these terms, it is not hard to see why Cavell describes the moment of Bloch's "perfect" Bach as one of the dawning upon him of a vision he will later call "Emersonian perfectionism," where what is "perfect" is not some preexisting gold standard of correctness (moral or aesthetic) to which conductors, musicians, editors, directors, actors, and the rest of us must strive to aspire; rather, it is the sense of the "perfectible"—the "perfect" or the "correct" as something always to be arrived at, and the quest for it as something we must take responsibility for, even if we (know we) are never to arrive there. What, then, is a text of Shakespeare's? In spite of, and even because of, all its textual variants, indeterminacies, and instabilities, a Shakespeare text is not something we can leave to the editor to determine: it is something each reader must take ownership of and responsibility for. Interpretive decisions, including editorial decisions, are down to us as readers, provided we are prepared to answer for the "correctness" of our "perfect" Shakespeare text. Moreover, we must be prepared to answer for the "perfection" of our text, knowing that its "perfectibility" may never be realized, at least not by us. And if this is so, then what Cavell calls a "Shakespeare text" is a deliberate refusal to acknowledge, and hence an avoidance of, the kind of entity that both the traditional editors, with their "definitive" versions, and the New Textualists, with their skepticism toward them, call by that name.

VI
The Actions of Their Characters

It is, roughly, an Aristotelian position to conceptualize a play as a complex whole comprising the deeds of characters, principally involving their actions and reactions to events. This, in short, is what is called a "plot," and a play of Shakespeare's can be thought of in this way. Consider the sheer number of adaptations, rewritings, retellings, and so on, that the Shakespeare play is heir to. Typically, aspects of the plot, consisting of the more fundamental actions of the principal characters, will be retained, albeit recast in some form that is different from, perhaps even alien to, Shakespeare's original conception.

Although Cavell is very much engaged with this phenomenon—as, for instance, in his recent essay on Eric Rohmer's adaptation of *The Winter's Tale* into the film *Conte d'Hiver*[41]—his understanding of Shakespeare is not primarily led by a plot-driven, Aristotelian view. As A. J. Cascardi explains, "Unlike that of so many of his predecessors, Cavell's interest in tragedy does not revolve around questions of action. . . . Cavell's work on Shakespeare shifts the ground of the analysis of tragedy to the questions of knowledge and doubt."[42] Whereas philosophers from Aristotle to Hegel place the plot and the characters' roles in it at the heart of their theories of tragedy, Cavell does not see it as the intellectual or aesthetic motor of the genre. If this seems problematic, then that may be because Cavell's notions of the dramatic or the tragic are themselves somewhat idiosyncratic. Cascardi, though, sees this idiosyncrasy as philosophically instructive rather than troublesome:

> Does the shift in focus away from matters of action somehow mean that the essentially *dramatic* quality of Shakespeare's plays is neglected? . . . Or, in Aristotelian terms, does Cavell make the mistake of privileging the "thought" (*dianoia*) of Shakespeare's works over and above matters of character and plot? Perhaps the best response that can be given to these questions is one that reveals them as relying on assumptions that are false. In Cavell's analysis, drama is not simply the representation of incidents in the form of a plot; rather, it is a mode of "poetry" that brings out as *dramatic* forms of human consciousness and experience that may not initially strike us as dramatic at all. . . . Understanding the dramatic qualities of Shakespeare's plays thus means understanding what drama is.[43]

Without wishing to disagree with any of this, I find its principal drawback to be its rendering our inquiry—"What is a play of Shakespeare's?"—as something of a begged question.

The emphasis on character is one part of the Aristotelian formulation that Cavell is zealously keen to hold onto, but, taking a "play" as a piece of dramatic literature, what emanates from characters is not so much their actions as their *words*. A Shakespeare play thus understood consists not so much of characters' actions boiled down to the kernel of a plot but of characters on stage exchanging speeches with one another. At the time Cavell began his engagements with Shakespeare, the New Criticism was still the dominant literary force in the American academy, and its close attention to the "words on the page" tended to abstract those words from the people saying them. An earlier generation of critics—principally A. C. Bradley—dwelled at greater length on Shakespeare's characters, and so Cavell begins his lifelong engagement with Shakespeare by drawing out the philosophical significance of a "shift from character to words" (*DK*, p. 39) in Shakespeare criticism. It is a shift he is deeply suspicious of, because (and this follows on in several ways from the previous section) it entails a flawed conception of a Shakespeare play as too straightforwardly a *text*.

Gerald Bruns correctly observes that "Cavell is not afraid to go back to an older, romantic way of reading Shakespeare, before absorption in character gave way to the unpacking of textual and contextual systems."[44] And indeed, some of Cavell's views on this matter might seem old-fashioned, or at least naively humanist, when read alongside contemporary criticism.[45] However, he is keen to distance himself from the standard humanist critique of the (then) New Criticism, which, to oversimplify, maintained that "the tendency of modern critics to treat metaphors or symbols rather than the characters and actions of Shakespeare's plays as primary data in understanding them . . . depends upon a neglect, even a denial, of the humanness of the play's characters" (*DK*, p. 44). Instead, Cavell is more interested in conducting an investigation into what critics (think they) are talking about when making a distinction between the characters in a play and the words in a play:

> My purpose here is not to urge that in reading Shakespeare's plays one put words back into the characters speaking them, and replace characters from our possession back into their words. The point is rather to learn something about what prevents these commendable activities from taking place. It is a matter of learning what it is one uses as data for one's assertions about such works, what kinds of appeal one in fact finds convincing. (*DK*, p. 41)

Cavell goes on to point out that the very same question arises for ordinary language philosophy: both New Critics and analytic philosophers are too frequently given to studying words in terms of appeals to form and structure, and although these terms mean completely different things in these disciplines—logical form and propositional structure in the case of analytic philosophy; literary, poetic, and symbolic structures and forms in the case of New Criticism—both tend to substitute theoretical entities for a more frank engagement with what particular human beings in particular circumstances say and mean by particular words. "That," Cavell remarks, "is all that 'ordinary' in the phrase 'ordinary language philosophy' means, or ought to mean" (*DK*, p. 42).[46] Accordingly, studying the words characters speak in isolation from, and even as an alternative to, studying the characters that speak them is actually a very *extra*ordinary thing to do:

> The most curious feature of the shift and conflict between character criticism and verbal analysis is that it should have taken place at all. How could any serious critic ever have forgotten that to care about a specific character is to care about the utterly specific words he says when and as he says them; or that we care about the utterly specific words of a play because certain men and women are having to give voice to them? Yet apparently both frequently happen. (*DK*, p. 41)

And so, Cavell implies, if we wish to understand aright what "a play of Shakespeare's" is, we ought to begin by asking two interrelated questions: "What has discouraged attention from investigations of character? What, apart from this, has specifically motivated an absorbing attention to words?" (*DK*, p. 40).

To take the second question first, Cavell plausibly suggests that

> one reason a critic is drawn to words is, immediately, that attention to characters has often in fact been given apart from attention to the specific words granted them, so it looks as if attention to character is a distraction from the only, or the final, evidence there is for a reading of a literary work, namely the words themselves. But it is then unclear what the words are to be used as evidence for. For a correct interpretation? But what would an interpretation then be of? (*DK*, p. 40)

One can hardly say that in denuding the analysis of a Shakespeare play of its characters in favor of its words one is interpreting a *play*, for surely the dramatis personae is the very basis of the play. At best, one is interpreting a *text*, which, as we have seen in the previous section, is not quite the same thing. Well may Gerald Bruns ask, "What, in shifting attention from character to language or text or context, are we (ourselves, as readers) turning away from, or trying to avoid?"[47]

To answer this question properly, we need to understand what a character *is*, what kind of entity it is and what kind of ontology it has. Cavell conducts a rigorous investigation of this question, but since it is the subject of detailed discussion later in this book, it makes little sense to render that discussion redundant by anticipating it here.[48] Suffice it to say that Cavell's writings on Shakespeare often seem to grant the characters an independent consciousness, intelligence, and existence of their own, so that, as Lawrence Rhu puts it, "his critics indict him for ingenuously connecting with a make-believe world and its denizens as though it were a real one and they were real people in it."[49] Whereas a better summary of Cavell's position would be that it is not so much that characters are real people with an independent existence but that in order to understand them aright, and hence to approach them aright, we need to confront them as if they made the same ethical and moral demands upon us as real people do. Anything short of this involves practicing a kind of avoidance of the claim of the other. "So," as Bruns puts it, "the idea is to read Shakespeare by confronting his characters."[50]

If there is indeed some form of avoidance at stake in sidelining the characters of a Shakespeare play, this places us in an uncanny complicity with tragic figures like Othello, Lear, or Leontes, who are themselves set on avoiding their knowledge of the other characters—that is the germ of their tragedy. But rather than suggesting that there is therefore an ethical imperative to return to character-oriented criticism, Cavell remains more committed to investigating why this state of affairs has come about. He ventures to suggest that

> one reason a critic may shun direct contact with characters is that he has been made to believe or assume, by some philosophy or other, that characters are not people, that what can be known about people cannot be known about characters, and in particular that psychology is either not appropriate to the study of these fictional beings or that psychology is the province of psychologists and not to be ventured from the armchairs of literary studies. But is any of this more than the merest assumption; unexamined principles which are part of current academic fashion? For what is the relevant psychology? Of course, to account for the behavior of characters one is going to apply predicates like "is in pain," "is ironic," "is jealous," "is thinking of . . ." to them. But does that require psychological expertise? No more than to apply these predicates to one's acquaintances. (*DK*, p. 40)

If this is indeed what has discouraged critics from attending to questions of character, then the psychoanalytically inflected approach sometimes adopted by Cavell might well be arraigned for taking a step too far in the opposite direction. Indeed, of the many occasions when Cavell suggests a psychoanalytic gloss on a character's words, actions, or motives, most range from the speculative to the crude, as when he suggests that "Coriolanus's erotic attachment to battle and to men who battle suggests a search for the father as much as an escape from the mother" (*DK*, p. 156), or when he reads Gloucester's blinding scene in *King Lear* in the reverse direction:

> It is by now commonly appreciated that Gloucester had, when that scene began, no plans for going to Dover. . . . The question is why *Regan* assumes that he is going to Dover. (Her husband, for example, does not: "Turn out that eyeless villain.") We may wish here to . . . suppose that she associates that name with the gathering of all her enemies. But the essential fact is that the name is primarily caught to the image of her father. In her mind, the man she is sending on his way to Dover is the man she *knows* is sent on his way to Dover: in her paroxysms of cruelty, she imagines that she has just participated in blinding her father. (*DK*, pp. 52–53)

If this is what counts as enriching armchair literary criticism with psychology, then it is not entirely clear that such armchair Freudianism constitutes much in the way of progress.

Arguably the most ambitious and detailed of Cavell's attempts to reanimate Shakespeare criticism by psychologizing characters is his reading of *Othello*. In a nutshell, the basic insight behind this reading is that "Othello kills Desdemona not because she is faithless . . . but on the contrary because she is faithful, because the very reciprocity of the thing he has elicited from her is what makes him feel sullied" (*IQO*, p. 138). This, I submit, is indeed an astute, perceptive, and insightful psychological interpretation of Othello's behavior, arrived at in large measure by interpretation of his words. However, the discussion does not rest here; indeed, it has barely commenced. Cavell builds on this insight to suggest that

> Othello's problem, following my suggestion that his problem is over success, not failure, is that Desdemona's acceptance, or satisfaction, or reward, of his ambition strikes him as being possessed, as if he is the woman. This linking of the desire of knowledge for possession, for, let us say, intimacy, links this epistemological problematic as a whole with that of the problematic of property, of ownership as the owning or ratifying of one's identity. (*DK*, p. 10)

The engagement with the problematic of property, we are then told, links Othello (and hence *Othello*) to the philosophies of Locke and Marx, while the anxiety around gender is related to questions Cavell raises repeatedly about the nature of Othello's sexuality:

> We of course have no answer to such questions. But what matters is that Othello has no answer; or rather he can give none, for any answer to the questions, granted that I am right in taking the questions to be his, is intolerable. The torture of logic in his mind we might represent as follows: Either I shed her blood and scarred her or I did not. If I did not then she was not a virgin and this is a stain upon me. If I did then she is no longer a virgin and this is a stain upon me. Either way I am contaminated. (I do not say that the sides of this dilemma are of equal significance for Othello.) (*DK*, p. 135)

Cavell's analysis, then, claims to identify Othello's psychological idiosyncrasies; to deduce from these a peculiar and contorted "logic" of virginity and its loss; to embed these in a psychoanalysis of Othello's sexuality; and to relate the whole lot to broader philosophical currents such as the concept of property or, more fundamentally, the concept of Cartesian skepticism. Crucially, all of this is attributed not to Cavell's interpretation of *Othello* but to Othello as a character, that is, to the man himself. As Cavell says, "I do not think that we must, nor that we can, choose among these possibilities in Othello's mind. On the contrary, I think Othello cannot choose among them" (*DK*, p. 132). Given that

Othello is unlikely to have had knowledge of Freud or Descartes, Locke or Marx, many critics would find it something of an understatement for Cascardi to observe that "it could be complained that Cavell gives us a Shakespeare . . . whose characters seem to be involved in intricacies of plotting that require motives far more recherché than they themselves might imagine."[51] Cavell's attempts to psychologize or psychoanalyze Shakespeare's characters sometimes go so far as to venture a claim as to what a given character is thinking in a given moment, and all too often what they are thinking turns out to impinge in some way on a philosophy or a philosopher close to the heart of Cavell's broader project.

It is at this level that I find Cavell's readings of Shakespeare to be at their weakest, as well as their least persuasive: while they are intriguing and entertaining as interpretations of characters' words and actions, their plausibility too often hinges on ideas or concepts voiced in philosophical texts whose relation to the play under discussion is not always rendered altogether intelligible. However, what makes them compelling interpretations nevertheless is, in part, the stark incontestability of the method in this madness, which Cavell basically derives from ordinary language philosophy. As Mulhall puts it, "His assumption [is] that the meanings of words spoken by characters in texts are a function of their significance as words and the significance of their being uttered at a given time by a given individual."[52] If we are truly to confront Shakespeare's characters, it seems undeniable that we must grant them and their words the same grounding in everyday language we would grant to anyone else whose meaning we seek to fathom. Yet when confronting someone who is in the process of uttering the most eloquent speeches ever penned in the English language, the (deceptively) simple intuition that their words must mean what they say may well start to feel shaky. The sheer power and beauty, the suggestiveness and allusiveness, of a speech from, say, *Hamlet* or *Othello* has a way of stopping this intuition in its tracks. What *does* Hamlet mean by asking, "To be or not to be?" or Iago by asking Othello, "Are you fast married?" It is not that the words are lacking in everyday sense but rather that the very everydayness of that sense seems inadequate both to the occasion and to the power of the words themselves. Is it possible, one often feels like asking, for language to get any *less* ordinary than Shakespeare's?[53]

But that is not quite the point. The point is rather to acknowledge the extraordinariness of these words not only as Shakespeare's (and perhaps not primarily as Shakespeare's) but as, say, Hamlet's or Othello's, in order to understand why they are saying these remarkable things and what they might mean by them. It is for this reason that I would disagree with Mulhall's contention that Cavell's interpretations of Shakespeare's characters "ground his overarching presupposition that the significance of the orderings of words which comprise a given text is something meant or intended by its author."[54] It is not that Cavell does not endorse this presupposition, nor that this presupposition is wrong—these, in any case, would be matters for discussion in the next section. It is rather that the remarkable degree of autonomy Cavell's readings grant Shakespeare's characters affords them a status of critical independence from the overarching intentions of their author.

In this respect, Cavell's treatment of Shakespeare's characters suggests an answer to our question "What is a play of Shakespeare's?" that resembles the architectonics of the Dostoevskian novel as described by Mikhail Bakhtin.[55] Here, characters are not subordinated as entities situated in order of importance within a designed hierarchy with a narrator or author at its pinnacle and the hero sitting on his right hand. Rather, the work consists of a plurality of characters of equal status with one another and with the author, each of whom brings to the work his or her voice, consciousness, philosophy, thoughts, and worldview, with the work then consisting of these autonomous characters entering into dialogue and polemicizing with one another in a manner that can only be called philosophical. This, it seems to me, is, *mutatis mutandis*, a good way to describe Cavell's critical treatment of the characters in a Shakespeare play. Moreover, if Shakespeare's characters are to be understood, not as subordinates to an overarching authorial design, but as free agents having equally valid voices within the realm of the Shakespearean text, then, thanks in part to Bakhtin, we have arrived at a view of a play of Shakespeare's as a speech community in which the characters play a role not unlike that of ordinary language philosophers, exploring the implications of our (and their) language and our (and their) knowledge, and our problems with the limits of both, which open the doors to skepticism. A. J. Cascardi, in fact, explores a similar linkage between Cavell's analyses of Shakespeare's characters and his philosophy of ordinary language when he asks:

> *How* do the characters in a play mean what they say? How can they *not* mean what they say? What are we to make of the meaningfulness of their words? Cavell's analyses of Shakespeare are all rooted in a conviction that Shakespeare's characters *must* mean what they say, and mean it thoroughly, unless of course they are in a posture of avoidance, in which case their words may reveal whatever it is they might wish to disown.[56]

Is Cavell's character-oriented approach to Shakespeare itself in a posture of avoidance? That is, is this character-based account of what a play of Shakespeare's is in some way at odds with literary critical answers to the same question? And since this account of a Shakespeare play is centered on characters, is there a sense in which what Cavell means by *character* is somehow at variance with what a literary critic means by this term? Certainly, few contemporary literary critics would consider it a good use of their time to speculate on characters' putative and anachronistic relationships with philosophical texts that neither they nor Shakespeare could have read, and if there are still psychoanalytic critics who attempt to account for characters' words and deeds by claiming to know, through psychoanalysis, what those characters are thinking, then thankfully those critics can hardly be held representative of the vanguard of psychoanalytic literary criticism. It is in these respects that Cavell's account seems to me unpersuasive. However, if I am right in seeing in his treatment of Shakespeare's characters an understanding of his plays as analogous to linguistic communities and its characters as analogous to agents within them, then this would chime closely with certain aspects of the Bakhtinian school of critical theory. It is worth qualifying this, though, by observing that since Shakespeare's characters are known to us through—and indeed essentially consist in—the words they speak, the relation in which a Shakespearean character stands to the words that form the text of a Shakespeare play could well seem a relation of identity. As Cavell puts it:

> Can Coleridge or Bradley really be understood as interested in characters *rather than* in the words of the play; or are the writings of Empson or G. Wilson Knight well used in saying that they are interested in what is happening in the words *rather than* what is happening in the speakers of the words? It is, however, equally easy and unhelpful to say that both ends of the tradition have been interested *both* in the characters *and* in their words . . . because this suggests that there are two things each end is interested in, whereas both would or should insist that they are interested only in one thing, the plays themselves. (*DK*, p. 39)

What might well differentiate Cavell's position from that of Bakhtinian theory, and what may ultimately mean that Cavell's idea of character is not the same as that of most literary critics, is that he is prepared to question the distinctions between the words that form the text of Shakespeare's plays, the characters that speak them, and "the plays themselves." For Cavell, not only do these coordinates need to be thought together and kept in the same frame but they may well turn out to be one and the same thing.

VII
Embodiments of Authorial Intention

Of all the aspects of Cavell's work on literature and on aesthetics more generally, his engagement with issues of authorship and intentionality are probably the most extensive, ambitious, and complex. What is more, this issue is one of the most live and emotive topics in the history of literary criticism: contributions to debates around authorial intention include such classic discussions as Wimsatt and Beardsley's "The Intentional Fallacy," Barthes's "Death of the Author," Foucault's "What Is an Author?," Knapp and Michaels's "Against Theory," and E. D. Hirsch's *Validity in Interpretation*. The subject is a hardy perennial for undergraduate essays in introductory critical theory courses, but Cavell's contribution to the debate seems to feature on the reading lists for such courses only rarely, if at all. Why is this?[57]

Having concluded each of the previous five sections by suggesting that Cavell's arguments differ in various more or less radical ways from the common parlance of literary criticism, I will now break the pattern by asserting it from the outset: the Cavellian approach to the issue of authorial intention is not simply an avoidance of but in some ways a direct critique of the way this issue has been handled by certain literary critics. His work on Shakespeare—given how the name *Shakespeare* has become loaded as that of the most preeminent author of Anglophone culture—is a good place from which to investigate this issue in depth.

To those well versed in the standard terms in which debates about authorial intention are conducted in literary theory, Cavell can sometimes seem downright self-contradictory. One of his earliest essays on aesthetics claims that "the first fact of works of art is that they are meant, meant to be understood" (*MWM*, pp. 227–28), and elsewhere he makes clear that they are meant by "the one doing the writing, backing it, fronting it" (*IQO*, p. 23), namely, the author. Mulhall, who, of all commentators on Cavell, is keenest to talk up the role of the author in Cavell's writings on literary texts, claims that Cavell "tends to treat each such text primarily as the intentional product of a single organizing intelligence, as the creation or composition of an individual human being," and that "the Cavellian emphasis upon a single controlling human intelligence behind the texts he studies is, at least in part, a reflection or displacement of his tendency to regard those individual texts and *oeuvres* as essentially integral and self-comprehending human compositions."[58] It is not hard to see why those teaching or studying the poststructuralist assault on the figure of the author rarely find time to make what appears to be a clear detour through Cavell, since his proauthorial stance could only take them out of their way. Indeed, if most of the classic literary theory on the issue of authorial intention has tended to downplay, critique, or reject the concept (E. D. Hirsch or Knapp and Michaels notwithstanding), Cavell, as Mulhall observes, "finds himself . . . strongly inclined to employ that concept in aesthetic discussions, and so equally strongly inclined to believe that only an erroneous theory of the nature of intentions could lead others to reject its legitimacy."[59]

Oddly, though, Cavell's writings also contain what appear to be some flat endorsements of a clearly *anti*authorial, anti-intentional position that would seem, at first blush, located in surprisingly close proximity to the coordinates of poststructuralism. As regards intention, one of his earliest essays states: "I should urge that we do justice to the fact that an individual's intentions or wishes can no more produce the general meaning for a word than they can produce horses for beggars, or home runs from pop flies, or successful poems out of unsuccessful poems" (*MWM*, pp. 38–39), while elsewhere he asserts that in interpretations of literature, "the goal is freedom from the person of the author" (*TOS*, p. 53). Is Cavell simply contradicting himself here? And if not, how is his position on the question of authorial intention related to those in the standard debates of literary theory?

Let us look closer at what Cavell is saying when he suggests that the goal of interpretation is to free a text from its author. Taken as a slogan, this seems to chime closely with the Barthesian view that the birth of the reader is bound up with the death of the author. Placed in its context, however, it is a rather more complex claim: the aim is not to establish a dialectical trade-off between author-bound, intention-directed criticism and reader-centered "free" engagement with the text. Rather, *both* kinds of interpretation are equally suspect, because "the motive of an interpretation, like what one might call the intention of the work . . . exists fully only in its satisfaction" (*TOS*, p. 62). We are making a basic methodological error if we think that either a reader-derived interpretation or an author-derived intention can ground a reading of a literary text, because that is putting the interpretive cart before the textual horse and hence begs the question, "But what is a text that it has this power of overcoming the person of its author?" (*TOS*, p. 53). We have already seen how, for Cavell, what counts in interpreting a Shakespeare play is not a particular picture of, say, historical context or of the conventions of drama; rather, what counts is how the *play* pictures these things. But what would it mean, though, to ask how *Hamlet* or *Coriolanus* pictures the intention of its author? How is this question anything more than an oddly phrased, cumbersome reiteration of the kinds of critical activity Cavell found troublesome in the first place?

Actually, it is not, and that is precisely the point. It makes no sense to ask how *Hamlet* pictures Shakespeare's intention, because Shakespeare has already offered us a perfect picture of that intention, and that picture simply *is* the play *Hamlet*, just as the same play is also a perfect picture of how and what its readers are supposed to interpret. In other words, the play's the thing. What is more, if "what Shakespeare meant by *Hamlet*" just *was Hamlet*, then poststructuralist readers who imagine they have dispensed with the author and are engaging in "free play with the text" are in fact responding directly to what Cavell calls "Shakespeare's melodramatic invitations to the competition of meaning" (*CT*, p. 169). (Perhaps it might be instructive here that Shakespeare gave some of his plays open-ended titles and subtitles like *As You Like It* or *What You Will*.) For Cavell, we have already lost our footing the moment we start to speak of an author's intention as something that can be conceived of apart from, as an entity separate from, the play itself. As Wittgenstein put it—and Cavell's view of intentionality does indeed appear to be shaped by Wittgenstein's, and to a degree Austin's—"An intention is embedded in its situation, in human customs and institutions. If the technique of the game of chess did not exist, I could not intend to play a game of chess."[60] Authorial intentions have no more autonomy from the texts in which they appear than do chess players' intentions, and literary critics bestow a false, metaphysical autonomy on them by regarding them in a different light from how intentions work in ordinary language. In other words, "a particular formulation of the problem of intention has been accepted," and this formulation is tautologous: "Because in what I have been urging, this alternative between 'what is intended' and 'what is there' is just what is being questioned" (*MWM*, p. 230). When Cavell began writing on aesthetics, it was common for critics to, in the words of Stephen Mulhall, "reject critical references to the artist's intentions because they picture an intention as existing in the artist's head and having only a causal relation to the artwork."[61] Cavell is quite happy to wield Occam's razor to this curious picture of intentionality. As Espen Hammer puts it, "Rather, what an artist intends is nothing more than that which we encounter when we watch, read, or listen to the work itself."[62]

What is at issue here can perhaps be seen more clearly if we move away from the poststructuralist position on authorial intentionality and turn instead toward the New Critics' position, with which Cavell's early writings on this subject engage directly. He pays tribute to what he calls "the decisive accomplishment, in literary criticism, of the New Critics, whose formalist program called for, and depended upon, minute attention concentrated on the poem itself" (*MWM*, p. 181), while pointing out that the success of the New Criticism has brought about:

> the realization on the part of anyone who knows what art is that many of the responses directed to works of art are irrelevant to them as art and that the artist's intention is *always* irrelevant—it no more counts toward the success or failure of a work of art that the artist intended something other than is *there*, than it counts, when the referee is counting over a boxer, that the boxer had intended to duck. (*MWM*, p. 181)

Now, whereas Roland Barthes's poststructuralist view envisaged a dialectical trade-off between the author's intention and the reader's interpretation—simplistically, cordoning off the former simultaneously opens up the way for the latter—Wimsatt and Beardsley saw *both* the "intentional fallacy" *and* the "affective fallacy" as equally misguided and equally irrelevant: the former, they claimed, confused a poem with its cause, and the latter confused a poem with its effect.[63]

For Cavell, this cause-and-effect view of literature is highly problematic, as well as deeply metaphysical.[64] If nothing else, it is metaphysical because it departs from the role "intentions" play in ordinary language and in our everyday lives. As Mulhall observes, "Cavell takes the notion of 'intention' with which he is working to be the ordinary, familiar one; so he takes recent critical attempts to dissuade us from so employing it to be based on metaphysical misinterpretations of this concept."[65] Wimsatt and Beardsley therefore

> appeal to a concept of intention as relevant to art which does not exist elsewhere: in, for example, the case of ordinary conduct, nothing is more *visible* than actions which are not meant, visible *in* the slip, the mistake, the accident, the inadvertence . . . , and by what follows (the embarrassment, confusion, remorse, apology, attempts to correct . . .). (*MWM*, pp. 226–27)

Of all the slips, mistakes, accidents, and inadvertences that ordinary language is heir to (one thinks of Spoonerisms, Freudian slips, malapropisms, and the like), all can be clarified by asking, "What did you mean?" or by explaining "What I meant was . . ." and hence are in some sense correctible. That this is not the case for a literary text, for a Shakespeare play, or for any kind of artwork does not in itself demand a different concept of intention for these works. And most importantly, in neither case is there a good ground to suppose that an intention behind the words can be readily isolated from the words themselves. Consider the following scenario:

> A man asks me for a candlestick from the mantel and I bring it to him; he looks and says, "No, I meant the other one." Did he? Does his saying this establish his intention? Not in the absence of an understandable continuation. If he simply puts the thing on the floor beside him and I cannot imagine to what point, nor can I imagine what he may want to use it for later, nor can I see what its difference is from the one he rejected, I am not going to say that he *meant* this one rather than the other one. (Perhaps his intention was to demonstrate the completeness of my subservience, obeying pointless requests.) What the continuation will have to be, how it establishes the intention, will vary in range and complexity, with the context. (*MWM*, p. 230)

The assumption that this man's intention can be identified in its own right as something separable from his words in the case of this straightforward, albeit idiosyncratic, request simply does not hold up, any more than the idea that we could hive off Shakespeare's intention in writing *Hamlet* from the play that is *Hamlet*. If Wimsatt and Beardsley think otherwise, as Mulhall says, "they thereby fail to see that intention and outcome are internally related."[66] Or as Cavell puts it, "What counts is what is *there*, says the philosopher who distrusts appeals to intention. Yes, but everything that is there is something a man has *done*" (*MWM*, p. 236).

And so the idea of Shakespeare's plays as "embodiments of authorial intention" is, *pace* a great deal of contemporary literary criticism and theory, a perfectly sound one, *provided* we do not make the mistake of imagining that Shakespeare's intention could ever be *dis*embodied. As Cavell says, "It doesn't follow that what we are interested in, being interested in his work, is not his intention" (*MWM*, p. 232), but nor does it follow that being interested in Shakespeare's intention, we can isolate it from Shakespeare's play. Least of all could it be disembodied by turning to the biographical speculation or pseudo-psychological mindreading that has guided certain Shakespeare scholars. Cavell would certainly concur with the New Critics and the poststructuralists alike in rejecting scholarship of this kind—controversies surrounding the authorship of Shakespeare's plays notwithstanding—because they too subscribe to an erroneous, positivistic view of Shakespeare's intention as detachable from Shakespeare's plays. We may very well have a hunch about a meaning Shakespeare intended by a certain passage in *Hamlet*, but the best evidence for it is surely *Hamlet*, and the relevance of psycho-biographical speculation is at the very least questionable:

"Whether he did intend it depends on what he *did*, on the work itself. . . . For there is no relevance to point out, in relation to a work of art, which the artist has not himself created" (*MWM*, pp. 233–34).

As an example of how Cavell puts this theoretical orientation into critical practice, consider some of his comments on the abdication scene in *King Lear*, which, Cavell says, "has always been known to be extraordinary, and a familiar justification of it has been we, as spectators, simply must accept it as the initial condition of the dramatic events and then attend to its consequences" (*DK*, p. 86). Throughout the history of Shakespeare criticism there have been a host of explanations for this scene,[67] and Cavell is not reluctant to offer one of his own, centering on shame, on love, and on its avoidance. Whether or not his interpretation is more or less plausible than any of its predecessors is not the point here—or, better, it is only incidentally the point. The key point is that "arguments ensue, in each case, about whether Shakespeare is justified in what he is asking his audience to accept" (*DK*, p. 57). In other words, one cannot wholly account for *what* we have to accept in this scene and *why* accepting it proves difficult if one insists on factoring out some sense of what it is that Shakespeare has put into the scene and, relatedly, why it is that he has put the scene into the play.

If there is such a pervasive sense that "the abdication scene strains belief" (*DK*, p. 87), then for Cavell this is better thought of as a "structural strategy in *King Lear*" (*DK*, p. 86). This phrase suggests a picture of a *strategist* and hence of authorial intention, which many critics will find objectionable, but Cavell does not shy away from it. (Nor does he seek to fudge the issue, as some contemporary critics do, by taking the authorial agency out of the word *strategy* and speaking instead of "textual strategies" or "discursive strategies"; this, surely, could only amount to an avoidance of Shakespeare, and moreover a metaphysical departure from what the term *strategy* would ordinarily be taken to mean.) Rather, for Cavell,

> this uncovers what I meant by the structural strategy of the play's opening scene: we *do* accept its events as they come to light; anyway we sit through them and we accommodate ourselves to them one way or another; after which, as a consequence of which, we have to accept less obviously extraordinary events as unquestionable workings out of a bad beginning. To speak of this as a strategy may suggest that Shakespeare intended it to have this effect; and do I want to make such a claim? But why not? A critic who strains at this claim will allow himself to swallow the notion that Shakespeare counted on the fact that he was only using

> an old story whose initial improbabilities he needn't be responsible for. Maybe. Only this raises, and makes unwelcome, urgent questions: Why does he use *this* story? What does he see in it? Why *show* the abdication rather than begin with various accounts of it? Whereas all I need as evidence for saying that Shakespeare intended the strategy of our accepting it (that is, all the claim comes to) is that he put it in there and we do accept it, if in confusion. (*DK*, p. 87)

That we accept this scene is all the evidence that is needed for the claim that Shakespeare succeeded in his intention here. It is simply not necessary—for either the audience or the critic—to settle on a definitive, detachable thought that Shakespeare had in putting it there. To think otherwise is to misunderstand the role that the word *why* plays in the above questions. As Cavell has it:

> Nothing could be commoner among critics of art than to ask *why* the thing is as it is, and characteristically to put this question, for example, in the form "Why does Shakespeare follow the murder of Duncan with a scene which begins with the sound of knocking?," or "Why does Beethoven put in a bar of rest in the last line of the fourth Bagatelle (Op. 126)?" The best critic is the one who knows best where to ask this question, and how to get an answer; but surely he doesn't feel it necessary, or desirable even were it possible, to get in touch with the artist to find out the answer. (*MWM*, p. 182)

Putting the matter in these terms demonstrates that regarding Shakespeare's plays as products of Shakespeare's intentions need not and does not problematize the kind of critical activity that relates to analyzing those plays. Rather, it is restoring to critical activity a grounding in a sense of design and artistry that critics from Wimsatt and Beardsley onwards have erroneously dismissed as anthropomorphic, humanist fallacies.

In summary, then, Cavell characterizes his position by stating:

> I assume that any complexity the average mortal finds in a play of Shakespeare's is something Shakespeare is capable of having placed there. The critical question is: How? By what means? The question whether an author intends any or all of what happens is a convenient defense against this critical question. (*DK*, p. 240)

What this suggests is that the sidelining of authors and their intentions in the literary criticism and theory of most of the last century amounts, in our terms and in Cavell's, to an avoidance of Shakespeare. And so Cavell, in his writings on Shakespeare and on literature and art more generally, is not advocating or practicing a "return to" the figure of the artist or the writer, if what is meant by that is the flawed picture of a biographically centered, deterministic approach to interpretation and analysis. Rather, Cavell is more concerned with avoiding an avoidance, and thereby bringing the idea of intentionality home from its metaphysical holiday and restoring it to the role it plays in ordinary language:

> Recent attacks on intentionality share the (metaphysical) picture of intention that they would criticize, one that makes its importance absolute, as if, if intention counts for anything in meaning, it counts for everything. . . . So let us say: Intention is merely of the last importance. Everything (else) has first to be in place for it to do what it does—as in putting a flame to a fuse. (*DK*, pp. 240–41)[68]

This picture of authorial intention, held by (supposedly) traditional New Critics and (supposedly) iconoclastic poststructuralists alike, is not so much false as it is empty, and though these critics were right to see that giving up the search for it is simply to give up a wild-goose chase, they did not see so far as to give up this flawed concept altogether—which is to give up exactly nothing. Like the idea of the "perfect Shakespeare text," this particular idea of Shakespeare's intention is "something Wittgenstein calls a house of cards" (*PDAT*, p. 36), predicated on what Mulhall rightly calls "a picture of a conceptual gap between intention and outcome that simply does not normally exist."[69]

But the matter does not entirely rest there, because, for Cavell, "it is not merely a bad picture of intention that makes this seem false or contentious or paradoxical, it is also a bad picture of what a poem is" (*MWM*, p. 227). Depriving artworks such as literary texts of the impulse behind them relegates them to mere things, analogous to physical objects (the New Critics' "verbal icons" and "well-wrought urns," for example).[70] This, once again, overlooks the way these literary objects have been crafted, according to some sense of design—or, in Cavell's term, the way they have been *meant*. Thus, rethinking our notion of intention can restore to the literary text (such as a Shakespeare play) a clearer sense of its status and its demands on us as readers. As Mulhall explains:

> Asking a question about the intention of a particular act typically does not drive us outside the action itself but further into it; in asking the question, we are asking about the meaning of that particular action, about its significance, and not about the existence or non-existence of a particular psychological episode. Correctly understood, talk of the author's intentions in the specific context of art is simply a way of focussing more closely upon the work of art itself.[71]

As regards Shakespeare and his plays, this insight is particularly apt, because Cavell has more recently asserted (in "The Interminable Shakespeare Text") that "Shakespeare's feats of creativity take place within fields of forces incommensurably beyond the power of finite intentions to effect" (*PDAT*, p. 35).

I take this, however, not to mean that intention is somehow irrelevant to the plays of Shakespeare, nor that Shakespeare's plays are somehow above or beyond the debate that has been conducted in this section, but rather as chiming with a remark of Wittgenstein's that Cavell cites and discusses in this essay, to the effect that "I do not believe that Shakespeare can be set alongside any other poet. Was he perhaps a *creator of language* rather than a poet?"[72] Maybe the reason why Wittgenstein needed the authority of Milton to convince him of Shakespeare's greatness, or the reason why he felt unable to speak of "Shakespeare's great heart" in the way he felt perfectly comfortable speaking of "Beethoven's great heart,"[73] is to be found in the following passage:

> The reason why I cannot understand Shakespeare is that I want to find symmetry in all this asymmetry.
>
> His pieces give me an impression as of enormous *sketches* rather than of paintings; as though they had been *dashed off* by someone who can permit himself *anything*, so to speak. And I understand how someone can admire that and call *it supreme* art, but I don't like it.—So if someone stands in front of these pieces speechless, I can understand him; but anyone who admires them as one admires, say, Beethoven, seems to me to misunderstand Shakespeare.[74]

It seems more than possible, on the evidence of these remarks, that Wittgenstein fails to connect with Shakespeare because, unlike, say, Milton's or Beethoven's, Shakespeare's works do not seem (to Wittgenstein, that is) to picture Shakespeare's designs, meanings, or intentions as clearly as (to paraphrase Wittgenstein) the human body pictures the human soul. Does this mean that Wittgenstein, whose remarks on intentions and intentionality are so clearly a major influence on Cavell's, has fallen prey to the metaphysical concept of authorial intention that Cavell corrects? On the contrary:

> It may be that the essential thing with Shakespeare is his ease and authority and that you just have to accept him as he is if you are going to be able to admire him properly. . . . If I am right about this, that would mean that the style of his whole work, I mean of all his works taken together, is the essential thing and what provides his justification.[75]

This is not altogether removed from the stance Cavell talks up in his view of the abdication scene in *King Lear*, as outlined above.

Finally, as a closing thought, if Wittgenstein is correct in seeing Shakespeare as a "creator of language" rather than a poet, then what Shakespeare's plays do is to create the conditions of possibility for intention, meaning, and design—which is why they strike Wittgenstein as sketches rather than as artworks. And if this is so, then it is highly instructive that Wittgenstein's preface to his own magnum opus compares it to an album of sketches and clearly does not consider *Philosophical Investigations* to be "a good book."[76] If I am right here, then Wittgenstein's description of Shakespeare's plays is in fact surprisingly close to his description of his own philosophy (he compares both to a set of sketches and also to a landscape, for example). That Cavell has been so constantly preoccupied and heavily influenced by both Shakespeare and Wittgenstein and that, taking his cue from Wittgenstein, he is unfashionably willing to pay heed to the "spirit" in which a philosophical investigation is conducted or a play is written may well help us to see why "meaning it" is such an important idea throughout his thought and why "intention" often plays the role in his writings on literary texts that "spirit" plays in his meditations on philosophy.

VIII

We have consistently seen in this chapter that the terms Cavell uses in his essays on Shakespeare invariably contest the way those same terms are pictured and employed in traditional and contemporary literary criticism and theory. The suggestion throughout has been that whereas Cavell's readings may seem to some critics and theorists to amount, in various ways, to an avoidance of Shakespeare—or to what is conventionally meant or pictured by that name in these contexts—Cavell is in fact exposing a number of avoidances that he finds are common currency in Shakespeare criticism. Harboring highly suspect metaphysical notions of what counts as a "text" or as an "intention," and using stale pictures of historical context or generic conventions to ground the plays, while avoiding their author and their characters, in many of its aspects the output of contemporary Shakespeare studies might well strike a Cavellian as knowledge well worth avoiding. Cavell's longstanding interest in Shakespeare's plays thus also involves a survey of nearly all that he sees as troublesome and misleading in literary studies today.

But if "What is a play of Shakespeare's?" is a timely question for Cavell to ask, there are nevertheless many further questions to be asked of his manner of posing it and answering it. Cavell says that part of his project in writing on

Shakespeare involves "investigating the act of criticism" (*DK*, p. 82), but his investigations themselves stand in need of further investigation, as Cavell is well aware. One pressing way in which the questions Cavell asks of Shakespeare might be investigated in their turn would be by posing questions like

> What does it betoken about what I mean when I say "literature" that my instances of the concept are so often works of Shakespeare . . . and in particular how do these instances bear on the more or less implicit theme of the relation (if that is the word) between philosophy and literature . . . ? (*IQO*, pp. 144–45)

Perhaps the answers to these questions might have to do with the status of Shakespeare as the foremost name among Anglophone writers, or that of drama as the most public of the genres of literature. Answering them in the detail they deserve, however, takes us far beyond the scope of this chapter. Instead, the next chapter turns, partly by way of a contrast, to a playwright whose works configure a relationship between literature, philosophy, and language that, if anything, is even more unique than that found in Shakespeare's plays—namely, to Samuel Beckett.

CHAPTER THREE

From the Sublime to the Ordinary

Stanley Cavell's Beckett

"Beckett shrugs his shoulders at the possibility of philosophy today." So claims Theodor Adorno in his rather abortive "Versuch, das Endspiel zu verstehen."[1] And yet, perhaps because of this very act of shoulder shrugging, the works of Samuel Beckett seem to have fired the imaginations of a great many philosophers. Discussions of Beckett feature prominently in the writings of such thinkers as Gilles Deleuze, Maurice Blanchot, Alain Badiou, and, of course, Theodor Adorno, and current work in Beckett studies has been dominated by contemplating, clarifying, and extrapolating these philosophical readings.[2] A recent book by Richard Lane, *Beckett and Philosophy*, is divided into two sections, one mapping out Beckett's significance for an array of French philosophers and one mapping out the same territory in German philosophy. Tellingly, there is no third section on Beckett's significance for Anglo-American philosophers, even though his works have drawn comment from leading thinkers like Stanley Cavell and Martha Nussbaum.[3] Indeed, since the publication of *Must We Mean What We Say?* forty years ago, Cavell's essay on *Endgame* has attracted the attention of only the smallest handful of commentators—a fraction of those who have written on Adorno's essay on the same subject. This chapter takes some steps toward redressing this imbalance by teasing out some of the implications of Cavell's position.

I

I want to start by taking a few caveats from Simon Critchley, one of the select few philosophers to have taken Cavell's reading of Beckett seriously. Critchley begins his philosophical discussion of Beckett with the following words of warning:

> The writings of Samuel Beckett seem to be particularly, perhaps uniquely, resistant to philosophical interpretation. . . . His texts continually seem to pull the rug from under the feet of the philosopher by showing themselves to be conscious of the possibility of such interpretations; or, better, such interpretations seem to lag behind the text which they are trying to interpret; or, better still, such interpretations seem to lag behind their object by saying too much: something essential to Beckett's language is lost by overshooting the text and ascending into the stratosphere of metalanguage. . . . It might well be that philosophically meditated meanings are precisely what we should *not* be in search of when thinking through Beckett's work.[4]

Critchley characterizes the danger besetting those of us who try to read Beckett philosophically as "saying too much and saying too little, saying too little by saying too much."[5] This is a warning we would do well to heed. A satisfactory approach to Beckett, it seems, must navigate between a Scylla and a Charybdis: on the one hand, the temptation to conclude that Beckett's works are essentially meaningless; and on the other, the compulsion to read into them layers and levels of supposedly "deeper," pseudo-philosophical, metaphysical meaning. It is between these two extremes—distant cousins, I suspect, of skepticism and metaphysics—that Cavell's reading of Beckett tries to plot its course, while acknowledging both the temptation and the compulsion that would lead it astray.

Perhaps the most striking aspect of Cavell's reading of Beckett is its insistence on taking Beckett as literally as possible.[6] Cavell steers deftly between the argument that Beckett's plays are meaningless and the argument that they have a supposedly "deeper" metaphysical meaning by pointing out that as often as not, Beckett's characters mean exactly what they say. *Endgame* is suffused with a property that Cavell terms "hidden literality" (*MWM*, p. 119), as in the following:

> HAMM: Did you ever think of one thing?
> CLOV: Never.

or

> CLOV: Do you believe in the life to come?
> HAMM: Mine was always that.[7]

This is what Cavell calls "Beckett's uncovering of the literal" (*MWM*, p. 120), and it is directly related to the claims he makes about the ordinariness of *Endgame*. As Cavell puts it, "The sort of method I try to use consistently in reading the play, [is] one in which I am always asking of a line either: What are the most ordinary circumstances under which such a line would be uttered? Or: What do the words literally say?" (*MWM*, p. 121). This strategy might reasonably be expected to stave off the threat of skepticism, but I find that it does rather the opposite. Faced with an assertion like "Beckett's plays mean nothing more and nothing less than what they say," a skeptic (or, for that matter, a bemused undergraduate) might reasonably respond with the question, "And what is that?" A meaningful answer to this question could well prove difficult to give.

How, then, are we to read *Endgame*? All too often, critics and philosophers spill rivers of hermeneutic ink in seeking to persuade themselves and others that they have uncovered a meaning to a literary text that is *more* than is said by the words at first sight. This exposes their widely held, problematic suppositions that our words can or could mean more than they say, opening up a metaphysical dimension for meaning in which proliferate unresolvable arguments about which supposedly "deeper" meaning the text is supposedly "really" about. It goes against more or less the entire bent of Cavell's thought to do this, particularly when the text under discussion is as enigmatic as Beckett's *Endgame*. Yet critics of Cavell have pointed out that this is precisely what he does in his own reading. In his essay, Hamm and Clov's shelter becomes Noah's ark; the play takes on the force of a theological parable on eschatology; and its eschatological dimensions evoke the specter of nuclear holocaust (see *MWM*, pp. 132–55). For Jay Bernstein at least, Cavell's reading of Beckett fails to practice what it preaches.[8] But this isn't the problem it seems at first blush. These excursive flights into exegesis surely exemplify the crux of Cavell's case: that there is a deep-seated compulsion to see in Beckett's words something more than they say, a need to get from them more than they have given us. As Cavell puts it, "We *have* to talk, whether we have something to say or not; and the less we want to say and want to hear the more wilfully we talk and are subjected to talk" (*MWM*, p. 161). To put it another way, Cavell successfully argues that there is no contradiction between Beckett's lack of faith in words and his going on to use them (see *MWM*, p. 161). By the same token, there is no more contradiction in Cavell's advocating that we take *Endgame* literally and his going on to read it allegorically.

In any case, for much of his essay, Cavell argues not that Beckett's play is incapable of meaning something *more* than it says but rather the opposite: that it is incapable of meaning anything *less*, that it is incapable of attaining the status of meaninglessness ascribed to it by so many critics. As Cavell puts it, "The discovery of *Endgame*, both in topic and technique, is not the failure of meaning (if that means the lack of meaning) but its total, even totalitarian, success—our inability *not* to mean what we are given to mean" (*MWM*, p. 117). It is this claim that strikes me as the most interesting aspect of the essay, and one that, along with the following assertion, invites further discussion: "Solitude, emptiness, nothingness, meaninglessness, silence—these are not the givens of Beckett's characters but their goal, their new heroic undertaking" (*MWM*, p. 156).

Critchley glosses these claims by relating them to the role of the ordinary in Cavell's thought. That is, *Endgame* is anchored in what Cavell highlights as the "ordinariness" (*MWM*, p. 117) of its events and its language, but that does not, in and of itself, stabilize its meaning or make it straightforward. Rather, for Critchley, here as elsewhere in Cavell's thought "the ordinary is the object of a quest, a task, something to be achieved and *not* an available fact." According to Critchley, "On Cavell's reading, Beckett is not telling us that the universe *is* meaningless, rather meaninglessness is a task, an achievement, the achievement of the ordinary or the everyday."[9]

Perhaps the obvious question to ask here would be, is this task achieved? Is this goal ever reached? Everything about Cavell's position seems to imply that the answer to this question is, and must necessarily be, no. If, as Cavell has it, Beckett's play is indeed imprisoned within the totalitarian confines of inescapable meaning, then the possibility of breaking free of these shackles does not and cannot arise. To think otherwise would be to lapse into the delusion that Beckett's words could somehow avoid meaning what they say. Moreover, if the answer were yes, then *Endgame* might indeed aspire to the condition of meaninglessness, an argument from which Cavell distances himself at the start of his essay, describing it as "impositions from an impression of fashionable philosophy" (*MWM*, p. 115).

It may seem perfectly in tune with the spirit and *timbre* of Beckett's plays to see within them an ongoing task that can never be accomplished, a distant goal that can never be achieved. But it is nonetheless a questionable move. Critchley's suggestion may encapsulate the predicament of Hamm and Clov perfectly, and it may well describe our experience in watching them, and perhaps that is all it needs to do. But by implication at least, it places Beckett alongside the likes of Emerson, Thoreau, Wordsworth, Coleridge, Wittgenstein, Austin, and Cavell himself, for whom to be in quest of the ordinary is to be in quest of the unattainable. It seems to me that there is something qualitatively different about what Beckett does that sets him apart from these writers and thinkers. I would suggest, *pace* Critchley, that Beckett's characters are not so much in quest of the ordinary as imprisoned within it, and their impossible task is not so much achieving the ordinary but aspiring beyond or beneath it. That this is an unattainable quest, an impossible task, is, perhaps, the tragedy of the everyday.[10]

Ultimately, whichever of these versions of Beckett we prefer, there are limits to an approach that takes Beckett *too* literally, and these are limits that are implicit in Cavell's own discussion. After charting the forms of hidden literality found in *Endgame*, Cavell goes on to diagnose a very different form of meaning in the play, in which the words do indeed seem to mean more than what they say. It is described as "the way an utterance which has entered naturally into the dialogue and continues it with obvious sense suddenly sends out an intense meaning, and one which seems to summarise or reveal the entire drift of mood or state of mind until then unnoticed or unexpressed" (*MWM*, p. 128). One of the examples Cavell gives of such a "climactic exclamation" (*MWM*, p. 149) is Hamm's enigmatic line, "To think it won't all have been for nothing" (*EG*, p. 108). Reflecting on the experience of such lines, Cavell says, "It would not be quite right to say that something was revealed; but there was as it were an air of revelation among us" (*MWM*, pp. 128–29).

Cavell is undoubtedly right to hear such moments with a sense of revelation about them peppered throughout Beckett's works; indeed, one can hardly watch a performance of *Endgame* without hearing them. But these moments might be seen as problematic for an approach that tries to take the play literally: they seem to imply that, at times, Beckett's words have the capacity to reveal something more than what they say, and yet that something is not necessarily a meaning that is recuperable within ordinary language. As a Wittgensteinian might put it, "It is not a *something*, but not a *nothing* either!"[11] Are these abortive epiphanies in Beckett's prose troublesome for an approach that takes as its working assumption the premise that his words mean no more and no less than what they say? In the next section, I explore this question with reference to what James Noggle has called "the Wittgensteinian Sublime."

II

Noggle takes one of the most traditional concepts associated with aesthetics—that of the sublime—and rethinks it in terms of the Wittgensteinian ideas of language games and the limits of language. Such a move might at first seem uncongenial to the bent of the *Philosophical Investigations*. After all, Wittgenstein warns us against the "tendency to sublime the logic of our language" and against the "tendency . . . to purify, to sublime, the signs themselves." But elsewhere he says that "these considerations bring us up to the problem: in what sense is logic something sublime?"[12] This is indeed a good question to ask of the author of the *Tractatus Logico-Philosophicus*. Noggle suggests that the vast, undiscovered country *wovon man nicht sprechen kann* is best thought of as the territory of the sublime. To use the well-known example of *Tractatus* 6.421:

> It is clear that ethics cannot be put into words.
> Ethics is transcendental.
> (Ethics and aesthetics are one and the same.)

This is a clear instance of the classic double bind of the *Tractatus*: on the one hand, we are aware of a vast, transcendental realm that appears to harbor all the metaphysical truths of philosophy; yet on the other, we are aware that this realm remains unattainable, incomprehensible, unspeakable, since, as Wittgenstein has just warned us in *Tractatus* 6.42, "Propositions can express nothing that is higher." For Noggle, this bind is closely analogous to the concept of the sublime. He argues:

> Our attempts to venture beyond language games . . . posit a supersensible domain of discourse. . . . But as Wittgenstein says, our apprehension of this domain is illusory. We attain an illusion of transcendence similar to the illusion experienced in the sublime, where the saturation of our cognitive or perceptual faculties *seems* to present the infinitely mighty or vast, but in fact can indicate no more than our inability to cognise or perceive infinitely.[13]

The experience of the sublime, it will be remembered, is not an experience with any positive content whatsoever; it is an experience of our incapacity to comprehend or to articulate it. Noggle compares it to what Wittgenstein calls the "bumps that the understanding has got by running its head up against the limits of language."[14] This remark in turn suggests how the experience of the sublime is, perhaps surprisingly, intimately related to the realm of ordinary language. As Noggle argues,

> In [Wittgenstein's] later work, philosophical utterances "sublime the logic of our language" not because they gesture outward toward some ineffable but metaphysically significant realm beyond the ordinary. Rather, they are an effect of language's failure to do so, to hint at anything truly metaphysical, truly beyond ordinary language games. Much as sublime experience according to Kant's third *Critique* offers not a true image of absolute power or the infinite universe but rather an instance of our failure to grasp such things, language "outside language

> games" is an outward venture that leads us nowhere but backward, to the untranscendental conditions of ordinary language—which is all there is. ("WS," p. 609)

Or to put it more succinctly, "Sublime language is a leap away from the ordinary, not into some alternative language of metaphor but into the void of meaning" ("WS," p. 614). And yet, of course, we find ourselves compelled to attempt such leaps in spite of, perhaps even because of, their futility. Like characters in a Beckett play, we strain to reach beyond the ordinary, though doing so can only result in meaninglessness.[15]

Noggle compares the experience of the Wittgensteinian sublime with Cavell's emphasis on encountering the limits of language games: "For Cavell, only by departing from language games can we grasp their significance" ("WS," p. 607)—which is not to say or imply that there is anything "beyond" or "outside" language games that we grasp instead. Such ventures are rather "(attempted) departures from that from which we 'cannot' depart" ("WS," p. 613).

To describe the Wittgensteinian sublime in these terms is to recognize that it is fundamental to the question of the limits of language and to the meaninglessness that lies beyond everyday language games. Yet it also highlights an interesting dialectical relationship that the Wittgensteinian sublime mediates between ordinary language games and meaninglessness, in that, for Noggle, "the sufficiency of language games reveals itself only if we subject ourselves to the metaphysical nonsense that would seem to negate them" ("WS," p. 614). This position is very close indeed to Cavell's, as is evident in the following short summary: "Ordinary language is both all the language we ever really have and radically in need of the extraordinary language of metaphysical illusion—which is useful only insofar as it proves from the perspective of ordinary language to be useless" ("WS," p. 611).

Interestingly, Noggle's delineation of the Wittgensteinian sublime takes inspiration from other aspects of Cavell's work, in particular a brief but suggestive passage from *This New Yet Unapproachable America*:

> Wittgenstein's appearance at this intersection of romanticism and skepticism and Kant is, so it seems to me, encoded in his concept of *subliming*. . . . But whereas in Kant the psychic strain is between intellect and sensibility, in Wittgenstein the straining is of language against itself, against the commonality of criteria which are its conditions, turning it as it were against its origins.—Thus a derivative romantic aesthetic problematic concerning the sublime moves to the center of the problematic of knowledge, or say wording the world; quite as if aesthetics itself claims a new position in the economy of philosophy.[16]

Cavell doesn't specify what this new position might be, but if Noggle is right, then the Wittgensteinian sublime might be that which both designates and demarcates the boundaries of the knowable, the thinkable, and the speakable. To attempt to aspire beyond these, as Hamm and Clov do—as from time to time we all do—is to take on the sublime, to try and bring it within the compass of language and of comprehension, in short, to try to turn it into something like the beautiful.

It is with these terms in mind that I return now to Cavell's literary aesthetic. The attempt, so common in literary texts but by no means peculiar to them, to use ordinary language to gesture beyond itself is, for Noggle, "best identified as a species of the sublime" ("WS," p. 605). After all, it has long been a critical commonplace that works of literature do their best to depart from the conventions of everyday language games, in quest of more striking meanings, and clearly the Wittgensteinian sublime gives us an intriguing way of conceptualizing how they (attempt to) do so. But a sensible objection to my line of argument at this stage would be that if Cavell is right, then, generally speaking, Beckett does *not* do this. Beckett's lines, Cavell argues, generally mean what they say; they ought to be taken literally, as pieces of ordinary language. A similar approach has been argued for in the movement toward a Wittgensteinian literary criticism articulated by Marjorie Perloff and others: that Wittgenstein's emphasis on the everyday helps us to appreciate the creativity of writers from the modernists to the language poets (and she explicitly includes Samuel Beckett among them)[17] who turned deliberately to ordinary language precisely in order to reject poetry's traditional, romantic attempts to get beyond it. Theirs, Perloff argues, is an aesthetic of the ordinary—what she calls "the 'ordinary language' poetics so central to our time"[18]—and the critic should embrace this aesthetic in approaching them. There would not appear to be much room for the Wittgensteinian sublime, or indeed for any other kind of sublime, if we adopt this critical emphasis on ordinary, everyday, literal language.

To think this way, though, is to set up a false opposition between Perloff's "'ordinary language' poetics" and Noggle's Wittgensteinian sublime—*and* to misunderstand Cavell's approach to Beckett. For it is in the nature of both Cavell's and Noggle's enterprises that they are neither stable nor sustainable. Both demonstrate, as does Perloff, that an emphasis on ordinary language is all-important. But the "ordinary" is not always straightforwardly or readily available in or on its own terms. Indeed, for Cavell the ordinary is most clearly grasped in the moment of its loss. Just as the Wittgensteinian sublime is an empty territory, a void of meaninglessness where we cannot dwell, and from which we pass back into the realm of the ordinary with a better, more sharply defined sense of its power and its limits, so too the everyday language of Beckett's Hamm and Clov is not and cannot be sufficient unto itself, but inevitably bumps up against the limits of language, as even the most "ordinary" or "everyday" work of literature must. To quote Noggle once again:

> At such extreme moments, in the *Investigations*' words, "language is like an engine idling," disengaged from the language games in which it has its life and therefore alienated from and useless to its user—a state of confusion that Wittgenstein also describes as "the bewitchment of our intelligence by means of language" (*PI* §109). But while such linguistic bewitchment or alienation by definition can never be seen as a language game in itself, Cavell's reading of Wittgenstein also stresses that we can never find a way of avoiding it once and for all, that we must confront it repeatedly—and he furthermore persistently suggests that literary works are especially good at provoking such confrontations. ("WS," p. 606)

Which is not to suggest that we should risk "equating good literature with bad philosophizing" ("WS," p. 607). It is rather to acknowledge the near inevitability of overstepping the limits of language and hence passing into nonsense in a literary text, even if—perhaps especially if—that text attempts to confine itself to the ordinary. "Thus," Noggle says, "the aesthetic power of language outside language games does not affect us in spite of its distinctness from ordinary concerns but rather consists in it" ("WS," p. 612).

III

So much for the philosophy. How then to support this argument with reference to Beckett's *Endgame* and Cavell's reading of it? Starting with Cavell, toward the end of his essay on *Endgame*, Beckett's use of words in his writing is described in these terms: "One could say: He doesn't use them just *any* way; and even: He doesn't *use* them at all (for example, to promise, to threaten, to pray, to apologise—the things words are used for) or sees how far he can go in not, in not saying more than the words" (*MWM*, p 161). In a telling choice of phrase, Cavell suggests that Beckett is not so much trying to take ordinary language as far as he can in terms of meaning but rather is trying to take it as far as he can in terms of *not* meaning something more, *not* going beyond it, as if acknowledging the inevitability of so doing, or as if the two were inextricably implicated in one another. A similar choice of phrase is in evidence when Cavell tells us that "to miss the ordinariness of the lives in *Endgame* is to avoid the extraordinariness (and ordinariness) of our own" (*MWM*, p. 119). Once again, there is the suggestion here that the ordinary and the extraordinary are linked and that the sense of each is gained from passing on into the realm of the other.

But as we see in *Endgame*, such a transition is an empty one, in that when Hamm's and Clov's words manage to depart from the ordinary, the result is a "coupling of their sublimity with their nonsensicality" ("WS," p. 617). Consider this line of Hamm's, taken from his final monologue: "Moments for nothing, now as always, time was never and time is over, reckoning closed and story ended" (*EG*, p. 133). The first part of the line—"now as always, time was never and time is over"—is a patent self-contradiction, a parcel of nonsense that, however poetic it sounds, says nothing intelligible. It is, I think, as clear an evocation of the unfathomable and incomprehensible nature of time, and hence of the sublime, as William Blake's rather more traditional exhortation to "Hold infinity in the palm of your hand / and eternity in an hour." And yet the second part of Hamm's line—"reckoning closed and story ended"—insists on the limits of knowledge and of language and seems to draw back from the abyssal depths hinted at in the first part. Perhaps this is nothing more than what Wittgenstein would have called "the transition from patent nonsense to something which is disguised nonsense,"[19] but it nevertheless hints at a transition from the sublime to the everyday.

A similar transition can be seen more clearly in the following piece of dialogue between Hamm and Clov:

> HAMM: Go and get the oilcan.
> CLOV: What for?
> HAMM: To oil the castors.
> CLOV: I oiled them yesterday.
> HAMM: Yesterday! What does that mean? Yesterday!
> CLOV: [*Violently.*] That means that bloody awful day, long ago, before this bloody awful day. I use the words you taught me. If they don't mean anything any more, teach me others. Or let me be silent. (*EG*, p. 113)

This exchange begins as a perfectly everyday, workmanlike piece of conversation. The dialogue about the oilcan and oiling the castors is as ordinary as a builder asking his workmate for a slab or a customer asking the shopkeeper for five red apples. But something extraordinary enters the conversation with the word *yesterday*: Hamm demands, "Yesterday! What does that mean? Yesterday!" The obvious way to read this line would be as the interjection of a hard taskmaster, something like "What's the good of telling me you did it yesterday when I want it done today?" Hamm throws the word *yesterday* back at Clov, as if he were scoffing at it. But, of course, given the context of the play, it is also a line haunted by the specter of metaphysics, a kind of philosophical question—"Yesterday! What does that *mean*? Yesterday!" It is not so much a question as an evocation of the sublime, the incomprehensible mystery of passing time. It broaches the domain of the infinite, and as a question it is, of course, unanswerable. But Clov refuses to hear either the scoffing or the evocation; he insists on answering the question literally by providing Hamm with a literal definition of the word *yesterday* as it is ordinarily used: "That means that bloody awful day, long ago, before this bloody awful day." He is, to paraphrase Wittgenstein, bringing Hamm's words back from their metaphysical to their everyday use, and thereby recuperating them from the realm of the sublime. Or as he puts it, "I use the words you taught me. If they don't mean anything any more, teach me others." Clov's words here recall Cavell reporting Esslin reporting Gessner reporting Beckett's response to a question about the insufficiency of language, to which Beckett replied, "Que voulez-vous, Monsieur? C'est les mots; on n'a rien d'autre" (see *MWM*, p. 161). And indeed, what else is there? Certainly, there are no more sugar-plums, no more bicycle wheels, no more pap, no more pain-killer.

If I appear to be investing too much significance here in the word *yesterday*, it is because this same word is used to (attempt to) evoke the same depths by Hamm's mother, Nell. Consider, once again, the transition between ordinary, workmanlike language and the evocative use of that word in the following exchanges between Nagg and Nell:

> NAGG: I've lost me tooth.
> NELL: When?
> NAGG: I had it yesterday.
> NELL: [*Elegiac.*] Ah yesterday!
> [*They turn painfully towards each other.*] (*EG*, p. 99)

Or, once again:

> NAGG: Could you give me a scratch before you go?
> NELL: No. [*Pause.*] Where?
> NAGG: In the back.
> NELL: No. . . .
> NAGG: . . . Could you not? [*Pause.*] Yesterday you scratched me there.
> NELL: [*Elegiac.*] Ah yesterday! (*EG*, p. 101)

With this one word, *yesterday*, Nell passes beyond what Cavell calls her "girlish re-rhapsodizing the beauties of Lake Como" (*MWM*, p. 118) and into an abyss of melancholy so deep it cannot be put into words; it can only be hinted at, evoked with the word *yesterday* spoken, as the stage direction requires, in an elegiac tone of voice. It is as if a whole world of pain were contained in the word, and yet that is not how Nagg uses it, nor how Clov defines it, nor how it fits into ordinary language. The world of pain that is contained within the word can never be given form, shape, or content.

I use the turn of phrase "a world of pain . . . contained in the word" because it is how Wittgenstein describes a similar experience. In his comments on Schubert's *Death and the Maiden* in his *Vermischte Bemerkungen* we find the following instance of the phenomenon I am describing:

> The last two bars of the "Death and the Maiden" theme . . . it's possible to understand this first as an ordinary, conventional figure before coming to understand its deeper expression. I.e., before coming to understand that what is ordinary here is filled with significance.
>
> "Fare well!"
>
> "A whole world of pain is contained in these words." How *can* it be contained in them?—It is bound up with them. The words are like an acorn from which an *oak tree* can grow.[20]

Here Wittgenstein's strategy is the exact opposite of Clov's: faced with his metaphysical expression—the sublime evocation of the whole world of pain that lies in just two words—he prefers to delve further into the territory of the meaningless than to bring the words back home to the ordinary. (Perhaps this makes Wittgenstein more of a romantic than a skeptic here.) He asks the question, "How *can* it be contained in them?" which sounds as if he is about to correct himself, but does the opposite, by answering the question with a parable of an acorn and an oak tree that is purely figurative and that, once again, evokes much but means nothing. It means nothing because, for Wittgenstein as for Beckett, this "whole world of pain" is itself a part of "what is ordinary." The gesturing toward an unspeakable sublime is here an unrecuperated gesture into meaninglessness.

A final example of what is at stake here is in evidence in one of Cavell's own examples. Consider this short exchange between Hamm and Clov:

> HAMM: I'll give you nothing more to eat.
>
> CLOV: Then we'll die.

HAMM: I'll give you just enough to keep you from dying. You'll be hungry all the time.

CLOV: Then we won't die. (*EG*, pp. 94–95)

According to Cavell, this is a signal instance of when Beckett's words at first blush mean something other than what they say. He argues:

> Clov can hardly be meaning what his words, taken together and commonly, would suggest, namely "It makes no difference to me whether I live or die; I couldn't care less." First in one sense that is *so trivial* a sentiment, at their stage, that it would get a laugh—at least from clear-headed Hamm. Second, it is not true. How could it make no difference when the point of the enterprise is to die to that world? . . . And he *could* care less, because he's *trying* to leave. (*MWM*, p. 125)

The alternative Cavell suggests is that Beckett's characters are deaf to implicatures, that is, that there is no implicit threat in Hamm's line "I'll give you nothing more to eat" and that, hence, Clov is simply commenting on the logical consequences of Hamm's decisions. The words mean what they literally say, that is, they mean less than they would ordinarily imply.[21]

While this is an interesting way of looking at this dialogue, I would suggest that we can both have our cake and eat it here. Clov is also doing something else in this extract, whether he or Beckett means him to or not. He is, once again, bringing Hamm's words back from their metaphysical to their everyday use, taking them from the sublime to the ordinary. To be more precise, we can retain the sense of the threat in Hamm's words—"I'll give you nothing more to eat"—*and* read Clov as commenting upon it as an ordinary statement. A threat to starve someone to death should evoke a reaction of shock, terror, and awe, emotions that would normally betoken the presence of the sublime, but Clov's reaction takes Hamm's threat away from the metaphysical and back to an ordinary statement, the tone of which is so banal as to become unsettling. Viewed this way, it is both a refusal to be drawn into the power that the sublime has to lead us away from the literal and an acknowledgment of that power. In fact, it puts Clov in a position not unlike that of the skeptic.

Indeed, Noggle suggests that there is a "comparison between sublime experience and the alienating and absorbing powers of skepticism" ("WS," p. 612), in that both seem to open up an abyss beneath our feet into which our securities are plunged, while simultaneously, and perhaps paradoxically, appearing inconsequential, since in both cases we soon emerge from the abyss unscathed. "Like Hume's skepticism," says Noggle, "the sublime aesthetic effect is distinguished by its capacity to alternately overturn everything and nothing at all, the proximity that it establishes between absolute precariousness and absolute security—the aesthetic unification of our terror of the ocean storm with our safety on shore" ("WS," p. 612).

This relationship between a Cavellian view of skepticism and a Wittgensteinian view of the sublime would be an apt way of drawing toward a conclusion. Since, for Cavell at least, skepticism is not (and cannot be) overcome by further knowledge, or certainty of belief, or insistence on either of these things, but only by a reframing of the ground of skepticism itself, so too the encounter with the meaninglessness beyond everyday language games that constitutes the Wittgensteinian sublime can be apprehended only by reframing the ground of the gesture toward the metaphysical and returning, albeit temporarily, to the ordinary and the everyday. What can we conclude from this about Beckett's *Endgame*? That Hamm and Clov's fraught relationship with the language they use encapsulates and lays bare the ceaselessly, inevitably shifting transition between sense and nonsense that characterizes the quest for certain forms of meaning. Like the very skepticism to which such a relationship with meaning must no doubt give rise, this quest is attainable only by the kind of therapeutic intervention that addresses the ongoing compulsion—to which readers of Beckett seem particularly addicted—of questing for such meanings in the first place.

Perhaps we would be right to take a skeptical view of the Wittgensteinian sublime, since, after all, we cannot *do* anything with it. Yet, at the same time, we cannot do *without* it either, so skepticism in this case is "*not* irrefutable, but obviously nonsensical."[22] Either way, it makes no difference *and* it makes all the difference in the world. We cannot help but plunge into the abyss of the Wittgensteinian sublime in search of so-called deeper meanings to our words. But there are no more of these than there are sugar-plums or pain-killers, and it is simultaneously the Wittgensteinian sublime that shows us this. This is why Cavell is right to describe Beckett's technique in *Endgame* as "not by supposing that there is a way out of language, but by fully accepting the fact that there is nowhere else to go" (*MWM*, p. 126). And yet I question whether anyone—even Beckett, even Hamm and Clov—can ever "fully accept" the limits of language so simply, since we are doomed, time and again, to find ourselves propelled from the ordinary to the sublime and back again. That is why the final sentence of Cavell's essay on Beckett is such an apt conclusion: "We hang between" (*MWM*, p. 162).

CHAPTER FOUR

How to Do Things with Wordsworth

William Wordsworth and his poems crop up repeatedly in various discussions that span the breadth of Cavell's career, from the early essays in *Must We Mean What We Say?*, through discussions of romanticism in *The Claim of Reason* and other texts of the 1980s, and on into the later work. Cavell's discussions of Wordsworth are often brief yet complex; he claims he is "reading texts of Wordsworth . . . as though they are responding to the same problems philosophers have, even responding in something like the same way (a way that cannot be dissociated from thinking)" (*IQO*, p. 7).[1] These discussions establish Wordsworth—on Cavell's reading—as a poet investigating the challenge of "ordinary language," a claim that puts his poetry in a similar orbit to that of the philosophy of J. L. Austin. Though this claim might at first seem counterintuitive—what, after all, could Austin, the most insistently ordinary of ordinary language philosophers, have in common with Wordsworth, a romantic poet?—I shall nevertheless be adding another claim to it, namely, that Wordsworth also shares a (loosely) Austinian awareness of the performative power of language itself, that is, an understanding of how we do things with words. Following Angela Esterhammer, I shall refer to this dimension of Wordsworth's poetry as the *Romantic performative*, and, building on her insights, I hope to demonstrate that this term can help us understand broader issues in Cavell's understanding of romanticism itself.

I

Wordsworth's well-known ode "Intimations of Immortality from Recollections of Early Childhood" is a poem to which Cavell turns at several moments in his writings. The first of these, and the earliest encounter with Wordsworth's poetry in Cavell's writings, is to be found in an essay entitled "Aesthetic Problems of Modern Philosophy" (see *MWM*, pp. 73–96). For the most part, the essay conducts itself as an alert sparring partner against various orthodoxies in the then dominant New Criticism, particularly Cleanth Brooks's concept "The Heresy of Paraphrase." Brooks's argument, which decries the idea that a poem can be taken as a kind of statement, with a content that could in principle be summarized, is deflated by Cavell in what could easily be read as a moment of satire:

> Someone is likely to burst out with: But *of course* a paraphrase says what the poem says, and an *approximate* paraphrase is merely a bad paraphrase; with greater effort or sensibility you could have got it exactly right. To which one response would be: "Oh, I can tell you exactly what the Ode means," and then read the Ode aloud. (*MWM*, pp. 75–76)

This response may sound facetious, but taken seriously, it contains several characteristically Cavellian insights: most obviously, that the "Intimations" Ode, like any other piece of language, must mean what it says; equally, that a moment of romanticism is intersected by a moment of skepticism. More importantly, though, if Wordsworth's poem is *not* reducible to a mere statement, then there is something about the poem that is not simply constative, which might imply that, in J. L. Austin's terms, it entails some sort of performative dimension. This much is suggested in the upshot of the recital alluded to at the end of Cavell's quote: someone who recites Wordsworth's "Intimations" Ode in this context is *not* telling us what it means so much as exposing us to its illocutionary force. Whether there is also a *per*locutionary aspect to this recital is difficult to ascertain for many reasons (e.g., it is not clear what securing uptake in this context could mean). Indeed, to follow Austin's crude test for perlocution, one cannot say "I poem you" in the way one can utter other performatives like "I promise you," "I bet you," or "I order you." Nevertheless, the poem itself is inscribed with various gestures toward the performative power of language, in ways that, I shall argue, expand our concept of performativity itself.

Cavell takes Brooks to task for suggesting, in spite of his views on paraphrase, that the "Intimations" Ode is a statement "about" the poet having "lost something." Nevertheless, the poem is best known for giving voice to the experience of loss: "It is not now as it hath been of yore" (line 6); "there hath past away a glory from the earth" (line 18); "The things which I have seen I now can see no more" (line 9). But it is how the Ode frames this experience of loss that is most interesting here: "Whither is fled the visionary gleam? / Where is it now, the glory and the dream?" (lines 56–57).[2] To ask questions such as these is to imply that what has been lost is being searched for or has become the object of a quest, and this underscores Cavell's description elsewhere of Wordsworth's poetry (specifically the *Prelude*) as "a quest myth, in which the goal of the quest is an understanding of the origin of the quest itself" (*TOS*, p. 143). This description applies more obviously to the "Intimations" Ode than to the *Prelude*, as is clear from the Ode's opening stanza:

> There was a time when meadow, grove, and stream,
> The earth, and every common sight,
> To me did seem
> Apparelled in celestial light,
> The glory and the freshness of a dream.
> It is not now as it hath been of yore;—
> Turn wheresoe'er I may,
> By night or day,
> The things which I have seen I now can see no more. (lines 1–9)

So the speaker of the poem mourns for a time when "every common sight" was viewed "in celestial light," and his quest is to recover that loss.

It is worth highlighting the adjective *common* here, since it is a near synonym for such key Cavellian terms as *ordinary* and *everyday*. Emphasizing this aspect of Wordsworth's writing, Cavell implies that to be a romantic is not to search for lofty poetic truths but rather to be in quest of the ordinary:

> The connection with romanticism . . . [is] my sense of the underwriting of ordinary language philosophy in the work of Emerson and Thoreau by speaking of an intimacy with existence, or intimacy lost—a signal recognizing the claim that the transcendentalism established in their pages is what became of romanticism in America.
>
> Accordingly, given my interest in putting Wittgenstein's and Austin's preoccupation with the ordinary and the everyday together with Emerson's and Thoreau's emphasis on the common, the near, and the low, it is understandable that I would eventually want to understand more about Wordsworth's notorious dedication of his poetic powers, in the preface to the *Lyrical Ballads*, to "[making] the incidents of common life interesting," and his choosing for that purpose "low and rustic life" together with the language of such men as lead that life, which he calls "a far more philosophical language than that which is frequently substituted for it by Poets." (*IQO*, p. 6)

According to Cavell, then, Wordsworth lines up alongside Austin as a champion of ordinary language, and "Wordsworth's sense in claiming for poetry the language of the rustic and the low" (*IQO*, p. 41) would compare to Austin's repositioning of philosophy in the territory of everyday speech acts.

This position may seem a difficult one to maintain, partly because it is hard to conceive of a philosopher with less of the romantic poet in his soul than J. L. Austin but also, and more importantly, because the way the moment of romanticism has been conceived traditionally emphasizes the creative, the inspirational, the sublime. Surely, then, romanticism emphasizes the *extra*ordinary, the exceptional? In *The Claim of Reason*, Cavell concedes this point and clarifies that "both the wish for the exceptional and for the everyday are foci of romanticism. One can think of romanticism as the discovery that the everyday is an exceptional achievement. Call it the achievement of the human" (*CoR*, p. 463). Nevertheless, it is worth asking—as Cavell does—"What is romantic about the recovery of, the quest for, the ordinary or everyday?" (*IQO*, p. 26).

As regards Wordsworth's "Intimations" Ode, it could reasonably be objected that what the speaker is in quest of is not "every common sight" but the "celestial light" in which it was once viewed, that is, that the quest is for something exceptional, which Wordsworth calls "glory" (lines 5, 18, 57, 64). Indeed, the "common" is precisely what is *not* sought, as is evident when the "celestial light" (line 4) from "our life's Star" (line 59) which is beheld by the growing boy (line 68) and the youth (line 71) is lost by the man, who "perceives it die away / And fade into the light of *common* day" (lines 75–76, my emphasis). Viewed this way, the common is what causes the loss, not what is lost, and it impedes the search for the light of "glory" rather than helping in its recovery.

Once again, however, Cavell is alert to this objection. He concludes his longest discussion of Wordsworth with the following observations:

> What remains of the "vision splendid" is that it "fades into the light of common day." Such is Wordsworth's construction of the ordinary. Shall we take this, as I suppose it commonly is taken, to be the same as a going out? But "fades into" does not *say* "fades out." . . . Wordsworth's construction is to replace the ordinary in the light in which we live it, with its shades of the prison-house closing upon us young, and its custom lying upon us deep almost as life, a world of death, to which we are dead—replace it accordingly with freedom ("heaven-born freedom"); and with lively origination, or say birth; with interest. How far can the vision be preserved and lived? What remains of interest to us? . . . We must turn to that. (*IQO*, p. 75)

The move Cavell makes here highlights a sense in which Wordsworth's concept of the common verges on the paradoxical. In the "Intimations" Ode, the "common light of day" appears to be opposed to the "celestial light" of vision, and even if, as Cavell hints, there might be the possibility of a symbiotic relationship between the two ("'fades into' does not *say* 'fades out'"), what interests the speaker and forms the object of his quest is principally the "vision splendid" rather than, or perhaps even at the expense of, the "common." But elsewhere, Wordsworth assigns a different value to the "common," one in which it is to become, as Cavell puts it, "of interest to us":

> When Wordsworth dedicated his poetry, in his preface to *Lyrical Ballads*, to arousing men in a particular way from a "torpor," the way he sought was "to make the incidents of common life interesting," as if he saw us as having withdrawn our interest, or investment, from whatever worlds we have in common, say this one or the next. (*IQO*, p. 32)

How, then, to reconcile these two conceptions of the "common," the "ordinary"? Can it be both the thing that is lost, mourned, searched for, quested after, and simultaneously the area the quester must search through for the thing that is lost? If the common and the ordinary are to be thought of as *both* the needle *and* the haystack, then how could any quest ever get under way? How could we even know what we were looking for? A classically Cavellian answer would be that the ordinary is to be discovered only in its loss and that romanticism shows us this paradox. To reiterate: "both the wish for the exceptional and for the everyday are foci of romanticism. One can think of romanticism as the discovery that the everyday is an exceptional achievement" (*CoR*, p. 463). And this would indeed describe the achievement of the "Intimations" Ode, in which, if I understand the implications of Cavell's analysis correctly, the "celestial light" that bathes the objects of "common sight" is something that "fades into" those objects. In other words, in remembering the "splendour in the grass" and "glory in the flower" (line 182), it is every bit as problematic to differentiate the "radiance which was once so bright" (line 179) from the ordinary grass and common flowers as it is to tell the dancer from the dance. And yet, *that* the ordinary grass and common flowers are viewed with such exceptional radiance is an achievement that Cavell describes as the achievement of the human.

But there is, I shall argue, a more ambitious way of understanding the complex and seemingly paradoxical nature of Wordsworth's invocation of the common, and that involves, once again, placing Wordsworth alongside J. L. Austin. Cavell asks us to

> look for a moment . . . at the magnitude of the claim in wishing to make the incidents of common life interesting. Beyond the word "common" take the words "make" and "interesting." Wordsworth's modest statement first of all carries on its face its competition with other conceptions of poetry, since the verb "to make" is forever being cited as what the word poetry declares itself to take on. Presumably this is meant to call attention to the fact that poems are made, invented, that they are created, hence by creators; this would be confirmed in such a remark as Auden's, that "poetry makes nothing happen." What the words "make interesting" say is that poetry is to make something happen—in a certain way—to the one to whom it speaks; something inside, if you like. That what is to happen to that one is that he or she becomes interested in something, aligns the goal with . . . the enterprises of such philosophers as Wittgenstein and Austin. They perceive us as uninterested, in a condition of boredom, which they regard as, among other things, a sign of intellectual suicide. (*IQO*, p. 7)

Here, then, we are to understand Wordsworth's poem as an utterance that makes something happen. We are to understand it as performative.

II

According to Angela Esterhammer, "The question of what language does, as well as what it describes, was already there to be asked during the Romantic period."[3] More specifically, she argues that "writers of the English Romantic period inhabited an environment marked by a new awareness of the bond between language and action" (*RP*, p. 23). Surveying a wide range of both writers and philosophers from British and German traditions of romanticism, her study *The Romantic Performative: Language and Action in British and German Romanticism* convincingly demonstrates the surprising extent to which "the notion that language is not merely descriptive of reality, but that it affects, shapes, alters, or even creates reality, underlies several interrelated currents of theory and practice from the 1780s onward" (*RP*, p. 23).

From aspects of the philosophies of language of, for example, Herder or Humboldt, to poems by Coleridge or Hölderlin, to political philosophers like Bentham or Godwin on the significance of promises, oaths, and contracts, to specific historical utterances like the Declaration of the Rights of Man, to disputes over its validity by the likes of Paine and Burke, Esterhammer calls attention to the extent and the importance of the romantic era's conceptualizing of language as doing something with words. "The understanding of language as a form of action is so pervasive, turning up in different but recognizable guises in such a wide range of late-eighteenth- and early-nineteenth-century writing, that it needs to be identified as the prevailing way of thinking and using language during this period," she claims (*RP*, p. xi). She diagnoses such an understanding of language as performative in the works of a dazzling array of writers and thinkers of the period, including Herder, Fichte, Bernhardi, Schelling, the Schlegels, Hölderlin, Kleist, and Humboldt in Germany, as well as Thomas Reid, John Horne Took, Bentham, Burke, Paine, Godwin, and Coleridge in Britain. Her "presentation of Romantic philosophy *as* a theory of the performative, and of Romantic literature in terms of that theory" (*RP*, p. xii) shows that much more is at stake than establishing that a theory of language as performative underpins the texts of romanticism. "It is not a matter of philosophy or linguistics providing a theory of language which poets then apply," as she puts it. "Rather, *both* linguistic and poetic texts are *both* analyses of language as action and instances of language as action" (*RP*, p. 3).

There is, of course, a name conspicuous by its absence from the above list: that of William Wordsworth. This is surprising since, as Cavell suggests, the Preface to *Lyrical Ballads*, itself one of the defining texts of British romanticism, contains several strong hints toward the performative nature of the task Wordsworth sets himself in his poetry and the language he uses to accomplish it. "What then does the Poet?" asks Wordsworth, in a question that almost sounds rhetorical, but for the fact that Wordsworth answers it thus: "He considers man and the objects that surround him as acting and re-acting upon each other."[4] That the poet *does* something in his poetry, that he considers himself "*acting* and re-*acting*" on the world and on other men as fundamental to the nature of his poetry and his status *qua* poet, suggests a conception of poetry as act. That this act is linguistic in nature is suggested by Wordsworth's characterizing the task of his Preface as "pointing out in what manner language and the human mind act and re-act on each other" (Preface, p. 120). He further claims that "each of these poems has a purpose" (Preface, p. 127), again implying a performative dimension to them. Wordsworth, then, seems to tally nearly perfectly with Esterhammer's diagnosis of a philosophy of performativity in the literature and thought of the romantic era.

It may well be objected hereabouts that what Wordsworth means by doing things with poems and what Austin means by doing things with words are qualitatively different from each other, and this is probably true. Esterhammer designates at least one major difference between Austin's thought and that of his romantic forebears when she points out that "the typical position adopted by

Romantic linguists is that individual speakers do things with language *while* language *also* does things to individual speakers. Accordingly, the speaking subject tends to be a much more fluid entity for them than it is in twentieth-century speech-act theory" (*RP*, p. 13).

This position can readily be seen in Wordsworth's Preface, where he seems to conceptualize the bond between a writer and his readers along the lines of a classically Austinian speech act, namely, a promise: he talks of "the promise which, by the act of writing in verse, an Author in the present day makes to his reader" (Preface, p. 122). Furthermore, such a promise, for Wordsworth at least, appears to carry the force of a contract, implying terms and conditions reminiscent of that most loaded of romantic-period debates, the social contract:

> By the act of writing in verse an Author makes a formal engagement that he will gratify certain known habits of association; that he not only thus apprises the Reader that certain classes of ideas and expressions will be found in his book, but that others will be carefully excluded. (Preface, p. 122)

Strangely, he freely and openly concedes the possibility that, *qua* poet, he might well appear to be in breach of this contract: "It will undoubtedly appear to many persons that I have not fulfilled the terms of an engagement thus voluntarily contracted" (Preface, p. 122). He considers such a breach of contract to be "one of the most dishonourable accusations which can be brought against an Author," because it involves "an indolence which prevents him from endeavouring to ascertain what is his duty, or, when his duty is ascertained, prevents him from performing it" (Wordsworth, Preface, p. 123), and he further claims to be writing the Preface to *Lyrical Ballads* primarily in order to exonerate himself from such a charge of dereliction of duty arising from breaking either promise or contract, or both.

Admittedly, what is at stake here is not a speech act in the sense of Austin's "I promise you . . ." Moreover, a book of poetry is not a contract in the sense that it must be prefaced with a waiver, or appended with its terms and conditions in small print, or signed with the reader's signature. And yet a promise has been made and, Wordsworth implies, will appear at least to some people to have been broken. A simple way of making sense of Wordsworth's point would understand him as saying that a poet is bound by his role *qua* poet—his "duty"—to a certain kind of writing. To call oneself a poet, and one's writings poetry, then, is not so much to stake a claim as to take on a contract to provide a reader with poems. It is to promise the reader poetry. If the reader doesn't see them as poems, then both contract and promise have been broken.

Here one can see why the Romantic performative encompasses a broader, and looser, sense of the term than Austin's. Austin would probably not have conceived that a promise or a contract could be binding in these circumstances; indeed, it is hard to see where or how an Austinian performative takes place in the Preface to *Lyrical Ballads*. But according to Esterhammer, the Romantic performative conceptualizes doing things with words more broadly:

> In Romantic-period philosophy of language [the] most crucial of these recurring concepts is that something *happens* when words are spoken. Verbal utterances have an effect on the addressee, the speaker, and the speech situation that needs to be described not just in terms of rhetoric or persuasion, but as the actual founding of the subject-positions of speaker and hearer, the establishment of their relationships to one another and to the external world. (*RP*, pp. xi–xii)

Thought of in this way, then, the Wordsworthian contract and promise could be paraphrased along these lines: to call oneself a poet is to use a word to position oneself in a certain way alongside one's interlocutor.[5] It is to posit that interlocutor as a reader and to posit the words one relays to the reader as poems. One cannot call oneself a poet without entering into a contract that promises poetry, so the word entails a performative dimension. Or as Esterhammer puts it,

> What the Romantics mean is that speakers are only defined—which is to say they only come to occupy an I-position in relation to a You, to other subjects, to the divine, to nature—in and through the act of speaking. Rather than taking the status of the speaker for granted, a Romantic speech-act theory considers utterance as an event that before all else shapes the subject's consciousness, determines the subject's relationship to the world and the hearer, and changes the environment that surrounds, and includes, the one who speaks. (*RP*, p. 13)

It is in these subtler, less explicit ways than the classic "I name this ship the Mr Stalin" that the Romantic performative operates.[6]

But it is not just in the sense that his words posit, position, create, or transform the identity of the speaking subject that Wordsworth's works might be called performative. To return to Cavell's engagement with Wordsworth, Cavell argues that the quest for something lost, and the work of mourning that loss, that he sees as so central to Wordsworth's poems, and to the "Intimations" Ode in particular, is bound up with the potential of poetry and of language to transform the world itself—a truly performative task.

III

Wordsworth, then, lived and wrote in an era when "a Romantic view of poetry and philosophy as expressions of energy and power" was deeply rooted in a view of language *as* this very energy and power itself, and this, according to Esterhammer, should "encourage, indeed compel, us to read Romantic literature with [the] concept of performativity in mind" (*RP*, p. 143). In the Preface to *Lyrical Ballads*, Wordsworth's stated goal is to transform the common and the ordinary in, by, and through the power of language in poetry—a task that can only be called performative, since what presents itself here as a transformation in language is in fact an ambition to transform the world. Indeed, the Preface states that "to prefix a systematic defence of the theory upon which the Poems were written" would in fact be impossible "without tracing the revolutions, not of literature alone, but likewise of society itself" (Preface, p. 121). So to change the world through the language of poetry is not just a performative task but a revolutionary one; indeed, Wordsworth implicitly relates the two by suggesting that "the Reader [will be] assisted in perceiving that the powers of language are not so limited as he may suppose" (Preface, p. 157).

Cavell's discussions of romanticism highlight a romantic tendency that resembles Wordsworth's ambitions here, namely, the idea that "language as such has fallen from or may aspire to a higher state, a state, say, in which the world is more perfectly expressed." He argues that this "vision that the world as a whole requires attention, say redemption, that it lies fallen, dead . . . [is] essential to what we call romanticism" (*TNYUA*, pp. 81–82). It is, he says, "an idea that . . . any Romantic would be lost without, that the world could be—or could have been—so remade, or I in it, that I could *want* it, as it would be, or I in it" (*IQO*, pp. 35–36). If this seems vague or abstract, then it is easy to find a concrete illustration of this vision of redemption and remaking the world. Cavell says that to exemplify "the romantic themes I have emphasized of reawakening or revival" we should "[begin] with the figure of the six-year-old boy of Wordsworth's Intimations Ode and the ode's idea of the adult's world as 'remains,' as of corpses" (*IQO*, p. 76).

Elsewhere in the poem, Wordsworth seems to suggest that it lies within the power of language to redeem or resurrect the fallen world lost in childhood. He describes the "shadowy recollections" (line 153) as "truths that wake, / To perish never" (lines 159–60), and *truth* used as a noun in this way can ordinarily only be applied to something expressed in or as a piece of language. These "truths," Wordsworth tells us, "*have power to make* / Our noisy years seem moments in the being/Of the eternal Silence" (lines 157–59, my emphasis). That is, they have the power to transform, and thereby to redeem, those "shadowy recollections," perhaps in, by, and through the act of turning "recollections" into "truths," pieces of language.

This, then, is what Wordsworth aims to do with words, his vision of language's performative power. His romantic quest is to redeem the world, save the world, change the world, or such like, and to do so through the language of his poetry. And so he must begin by describing what Cavell calls "our worldlessness or homelessness, the deadness to us of worlds we still see but, as it were, do not recollect (as if we cannot quite place the world)" (*IQO*, p. 32). Cavell goes on to say that the cure for this condition "will require a revolution of the spirit," and it is true that he considers Wordsworth a writer of revolutionary ambitions.[7] But a revolution, whether in language, in poetry, in spirit, or just in France, will not, Cavell implies, form a satisfactory resolution to Wordsworth's quest, because the conditions of worldlessness, homelessness, and deadness he describes are not conditions that can be defeated by revolutionary means: they are, he says a "description . . . of skepticism" (*IQO*, pp. 32–33), and it is primarily as such that they are of interest to Cavell, and to the Cavellian conception of romanticism itself.

One cannot overstate the importance of what Cavell calls "my use of the skeptical problematic as my opening into romanticism" (*IQO*, p. 58). He argues that "romanticism generally is to be understood as in struggle with skepticism, and at the same time in struggle with philosophy's responses to skepticism" (*IQO*, p. 175). More specifically, what makes romanticism such a dynamic and challenging movement is that both the poets and the philosophers of the romantic era are contending with one another, and the ground of their contention is skepticism:

> I take romanticism to mark the (modern) struggle of philosophy and poetry for and against one another, for and against their own continued existence. Why there is, or comes to be, such a struggle is, it is implied, a philosophical and a poetic, no less than a historical, issue. The cause is something to which I assign, or extend, the name skepticism. (*IQO*, p. 145)[8]

How is this relevant to Wordsworth's quest, in the "Intimations" Ode, to redeem the common and the ordinary from their loss? Clearly, the Ode, insofar as it describes a crisis of faith and belief, describes an experience of skepticism, and skepticism regarding the very identity of the soul at that. Cavell sees such an experience of skepticism about human selfhood—in Wordsworth's

Ode, a loss of faith in the destiny of the soul—as an experience characteristic of romanticism:

> That types of the passive skeptic should naturally present themselves as typical figures of romanticism registers (whatever else romantic self-assertion shows) the apprehension that human subjectivity, the concept of human selfhood, is threatened; that it must be found and may be lost; that if one's existence is to be proven it can be proven only from oneself; and that upon that proof turns what proof there is in the continued existence of the human as such. This is what happens . . . in romanticism. (*CoR*, p. 465)

This passage gives us to see why romanticism is such an important phenomenon for Cavell to deal with: whereas one of the main currents in his philosophy involves tackling the issue of skepticism toward other minds (most obviously in *The Claim of Reason*), romanticism appears to offer Cavell a more thoroughgoing skepticism to address, a skepticism directed toward the nature and existence of one's *own* mind, or soul, or self. But there is also another classic variety of skepticism to which romanticism is vulnerable, and that is skepticism toward knowledge of the world:

> Fundamental to romanticism, especially to . . . its sense of estrangement, is first of all, say, the relation of knowledge and the world; whether accordingly self-consciousness is the cause or the effect of skepticism, or whether they are simultaneous, or whether one or other of these possibilities leads from and to one or another version or notion of romanticism. (*IQO*, p. 45)

For Cavell, then, romanticism arises from skepticism, directed both toward knowledge of the self and toward knowledge of the world, and from the quarrel with philosophy that this skepticism occasions.

Such a description might well apply to the "Intimations" Ode: it does indeed describe the loss of a certain kind of knowledge of the soul, intimately related to a loss of a certain kind of knowledge of the world—in short, the onset of skepticism. Yet the description fits almost too well, or at any rate too neatly, to do justice to the importance of skepticism in the poem. For skepticism in the Ode is not seen as the loss of the soul and the world, from which the quester must recover it, nor even as the loss of the "extraordinary" ordinariness that knowledge of soul and world once constituted. Instead, skepticism is figured in the "Intimations" Ode as something to be lived through and celebrated. It is telling that the speaker will "raise / The song of thanks and praise" (lines 143–44) not for the "Delight and liberty" (line 140) or "new-fledged hope" (line 142) of childhood, but rather

> . . . for those obstinate questionings
> Of sense and outward things,
> Fallings from us, vanishings;
> Blank misgivings of a Creature
> Moving about in worlds not realised, (lines 145–49)

which can only be described as charting the experience of skepticism. Moreover, these "obstinate questionings" are connected to the "truths that wake" (line 159) to transform our experience and our knowledge, as if the experience of skepticism were symbiotically connected to the process of overcoming skepticism, and therefore as much part of the solution as part of the problem.

Such a figuring of skepticism may seem curious for a poem that describes the anguish of a loss of spiritual faith. But the following extract from *In Quest of the Ordinary* describes how the surmounting of skepticism takes place not through repudiating it but by reclaiming the way skepticism sets itself up in the first place:

> The recovery of the (my) ordinary (voice) from skepticism, since it is itself a task dictated by skepticism, requires the contesting of skepticism's picturing of the task. . . . In philosophy the task is associated with the overcoming, or say critique, of metaphysics, and in literature with . . . the transcendentalizing of the domestic. . . . This communication between philosophy and literature, or the refusal of communication, is something that causes romanticism, causes at any rate my present experiments with romantic texts. (*IQO*, p. 27)

It is precisely by "transcendentalizing the domestic" that Wordsworth's "Intimations" Ode contests the insidious onset of skepticism. The domestic tedium of the daily grind brings its "inevitable yoke" (line 128) of "custom," which lies "with a weight / Heavy as frost, and deep almost as life" (lines 131–32), and yet this tedium of the everyday can be vanquished with something equally everyday, like "the meanest flower that blows" (line 206). If this double aspect of the ordinary (what Wordsworth calls the "common") seems paradoxical, and thus to give rise to further skepticism, it should be reflected that the ordinary is not a straightforward object of knowledge here; if it were, it could not be the antidote to skepticism, since skepticism is precisely what such knowledge is subjected to. Instead, as Cavell puts it, "the world I think, is not presentable as the empirical content of a concept—it is not a piece of what is called knowledge (a Kantian assertion). Then what constitutes the search for it (a romantic quest(ion))?" (*TNYUA*, p. 10). And this takes us back to where we started—to Wordsworth's search for something that is lost. Skepticism is overcome here by the recognition that what is lost in skepticism is *not* knowledge, merely a certain picture of it. So what, then, is at stake in the recovery of (or, better, from) skepticism? Here, as so often in the romantic period, all roads lead to Kant. I turn now to what Cavell describes as "the thought of romanticism as working out a crisis of knowledge, a crisis I have taken to be (interpretable as) a response at once to the threat of skepticism and to a disappointment with philosophy's answer to this threat, particularly as embodied in the achievement of Kant's philosophy" (*IQO*, p. 52).

IV

"The connection between romanticism and skepticism takes one of its ways from Kant," claims Cavell (*TNYUA*, p. 57). Kant figures so prominently in the debate between romanticism and skepticism because his philosophy transforms the very ground of what we might mean by *knowledge*, to the point that, as Cavell observes, "it is habitually said, I suppose correctly, that what we think of as romanticism is a function of (whatever else) how we conceive the philosophical settlement proposed in the achievement of Kant" (*IQO*, p. 29). It is worth quoting Cavell on the Kantian settlement at full length, since his argument impinges directly on so many aspects of our reading of the "Intimations" Ode—its quest for knowledge lost, for a world or home beyond the experience of worldlessness and homelessness—and moreover on the centrality of these concerns to romanticism itself:[9]

> The dissatisfaction with such a settlement as Kant's is relatively easy to state. To settle with skepticism . . . to assure us that we do know the existence of the world, or rather, that what we understand as knowledge is *of* the world, the price Kant asks us to pay is to cede any claim to know the thing in itself, to grant that human knowledge is not of things as they are in themselves (things as things, Heidegger will come to say). You don't—do you?—have to be a romantic to feel sometimes about that settlement: Thanks for nothing.
>
> The companion satisfaction with the settlement is harder to state. It is expressed in Kant's portrait of the human being as living in two worlds, in one of them determined, in the other free, one of which is necessary to the satisfaction

of human Understanding, the other to the satisfaction of human Reason. One romantic use for this idea of two worlds lies in its accounting for the human being's dissatisfaction with, as it were, itself . . . that we want unappeasably to be lawfully wedded to the world and at the same time illicitly intimate with it, as if the one stance produced the wish for the other. . . . Another romantic use for this idea of our two worlds is its offer of a formulation of our ambivalence toward Kant's ambivalent settlement, or a further insight into whatever that settlement was a settlement of—an insight that the human being now lives in *neither* world, that we are, as it is said, between worlds. (*IQO*, pp. 31–32)

It is important to note that Cavell's engagement with the "Intimations" Ode involves, in a sense, negotiating (or renegotiating) the terms of the Kantian settlement. He tells us that "the texts I am using as examples of romanticism I understand as monitoring the stability of this settlement—both our satisfaction in the justice of it and our dissatisfaction with this justice" (*IQO*, p. 31).

Interestingly, Angela Esterhammer argues that it was precisely in response to the settlement proposed in Kant's philosophy that philosophers and writers turned in his wake to language, and to rethinking it as an active force that alters the terms of that settlement. While acknowledging that "Kant did not concern himself with language per se in his investigation into the conditions of possibility for human knowledge" (*RP*, p. 68), Esterhammer nevertheless argues that "Kant's central hypothesis of the synthetic power of the human mind introduces a moment of creative action, construction, or positing into the cognitive process that could be seen as the germ of the Romantic performative" (*RP*, p. 74),[10] which in turn "brings about a recognition of how and why speech-act theory and the concept of performativity is rooted in eighteenth-century, above all in Kantian epistemology" (*RP*, p. 331).

These are big claims to make, and it is important to clarify them. Esterhammer's study attempts

to locate the roots of the performative in late-eighteenth-century epistemology and political philosophy, especially in Kant's account of the mental faculties. . . . In response to Kant's theory that the mind actively produces phenomena by processing intuitions in accordance with *a priori* forms of understanding, both his critics and his followers speculated that language must be ultimately involved in this process. More accurately—and more radically—philosophers like Hamann, Herder, and Humboldt recognized that language must *be* the process through which we articulate and conceptualize elements of the material world. While they defined cognition as essentially verbal, they also defined verbalization as essentially communicative. The mind's dialogue with the external world, and one speaker's dialogue with another, are bound together at the very origin of Romantic philosophy of language. (*RP*, p. 329)

This description of the renegotiation of what Cavell calls the Kantian settlement does indeed place language at the center of our relationship to the world and affords it an active role in shaping that relationship. But to use Austin's concept of the performative to describe this role might seem something of a stretch. Esterhammer nevertheless demonstrates that there are points of comparison between crucial aspects of Austinian and Kantian thought:

> There is an intriguing structural parallel between Kant's claim that "I think" accompanies all our mental representations, and can always potentially be made explicit, and Austin's claim that "I state that . . ." implicitly accompanies all our verbal representations, whether or not it is actually articulated. Making the "I think" explicit reveals the active role of the understanding in forming representations; making the "I state" explicit reveals the active role of the speaker in forming sentences. In both cases, the act-character of the (cognitive or verbal) judgment is bound up with a reference to the first-person subject—and the centrality and asymmetry of the first person in both speech-act philosophy and Kantian-Romantic theories of cognition is a key issue for a theory of the Romantic performative. (*RP*, p. 75)[11]

Esterhammer goes so far as to claim that "Austin and Searle only gave explicit and systematic form to a concept that is deeply rooted in Kantian and post-Kantian philosophy, as well as in German idealism and Romanticism" (*RP*, p. 70). There is not space here to give the validity and the significance of this claim a full hearing, but it certainly corroborates Cavell's diagnosis of the relationship between romanticism and the Kantian settlement and underscores the importance of the role of language in challenging the skepticism that settlement confronted in the first place. With this in mind, it will be instructive to observe the Romantic performative at work in the poetry of Wordsworth, comparing these instances of how Wordsworth does things with words with Cavell's analyses of his poetry.

V

In contrast with the famously problematic and ambiguous status of poetry in Austin's discussions of the performative, Esterhammer sees poetic language as an essential dimension of the Romantic performative. This chimes closely with Cavell's interpretation of Wordsworth's task as transforming or redeeming the world through the language of his poems. Or as Cavell puts it:

> Against a vision of the death of the world, the romantic calling for poetry, or quest for it, the urgency of it, would be sensible; and the sense that the redemption of philosophy is bound up with the redemption of poetry would be understandable: the calling of poetry is to give the world back, to bring it back, as to life. Hence romantics seem to involve themselves in what look to us to be superstitious, discredited mysteries of animism, sometimes in the form of what is called the pathetic fallacy (*IQO*, pp. 44–45)

To single out the pathetic fallacy in this way is an instructive move, not least because Wordsworth's "Intimations" Ode is replete with examples of it. But Cavell's view of the nature of the pathetic fallacy is, to say the least, unconventional. He sees it in terms of a relationship to the world that he calls "animism" and sees in this a romantic challenge to the Kantian position sketched above. "The price of animism is an aspect of the romantic settlement" (*IQO*, p. 54), claims Cavell, because it represents "romanticism's bargain with the Kantian (buying back the thing in itself by taking on animism . . .)" (*IQO*, p. 65). It is a way of renegotiating the terms of the Kantian settlement by confronting the skepticism that Kant sought to placate, or, as Cavell puts it, "bringing out an animism already implicit in the idea of doubting [the world's] existence" (*IQO*, p. 55).

This is a complex argument, and perhaps in part a counterintuitive one. As Cavell puts it, "There seems to be no shaking the sense that I have transformed the issue of skepticism into the issue of animism, exchanged one form of craziness for another" (*IQO*, p. 55). More pressingly, it involves a certain ambiguity in Wordsworth's conception of his task as a poet:

> The matter of animism is not going to be simple to state, because it has seemed badly misconceived . . . as something romantics embrace—whereas Wordsworth's endlessly discussed remarks concerning poetic diction are in practice as much *against* the pathetic fallacy, against certain accessions to it, as in theory they are *for* the imitation of the rustic and the low, and perhaps the one because of the other. (*IQO*, p. 54)

And yet the "Intimations" Ode appears to be equally committed to redeeming the "rustic," the "low," the "common," and the "ordinary" *and* to the trope of pathetic fallacy, and perhaps the one through the other.

Consider the following passage from the poem, singled out by Cavell as a salutary example of the pathetic fallacy because in it "Wordsworth apparently claims to find not only that flowers feel but that they speak" (*IQO*, p. 69):

> —But there's a Tree, of many, one,
> A single Field which I have looked upon,
> Both of them speak of something that is gone:
> The Pansy at my feet
> Doth the same tale repeat:
> Whither is fled the visionary gleam?
> Where is it now, the glory and the dream? (lines 51–57)

It would be hard to conceive of a clearer case of the pathetic fallacy than this. Wordsworth appears to invest not just a level of sentience and feeling in nature itself, but affords it the status of a speaking subject, and not just as a speaker he might commune with in dialogue but as a speaker that actually accosts him. And this enables us to see how the trope of pathetic fallacy expresses the tendency toward animism that Cavell describes: by personifying the tree, the field, and the pansy, and bestowing on them the anthropomorphic trait of language, Wordsworth can be understood as restoring a form of communion with the Kantian "thing in itself."

It is nevertheless instructive to refract Cavell's understanding of the nature of animism through the lens of Esterhammer's diagnosis of the performative aspects of the romantic view of language, because it is surely significant that the anthropomorphic trait bestowed on these things is not a capacity for thought or feeling or the immortality of the soul but the power of language. But it is also significant that this bestowing is carried out through language itself, that is, through the speech acts of Wordsworth's poem. And it is even more significant that the "Fountains, Meadows, Hills, and Groves" (line 191) are conceived as having the power to use not just language but performative language at that, and that Wordsworth appears to be able to use performative language in return when addressing them.

In claiming that nature converses with him, Wordsworth is in good company, since similar claims can be found throughout the romantic period:

> In Herder's essay on the origin of language, elements of the natural world impress themselves on human consciousness by uttering a word, . . . Coleridge emphasizes the way roses or nightingales announce themselves as "speaking" subjects, . . . By characterizing roses and nightingales as speaking subjects,

> Coleridge also lines up with Humboldt, Friedrich Schlegel, and other German Romantic philosophers who considered dialogue the model for reflective thought. (*RP*, p. 179)

The claim that the natural world pronounces speech acts is one that is unlikely to find much sympathy in classic speech act theory, with its emphasis on the speaking subject, on conventions, and on context. It is hard to imagine how, on this view, the romantic conversation with flowers and birds would qualify as language at all, let alone as performative. As Esterhammer says, "Searle would be unlikely to ascribe intentionality to a rose or a nightingale—but this in itself highlights the flexibility of the Romantic conception of utterance" (*RP*, pp. 179–80).

Yet Esterhammer argues that the ability of language to bestow the status of subject on the world is an important dimension of the Romantic performative, indeed that such a bestowing *is itself* performative. Moreover, she argues that certain romantic views of language—and especially the language of poetry—see this bestowing not as mere postulating but as *creating* the new state of affairs language bestows upon the world. She claims, interestingly, a Kantian genealogy for this view:

> Taking their cue from Kant's analysis of the understanding as the faculty that creates representations of the world through synthesis, linguistic philosophers analyze language as a counterpart to the understanding that creates representations through its own synthetic process. They stress the way language not only represents but *recreates* being, where "being" is itself not a static but a dynamic principle, a constant coming-into-being. The result is a revised view of utterances, particularly propositions, that regards them not as (passively) referring to reality but as (actively) creating a represented reality, an ideal reality, or—in the most radical view, which is generally reserved for poetic utterance—simply *creating reality.* (*RP*, pp. 95–96)

So the statement in a poem that a pansy or a field or a tree speaks is a moment where language actively "has the ability to create *in reality,* to confer reality on what were internal and not yet fully existing concepts. . . . Thus, the sentence 'Mind is immortal' *creates mind* as an entity that can be thought and responded to. That *is* its reality, a reality it did not have before the utterance took place" (*RP*, p. 122). Viewed in this way, the "Intimations" Ode *actively creates* a speaking subjectivity for fields, trees, pansies, fountains, meadows, hills, and groves with a linguistic power closely related to that which, for example, creates a state of union between people who are pronounced man and wife. This power must surely be called performative, albeit loosely, and it demonstrates an important way in which Wordsworth's "Intimations" Ode does things with words.

If Esterhammer's analysis of the Romantic performative is accepted, then I would argue that it enables us to refine Cavell's reading of Wordsworth's animism, Kantianism, and even romanticism. If I understand it correctly, Cavell's argument is that in the wake of the loss of the Kantian "thing in itself," romanticism seeks to reclaim knowledge of the natural world by repicturing it in anthropomorphized forms of animism, which find their expression in the poetic device of the pathetic fallacy. To adopt Esterhammer's view, though, is to see *language itself* as that which enables animism: animism belongs to language since language is that which animates the inanimate world, and the power to animate the world in this way is performative. The romantic quest, then, is not so much to retrieve the world it had lost thanks to Kant but to reanimate (and thereby redeem) the world in and through language—the field of cognition unplowed by Kant but harvested by his romantic successors.

To put the point more clearly, here is a succinct summary of the Cavellian position:

> Romanticism's work here interprets itself . . . as the task of bringing the world back, as to life. This may, in turn, present itself as the quest for a return to the ordinary, or of it, a new creation of our habitat; or as the quest, away from that, for the creation of a new inhabitation: Wordsworth and Coleridge would represent the former alternative; Blake and Shelley, I believe, the latter. . . . But romanticism in either direction makes its own bargain with the concept of knowledge and the threat of skepticism, one which a philosopher may feel gives up the game, one that accepts something like animism, represented by what seems still to be called, when it is called, the pathetic fallacy. (*IQO*, pp. 52–53)

What I am suggesting is that this is a bargain made not merely with knowledge but also, indeed primarily, with language and that the threat of skepticism is directed as much toward the effectiveness of language and its power (not least its power to redeem the world) as toward the certainty of knowledge.

Consider the opening of the final stanza of the "Intimations" Ode, where the speaker addresses the landscape and, in keeping with the animism Cavell detects in romanticism's use of the pathetic fallacy, imparts once again onto inanimate nature the ability to use language: "And O, ye Fountains, Meadows, Hills, and Groves, / Forbode not any severing of our loves!" (lines 191–92). Cavell glosses these lines thus: "'Forbode' means fortell, or portend, so here speaking is interpreted as, let us say, bespeaking, forming an omen of something" (*IQO*, p. 71). So an animistic communion with the world in itself is enabled not just through the trope of pathetic fallacy but, more specifically, through admitting the world into the order of language as a speaking subject.

It is telling that Wordsworth is investing the landscape not merely with the power to speak but with the power to use the performative—to foretell, to predict. But while it may be (relatively) easy to imagine the earth speaking as an oracle, it is harder to imagine a poet speaking back. Yet Wordsworth does this too, and, moreover, he does so by addressing the fountains, meadows, hills, and groves with a performative. Cavell draws attention to this when he says that when "the poet speaks to things, what he speaks to them about is their speaking, their foreboding. He commands them, or beseeches them, not to be omens of severing, presumably because he knows that severing is a reasonable thing for them to foretell" (*IQO*, p. 72). *Both* the landscape's ability to forebode or foretell *and* the poet's ability to beseech or command involve clearly performative speech acts. Moreover, bestowing on both landscape and poet the ability to communicate with each other would be a good instance of Esterhammer's Romantic performative, since it is "a speech act that paradoxically founds the conditions within which it operates in the very moment when it is uttered" (*RP*, p. xiii).

It could be argued that conceptualizing the speakers this way invalidates the status of the landscape's foretelling and the poet's beseeching/commanding, because there are no conventions involved—no criteria by which the poet could interpret the landscape's foreboding and none by which the poet could command or beseech the landscape. There is thus no way in which either the poet or the landscape could either have or lack the authority to command or predict, nor is there a way to assess the success or the failure of their speech acts *qua* performatives or even *qua* speech acts. The issue of skepticism, then, bedevils the Romantic performative as ferociously as it does Kantian epistemology.[12] But just as Cavell shows that living with a certain form of skepticism is the inevitable corollary of the Kantian settlement, so too I wish to build on Esterhammer's diagnosis of the Romantic performative and its awareness of the power of language by suggesting that in this instance it is haunted as much by the possibility of the *failure* of that power.

The lost communion with the world forfeited by Kant is staged here as an encounter in and through language, in and through its ability to act and react on speakers and on the world. The poet's beseeching or commanding must be predicated on positing that the fountains, meadows, hills, and groves will listen and oblige him; yet, reciprocally, their foreboding must be predicated on positing their addressee—is it stretching too far to call him Wordsworth?—as someone who will notice, hear, interpret, and pay heed to their omen. Both of these assumptions, though, are hopelessly fraught, given their context in a poem that is precisely about the *loss* of such an intimate communion with the world, about the failure or breakdown of communication with it. The poet beseeches or commands the world because he knows that retaining an intimate communication with it is impossible (the bulk of the Ode demonstrates just this), and this is paradoxical. But more paradoxical yet is that if the earth *were* to forebode the dreaded severing, then the poet would not—could not—know this and thus could not read or interpret their omen, because the connection between them would be severed. So in the "Intimations" Ode these Romantic performative speech acts, when founding the conditions of their own possibility, simultaneously found the conditions of their *im*possibility.

Cavell suggests that "the intellectual drive of a work like the Intimations Ode" (*IQO*, p. 41) can be understood as a working through of the problem of the pathetic fallacy, and I could not be more in agreement with this assessment. Furthermore, he relates this working through to the romantic quest for the ordinary, and this is indeed an important connection to make:

> This poem as a whole may be taken as a process of understanding and overcoming the unabashed pathetic fallacy that occurred in its opening stanzas, where the moon looks round her with delight, and land and sea give themselves up to jollity, and every beast keeps holiday. But in favour of what is this overcome, and why is it so hard? I mean, why is it, or why was it, when we were children, *natural* to us; an ordinariness which a new ordinariness must replace? (*IQO*, p. 71)

The ambiguity here has as much to do with the already-noted paradox involved in Wordsworth's conception of the ordinary as with animism or the pathetic fallacy. For in his Preface to *Lyrical Ballads*, Wordsworth defends his decision "to choose incidents and situations from common life, and to relate or describe them, throughout, as far as was possible in a selection of language really used by men" (Preface, p. 123) in terms that imply his commitment to an aesthetic of the ordinary. And yet he defends this decision in terms that seem to contradict this aesthetic: "The language of such Poetry as is here recommended is, as far as is possible, a selection of the language really spoken by men; . . . this selection, wherever it is made with true taste and feeling, will of itself . . . entirely separate the composition from the vulgarity and meanness of ordinary life" (Preface, p. 137). The only way to resolve this apparent contradiction is to note that

Wordsworth's target here is "the *vulgarity* and *meanness* of ordinary life," and not ordinary life in itself. But this is tantamount to saying that it is ordinary language that must redeem the ordinary, which seems simply to replace one paradox with another. Wordsworth's assertion that "ordinary things should be presented to the mind in an unusual aspect" (Preface, p. 123) encapsulates the problematic: it is only in exiting from the ordinary that the ordinary can be redeemed. This is why Wordsworth must ultimately be thought of as sharing *both* Austin's concern with the ordinary *and* Cavell's interest in its loss, and his poetry must be thought of as both enabled by the performative power of language to transform the world *and* curtailed by the failure of that power.

CHAPTER FIVE

What Did Cavell Want of Poe?

In a lecture given at Stanford some years ago, Stanley Cavell added his name to the list of thinkers who have endeavored to read Poe philosophically, an impressive list that already included Derrida, Lacan, and Barbara Johnson.[1] Yet Cavell's engagement with Poe does not amount to a "reading" in any straightforward, positivistic sense of the term. Focusing largely on one of Poe's lesser-known stories, "The Imp of the Perverse,"[2] he gives three "directions for reading" the story, followed by three questions, which, Cavell says, the text invites.[3] However, none of the questions meets with an apparent answer, nor are the suggestions he makes as "directions for reading" followed up. "What did Cavell want of Poe?" is, then, a genuine question. But it is also a citation. In a more recent piece entitled "What Did Derrida Want of Austin?," Cavell's reading of Austin's *How To Do Things With Words* contains an insight that, applied to "The Imp of the Perverse," opens up new dimensions to his engagement with Poe.[4]

"The Imp of the Perverse" is an unusual example of its genre. Indeed, it is scarcely a tale at all. It is largely a meditation on "an innate and primitive principle of human action . . . which we may call *perverseness*" ("Imp," p. 284). It contains a story only as a brief coda. Its philosophical narrator takes great pains to expound his notion of perverseness as "the *prima mobilia* of the human soul" ("Imp," p. 283); to argue that "the phrenologists," together with "all the moralists" and "all metaphysicianism" ("Imp," p. 283), have ignored this propensity of mankind—indeed, "In the pure arrogance of the reason, we have all overlooked it" ("Imp," p. 283); to imply that this oversight constitutes a major gap in our knowledge of ourselves; and to describe, partially by exemplification, the nature and importance of our impulse toward the perverse. It is only after this that the story proper begins: the narrator reveals himself to be making a confession from a prison cell on the eve of his execution for murder. He has committed the perfect crime, poisoning his victim with vapors emitted from a toxic candle and inheriting his wealth. Since there is no possibility of his detection, he repeats to himself, mantralike, the phrase "I am safe," until one day, "In a fit of petulance, I re-modelled them thus:—'I am safe—I am safe—yes—if I be not fool enough to make open confession!'" ("Imp," p. 287). At this point, the spirit of perverseness seizes hold of him, and he finds himself driven by it to make, against every other basic instinct, the confession that brings him to his cell and ultimately to the narrative we are reading.

The story component of the tale is about half as long as the meditation, and since the meditation participates largely in the genre of philosophical discourse, it is not hard to see why this hybrid text should appeal to a philosopher such as Cavell. Cavell's three suggestions for reading the text are as follows: firstly, that "the fiction of the writer's arresting himself and wearing fetters and tenanting the cell of the condemned and the fiction of providing a poisonous wax light for reading are descriptions or fantasies of writing, modeled by the writing before us" (*IQO*, p. 123); secondly, that, in a reversal of Descartes, thinking leads to the annihilation of the subject—"I think, therefore I am destroyed" (*IQO*, p. 124)—and so the story narrates "a kind of negation or perversion of the cogito" (*IQO*, p. 123); and thirdly, that language itself is perverse (*IQO*, pp. 124–25).

As can be seen from Cavell's reading, the hybridity of the tale in terms of its mixing of philosophical and narrative genres complicates our approach to it as readers. If we read "The Imp of the Perverse" as essentially a philosophical discourse, then we are likely to view the story with which it concludes as carrying the force of an exemplum and therefore to interpret it along the same lines as the scenarios outlined by the narrator earlier on as instances of perverseness (feeling the urge to jump off a cliff, or inexplicably procrastinating an urgent task). Yet to read it as such is to miss the force that Poe's narrator attaches to his own story; the philosophical discourse is rather a pretext, a "mere" introduction to it:

> I have said thus much, that in some measure I may answer your question—that I may explain to you why I am here—that I may assign to you something that shall have at least the faint aspect of a cause for my wearing these fetters, and for my tenanting this cell of the condemned. Had I not been thus prolix, you might either have misunderstood me altogether, or, with the rabble, have fancied me mad. As it is, you will easily perceive that I am one of the many uncounted victims of the Imp of the Perverse. ("Imp," p. 286)

In many ways, this paragraph is the pivotal moment of the tale and therefore central to Cavell's reading of Poe. It gives the tale a purpose, "—that I may explain to you why I am here—," an explanation that Cavell points out is unsolicited (*IQO*, p. 123) and that can be interpreted as a philosophical undertaking. It also introduces the figure of the condemned, imprisoned, fettered writer, which constitutes, for Cavell, a description/fantasy of writing itself. Most importantly, it marks the turning point between the literary and philosophical halves of the text. For this reason, I shall call it the "hinge paragraph."

All three of the "questions" Cavell puts to Poe's text hinge in some way on this paragraph: "First, what does it betoken about the relation of philosophy and literature that a piece of writing can be seen to consist of what is for all the world a philosophical essay preceding, even turning into, a fictional tale—as it happens, a fictional confession from a prison cell?" (*IQO*, p. 126). Cavell suggests that the answer is to be found in

> the paragraph . . . in which Poe pivots from the essay to the tale, insinuating that we are failing to ask a question about the origin of the writing and claiming that without the philosophical preface—which means without the hinging of essay and tale, philosophy and fiction—the reader might, "with the rabble, have fancied me mad," not perceiving that he is "one of the many uncounted victims of the Imp of the Perverse." (*IQO*, p. 126)

The second of Cavell's questions is, "What does it betoken about fact and fiction that Poe's writing of the Imp simultaneously tells two tales of imprisonment . . . as if they are fables of one another?" (*IQO*, p. 127). The hinge paragraph is where the narrator reveals to us the fact of his imprisonment, so it is crucial in this respect too. Finally, the third of Cavell's questions is, "What does it betoken about American philosophy that . . . Poe may be seen as taking upon [himself] the problematic of the cogito (. . . by perverting or subverting it) and as sharing the perception that authoring—philosophical writing, anyway, writing as thinking—is such that to exist it must assume, or acknowledge, the proof of its own existence?" (*IQO*, p. 129). Since the hinge paragraph introduces the theme of "why I am here," it is thus, once again, central to Cavell's line of enquiry. (It will also be seen that the first two of Cavell's "directions for reading" are also rooted in the hinge paragraph.)

The hinge paragraph, more than anywhere else in Poe's tale, is the moment where, as Cavell says, "philosophy and literature have come together" (*IQO*, p. 127). But it is also the moment where, as Cavell also argues, the philosophical essay turns into a fictional tale, with an attendant discursive transition from philosophy to fiction (*IQO*, pp. 122, 126). As such, it is quite literally the pivotal moment in Poe's text, and there is no questioning its importance. Yet Cavell's reading places a level of stress on it that is indeed questionable. At the risk of appearing perverse, I want to suggest that the hinge paragraph is *not* a moment of transition from a philosophical genre to a literary one. To claim that is to register our assumptions and preconceptions about the distinctions (and distinctiveness) of the genres of philosophy and literature that Poe's text neither bears nor shares.

The key to my argument is that Poe's text is first and foremost a *confession*, and the disputed paragraph reveals it to be such. Cavell is aware of the confessional aspects of the tale,[5] but he does not explore their implications to any degree. This is surprising, given that Cavell is a sensitive reader of the confessional aspects of philosophical texts:

> Serious confessions must [contain] the full acknowledgement of temptation . . . and a willingness to correct them and give them up. . . . In confessing you do not explain or justify, but describe how it is with you. And confession, unlike dogma, is not to be believed but tested, and accepted or rejected. Nor is it the occasion for accusation, except of yourself, and by implication those who find themselves in you. There is exhortation . . . not to belief, but to self-scrutiny. (*MWM*, p. 71)

Admittedly, Cavell is describing here not the legal confessions found in crime fiction but the genre of religious confession and its influence on philosophical confession, specifically in Wittgenstein's *Philosophical Investigations*. Nevertheless, according to the above definition, "The Imp of the Perverse" would *not* count as a confession. It does not "acknowledge temptation," pointing instead toward a philosophical/psychological necessity—the impulsion of the perverse—which can neither be "corrected" nor "given up." (Indeed, its accusations are leveled not against the narrator's own self but against the Imp of the Perverse). It moves not from the particular ("describe how it was with you") to the general ("and by implication those who find themselves in you") but rather in the reverse direction. Poe's text, then, does not sit easily with Cavell's account of confession.[6]

Yet the genre of confession nevertheless provides a framework for reading "The Imp of the Perverse," one that avoids the schism between literature and philosophy since it contains elements that are both narrative and philosophical in nature. Cavell's discussion of confession in *Must We Mean What We Say?* demonstrates a keen sense of their interrelation, but this is precisely what is overlooked by his division of Poe's text into two separate and distinct halves, a "philosophical" and a "literary" one. If what Cavell wanted of Poe was a segregation between the genres of philosophy and literature (a segregation highly uncharacteristic of his thought), then he is likely to have been disappointed, since Poe's *oeuvre* resists any such thing. The discussion of "the analytical power" that prefaces "The Murders in the Rue Morgue," the dialogues on "self-evidence" that intersperse "The Purloined Letter," and even the brief paragraph of reverie with which "Berenicë" opens configure different relationships between philosophical and narrative discourse, and rarely are the two separate or separable.[7] That this is particularly the case with the genre of confession can be seen in the following (related) passage from "The Black Cat," also quoted by Cavell,[8] which uses confession to blend storytelling and philosophizing effortlessly:

> In the meantime the cat slowly recovered. . . . He went about the house as usual, but, as might be expected, fled in extreme terror at my approach. I had so much of my old heart left, as to be at first grieved by this evident dislike on the part of a creature which had once so loved me. But this feeling soon gave place to irritation. And then came, as if to my final and irrevocable overthrow, the spirit of PERVERSENESS. Of this spirit philosophy takes no account. Yet I am not more sure that my soul lives, than I am that perverseness is one of the primitive impulses of the human heart—one of the indivisible primary faculties, or sentiments, which give direction to the character of Man. Who has not, a hundred times, found himself committing a vile or a silly action, for no other reason than because he knows he should *not*? Have we not a perpetual inclination, in the teeth of our best judgment, to violate that which is *Law*, merely because we understand it to be such? This spirit of perverseness, I say, came to my final overthrow. It was this unfathomable longing of the soul *to vex itself*—to offer violence to its own nature—to do wrong for the wrong's sake only—that urged me to continue and finally to consummate the injury I had inflicted upon the unoffending brute. One morning, in cool blood, I slipped a noose about its neck and hung it to the limb of a tree;—hung it with the tears streaming from my eyes, and with the bitterest remorse at my heart;—hung it *because* I knew that it had loved me, and *because* I felt it had given me no reason of offence;—hung it *because* I knew that in so doing I was committing a sin—a deadly sin that would so jeopardize my immortal soul as to place it—if such a thing were possible—even beyond the reach of the infinite mercy of the Most Merciful and Most Terrible God.[9]

This confession, however, is not as complex as that in "The Imp of the Perverse." Unlike the above example from "The Black Cat," the confession in "The Imp of the Perverse" is hardly the confession of a *crime* at all.

A typical example of the crime-confession genre might begin with the perpetrator confessing to a crime that his better judgment told him not to commit but that he committed anyway, subsequently feeling the remorse that leads to the confession, through which he embarks on the path of penitence. Yet this is not what we find in "The Imp of the Perverse." Poe breaks with these generic patterns by having his narrator make a confession of a confession, in which the moment of confession being confessed to occupies the status normally associated with the crime. In fact, the original crime (the murder) is committed without any compunction whatsoever, and the narrator rather revels in it than feels shame at it:

> It is impossible that any deed could have been wrought with a more thorough deliberation. For weeks, for months, I pondered upon the means of the murder. I rejected a thousand schemes, because their accomplishment involved a *chance* of detection. . . . The idea of detection never once entered my brain. . . . I had left no shadow of a clue by which it would be possible to convict, or even to suspect me of the crime. It is inconceivable how rich a sentiment of satisfaction arose in my bosom as I reflected upon my absolute security. For a very long period of time, I was accustomed to revel in this sentiment. It afforded me more real delight than all the mere worldly advantages accruing from my sin. ("Imp," pp. 286–87)

This feeling is shattered by the perverse confession, which now functions exactly as the crime would in a more straightforward example of the genre: the narrator makes a confession that his better judgment and every instinct tell him not to, and having confessed anyway, he subsequently feels the remorse that leads to the confession of the confession, that is, the story we are reading. This strategy enables the narrator, a calculating murderer, to cast himself in the role of victim ("one of the many uncounted victims of the Imp of the Perverse"), and through expressing remorse for his confession, he neatly avoids having to make any statement of remorse regarding his original crime of murder. Poe's manipulation of confessional discourse, then, is startling and effective.

As Paul de Man has noted, the genre of confession is related to the genre of *excuse*. The relationship—and the difference—is bound up with the relationship between referential language and performative language.[10] According to de Man, confessional discourse is fundamentally referential: it makes statements about acts performed, deeds perpetrated, crimes committed, and it is necessary to confession that they be true. But in order for a confession to achieve its results, it must be accepted, and it must therefore persuade its audience of the speaker's sincerity and penitence. To this extent it is performative, and de Man, citing J. L. Austin, calls this aspect of confession the "excuse":

> The difference between the verbal excuse and the referential crime is not a simple opposition between an action and a mere utterance about an action. To steal is to act and includes no necessary verbal elements. To confess is discursive, but the discourse is governed by a principle of referential verification that includes an extraverbal moment. . . . No such possibility of verification exists for the excuse, which is verbal in its utterance, in its effect and in its authority: its purpose is not to state but to convince.[11]

As with all performatives, when we excuse ourselves and ask to be excused—and any serious reader of Cavell will want to use scare quotes here—"we must mean it":[12] we must lay bare our feelings of penitence, and those feelings must be sincere. But unlike in the genre of confession, which deals in admitting verifiable facts, in the genre of excuse our audience can only "take our word for it." "The distinction between the confession stated in the mode of revealed truth and the confession stated in the mode of excuse is that the evidence for the former is referential . . . whereas the evidence for the latter can only be verbal."[13] Accordingly,

> confessional language can be considered under a double epistemological perspective: it functions as a verifiable referential cognition, but it also functions as a statement whose reliability cannot be verified by empirical means. The convergence of the two modes is not a priori given, and it is because of the possibility of a discrepancy between them that the possibility of excuse arises. The excuse articulates the discrepancy and, in so doing, it actually asserts it as fact.[14]

This, for de Man, sets up a tension between the two genres based on their differing uses of language:

> It is not enough to *confess*, one also has to *excuse*. . . . The only thing one has to fear from the excuse is that it will indeed exculpate the confessor, thus making the confession (and the confessional text) redundant as it originates. *Qui s'accuse s'excuse*; this sounds convincing and convenient enough, but, in terms of absolute truth, it ruins the seriousness of any confessional discourse by making it

> self-destructive. Since confession . . . exists only as a verbal utterance, how then are we to know that we are indeed dealing with a *true* confession, since the recognition of guilt implies its exoneration in the name of the same transcendental principle of truth that allowed for the certitude of guilt in the first place?[15]

In "The Imp of the Perverse," as we have seen, confession is indeed "self-destructive" in a far starker sense than de Man intends here; after all, a second confession is needed to express regret for the (self-)destruction caused by the first. Or rather, since the first confession is basically referential, but the second seeks to *excuse* the narrator to the reader, this is perhaps an excuse for a confession as much as a confession of a confession.

But how does de Man's understanding of the confessional genre help us to read Cavell's reading of Poe? The answer, I maintain, lies in the nature of the excuse, and it is interesting in this respect that de Man's deconstructive engagement with the subject references the very text that Cavell criticizes arch-deconstructor Jacques Derrida for not reading, namely, J. L. Austin's "A Plea for Excuses."[16] Cavell argues a relation between the theory of excuses and the idea of tragedy: "Excuses mark out the region of tragedy, mark it as the beyond of the excusable, the justifiable, the explainable, (the sociable?)" (*PP*, p. 54). Which is not to suggest that Poe's narrator is any kind of tragic hero, even though his crime inhabits all of these "beyonds." Rather, what he cites as his excuse—the perverse, the force it exerts over us, and especially our obliviousness to both—is a clear demarcation of these "beyonds" and is accordingly presented as tragic.

As we shall see in this book's final two chapters, the concept of tragedy often functions in Cavell's thought as a moment of intersection between literature and philosophy, so it is unsurprising that his critique of Derrida homes in on the latter's inattention to a line from Greek tragedy cited by Austin:

> The Greek sentence Austin calls classic and cites from Euripides and translates as "My tongue swore to, but my heart did not," is Hippolytus's reply to Phaedra's nurse when she reminds him of his oath to keep her revelation a secret. Austin uses this distinction between tongue and heart as a type of the philosophical use of profundity (call it metaphysics) to exempt yourself, or exclude yourself, from the everyday responsibilities or accountabilities that make civilized life possible—giving an out to bigamists, welshers, con artists of every stripe. But Austin himself seems to be forgetting something about the *Hippolytus*, since he apparently attributes the line to Hippolytus as a species of excuse, whereas Hippolytus never uses it so, and indeed the pity and terror involved are some

function of the knowledge that the most *casual* of utterances may be irretrievable: so my tongue swore without my heart—*nevertheless I am bound.* (*PP*, p. 62)

The nature of the oath or promise need not interest us here. Rather, as Cavell points out, the line "My tongue swore to, but my heart did not" resembles an *excuse*. Understood in this way, it carries the same force as Poe's narrator's protestations in "The Imp of the Perverse."

The confession to which Poe's narrator is confessing would seem to provide a classic case of one's tongue saying words to which one's heart or mind or soul does not assent, with all the attendant bad consequences of speaking insincerely magnified so as to amount to the speaker's downfall. Furthermore, it exhibits precisely the kind of suspect metaphysical gesture that Cavell (as well as Austin and Derrida) objects to, namely, the appeal to a metaphysical entity as a get-out clause from being held to one's word: "Hippolytus enacts the claim that a metaphysician—the metaphysician in each of us—will use metaphysics to get out of . . . our ordinary moral obligations" (*PP*, p. 75).[17] Poe's narrator could similarly be read as excusing himself from his perverse confession because, like Hippolytus, he did not "mean" his words in his heart but was rather set on by "some invisible fiend," "the spirit of the *Perverse*" ("Imp," pp. 288, 286). We have, then, somebody (sincerely) excusing himself from a confession on the grounds that he was insincere when he made it, but the confession nevertheless stands, with the same effective consequences regardless of whether it was uttered merely from perverseness. Such a reading of Poe's story would fit neatly alongside Cavell's essay "Must We Mean What We Say?," which also begins by scrutinizing notions of "voluntary" and "involuntary" actions for which we are or are not held "responsible."[18] (And, tellingly, this essay is also explicitly indebted to Austin's "A Plea for Excuses.") This would add a moral dimension to Cavell's reading of Poe, and more importantly, it would do so without opening the door to the metaphysics of which Cavell and Austin (and Derrida and de Man) are so wary.

However, such a reading will not quite do. The inaccessibility, and therefore the sincerity, of one's "inner feelings" that de Man identified as problematic comes into play here. How can we know, except by taking his word for it, that Poe's narrator is being sincere when he excuses himself from being insincere? How can we be sure, if he pleads that he confessed from perverseness instead of from the heart or soul, that he is not doing so again? Poe's masterful use of unreliable narrators aside, the text is keen to upset the very terms we might use to differentiate between words spoken from the heart or soul and words spoken from perverseness. The narrator, indeed, situates perverseness within the human heart and soul itself. At first, the location of this mysterious tendency is withheld:

> We first determined, naturally enough, that it was the design of the Deity that man should eat. We then assigned to man an organ of alimentiveness, and this organ is the scourge with which the Deity compels man, will-I nill-I, into eating. Secondly, having settled it to be God's will that man should continue his species, we discovered an organ of amativeness, forthwith. And so with combativeness, with ideality, with causality, with constructiveness,—so, in short, with every organ, whether representing a propensity, a moral sentiment, or a faculty of the pure intellect. ("Imp," p. 283)

So if every human capacity has its organ, where does our impulse toward perverseness reside? Eventually the answer is supplied:

> An appeal to one' s own heart is, after all, the best reply to the sophistry just noticed. No one who trustingly consults and thoroughly questions his own soul, will be disposed to deny the entire radicalness of the propensity in question. ("Imp," p. 284)

When the narrator finally succumbs to perverseness, he describes the experience thus: "I felt an icy chill creep to my heart. I had had some experience in these fits of perversity" ("Imp," p. 287). Eventually, he says, "the long-imprisoned secret burst forth from my soul" ("Imp," p. 288). Perverseness, then, resides right in the human heart and soul. Indeed, it is the "*prima mobilia* of the human soul" ("Imp," p. 283).

This would imply that when we speak from perverseness, we are *also* speaking from the heart, that we are actually being true to our hearts and souls when we are being perverse. This, no doubt, is why Poe's narrator places such heavy emphasis on perverseness as fundamental to human action. Indeed, reading the story along Cartesian lines (this is the second of his "directions for reading"), Cavell argues that for Poe perverseness is fundamental to the makeup of the cogito:

> It seems reasonably clear that Poe's (narrator's) search for a proof of his (her?) existence (in the confessional tales I was citing) is for a proof that he breathes, that is, that he is alive. "I am not more certain that I breathe, than that the assurance of the wrong or error of any action is often the unconquerable *force* which impels us, and alone impels us, to its prosecution." Assume that he

> is betraying here an uncertainty that he breathes; and then turn around his comparison of certainties. The imp of himself here apparently gives him to think that he is not *less* certain that he breathes than that there is the impulsion in question. So his certainty of breathing becomes dependent on his impulse to wrongdoing. (*IQO*, p. 142)

One can take this logic even further. A similar sentence in Poe's story "The Black Cat" (the source of Poe's other major engagement with the perverse, and a source that Cavell is familiar with) reads: "I am not more sure that my soul lives, than I am that perverseness is one of the primitive impulses of the human heart."[19] Turning this sentence around, as Cavell advises, suggests that the narrator's certainty of the very existence of his own heart and soul depends on that heart and soul's propensity to wrongdoing: "I am perverse, therefore I am."

De Man's problematization of sincerity then becomes beside the point: a perverse excuse or confession is not just indistinguishable from a genuine one; it *is* genuine and sincere ("from the heart"). Hence, there is no metaphysical opening to be appealed to, since our "hearts" and "souls" are not unsullied refuges of truth and sincerity but are themselves perverse through and through. This renders the very possibility of "opening the soul" in confession and "speaking from the heart" in excuse suspect. Nor does "The Imp of the Perverse" allow us to abandon the more performative aspects of the excuse and take refuge in a stabler, referentially grounded genre of confession. In this case, the narrator has committed the perfect crime (he is "safe"), and there is no way of establishing the facts of the confession except that by which we also accept the sincerity of the excuse, namely, by taking his word for it. *Pace* de Man, confession and excuse cannot be distinguished, separated, *or* verified in this case. The confession may be as false as it is perverse, but its practical consequences are binding nevertheless. Poe's tale, then, undermines any attempt to assert the mastery of a metaphysical subject over the institution of language, and it does so not just along the lines of Cavell's reading of *Hippolytus* but also, and more radically, by problematizing the very idea of genuine sincerity and intentionality on which the speaking subject so often comes to rest.

What, then, did Cavell want of Poe? Well, if the site of the perverse is to be located in the very organ we use to vouch for our sincerity, then "The Imp of the Perverse" threatens the possibility of determining whether and how we can truly be certain that we mean what we say (or rather, that our interlocutor means what he or she says), as opposed to "merely" being perverse. And if being perverse *is* being sincere and genuine, then we can be sincere and genuine without meaning, or indeed wanting, to be. However, in any case, our words still mean what *they* say, regardless of the organ from which they were spoken. Put in these terms, Poe's tale confronts Cavell's thought with the very aspects of language he finds most philosophically challenging, and it can be no coincidence that his "directions" and "questions" address many of these: the suggestions that language itself is perverse, that the subject is self-destructive, that writing is a form of both crime and punishment and the writer is figured by the imprisoned self, and the related question about the troublesome relation between fact and fiction are all responses to the challenges Poe's story makes to these quintessentially Cavellian themes. Does the very institution of performative language rest on a myth of sincerity? What if we are victims rather than masters of it? "The Imp of the Perverse" provides Cavell with something of a limit case for these ideas, on which much of his philosophy is based. That is probably why his reading of it, like Poe's text itself, raises more questions than it answers.

CHAPTER SIX

"Politics as Opposed to What?"

Social Contract and Marriage Contract in A Doll's House

Let us begin this chapter from the same starting point as Cavell himself, who begins his longest discussion of *A Doll's House* with the obvious question, "Why Ibsen?" (*CoW*, p. 247). Unlike the questions Cavell asks of Poe's "The Imp of the Perverse," explored in the previous chapter, and unlike some of his questions that will come up later in this one, the question "Why Ibsen?" gets a prompt and relatively straightforward reply:

> It matters particularly to me that Ibsen became the most significant playwright in the lapse of time from Shakespeare and Racine to the middle of the nineteenth century, by taking as his subject for observation what can be seen precisely as a sequence of debasements of the search for a perfectionist existence. (*CoW*, p. 247)

Ibsen's plays, then, serve "to rebuke philosophy . . . for its comparative shunning of the perfectionist strain in moral thinking" (*CoW*, p. 247), and among his *oeuvre*, *A Doll's House* is of particular interest as "an exposure of the harm caused in failing to honor or recognize perfectionist longings" (*CoW*, p. 248). Accordingly, Cavell's more substantial engagements with Ibsen are essays in a philosophy he terms moral perfectionism, and as such, they are sketches of the moral questions and principles raised by Nora's shutting the door, literally and metaphorically, on her marriage in order to try and fulfil what she calls "My duty to myself."[1]

Although it will be important to enumerate and discuss these moral principles and questions, it is equally important to make clear from the outset that the main thrust of this chapter is not directly concerned with the Cavellian account of Nora's moral perfectionism. That aspect of Cavell's philosophy is explored in greater detail in the conclusion of this book, where it is discussed in connection with another classic of the modern stage, Arthur Miller's *Death of a*

Salesman. Instead, for reasons I shall set out in due course, my aim in this chapter is to reframe Cavell's discussions of *A Doll's House*, and of Nora's actions in particular, as a contribution to a debate that is essentially political rather than moral, concerned primarily with a political interpretation of Ibsen's play. That is not to say that we will be parting company with Cavell's writings on Ibsen; rather, I shall attempt to show how they provide answers to a different set of questions—political questions—from the set of moral questions Cavell asks of Ibsen.

What, then, are the questions Cavell poses to *A Doll's House*? Almost all of them are derived from what he calls the "unavoidable question," namely, "Is Nora right or wrong to leave the house? Is it good or bad of her?" (*CoW*, p. 249). Initially, Cavell tackles the question in terms that are disappointingly familiar and perhaps even hackneyed: he invokes the dispute between Kantian and utilitarian conceptions of morality that has formed the staple of countless essays and exam questions in undergraduate philosophy classes. But Cavell deploys these well-worn terms only to demonstrate that neither school of philosophy can do justice to Nora and her actions. Mill's famous utilitarian precept that "actions are right in proportion as they tend to promote happiness; wrong as they tend to produce the reverse of happiness" seems to provide concrete mathematical grounds on which to condemn Nora outright. "Shall we calculate for her?" Cavell asks. "Let's see: she will cause intense pain to at least four people we know about (one husband and three children), perhaps for the rest of their lives. And . . . for herself . . . she anticipates something like isolation and desolation. So she is creating displeasure all the way around" (*CoW*, pp. 249–50). The utilitarian view of morality finds Nora clearly in the wrong; conversely, if Nora is indeed justified in her actions, then utilitarianism as a moral philosophy would be little short of bankrupt.

Yet the great rival to the utilitarians' theory of morality—Kant's deontological philosophy—does not fare much better in trying to address itself to Nora's situation. The Kantian precept of the categorical imperative, no less famous than Mill's, states that the "universal imperative of duty" bids us to "act only in accordance with that maxim through which you can at the same time will that it become a universal law."[2] This creates something of a problem for someone in Nora's position, because the society in which she lives, and for which her husband Torvald Helmer is the play's principal spokesman, clearly regards her as abandoning the imperatives of duty and the universal laws of morality, grounded on family, religion, and what he calls "moral sense" (*ADH*, p. 228). While Nora repudiates the laws and duties Torvald invokes, she does not give voice to an alternative formulation of her own that guides her in doing so. "How then shall we articulate the maxim of her action?" Cavell asks (*CoW*, p. 252). He suggests various possibilities, ranging from the simplistic "If your husband disappoints you, leave him" to more complex and intricate suggestions with a more specific fit to Nora's case (see *CoW*, p. 252). But each of them seems a poor candidate for a universal law, because, if applied across the board, each of them could, at least potentially, abrogate the institutions of marriage and family, which form the bedrock of so many people's everyday lives. So someone in Nora's position cannot invoke Kant's categorical imperative without asking us to envision the possibility of the ordinary fabric of many (most?) people's ordinary arrangements for ordinary living being threatened with dissolution, if not crumbling away altogether. Hence, Cavell concludes that "there does not appear to be an obviously satisfying Kantian solution to Nora's dilemma" (*CoW*, p. 253).

So what are we to make of the question Cavell asks of *A Doll's House*? Is Nora in the right or not? "My answer must be," he says, "that we have no grounds for an answer. No utilitarian or Kantian grounds. The former is repudiated; the latter begs the question of what is dutiful" (*CoW*, p. 255). Cavell goes on to assert that "a perfectionist answer remains possible: that Nora feels the force of an unattained but attainable self" (*CoW*, p. 255). But there is also another possible solution, namely, that the questions we are asking of *A Doll's House* are not exclusively moral questions, and that they can be answered equally well, and perhaps even rather better, by regarding them as political questions, which is to say, as pertaining to the political interpretation of literature.

II

There is much to be said against seeking to elaborate a Cavellian politics of literary interpretation. In the first place, when asked to contribute to a symposium entitled "The Politics of Interpretation" in the literary journal *Critical Inquiry*, Cavell clearly stated in his essay that "I am still not ready to try a systematic account of what I understand either politics or interpretation to be" (*TOS*, p. 28). What is more, some philosophers have found Cavell an essentially apolitical philosopher, on the grounds that he "refuses to think of art or philosophy in directly political terms."[3] This criticism, as I hope this chapter will demonstrate, is unjustified, and there is in fact a steadily growing debate about the Cavellian contribution to political philosophy.[4] Nevertheless, the fact remains that Cavell's discussions of literary texts display relatively little interest in, or patience with, the kinds of interpretations of literature that are traditionally called political: "A political reading is apt to become fairly predictable once you know whose side the reader is taking" (*DK*, p. 145), he observes in his writings on Shakespeare. More discouragingly, he remarks that "the politics of the play is essentially the politics of a given production, so that we should not expect its political issues to be settled by an interpretation of what you might call 'the text itself'" (*DK*, p. 146), and while this is in the first instance a remark about Shakespeare's *Coriolanus*, it does not offer any grounds to exempt Ibsen's plays from its argument. It is from this decidedly unpromising start that my engagement with *A Doll's House* must begin to set out its case for a Cavellian interpretive politics.

The best place from which to embark on this journey is the essay Cavell contributed to the "Politics of Interpretation" symposium: the aptly entitled "Politics as Opposed to What?" Rather like the questions asked of Poe in the previous chapter, this is a question Cavell does not answer explicitly, if at all.[5] Leaving aside for a moment the question of what Cavell takes "politics" to mean, the essay is probably more interesting for what it says about interpretation and the act of reading. Espen Hammer summarizes this well: "In 'Politics as Opposed to What?' . . . Cavell extends his notions of reading and being read. . . . Reading is in this essay less understood as a process of interpreting a text than as one of being interpreted by it."[6] What this suggests is that a political interpretation of literature can be better articulated not, as so many literary critics of varying political persuasions have done, as a reading that a critic places upon a text in order to exemplify or elucidate a political position he or she is inclined to take up; rather, a political interpretation is how a text elucidates the politics of its critics. Cavell therefore provisionally defines "the politics of interpretation" along the following lines: "The politics of interpretation studies the public conditions of one's discourse, the forces it musters against the forces against it, where the victory of discourse consists in bringing those conditions to light" (*TOS*, p. 27).

The work of interpreting literature politically, then, is to be understood as the work of literature itself—as part of, to quote my own title, the claim of literature. And, *pace* Cavell, the claims that I find Ibsen's *A Doll's House* makes upon us are not primarily claims about the nature of morality, nor are they "an exposure of the harm caused in failing to honor or recognize perfectionist longings" (*CoW*, p. 248). They are rather claims about politics, where politics is to be understood not as a particular agenda or program for good governance but as defining what constitutes membership in a polis and whether or how the polis is determined by our participating in it, or by our specifically refusing to. Happily, I can still claim some kind of Cavellian provenance for this reading, in that Cavell's political interpretation of Shakespeare's *Coriolanus* sets out to address these very questions:

> This is not a play about politics, if this means about political authority or conflict, say about questions of legitimate succession or divided loyalties. It is about the formation of the political, the founding of the city, about what it is that makes a rational animal fit for conversation, for civility. (*TOS*, p. 84)

That is precisely the kind of investigation I see pursued by Ibsen in *A Doll's House*, although, unsurprisingly, the answers he arrives at turn out to be different from Shakespeare's.

Viewed in this way, Cavell's writings on Nora's situation in *A Doll's House* turn out to have a large political dimension to them, in that "her play takes place in the mode of conversation" and therefore "demands not the application of a law but the offer of conversation" (*CoW*, p. 257). If we take conversation to be what fits us for membership in the polis and therefore, according to Cavell, the very basis of democracy, *A Doll's House* in my view becomes a play about the very nature of politics precisely because its protagonist, Nora, finds that the bare possibility of conversation is refused her: "The person with whom Nora could imagine having such a conversation is precisely the one with whom such a conversation is not possible" (*CoW*, p. 254). Her realization that there is thus no conversation to be had dawns at the same time as her realization that she is not, and never has been, regarded as a member of society in her own right, as having a say in her polis.

For Cavell, Nora's decision to end a conversation that cannot truly begin is an important step in a journey of moral perfectionism, and since that conversation is withheld from her in *A Doll's House*, the play makes a moral call to us readers and viewers to engage in that conversation on Nora's behalf. But is he right that the claim *A Doll's House* makes on us is essentially a *moral* one?

> A moral response to Nora . . . seems to require not the construction of a [moral] law . . . but an offer of conversation . . . to help determine whether what may appear as conditions of such a law are in fact determinative and fixed conditions of her life, or whether there are possibilities of change other than the ultimate change she has arrived at. (*CoW*, p. 253)

To my ear, Cavell's vocabulary here—of laws and the possibilities of changing them—suggests a clear case for regarding this as more a political than a moral conversation, because the laws governing the conditions of Nora's life are not exclusively moral ones. The play's complicating action, in fact, depends precisely on Nora's choosing what she sees as a moral law (a wife's right to save her husband) over the law Krogstad wields against her (the legal code that defines forging a signature as a crime). Nora appears to have made this choice while having no clear idea that she was subject to the laws of the polis. Her "education"—a term that, in Cavell's perfectionist reading, is just as important as the term *conversation*—is an education in what it means to be a member of society and to be a political subject. These, together with the companion themes of being an outcast of society and a political mute, are the themes I read *A Doll's House* as wishing to converse with us about.

I can imagine being asked at this point, What difference does it make? That is, both moral philosophy and political philosophy are concerned—or at any rate profess to be, and should be, concerned—with regulating human actions, with debating how we determine what course of action is right, just, and for the best under the given circumstances, with arriving at what ought to be done. That is why it makes sense to use the word *law* in both contexts. To insist on the difference between a moral reading of Ibsen and a political reading of Ibsen might well court the charge of imposing artificial distinctions derived from philosophy onto a literary text that is better off without them, and to respond to this charge by demonstrating, as I hope to, that Cavell's writings on Ibsen themselves lend support to a political interpretation as much as a moral one may make the distinction seem like hair-splitting. But the difference, I feel, is worth insisting upon. It consists largely in the fact that in a democracy a political statement is essentially a claim to be *representative*, whereas a moral claim need not be. The question then becomes whether we are to regard *A Doll's House* as asking its audience whether or not Nora is justified in her words and her actions (or perhaps vindicated by them)—in which case we are indeed dealing with matters of morality—or whether it raises stakes that are political in asking us to view Nora's plight as an indictment of the social order and the politics that regulates it.

In fact, Cavell sees this matter in both ways. Or, more accurately, he takes different views on the question in his different writings on Ibsen. In his longest and latest discussion of *A Doll's House* he states that "Nora finds herself helpless to claim that her case represents a brief against the world; she cannot claim her suffering to be representative" (*CoW*, p. 263). The play supports this view, because Nora does indeed say, "All I know is that this is necessary for me" (*ADH*, p. 227), a statement that surely deflates any political dimension to her words and deeds. But a few moments after this, Nora makes a comment that, in his earlier discussion of *A Doll's House* in *Conditions Handsome and Unhandsome*, leads Cavell to the very opposite conclusion. When she responds to her husband Torvald's comment that "no man would sacrifice his *honour* for the one he loves" with the rejoinder "Thousands of women have" (*ADH*, p. 230), Cavell notes "that Nora feels herself representative beyond herself, . . . and representative, it seems to me, beyond the sphere of women" (*CHU*, p. 110). His aim is "to warn against a hasty impulse to dismiss Nora and Torvald's case as unrepresentative" (*CHU*, p. 111). And if Nora's case *is* representative, and Nora can indeed be taken as speaking for the plight of others besides herself (and it would seem decidedly odd to deny this, given the play's highly politicized history), then we are dealing with a play that moves beyond the moral and into the political, as the following quotation makes clear:

> The moral importance of Nora's outrage is not confined to the manifest content of the explicit moral argument she has with her husband, concerning whether she was right to borrow money in secret in order to save her husband's life and spare her dying father's feelings, and then to skimp household and personal expenses in order to maintain interest payments on the debt. Such an issue is the staple of domestic melodramas or, say, soap operas. In *A Doll's House* the thematics of Nora's climactic charges against her husband, Torvald Helmer, put the social order as such on notice. (*CHU*, pp. 108–9)

It seems to me that this forms a reasonable basis for reading *A Doll's House* politically. By following up hints such as these in Cavell's discussions of Ibsen, it should be possible to construct a Cavellian reading of the play that takes the political fork rather than the moral fork in the interpretive path.

III

In a recent study of Ibsen that is explicitly indebted to Cavell, Toril Moi suggests a case for reading *A Doll's House* as an investigation of the political via an engagement with Hegel.[7] Citing Hegel's *Elements of the Philosophy of Right*, Moi sees Torvald's assertion that "before everything else, you're a wife and a mother" as epitomizing the Hegelian view of women and their place in the world, and Nora's riposte that "before everything else I'm a human being" (*ADH*, p. 228) as a rebuttal of that view. Specifically, Hegel claimed that women are defined first and foremost by their family roles (daughter, wife, mother) and are thus not sufficiently individuated to attain full self-consciousness in their own right. Their family ties mean that they cannot attain the universal (so women, for Hegel, cannot become artists or philosophers) and, more to the point, that their loyalties lie primarily with the family, whose function defines them, overriding their loyalty to the state. According to Hegel, then, women are not fit for membership in the polis. Yet Moi points out that Krogstad teaches Nora that she is subject to the laws of the polis nevertheless and that fulfilling her role as a loving wife who did what it took to save her husband does not excuse her from what Hegel would call the universal law. Nora's response, thus read, constitutes a withering critique of the place assigned to women in Hegelian political theory. Moi follows Cavell's moral perfectionist reading in noting the importance Nora attaches to acquiring an education for herself—something Hegel thought was wasted on women—but the overall thrust of her argument is nonetheless inherently political.[8]

Moi's work on Ibsen is immensely valuable in highlighting key themes in his plays that are equally central in Cavell's thought.[9] The political dimensions to *A Doll's House* that her reading opens up thus deserve exploring in more detail. In doing so, however, I do not propose to follow Moi in making the detour through Hegel, which I find a slightly question-begging move, because if we invoked the terms Hegel uses of dramatic texts in a discussion of Ibsen, we would end up having to explain why the play is not a tragedy. Put simply, Hegel defines a tragedy as a play whose hero finds himself (or herself, since his prototype is often Antigone) caught between two conflicting ethical positions, the claims of each of which are just but overlook the validity of the claims of the other and, to the extent that they do so, end up being unjust. Thus, a tragic hero begins by taking a course of action that is justified but follows it through beyond the point where it ceases to be justifiable, and therein lies tragedy. The balance and order of the absolute can only be restored with the downfall of a hero who has staked his life on a one-sided ethical position.[10]

This is exactly how Cavell's moral reading of *A Doll's House* views Nora—as caught between two conflicting and ultimately one-sided moral claims. He cites George Bernard Shaw, who puts this point in a nutshell: "When you have called . . . Nora a fearless and noble-hearted woman or a shocking little liar and an unnatural mother, [and called] Helmer a selfish hound or a model husband and father, according to your bias, you have said something which is at once true and false, and in both cases perfectly idle" (*CoW*, p. 257). So, regarding *A Doll's House* as a critique of Hegel would entail clarifying why it is not a tragedy—and saying something more substantial than that it doesn't fit the conditions Cavell describes as tragic, which form the subject of my next chapters.

Cavell neatly sums up Nora's relationship to what the Hegels and Kants of this world call "the moral law" by pointing out that "everyone else legislates for her, but in such a way as to deny reciprocity with her own powers of legislation" (*CoW*, p. 255). If, as the categorical imperative has it, we should act as if each of our moral judgments were "legislating for humanity," then for Cavell it follows that "in being subject to these laws each is subject to laws each has, as it were, promulgated; each is both the sovereign and a subject" (*CoW*, p. 255). But Nora will find out that subject though she may be, she is no sovereign and has no powers of legislation with the moral law. The vocabulary Cavell uses to describe Nora's situation—*subject* and *sovereign*, *laws* and *legislating*—is an essentially political vocabulary, and so it is not unreasonable to suggest that his description of "Ibsen's staging the moral stakes as one of Nora's finding her voice" (*CHU*, p. xxxvi) is also a description of the political stakes of Nora's finding a political voice. If we grant this, then since the upshot of Nora's discovering a voice that is not simply the "clear voice" that Torvald demands "a songbird must have . . . to sing with" (*ADH*, p. 177) is that "she demands an education and leaves to seek one that she says her husband is not the man to provide,"[11] it makes sense to view her education not just as an Emersonian journey into moral perfectionism but as an equally political education. Perhaps a better way of putting it would be that she leaves to seek a moral (re)education *because* her political education has brought about her awakening. Whereas this moral education takes place in an indefinite, projected future that Cavell is obliged to "imagine" for the characters (see *CHU*, pp. 112–16), the political dimensions of it are more rooted in the present. We have, in fact, watched Nora undergo this political education and develop as a result of it: it consists of the three acts of *A Doll's House*.

If Cavell's suggestion is valid—namely, that to offer a political reading is to show how a play investigates the nature of the polis and the "formation of the political" (*TOS*, p. 84)—then the following paragraphs lay the foundation for such a political reading of Nora's journey. (I would even suggest that perhaps there is no way of reading *A Doll's House* that is *not* in some sense a political reading.) In act 1 we meet our heroine. At this stage she is scarcely aware that she is part of a society at all. When asked by Dr. Rank, "Do you really know what the community is?" she laughs, "What do I care for your dreary old community?"—an expression of indifference even more sociopathic than Dr. Rank's quip about "the sort of theory that's turning the community into a regular hospital" (*ADH*, p. 165). Her obliviousness toward the social bonds that make this community a polis is nowhere clearer than in her attitude toward the play's complicating action and its consequences, that is, the obligations and responsibilities incurred when one member of society borrows money from another member. At the very start of the play, Torvald asks Nora what would become of their creditors if they were forced to default on the loan she suggests they take out. "Them? Who bothers about them? They're just strangers," she replies (*ADH*, p. 149), and she demonstrates the same indifference toward her actual creditor as toward her hypothetical ones: "I wasn't thinking about you at all," she responds to Krogstad's pointing out that she was tricking him (*ADH*, p. 175). The Nora we meet at the start of act 1 has simply no awareness whatsoever that she is a member of a community, that this community is organized by laws, making it a political entity or polis, and that as a member of it she is subject to those laws.

This situation has changed by the end of act 2. Just before her celebrated Tarantella scene, she confesses to her friend Kristina Linde that she has broken the law.

> I forged a signature. There's just one thing I want to say, Kristina, and you shall be my witness. . . . If I were to go mad—as I easily might . . . or if anything else were to happen to me, so that I shouldn't be here. . . . And in case there was someone else who tried to take it all on himself—all the blame, you understand . . . —then, Kristina, you must bear witness that it isn't true. I'm perfectly sane, and I know exactly what I'm doing now, and I tell you this: no one else knew about it—I did it all by myself. Remember that. (*ADH*, p. 201, Mrs. Linde's interjections omitted)

In making this confession, Nora recognizes the existence of a law—implicitly but nevertheless unambiguously—and that it is binding upon her, that she has broken it, that there are consequences to this, and that she is to be held responsible for them; in other words, she recognizes that she is a part of civil society within a polis. This recognition brings with it the automatic reaction that goes with living in a polis that has unjust laws, namely, dissent: "It must be a very stupid law," she protests upon discovering it (*ADH*, p. 175).

By the end of act 3, however, Nora's relationship to the politics of her society has developed further yet. She tells her husband that he and her father—the patriarchal representatives of the social order—"have committed a grievous sin against me" (*ADH*, p. 226), but since there is no possibility, within the laws of her polis, of getting any kind of redress for this wrong, and no probability that her dissent will change those laws, she chooses instead—using Cavell's phrase—to "put the social order as such on notice" (*CHU*, pp. 108–9) and to renounce it altogether. That is, once Nora discovers that she lives in a polis where she is answerable to laws that the polis gave her no say in, her reaction voices a wish to withdraw or revoke her membership in such a polis. This means that *A Doll's House* begs some crucially important political questions: How do you renounce your membership in a polis? Indeed, is it even possible to renounce membership in a polis that never granted you full membership in the first place? And if the polis will not recognize your voice as valid, then how can your renunciation of it carry any force?

A good way to debate these questions would be to explore the contractual nature of Nora's predicament and the consequences that arise from a breach of contract. The contract I have in mind, though, is not (or not yet) the bond bearing the signature she forged, which gives Krogstad power over her. It is a document that is no less legally binding on Nora and no less problematic for her, but unlike the bond, it has no explicit content, nor did she ever put her signature to it, nor does it even have a material existence. It nevertheless plays a central role in the political aspects of Cavell's thought, and it has been known to political philosophers since the birth of modernity as the social contract.

IV

What does it mean to be bound by a contract that has never been written? Is the very idea of such a nonexistent contract perhaps dismissible as a mere myth, a legal fiction, or a collective psychosis? For Cavell, the social contract's nonexistence actually serves as an important reminder that definitive justifications for political systems are also nonexistent and that every polis is thus ultimately without foundation:

> The essential message of the idea of a social contract is that political institutions require justification, that they are absolutely without sanctity, that power over us is held on trust from us, that institutions have no authority other than the authority we lend them, that we are their architects, that they are therefore artifacts, that there are laws or ends, of nature or justice, in terms of which they are to be tested. They are experiments. (*SoW*, p. 82)

In his longest and most explicit discussion of the social contract, near the beginning of *The Claim of Reason*, Cavell gives a new slant to the debate by suggesting that the significance of what we have consented to is bound up with the significance *that* we have consented. He contends:

> What I consent to, in consenting to the contract is . . . membership in a polis, which implies two things: First, that I recognize the principle of consent itself; which means that I recognize others to have consented with me, and hence that I consent to political *equality*. Second, that I recognize the society and its government, so constituted, as *mine*; which means that I am answerable not merely to it, but for it. So far, then, as I recognize myself to be exercising my responsibility for it, my obedience to it is obedience to my own laws; citizenship in that case is the same as my autonomy; the polis is the field within which I work out my personal identity and it is the creation of (political) *freedom*. (*CoR*, p. 23)

To give consent to the social contract, then, is to acquire a political voice, and in a democracy that political voice simultaneously entails rights and responsibilities; having a right to a say in how the polis is run means we cannot avoid responsibility for how the polis is run. That such rights and responsibilities are given to all individuals who consent to the social contract means that the polis is born of a relational collectivity. The best summary of this aspect of Cavell's political thought is given by Stephen Mulhall:

> Political participation is thus pictured as a matter of simultaneously giving voice to the polis and giving one's voice *to* it; and its existence or reality is demonstrated in one's recognition that one's political voice is the voice of a political community. . . . By the same token, one cannot possess a political voice without allowing that others may speak for you, since being a citizen involves consenting to be identified with the words and deeds of one's fellow citizens.[12]

To participate in the life of a democratic polis, then, is essentially to engage in an activity I earlier described as "claiming," that is, to voice one's beliefs in publicly made statements that one expects, or at any rate hopes, will be validated by the agreement of others in the community.[13] But there is another, concomitant aspect of the activity of claiming in a democracy, in that the claims made by other members, insofar as they are made on behalf of the polis, are claims that are made in the name of each individual member of it. This may well put us, both individually and collectively, in some uncomfortable positions:

> To speak for oneself politically is to speak for the others with whom you consent to association, and it is to consent to be spoken for by them—not as a parent speaks for you, i.e., instead of you, but as someone in mutuality speaks for you, i.e., speaks your mind. . . . To speak for yourself then means risking the

> rebuff—on some occasion, perhaps once for all—of those for whom you claimed to be speaking; and it means risking having to rebuff—on some occasion, perhaps once for all—those who claimed to be speaking for you. (*CoR*, p. 27)

Phrasing the issue as a matter of *voice*—of speaking for and being spoken for—highlights the central importance of the term *conversation* to Cavell's sketch of the formation of the democratic polis. For reasons that will, I hope, become apparent in due course, this term will also turn out to have a central importance in the latter part of this chapter.

The conversation of democracy, in this liberal conception of it, may well strike the skeptic as something of a risky business: we are bound by collective responsibility to laws we did not make and to strangers we do not know. The social contract was supposed to guarantee the polis and its members a certain freedom from the arbitrary actions of an unjust ruler, but if, in a democracy, *anyone* can claim the right to speak and act for the polis, then it does not and cannot do this in and of itself. Cavell is well aware that the idea of a social contract is as apt to raise questions as to answer them: "The problem is . . . how I know with whom I am in community, and to whom and to what I am in fact obedient. The existence of the prior contract is not the explanation of such facts. On the contrary, it is . . . consequently the discovery of a new mode of ignorance" (*CoR*, pp. 25–26). If, as Cavell put it earlier, the social contract gives us to see that our political institutions are experiments, it does not follow that it can show us which of these experiments are successes, and which are failures. Moreover, since it is in the nature of the democratic conversation that it will seek to reform, or reformulate, the nature of the polis itself, by extending and restricting our rights and responsibilities on an ongoing basis, then it follows that in lending obedience to a social contract, we literally don't know what we've signed up for.

Of course, this needn't be a problem in and of itself: the democratic polis is a conversation that thrives on calling its foundations into question, and a certain amount of disagreement, or even skepticism, is essential to its healthy function. This is what is called dissent. Dissent, for Cavell, "is not the undoing of consent but a dispute about its content, a dispute within it over whether a present arrangement is faithful to it" (*CoR*, p. 27). It is thus a rebuking of the claims of others to speak for me, rather than a withdrawal of my consent to be spoken for by others at all. Espen Hammer puts the matter rather better when he observes that in Cavell's view, dissent "amounts to a continuation of the attempt, called for by the myth of the social contract, to make the laws of the polis one's own."[14] But what happens if one simply *cannot* make the laws of the polis one's own? What if one's disagreement with the makeup of the polis is too far-reaching for one to identify with it at all? If there is legitimacy to the Cavellian requirement that I, *qua* member of the polis, am to take responsibility for the political state of my society, then it follows that "a compromised state of society, since it is mine, compromises me" (*CHU*, p. 28). But this merely begs the question, what am I to do if I find myself so compromised?

It turns out that, for Cavell, there is no exit from the conversation of democracy, however compromised, sullied, or disenfranchised by it one may feel. This is because in the act of renouncing one's membership in the polis one is also denouncing it—denouncing it publicly, to others. Making such a statement of grievance is, precisely, to enter a claim in the conversation of democracy and thus to continue it rather than to withdraw from it. As Cavell has it:

> Since the granting of consent entails acknowledgment of others, the withdrawal of consent entails the same acknowledgment: I have to say *both* "It is mine no longer" (I am no longer responsible for it, it no longer speaks for me) *and* "It is no longer ours" (not what we bargained for, we no longer recognize the principle of consent in it, the original "we" is no longer bound together by consent but only by force, so it no longer exists). (*CoR*, p. 27)

Since to say these things is to participate in the conversation of democracy and hence to further it, that conversation cannot be withdrawn from or abrogated. Hence, in the Cavellian democratic polis "the alternative to speaking for yourself politically is not: speaking for yourself privately. . . . The alternative is having nothing (political) to say" (*CoR*, p. 27).

The vexed question whether consent to the social contract and to the polis can be withdrawn by an individual is one Cavell's thought struggles to answer.[15] It is nevertheless important because I am about to argue that this is precisely what Nora wishes to do, and seeks to do, at the end of *A Doll's House*. The play's final scene—the one that is so pivotal to Cavell's reading of the play—is contentious partly because it dramatizes the impossibility of her fulfilling this desire. The passage of the play that I see as central in this regard takes place between two lines that are of central importance in Cavell's moral perfectionist reading of *A Doll's House*. It begins with Torvald asserting, "Let me rouse your conscience. You must have *some* moral sense," to which Nora responds, "Well, Torvald, it's hard to say. I really don't know" (*ADH*, p. 228). It ends with Torvald insisting, "You're talking like a child; you don't understand the world you live in," to which Nora replies, "No, I don't. . . . I must find out which is right—the world or I" (*ADH*, pp. 228–29).

The significance of these lines for Cavell's reading is reasonably clear: they represent a repudiation of what the world calls morality in favor of a quest for a self's more perfectionist understanding of it. Between these lines, however, Nora declares: "Now I find that the law is quite different from what I thought, and I simply can't convince myself that the law is right. That a woman shouldn't have the right to spare her old father on his deathbed, or to save her husband's life! I can't believe things like that" (*ADH*, p. 228). This I take to be tantamount to a renunciation of Nora's consent to the formation of her polis. The final sentence of this extract does not read to me as an expression of incredulity—"I can't *believe* that!"—as if she had just discovered the injustice of her situation. (She discovered that the day before, in act 1, from Krogstad, and there her statement "I simply don't believe that" [*ADH*, p. 175] does function as such an expression.) Rather, "*I* can't believe things like *that*" serves to express the gulf that has emerged between Nora's beliefs and the values of her society, so that what she is saying is that she no longer *believes in* her polis—it no longer stands for her beliefs, and she cannot consent to its constitutive laws.[16] Nora's problem, as she is about to discover, is that voicing her need to distance herself from the polis is taken by the membership of that polis (represented here by Torvald) as calling into question the validity of her voice, *not* the validity of the polis.

We have seen that for Cavell the principal issue in this scene is "one of Nora's finding her voice" (*CHU*, p. xxxvi), but in fact the scene consists of Torvald's repeated attempts to silence that voice. He compares her to a "young girl" (*ADH*, p. 228) and a "stupid child" (*ADH*, p. 230), that is, someone who has not yet reached the age of consent, the age at which one becomes competent to give consent to the social contract, which according to Cavell is what the polis considers essential to membership (see *CoR*, pp. 26–27). And if, as Torvald suggests, Nora is not acting as someone of the age necessary to be capable of expressing her consent, she cannot be capable of withdrawing that consent either. Cavell makes a similar point when he observes that "Torvald's judgment, 'You're talking like a child,' is of Nora's incompetence as a moral agent" (*CHU*, p. 114) and that this lack of what Torvald calls "moral sense" (*ADH*, p. 228)—a lack Nora does not seek to deny—"amounts to the lack of that possession of speech which Aristotle declares fits one for membership in a polis" (*CoW*, p. 261). Torvald further tries to repudiate Nora's voice on grounds of incompetence by suggesting she is insane. "You're out of your mind" (*ADH*, p. 227), he tells her. "You're ill, Nora—you're feverish. I almost believe you're out of your senses" (*ADH*, p. 229), and his words should not be taken lightly, as merely the stereotypical patriarchal reaction to a stereotypical hysterical woman in a moment of stereotypical melodrama. Mental illness has always been grounds for excluding someone from participation in the polis, but Torvald's reaction here suggests the converse: that someone who wishes to renounce the polis is to be regarded as mentally ill. Stephen Mulhall makes a similar point to Torvald's, to the effect that those who refuse to participate in the Cavellian polis are "crazy—crazy because, in failing to act on behalf of the polis, we are failing to act on behalf of a community which acts in our name and so are acting against ourselves, opposing one aspect of our identity with another, splitting our personality."[17] It need hardly be added that someone who is crazy, out of his or her mind, feverish, or so on, as Nora is said to be, is not competent to renounce membership in the polis either.

Torvald's reactions dramatize the basic lesson of Cavell's writings on the social contract. They show that, as Espen Hammer puts it, "in the absence of the recognition of a particular community as one's own, there can be no political answerability, and hence no political self or voice,"[18] and that having a voice within a polis is a condition of possibility for politics itself. Outside the polis there is no such thing as a political voice. The only alternative, as Nora discovers here, "is having nothing to say, being voiceless, not even mute" (*CoR*, p. 28). It would be one thing to say that politically she is given a simple Hobson's choice in the running of her polis—take it or leave it—and she chooses to leave it, by closing the door on her husband, her marriage, and the society they represent. But this view, comforting though it may be, is inaccurate, in that it gives Nora an alternative she does not in fact have. As Cavell observes, "Mere withdrawal from the community (exile inner or outer) is not, grammatically, the withdrawal of consent from it" (*CoR*, p. 27). So the more accurate thing to say would be that the social contract, for Nora and for all of us, has a clause in it that functions just like the Catch-22 that prevents Yossarian from getting excused from combat duty: the right to leave is only a theoretical right, because nobody could ever take up a position from which they could successfully exercise it.[19] It is hard to avoid the conclusion that "Politics as opposed to what?" is an empty rhetorical question, because there is just no alternative to the polis.

The problem with this conclusion is that it leaves Nora entrapped. This in turn means that the Cavellian view of the social contract acts as yet another force binding her to her impossible situation—a force that lines up alongside her religion, her family, and nineteenth-century morality to keep her in her place. If Nora's finding a voice is the crucial element in the Cavellian reading of the play, then it is precisely the Cavellian conception of the conversation of democracy that deprives her of that political voice, by not recognizing the validity of her desire to renounce the polis. Conversely, if to offer a political reading of the play is to demonstrate how the text investigates our concept of politics, then surely it involves a critique of precisely the kind of formation of the political conversation elucidated and championed by Cavell. Perhaps this is why Cavell is interested in having a moral conversation with Nora rather than a political one (*CoW*, p. 257). In order to have a political conversation with Nora, I contend, it would first be necessary to find a way of granting the validity of what she has to say, namely, that she wants out of our polis. Such a statement, on the Cavellian view, might be called "ungrammatical." But it is more than possible that Nora can teach Cavell some grammar lessons of her own. Nora's plight shows us that it is indeed idle to talk of withdrawing or revoking one's consent from one's society, not because it is not the done thing or because it cannot be done, but because there is nothing that would count as doing it. But if consent cannot be revoked, then it is not meaningful to speak of *giving* it either: it is not a gift, because a gift is something freely given, whereas there is no alternative to consenting to the polis. Which suggests, in its turn, that the picture Cavell has of consent to the social contract is itself ungrammatical, or, to use a more loaded term, flawed.

V

Succinctly put, Cavell cannot coherently hold to his views on the social contract *and* wish to have a conversation with Nora, because the social contract as Cavell sees it is precisely what stands in the way of the kind of political conversation she wishes to have. So perhaps we have been looking at the wrong contract. There are, in fact, two other contracts that feature prominently in the play and that force Nora toward her crisis. The first is her contract of marriage, which puts her in thrall to Torvald, and the second is the bond she signed in her father's name, which puts her in thrall to Krogstad. Each of these contracts is clearly bound up with the laws and institutions of her society, and to that extent each has a political aspect. Moreover, each impinges on a different aspect of Cavell's philosophy, enabling us to look at *A Doll's House* from different angles.

Let us begin, then, with another contract, one that Nora tries more explicitly to revoke at the end of *A Doll's House*:

HELMER: But you're my wife—now, and whatever becomes of you.

NORA: Listen, Torvald: I've heard that when a wife leaves her husband's house as I'm doing now, he's legally freed from all his obligations to her. Anyhow, *I* set you free from them. You're not to feel yourself bound in any way, and nor shall I. We must both be perfectly free. Look, here's your ring back—give me mine. (*ADH*, p. 231)

Clearly, this is the point at which Nora declares her marriage to be over, or, more accurately, that her relationship to her husband does not amount to, and has never in fact been, "a real marriage" (*ADH*, p. 232). As such, it is a moment that assumes a crucial significance in Cavell's thought, by posing the question what can be said to constitute a marriage.

The answer to this question for Cavell is that marriage is *not* a contract. The cynical modern view that "marriage is just a piece of paper" is one that has only been possible since Luther launched the reformation that made divorce a possibility, and while that possibility indeed draws attention to the contractual nature of marriage, it no more explains what a marriage is than a landlord's giving notice to his tenant explains what real estate is. Or to put it differently, taking the words "I now pronounce you man and wife," uttered by the correct person under the correct circumstances, as the basis of a marriage will turn out, for Cavell, to give us a very poor picture of what constitutes a marriage, just as perlocutions in the form "I decree that . . . ," "I judge that . . . ," "I order that . . . ," and so on, give us either a poor picture of the institutions of politics or else a picture of a poor politics with poor institutions. In both cases, what counts is the orientation of our everyday lives toward the claims made on us, both by marriage and by the polis.

Cavell's clearest articulation of his ideas about marriage can be found not in his writings on literature but in his writings on film. In *Pursuits of Happiness* and *Contesting Tears* he looks at a number of classic Hollywood movies that share a central characteristic, in that the relationship between leading man and leading woman is in each case in crisis. These films can therefore be read as asking what constitutes a marriage. Cavell argues that what constitutes a marriage is a "willingness for remarriage" (*CT*, p. 11), that is, an everyday commitment to reaffirming and rediscovering what brings and binds the couple together. Simply put,

> what makes marriage worth reaffirming is a diurnal devotedness that involves friendship, play, surprise, and mutual education, all manifested in the pair's mode of conversing with each other (not just in words), which expresses an

> intimacy or understanding often incomprehensible to the rest of the depicted world, but in which consists the truth of the marriage. (*PDAT*, pp. 121–22)

Being in a marriage, then, is not the blind acceptance of the institution of marriage but the everyday questioning of why one is in this relationship and, more to the point, whether the relationship ought to continue. This philosophy implies that the unexamined married life is not worth living. In some of the films Cavell studies—constituting the genre of "comedies of remarriage"—the answer to the question whether the man and woman should continue their relationship is "a conditional Yes," while in others—constituting the genre of "melodramas of the unknown woman"—the answer "is an unreserved No" (*CT*, p. 11).[20] Both possibilities, and hence both genres, are, in Cavell's view, descended from an originary dramatic moment in which a woman is faced with a crisis of faith in her marriage, which poses her the choice of whether to continue in it or not. That moment is, of course, the denouement of *A Doll's House*, in which

> a woman climactically discovers that her eminently legal marriage is not comprehensible as a marriage, and therefore, before her own conscience, that she is dishonored. She demands an education and leaves to seek one that she says her husband is not the man to provide. They could find a life together (and so perhaps find or create marriage between them) only on the condition that a miracle of change take place. (*PoH*, pp. 22–23)

For Cavell, this change needs to take place either outside the conversation of marriage—in which case we are dealing with melodrama (see *CT*, pp. 6–7)—or else within it, thereby reconfiguring and redeeming the conversation of marriage—in which case we are in the presence of remarriage comedy. Either way, the godmother of each genre is Ibsen's Nora.

This way of thinking shows us that married life, rather like life in a polis, entails a risk. We bind ourselves to a lifelong commitment to an everyday questioning of that commitment, where "commitment" involves commitment to living one's life with others who are, or at any rate may turn out to be (as Nora describes Torvald after no less than eight years of marriage), "strangers" (*ADH*, p. 232). Indeed, the comparison between a marriage and a democracy is one that Cavell comments on himself, and one that most of his explicators have noted. Cavell traces the comparison to the analogy Milton draws, in his tracts on divorce, between a commonwealth and a marriage, and it is significant that what grounds a marriage for Milton is precisely what grounds a democracy for Cavell, namely, "conversation."[21] In Cavell's thought, then, the conversation of marriage and the conversation of democracy are analogous, to the point where the investigations of marriage he finds in Hollywood film "are understandable as studying the possibility of a perfectionist life in a democracy" (*PDAT*, p. 119). Both conversations are predicated on an everyday consenting and reconsenting to furthering the conversation, and to contributing the best one can to it.[22]

Clearly, there is an important difference here, in that consent can be readily and explicitly withdrawn from a contract of marriage, whereas there is no such thing as withdrawing one's consent from the social contract: one cannot file for a divorce from one's polis, after all. But that does not mean that we are dealing with two different kinds of consent, or that consent to a marriage can be given partially or hedged—any more than can consent to the polis. In both cases, "the idea is not to hedge consent, as if your commitment were incomplete, but to give it in the knowledge that its object is still in essential part idea, its existence incomplete" (*PDAT*, p. 108), which in turn means that insofar as they are conversations, both democracies and marriages are best seen as works in progress. As such, they are imperfect and hence in need of further discussion or conversation. Consequently, according to Cavell, we should not regard a marriage or a polis as unsatisfactory because in its ordinary, everyday existence it fails to live up to the promise of some utopian democracy or marriage *à venir*. Taking this stance would lay one open to Cavell's "friendly amendment of John Rawls's claim concerning . . . the Social Contract" (*PDAT*, p. 107), which he frames in these terms:

> In Rawls's view consent is directed to the principles of justice, rather than to a given state of society, no one of which on earth—as Socrates declares in the *Republic*—can be expected to realize perfect justice. But my claim is that consent cannot be hedged or proportioned in this way (as if one could coherently consent to one's society *to the extent that* it is just); hence your consent at best is to a given society whose partial compliance with the principles of justice you judge good enough to meet the promise of necessary reform. Consent is, on earth, always a risk, as democracy is, and hence is always accompanied by a knowledge of being compromised. So understood, consent is the show of a readiness for change, of allegiance to a state of society responsive to a call for change. This is how I present the enduring comedies of remarriage in their conversation with society. (*PDAT*, p. 107)

With this in mind, and in a similar spirit of "friendly amendment," it is worth briefly correcting the suggestion Lawrence Rhu has made that Cavell regards the state of marriage as a "utopia." According to Rhu, the "role of marriage in its political dimension is utopian for Cavell inasmuch as such relationships stand for an eventual human community rather than one already attained." Importantly, it is also "a utopian ideal that we employ both as a rebuke of things as they are in our present political arrangements and as a sign of an eventual human community we may aspire to create."[23] Rhu is certainly right about the resemblance between a Cavellian marriage and the Kantian "kingdom of ends," which has an implicitly utopian character. But if the everyday willingness toward reconsent and remarriage is to be seen as rooted in a utopian image of an eventual marriage *à venir*, then Rhu's understanding of what it is we consent to in remarriage is the same as Rawls's view of what it is we consent to in the social contract: both ground our commitment on a set of ideals that, in any given case, we will not (and cannot) have actually realized. For Cavell, as we have seen, this is a "hedge." In the case of marriage, it is a hedge because the emphasis should fall on the everyday, ordinary, diurnal circumstances that, in amounting to remarriage, make a marriage a marriage. Cavell is quite clear about this: "Marriage, as I have argued, is an image of the ordinary in human existence," he states (*CoW*, p. 422). That, essentially, is why Rhu's utopian reading of marriage needs amending: notwithstanding Cavell's emphasis, in his reading of Ibsen, on the wonderful and the miraculous as bound up with the process of remarriage, this process is in fact rooted in the ordinary and the everyday, at least as Cavell sees it. Which is not to set up a (false) opposition between the utopian and the ordinary, since, as we shall see shortly, there are indeed utopian moments in the Cavellian conception of the ordinary. Rather, *pace* Rhu, marriage can be understood as utopian only to the degree that there is something utopian in the character of the ordinary itself.[24] To think otherwise is to confuse perfectionism with perfection.

So, is the conversation of marriage a better model for the kind of conversation Cavell wishes to have with Nora than the conversation of democracy? On the face of it, it would appear to be. Even if divorce is a poor substitute for revolution, Nora's marriage contract nevertheless affords her the political agency she needs to revoke it, as her actions in the climactic scene make clear, and in this respect it offers a better model than the social contract. But marriage too begs its questions for Cavell's reading of *A Doll's House*, in that his interest in the everyday nature of remarriage paints a rather different and more complex picture of Nora's actions in leaving her husband's house than the straightforward ending of a contract. According to Cavell's interpretation, Nora does not end her conversation of marriage by refusing her everyday consent to remarriage;

she ends it by declaring that she has never been in a "real marriage" in the first place (*ADH*, p. 232). That is, in observing to Torvald that "we two—you and I, man and wife—have . . . never exchanged a serious word on any serious subject" (*ADH*, p. 225), she is announcing that their marriage has never involved the sort of conversation that would make it a (Cavellian) marriage. This means that their first conversation of marriage will also be their last. Or as Cavell puts it: "For them to have the conversation that would save their marriage they would already have to be (in effect) married. And they, she announces, have never been in that state" (*CoW*, p. 254). If this view of Nora's marriage is accurate, then the correct term for ending it is not *divorce* but *annulment*, because the marriage has been a "sham" (*CoW*, p. 257) from the get-go. The difference is worth insisting on, because it returns us to the problematic question of the withdrawal of consent with which we ended the previous section: whereas a divorce involves the withdrawal of consent, annulling a marriage is more the recognition that there is no valid object for such consent in existence. This nuance adds a complexity to the play on which, I would argue, Cavell's reading of Ibsen will be found to hinge.

The problem, as I see it, lies in the comparison Cavell draws between marriage and democracy, grounded on the analogy that both involve free conversation between equals. If this is true, then to withdraw unilaterally from the conversation of marriage, as Nora does, is an inherently antidemocratic act. That is, declaring an end to a free conversation of equals is something that, politically, tyrants and despots do, and so when thought through, the Cavellian analogy results in a view of divorce as something akin to a *diktat*.[25] But this is a poor description of Nora, whose dialogue with Torvald in the play's closing scene advocates the freedom of the individual and the right to self-determination. So something is out of joint. Cavell's suggestion that the Helmers are not actually married (in any meaningful sense) in the first place may seem a neat solution to this problem: it seems to sidestep the inconsistency, because it implies that Nora is leaving a conversation that was not democratic and hence not really a *con*versation at all. But in fact this only begs, or at any rate raises, some more difficult questions. If, as we have just seen, Cavell is suggesting that the Helmers are not in a state of marriage,[26] then Nora does not (and cannot) end her marriage to Torvald, because there is nothing there for her to end. Accordingly, her departure from Torvald's house is not in any way an action that effects a change, whether political or otherwise; it is merely a recognition of the status quo. Two consequences arise from this. Both are potentially ruinous for my attempt at a political reading of Cavell's Ibsen, and the second is potentially ruinous for Cavell's reading of Ibsen itself. These consequences are (1) that it is no more possible to end a marriage (as Cavell understands the term) than it is to withdraw from the social contract (as Cavell understands the term); and (2) that the play from which Cavell claims to trace the genealogy of his conception of marriage in fact contains no such thing as a marriage at all. And if this latter point is true, then it follows that marriage cannot possibly function as an image of democracy in *A Doll's House*, since there is no marriage in the play.

Taking the first of these points first, if Nora's case is paradigmatic—and Cavell certainly suggests that it is—then there is a Catch-22 clause in a marriage similar to that preventing withdrawal from the social contract. Succinctly, what Cavell's reading of *A Doll's House* implies is that to end a marriage, one must (1) be married (since one cannot end one's marriage if one is not in a marriage); and (2) realize that one is not in fact married (because the marriage is over, it is no longer a "real" marriage, or perhaps it never has been). Nora, then, cannot end her marriage any more than she can revoke her membership in the polis. We might perhaps call this "Nora's paradox," and it suggests that the Cavellian view of marriage, or at least of divorce, is incoherent. More to the point, if Cavell is right to observe that for the Helmers to have the conversation that would save their marriage, they would need already to have a marriage that is a conversation, then the analogy between the conversation of marriage and the conversation of democracy impels us to the unsatisfactory conclusion that to participate in a conversation of democracy, one must already live in a society that permits democratic conversation. This is an uncomfortable conclusion to reach, because, once again, it fails to give Nora—or anyone else who finds him- or herself excluded from participation in the conversation of democracy—a means of asserting her right to political agency.[27] There is, however, an alternative conclusion to draw, and this is a point to which I shall return in the final section of this chapter. The conclusion is that the term *conversation* is in fact a poor one on which to base an account of marriage or, more seriously, of democracy.

The second of these consequences is the shakier of the two. In fact, *A Doll's House* actually offers us a clear and dramatic example of a Cavellian marriage, but it is easily overlooked by focusing exclusively on the Helmers—as Cavell's reading does, and as this discussion has hitherto.[28] In the final act, Nora's melodramatic exit from her marriage is contrasted with a classic comedy of remarriage, because, in Moi's words, "Mrs. Linde and Krogstad are counterpoints to Nora and Helmer."[29] At the start of act 3 we see Kristina Linde and Nils Krogstad resuming a life together that ended "years ago" (*ADH*, p. 164) when Kristina left Krogstad for a richer man (*ADH*, p. 208). What is remarkable about this scene is that the vocabulary they use to describe their remarriage is set up as a mirror image to that of the Helmers' marriage, and as a result it coincides with the terminology with which Cavell describes remarriage. For example, whereas Nora and Torvald's marriage ends because of the impossibility of conversation between them, Ibsen casts the remarriage of Kristina and Krogstad as the resumption of a conversation:

> MRS LINDE: Well, Nils, let us have a talk.
>
> KROGSTAD: Have you and I got anything more to talk about?
>
> MRS LINDE: A great deal. (*ADH*, p. 207)

Where Nora's observation that "you don't understand me. And I've never understood you" (*ADH*, pp. 224–25) is taken by her as grounds to end her conversation of marriage, Kristina takes the same phrase—"you never really understood me" (*ADH*, p. 207)—as grounds to resume her conversation with Krogstad so as to set the record straight. Where Nora tells Torvald she has been treated as a mere caricature of herself, an image that misrepresents her to suit his needs ("your little songbird, your little doll," she says [*ADH*, p. 230]), Kristina says to Krogstad that "I have faith in you—the real you—Nils" (*ADH*, p. 210). Nora is quite clear that her duty to herself gives her the right to leave her husband (*ADH*, p. 228), whereas Kristina says of leaving Krogstad that "I've often asked myself if I had the right. I really don't know" (*ADH*, p. 208). (This means that both Kristina and Nora are therefore uncertain as to what is *right* but clear as to what is *necessary*.)

Perhaps the most important of these contrasts, however, is the idea of the "miracle of change" (*PoH*, p. 23) that Cavell says is the key to the comedy of remarriage. According to his reading, the significance of *A Doll's House* to this genre is that it makes explicit the importance to the idea of remarriage of a miraculous change, a change that Nora no longer believes in (*ADH*, p. 232). The Norwegian noun Ibsen uses is *det vidunderligste*, which is often translated as "miracle" and is consistently taken in this sense by Cavell. According to Toril Moi, who attaches roughly the same importance to the term as Cavell, this is a mistranslation, as its connotations are "somewhat too religious," and the term could more accurately be rendered as "the most wonderful thing."[30] Significantly, that is more or less the phrase that Krogstad uses to describe his remarriage: "Kristina, this is the most marvellous thing that's ever happened to me" (*ADH*, p. 211). Whereas Nora says of Torvald that he is capable of change only if she leaves him (*ADH*, p. 230), Kristina says of Krogstad that he might become "a different man" if they "join forces" and resume their relationship (*ADH*, pp. 209–10). In sum, then, *A Doll's House* offers us *both* a melodrama of an unknown woman *and* a comedy of remarriage. And it is in the interplay between these two genres that the play's most explicitly political aspects can be found.

I have in mind the significance of the relationship between Nora and Krogstad. Their conversations are fraught (as is no doubt to be expected when the leading woman in a melodrama about a failed conversation of marriage converses with the leading man in a comedy about a resumed conversation of marriage), but politically they are essential to the play. Cavell fleetingly suggests that Torvald recognizes "his own double" in Krogstad (*CoW*, p. 259), so it makes sense to ask, in what way is Krogstad to be understood as Torvald's double? The suggestion I am about to make may seem odd, given his initial role as Nora's antagonist in the play, but in Cavell's terms, Krogstad is an image of the husband that Nora never had. I say this because in their conversations he treats her as an equal, and what is more, his conversation gives Nora the principal thing that she later says she lacks and that Torvald cannot supply: it provides her with an education, or at least it educates her regarding her need for such an education. Equality and education are among the foremost conditions of a Cavellian conversation of marriage, and Nora receives both of these from Krogstad. That is what I take Moi to be asserting when she observes that "the only man in this play who treats Nora as a fully thinking human being is Krogstad, the man who taught her that they were equal in the eyes of the law."[31]

Thus, it is to Krogstad—the villain of the piece, the man who we are told is "rotten to the core" (*ADH*, p. 165) and who drives Nora to the very brink of suicide—that we owe the philosophical, educational, and political aspects of the text that lay the foundations for Cavell's account of marriage and its analogy with democracy. If this seems an overstatement, the following passage from *The Claim of Reason*'s discussion of the social contract applies perfectly to the changes Nora undergoes in response to the upshot of her conversations with Krogstad:

> The philosophical significance of the writing lies in its imparting of political education: it is philosophical because its method is an examination of myself by an attack upon my assumptions; it is political because the terms of this self-examination are the terms which reveal me as a member of a polis; it is education not because I learn new information but because I learn that the finding and forming of my knowledge of myself requires the finding and forming of my knowledge of that membership. (*CoR*, p. 25)

And so, looked at from this point of view, the analogy between marriage and democracy still stands, but with a certain proviso: there is indeed a vision of a successful conversation of marriage in *A Doll's House*, and its hero (if such we can call Krogstad) makes possible a concomitant conversation of democracy. But paradoxically, the man who makes this possible is himself deprived of a voice in this conversation, reviled as a "moral outcast" (*ADH*, p. 179), regarded by his society as scarcely fit for membership in the polis himself. In this sense, the play's only true, committed democrat turns out to be Krogstad—Krogstad the blackmailer, the loan shark, the fraudster.

VI

We have seen, then, that Nora's marriage contract fails as clearly as the social contract to give Nora the kind of political agency she needs, because the Cavellian view of both marriage and democracy is (problematically) conversational rather than contractual. There remains a third contract for discussion: the piece of paper that Krogstad wields in act 1, the note of hand bearing the forged signature of Nora's late father.

What kind of a thing is this contract? It scores over the social contract in that it has a material existence: Nora looks forward to the day when she "can tear it into little pieces and burn it—the horrid filthy thing" (*ADH*, p. 186). It is legally binding: Krogstad threatens to "produce this paper in court" (*ADH*, p. 175). In the eyes of the respectable society Torvald represents, it makes Nora "a liar, a hypocrite—even worse—a criminal!" (*ADH*, p. 221), just as repugnant, in fact, as Krogstad, who committed the same offense. So this contract is evidence of a crime, one that Nora has perpetrated. That she did so unwittingly, and out of the best intentions, is immaterial—and not just because, as Krogstad tells her, "The law is not concerned with motives" (*ADH*, p. 175), but because Ibsen leaves us in no doubt that even if the signature were genuine, the bond compromises Nora anyway. This is because borrowing money is something that "our worthy Torvald" (*ADH*, p. 197) and so presumably all such "respectable" members of society refuse to do. At the start of the play, we see Torvald refuse to borrow money even though he is in a position to repay it (*ADH*, pp. 148–49), and we soon learn that he refused to borrow money even when his life depended on it (*ADH*, pp. 160–61). This is probably because he believes that "there's something constrained, something ugly even, about a home that's founded on borrowing and debt" (*ADH*, p. 149). Whereas for Mrs. Linde, Nora's friend and confidante, what is reprehensible about the bond is not the borrowing of money or the forging of a signature, but Nora's lying to Torvald about it: "Helmer must know the whole story. This wretched secret must be brought into the open so that there's complete understanding between them. That'd be impossible while there's so much concealment and subterfuge" (*ADH*, p. 211).

In sum, then, this contract is a record of Nora's debt to Krogstad and her promise to repay him; it is evidence of criminal activity; it bears witness to a lie; and it partakes of a socially unacceptable practice. Borrowing and lending, promises of repayment, secrets and lies, threats of exposure—*A Doll's House* is predicated on the relationship between performative language and its attendant slips and glitches and is therefore as much as anything else a play about the way social practices are embedded in our ordinary language.

Insofar as our social practices are intimately related to the formation of our polis, this means that ordinary language is partly a political matter. As Cavell puts it,

> Language is . . . what puts us in bonds. . . . With each word we utter we emit stipulations, agreements we do not know and do not want to know we have entered, agreements we were always in, that were in effect before our participation in them. Our relation to our language—to the fact that we are subject to expression and comprehension, victims of meaning—is accordingly a key to our sense of our distance from our lives, of our sense of the alien, of ourselves as alien to ourselves, thus alienated. (*IQO*, pp. 39–40)

We see this happen in *A Doll's House* time after time. Consider the act of promising as an example: the bond would ordinarily amount to a promise Nora made to Krogstad to pay back the money he lent her. It leads her to what Torvald calls "making him promises" that are "irresponsible" (*ADH*, pp. 177, 187), that is, promising Krogstad to persuade her husband not to dismiss him (though Nora has not in fact actually done this), which leads Torvald to forcibly extract a promise from her "not to plead his cause" (*ADH*, p. 179). Then, having declared his intention to dismiss Krogstad, Torvald feels obliged to keep his word (*ADH*, p. 188). Since this is basically the concatenation of events and circumstances that places Nora in an impossible position, *A Doll's House* shows us how the ordinary practice of giving one's word, of holding to it and being held to it, can at times lead people into untenably destructive situations. So it is not too much of an exaggeration to say that Nora's political crisis is precipitated by a crisis in performative language.[32]

We might, then, wish to see Nora as falling victim to the ordinary linguistic and social practices of her community. But to see Nora as a victim is once again to deny her her agency. And perhaps it is also to misunderstand what is meant by ordinary language philosophy, as if that simply consisted in policing the usage of ordinary language. This misunderstanding is no doubt why some of the first reactions to this school of thought back in the early 1960s held that "ordinary language philosophy was politically conservative" (*TOS*, p. 28), a misunderstanding all too easily nourished by Cavell's insistent demonstration that ordinary language was something "normative."[33] Describing ordinary language use as something "normative" has unhelpful connotations and can present a (misleading) picture of reactionary philosophers simply castigating or dismissing those who break the rules of what we ordinarily say when. Were this true, Nora's relationship to ordinary language would be more or less the same as her position vis-à-vis the social contract: her language gives her a set of rules whose inflexibility amounts to a Hobson's choice (to borrow Saussure's phrase in his *Cours de linguistique generale*) of what she should say when, except that it is not really a Hobson's choice between "take it or leave it," because she cannot leave her language (to simplify what Wittgenstein says in his *Tractatus Logico-Philosophicus*). So, someone who finds him- or herself out of kilter with the rules of his or her language can no more repudiate the rules that constitute that language than someone who finds him- or herself out of kilter with the laws of his or her polis can renounce his or her membership in that polis. Both are stuck with what they've got. They cannot readily leave their political or linguistic community, though they are likely to find themselves castigated by their community, who will view them as simply being in the wrong. That is surely what happens to Nora, both politically and linguistically: she broke the law when she broke her word (or, more precisely, when she gave her father's word as her own).

If this were an accurate characterization of ordinary language philosophy, it would indeed be politically conservative, and Nora could indeed be judged a victim of its conservatism. But it is worth exploring this picture in a little more depth in order that its inaccuracies delineate themselves more clearly. Certainly, it is true that Cavell's view of ordinary language philosophy has a certain amount in common with his view of the social contract. Mulhall correctly points out that "Cavell's elucidation of contractarian conceptions of the relationship between citizen and polis provides a striking set of parallels with the ordinary language conception of philosophy" because the "conjunction of self-knowledge and knowledge of others in politics is . . . precisely analogous to the methodology of ordinary language philosophers."[34] Since the social contract has been such a bone of contention in this chapter, his comparison may well appear problematic. According to Mulhall, the similarities are as follows:

> In both domains, claims drawing upon self-knowledge are made in the first-person plural mode, but the range of reference of the "we" is a matter to be decided by the responses others make to our claims to speak for them, to speak their minds; in both, the self-knowledge concerned is worked out rather than simply assumed; and in both that working out is inseparable from the working out of the limits of one's agreement with others.[35]

It is also worth adding that in both domains, even if it should turn out that we found ourselves in complete disagreement with these others, we cannot repudiate the community (see *CoR*, p. 28). Nor can we leave it. But whereas the existence of the polis can be abrogated by a revolution, the existence of ordinary language cannot. This does not mean that there are no revolutions in ordinary language, a conclusion the conservative might welcome. It means, rather, that the revolution that is to take place lies in our relationship to the ordinary.

Reflecting on the all too common (mis)interpretations of Wittgenstein as a conservative—the philosopher who counsels us simply to accept our language and form of life as given, to say that "this is simply what I do" rather than to try doing something else, to recognize that philosophy leaves everything exactly as it is, and so on[36]—Cavell correctly draws our attention to Wittgenstein's calls for "transfiguration" and "revolution" in our relationship to the ordinary (see *TNYUA*, pp. 43–44). How can such things be possible if ordinary language is in fact "normative"? The question reveals that it is a misunderstanding to read *normative* as a synonym for *conservative*. A better synonym would be *criterial*. And here a revolution *is* possible. If our criteria are what teach us what we would ordinarily say and what we would ordinarily mean by it, then a revolution in our relationship to the ordinary is not just possible but even necessary. Nora teaches us this; we see her undergo such a revolution right before us, on the stage. It starts, symbolically, when she removes the fancy dress in which she enacted a performance of her gender that theatricalized her femininity, then replaces it with her ordinary "everyday" dress and observes that she has "changed" (*ADH*, p. 224).[37]

The final scene of *A Doll's House* can be read as precisely the kind of philosophical investigation of the ordinary that results in its transformation. Like Wittgenstein's investigations, it takes place in dialogue form. Nora begins it by declaring that "we've never sat down in earnest together to get to the bottom of a single thing" (*ADH*, p. 225), and that is what she intends to do now: to get to the bottom of things, or, Wittgenstein would say, to reach bedrock. In the dialogue that ensues,[38] Nora questions what "we"—the community she now feels estranged from—would ordinarily call "love," "marriage," "happiness," "duty," "religion," and "morality" in turn. She is, in short, rejecting—or, better, reclaiming—the criteria by which her community frames the key concepts that frame the life of women in society. She shows her audience that these terms have come to be used in ways that are stacked against her, and against women in general, but that beneath them lies another sense that she can use to articulate what is wrong with how they have come to be used. Their ordinary sense—what Mulhall calls "the actual everyday"—is shown up as bankrupt in the light of an "eventual everyday" that reframes the grounds of the ordinary. As Mulhall says:

> The actual everyday may have to be overthrown if the eventual everyday—the real possibilities of the distinctively human life form that are covered over by particular cultural formations . . . —are to be realized. . . . The form of philosophical practice that is required . . . therefore need not be a reactionary reiteration of whatever happens to be the case, but might rather revolutionize our ordinary life with language.[39]

Nora's unflinching investigation of what we ordinarily say and what we ordinarily mean when we say it constitutes just such a revolution, brought about through the methods of ordinary language philosophy. Nora declares her intention to "think things out for myself" (*ADH*, p. 228), and she does so by querying definitions ("What do you consider is my most sacred duty?" she asks Torvald [*ADH*, p. 227]), by calling attention to the emptiness of the concepts she has been given ("Ah, Torvald, I don't really know what religion is" [*ADH*, p. 228]), by insisting on crucial differentiations between deceptively similar concepts (as when she highlights the distinction between being "happy" and being "gay" [*ADH*, p. 226], or between "love" and "in love" [*ADH*, p. 225]), and the end result of her philosophical investigation is that the dialogue brings about clarity ("I've never seen things so clearly and certainly as I do tonight" [*ADH*, p. 229]). Looked at this way, this scene is surely one of the clearest examples that literature has to give us of the politically revolutionary nature of ordinary language philosophy.

VII

I suggested earlier that Cavell's idea of "conversation" gives us a poor term on which to ground an account of marriage and of democracy, especially in the context of *A Doll's House*. This is because Nora has no wish to continue her participation in either her marriage or her polis, and so Cavell's conceptualizing these institutions as predicated on the furthering of a conversation seems ill-suited to her needs. As readers we may very well desire, as Cavell does, to talk things over with Nora and to offer her the kind of conversation of which her husband is incapable, but nowhere does Ibsen give us any indication that she would wish to converse with us. On the contrary, Nora's investigation of the ordinary language underpinning the social and political institutions and conventions that are her shackles and fetters makes available the basis for a critique of this term *conversation* and hence for a political reading of *A Doll's House* that would finally do justice to her claims. That this investigation ends with what Cavell calls "the abandoning of words, and of the house of words" (*PoH*, p. 24) allows us to see that whatever has happened in the Helmers' house, it has not been a conversation. If a conversation ends with one party repudiating the words that constituted it—the common terms that made for the very possibility of conversation—then what took place between the parties was not a *con*versation.

To an extent, Cavell is aware of this. His reading of *A Doll's House* acknowledges that the play raises political issues that take Nora and Torvald beyond the kind of dissent that makes for a conversation of democracy: "I recognize that at some time my sense of my society's distance from the reign of perfect justice, and of my implication in its distance, may become intolerable. Then if an argument should not take place . . . what should take its place? (I assume that constitutional debate is not here in order.)" (*CHU*, p. 110). This is a reasonably explicit acknowledgment that *A Doll's House* takes us beyond the kind of democratic conversation Cavell calls "dissent," a conversation essentially about the makeup of the polis and the content of whatever social contract its members must consent to (see *CoR*, p. 27). Argument and constitutional debate are no longer of use, because one party in the conversation (Nora) feels there is nothing left to argue about. But this is not just because she finds her polis to be irretrievably unjust and politically bankrupt—irretrievably unjust and politically bankrupt though she finds it. It is also because the terms of the conversation are determined and dictated by the terms of the polis, by its laws and its mores, and these are terms to which Nora can no longer consent. The conversation ends because there cease to be any common terms on which to hold it. It is a *con*versation no more.

And so Nora finds herself in an impossible position: because the terms on which her conversation depends are terms set out by her polis, and because she rejects her polis and its terms, she effectively has no terms of her own in which to frame her grievances, state her case, and demand her rights. She is thus precisely in the position of someone without membership in a polis—"voiceless, not even mute" (*CoR*, p. 28). Cavell recognizes this when he asks,

> Do we feel that Nora's expressions of dishonor and outrage at the state of her so-called marriage require that she be prepared to show why certain institutions (here the institution of marriage) are unjust or how others have injured her? But when Nora tries to show this to Torvald he replies that she is talking like a child, that she does not understand the world she lives in (with which she agrees . . .) . . . Nora has no reasons that are acceptable, and she surely knows all the reasons that can be given her. (*CHU*, p. 109)

In a sense, then, since Nora has in effect been silenced by the gulf between her values and the values to which a member of her polis consents, what renders her voiceless is, precisely, consent—the consent on which her polis is founded. "Deprivation of a voice in the conversation of justice," Cavell observes, "is the work of the moral consensus itself, spoken for by the respectable Torvalds of the world (in us)" (*CHU*, p. xxxvii). And what this shows us, I would suggest, is that a consent-based conversation of democracy as Cavell describes it is founded on the silencing of certain voices, namely, those voices that cannot consent to the terms on which the conversation is held.

One of the political lessons of *A Doll's House* is that there are several conditions under which participants in this conversation can be rendered voiceless. One—the most obvious, perhaps—is when they are deemed incapable of participating in it, as Ibsen's salient dramatization of the predicament of women shows us. Another, as I have been arguing, is when their disagreement with the terms of the conversation is acute enough for them to wish to retract their voice from it, as seems to be the case for Nora. Yet a third is when society withdraws the privilege of participation from a member of the polis. Once again, Krogstad is a case in point here. We know that he forged a signature; he tells us so. But we also know that "it never came to court" (*ADH*, p. 172), which means that legally he is unblemished as a member of the polis. Nevertheless, because "he tried to wriggle out of it with tricks and subterfuges" (*ADH*, p. 179), he is regarded by Torvald, and presumably by the "moral consensus" Torvald represents, as a "moral outcast" (*ADH*, p. 179), and all doors have been closed to him (*ADH*, p. 172), presumably because there is a moral consensus among the members of the polis that, like Torvald, one should have nothing to do with anyone who "isn't absolutely respectable" (*ADH*, p. 155). So it is clear that if his society is indeed to be pictured as a conversation, it is a conversation that withdraws the right to speak from certain people, whether they have been convicted of breaking its laws or not. It is a conversation that creates "outcasts," or that casts people out. Cavell considers the position of the outcast toward the end of *The Claim of Reason*:

> So far as we think that the human being is naturally a political being, we cannot think that some human beings are naturally outcasts. . . . So if there are outcasts, we must have, or harbor, *sub specie civilitatis*, some explanation of their condition. One explanation is that their condition is deserved. Another is that their condition is undeserved but sheerly unfortunate, doomed or damned. Another is that the inhabitants of that condition are not quite or fully human. Another is that they are mysteriously in league with one another. Another is that my society is doomed or damned. Another is that my society is unjust; but not sufficiently unjust to be doomed or damned. (*CoR*, p. 437)

Whichever of these explanations any given member of any given polis subscribes to, surely the basic point is that, as Cavell says, once we have called someone an outcast, we have acknowledged ourselves as people who cast others out (see *CoR*, p. 436). And so by showing us that there are people who are excluded from participation in civil conversation, it is Krogstad—described earlier as perhaps the only true and committed democrat in the play—who demonstrates just how undemocratic this conversation can be.

In all fairness to Cavell's reading of Ibsen, however, it is worth highlighting moments in that reading when attention is drawn to the factors that are stacked against the possibility of conversation between Nora and Torvald: "When, in effect, at the denouement of *A Doll's House*, . . . Torvald claims that he is beyond reproach, that Nora has no claim against him, or against the institutions of their society, he is closing a door to which Nora's ensuing, more explicit, closing of a door is the mirroring action" (*CHU*, p. xxv). This astute observation appears to recognize that Torvald's stance forecloses the possibility of a conversation with Nora. Because "the legal rules are on his side" (*CHU*, p. 114), Nora has no basis for stating her case: the polis does not accept the terms she uses to justify herself. So it becomes "part of the resentment that there is no satisfactory hearing for the resentment" (*CHU*, p. 108). Cavell seems implicitly to acknowledge here that since Nora cannot put her side of the story within this conversation, it is a conversation so one-sided as to fail to count as a conversation at all.

This pattern of one-sidedness calls to mind the Hegelian position discussed earlier, whereby *A Doll's House* seems to contain a structure of two one-sided moral positions, each partially justified and justifiable, but for the fact that each overlooks the equally justified and justifiable terms of the other. We may be no closer to explaining why the play is not a (Hegelian) tragedy, but we can, I hope, see more clearly how and why it bears the marks of such a structure. Cavell argues that "Nora's enactments of change and departure . . . exemplify that over the field on which moral justifications come to an end, and justice, as it stands, has done what it can, specific wrong may not be claimable; yet the misery is such that, on the other side, right is not assertible" (*CHU*, p. 112). So, as in a Hegelian tragedy, each position is essentially incomplete.

This incompleteness, I suggest, comes from a lack of common terms between Nora and Torvald. Nora finds that the laws and mores of her polis have deprived her of terms with which to articulate how she has "been dreadfully wronged" (*ADH*, p. 225), while this same lack deprives Torvald of the terms he needs to understand this wrong and to see that she is not being "unreasonable" and "ungrateful" (*ADH*, p. 226). Torvald gives voice to this lack of common terms when he states that "there truly is a gulf between us" (*ADH*, p. 230). He has been brought to this understanding by what in the previous section was characterized as a politically driven lesson in ordinary language philosophy. The lesson he has learned—the lesson that we, the audience or readership of the play, must also come to learn—is that this "gulf" is a lack of shared and agreed meanings to the terms they use, which in turn is the reason why what takes place between Nora and Torvald is not, and should not be called, a conversation.

Clearly, then, we need a better word than *conversation* to provide an analogy for the kind of politics Ibsen sets out in *A Doll's House*. One possible candidate for such a word can be found in the thought of Jean-François Lyotard. The lack, or in Torvald's phrase the "gulf," between the parties, which means that neither side can ultimately ground its claims against the other side, recalls Lyotard's concept of the "differend." The differend is, precisely, a "negative formulation,"[40] denoting the absence of a common ground between factions engaged in a dispute. As Lyotard has it,

> A differend would be a case of conflict between (at least) two parties, that cannot be equitably resolved for lack of a rule of judgment applicable to both arguments. One side's legitimacy does not imply the other's lack of legitimacy. However, applying a single rule of judgment to both in order to settle their differend as though it were merely a litigation would wrong (at least) one of them (and both of them if neither side admits this rule). . . . A wrong results from the fact that the rules of the genre of discourse by which one judges are not those of the judged.[41]

Lyotard claims that "a universal rule of judgment between heterogeneous genres is lacking in general,"[42] especially in the wake of modernity, and that what is needed is a philosophy that rises to the challenge of thinking the "incompossibility"[43] of voices engaged in political and juridical dispute. His notion of the differend is meant as a step in the direction of such a philosophy. So would it provide a better term than *conversation* to describe the agonistics of Nora and Torvald in *A Doll's House*?

To gauge what might count as an answer to this question, it is worth comparing the diverging ways in which Cavell's reading of Ibsen's and Lyotard's accounts of the differend start out by targeting the same philosopher for critique, namely, Immanuel Kant. For Lyotard, the differend comes into being because there is no possibility of acting in accordance with Kant's categorical imperative such that our deeds would comply with a universal law. There is no possibility of doing this because there is no such thing as what Kant calls universal law in the first place. Instead, there are only false claims to universality that overlook the (no doubt equally false) claims of others who invoke different interpretations of a putatively universal law. That is how the differend finds its way into a dispute.[44] Applied to *A Doll's House*, this would mean, for example, that there is a differend between what Nora claims as "a woman['s] . . . right to spare her old father on his deathbed, or to save her husband's life" (*ADH*, p. 228)—rights she is convinced must be enshrined in law[45]—and the law, which, as Krogstad explains, "is not concerned with motives" (*ADH*, p. 175). Both positions seem quite reasonable, yet, *pace* Kant, there is no possibility of formulating a common law or rule between them; they are separated by a differend.

Now, Cavell, for his part, would certainly agree with Lyotard that we cannot articulate a formulation whereby Nora's actions would conform to any kind of universal law; indeed, he expends a great deal of effort making this very point (see *CoW*, pp. 250–55). So far, so good. But he does not draw Lyotard's conclusion that the idea of a universal law is all but a chimera. He concludes instead that "a moral response to Nora . . . seems to require not the construction of a law she is prepared to see become universally controlling, but an offer of conversation" (*CoW*, p. 253). So, in other words, whereas for Cavell the absence of a law is an opening for conversation, for Lyotard this absence is precisely what makes any just or satisfactory resolution to such a conversation impossible.

Although we have seen, time and again, that such a just and satisfactory resolution to the conversation of democracy in *A Doll's House* is indeed impossible, we should not be too hasty to conclude that Lyotard is altogether right here. There is something worth holding on to about Cavell's contention that the application of a law is inappropriate to Nora's case. I take that "something" to be revealed in Nora's investigations of ordinary language, which reveal that the issue is a lack of common *terms* rather than the lack of a common *law*. To put it another way, the "gulf" between Nora and Torvald is a gulf that is *prior to* the law and hence prior to the problem of its presence or its absence, its (in)validity or its (in)applicability. It is therefore a gulf that matches the description Jacques Rancière gives of certain kinds of political dispute: "Before any confrontation of interests and values, before any assertions are submitted to demands for validation between established partners, there is the dispute over the object of the dispute, the dispute over the existence of the dispute and the parties confronting each other in it."[46] Rancière has a convenient term for disputes of this nature: *disagreements*.

This concept of "disagreement" is often compared to, or even aligned with, the idea of the differend, but in fact Rancière takes pains to differentiate the two: "Disagreement differs from what Jean-François Lyotard has conceptualized as a differend. Disagreement is not concerned with . . . the presence or absence of a rule for assessing different types of heterogeneous discourse. It is less concerned with arguing than with what can be argued, the presence or absence of a common object between X and Y."[47] It is therefore a concept that operates at precisely the level of the "gulf," such as that between Nora and Torvald. The gulf is not, *pace* Lyotard, the lack of a common law whereby to judge their respective claims; the gulf is in the very terms in which those claims are made. That is why what takes place between Nora and Torvald might better be characterized as an instance of Rancièrean disagreement rather than of Lyotardian differend. According to Rancière's definition, a disagreement is a

> kind of speech situation . . . in which one of the interlocutors at once understands and does not understand what the other is saying. Disagreement is not the conflict between one who says white and another who says black. It is the conflict between one who says white and another who also says white but does not understand the same thing by it or does not understand that the other is saying the same thing in the name of whiteness.[48]

If, as I have argued, the dialogue in the closing scene of *A Doll's House* can be characterized as a politically driven exercise in ordinary language philosophy, then a large part of what it reveals is that there is precisely such a Rancièrean structure of disagreement between Nora and Torvald: it highlights the divergences in the ways they understand and use terms such as *right, duty, moral sense*, *religion*, *love*, and, perhaps more importantly, in light of an earlier discussion, *marriage*. Nora says that Helmer doesn't understand her (*ADH*, p. 225), but because he does not understand what she means by *understand*, he cannot understand that he does not understand her, even when admitting to her, as he does a few moments later, that he doesn't understand what she's saying (*ADH*, p. 229). Torvald, on the other hand, says that Nora doesn't understand the world she lives in (*ADH*, p. 228), and she concurs, effectively acknowledging the gulf between his terms and hers. And so if we require a better word than *conversation* to describe what takes place in *A Doll's House*, then it seems to me a reasonable surmise that the word *disagreement*, taken in the sense of the term that Rancière applies to political situations of this kind, would be a good one to use instead.

The aptness of the term *disagreement*, however, does not reside solely in the fact that "the interlocutors both understand and do not understand the same thing by the same words."[49] Its aptness resides in a certain structural analogy to the procedures of ordinary language philosophy. If we take ordinary language philosophy to designate, roughly, investigations of what we ordinarily mean when we say X, then, as Cavell (following Wittgenstein) makes abundantly clear throughout his work, the semantics or content of the "what" is internally related to the identity of the "we." Politically, this means that a disagreement about the content of the "what" can be bound up with an exclusion from the "we." And, as we have seen Cavell argue, if one is excluded from the "we" of the polis, then one no longer has a voice with which to "say" anything at all. And so, in short, just as the meaning of words is bound up with membership in a linguistic community, so too the issue of what political terms are taken to mean is bound up with membership in a polis.

Rancière does not put the matter in these terms, but his idea of disagreement can be read as exploring the consequences of such a view. "Disagreement clearly is not to do with words alone," he explains. "It generally bears on the very situation in which speaking parties find themselves."[50] More specifically,

> the problem is not for people speaking "different languages," literally or figuratively, to understand each other, any more than it is for "linguistic breakdowns" to be overcome by the invention of new languages. The problem is knowing . . . whether the common language in which they are exposing a wrong is indeed a common language. The quarrel has nothing to do with more or less transparent or opaque linguistic contents; it has to do with consideration of speaking beings as such.[51]

It seems quite clear, then, that a Rancièrean disagreement is not merely semantic, occurring over the "what" of "what we say." It also involves the "who" of who is saying it, and whether this "who" is to be recognized as part of the "we" that is the polis, and, hence, whether they can be understood as having the right to "say" anything at all in the first place. Or in Rancièrese, "The structures proper to disagreement are those in which discussion of an argument comes down to a dispute over the object of the discussion and over the capacity of those who are making an object of it."[52]

The process of political subjectivization that leads to equality is, for Rancière, a process characterized by dispute and dissensus rather than by conversation.[53] Conversation cannot be a model if one party is not considered capable of speech. Rather, "disagreement occurs wherever contention over what speaking means constitutes the very rationality of the speech situation."[54] Nora is faced with just such a situation in *A Doll's House*—what Cavell calls "Nora's finding her voice" (*CHU*, p. xxxvi). Her position thus resembles the examples of disagreements that Rancière gives, taken mostly from the historic struggles of the proletariat in the nineteenth century, whose representatives were not recognized as representatives precisely because there was no recognition of the people, or *demos*, they were said to represent and whose grievances were not considered grievances because they were voiced by a "political subject" whose voice was considered inadmissible. Much the same could be said of Nora.

The only voice Torvald will grant Nora is that of "my little songbird"—as in "A songbird must have a clear voice to sing with" (*ADH*, p. 177). She is also a "little skylark twittering" (*ADH*, p. 148), a "squirrel" who "will scamper and do all her tricks" (*ADH*, p. 187), a "fairy" who will "dance on a moonbeam" (*ADH*, p. 187), and, most significantly, a "doll" who is not allowed to have opinions of her own (*ADH*, p. 225). Irrespective of whatever political rights were granted to or withheld from women under the Norwegian constitution at the time the play was written, what these terms demonstrate is that Nora is not seen by her community as *saying* anything; that is, she is not regarded as capable of (political) speech. One cannot converse with a skylark, a songbird, a squirrel, or a doll, and if such creatures could talk, then, as Wittgenstein says of his lion, we could not understand them. In this sense, the "disagreement" in the play is partly prelinguistic: it concerns not just the meaning or semantics of terms, and whether these are common to both parties or not, but primarily whether Nora is to be regarded as having the capacity to say things that count, which is bound up with whether she is firstly counted as *saying* things at all. So the disagreement, as well as taking place over the terms that the parties use in such different ways, also (and more fundamentally) concerns membership in the "we," both the linguistic community and the polis.

Wittgenstein, albeit in the context of a rather different debate, asserts that "it is what human beings *say* that is true and false; and they agree in the *language* they use. That is not agreement in opinions but in form of life."[55] Perhaps the disagreement between Torvald and Nora could be framed as a disagreement not in opinions but in form of life. That is, if we follow the precept by which Cavell reads Beckett and take the words of the play as literally as possible, then Torvald sees his wife as a cute little animal, as a pet or a character from a children's story. He does not appear to regard her as sharing a form of life with competent agents of the polis such as himself, hence, following Wittgenstein, as sharing the terms of the polis's language. But it is worth pausing before jumping to such a conclusion in order to ask, as Cavell does in part 4 of *The Claim of Reason*, what exactly is meant, and whether anything coherent *could* be meant, by refusing to acknowledge that one shares one's form of life with another human being.

The case Cavell asks us to consider is that of slave owners and their slaves. The institution of slavery came ultimately to rest upon a claim that slaves were not human—upon a claim that they were "chattels," or "livestock," or some other such repugnant term. This claim was used to justify keeping human beings as slaves, with all the maltreatment and injustice this involved. "But," observes Cavell, "it is none too clear what possibility is being envisioned here" (*CoR*, p. 372). The slave owner's behavior toward his slaves may be brutal, but it is not the same as his behavior toward his livestock. He may rape his slaves violently, or take them as his concubines; he may convert his slaves to Christianity, forcefully or otherwise, or he may take steps to keep the Gospel from them. But he would not behave in any of these ways toward his horses, his cattle, or his pigs, nor would he allow these animals to cook his food, clean his house, or serve him his dinner (see *CoR*, p. 376). This gives the lie to the slave owner's attempt to justify his maltreatment of his slaves on grounds that theirs is a different form of life from his. Moreover, says Cavell, the same can be said of the subjection of women:

> It is sometimes imperative to say that women or children or black people or criminals are human beings. This is a call for justice. For justice to be done, a change of perception, a modification of seeing, may be called for. But does it follow that those whose perceptions, or whose natural reactions, must suffer change have

> until that time been seeing women or children or black people or criminals as something *other* than human beings? (*CoR*, p. 372)

To use our present text as an example, Torvald may call Nora by pet names, and these pet names may cast her as a pet, but, however literally we may take these terms, Nora is *not* treated as a pet by Torvald: he does not stroke her back, or take her for walks, or keep her in a hutch, or change her straw regularly, or throw her bones and scraps from his plate, or scold her for sitting on the furniture, or throw sticks for her to fetch. "So what is this about 'not human beings'?" (*CoR*, p. 376), we might ask. "What else could a person be other than a person?" (*CoR*, p. 372). The suggestion that certain human beings are not in fact human beings "means, and can mean, nothing definite" (*CoR*, p. 376).

Why, then, does Nora have to spell out so explicitly to Torvald that "before everything else I'm a human being—just as much as you are" (*ADH*, p. 228)? Because what is entailed by Torvald's assertion that "before everything else, you're a wife and mother" (*ADH*, p. 228) is none too distant from what is entailed by the slave owner's assertion that before everything else, certain human beings are slaves: "He means, indefinitely, that they are not *purely* human. He means, indefinitely, that there are *kinds* of humans. (It is, I take it, to deny just this that Marx, adapting Feuerbach's theology, speaks of man as a species-being. To be human is to be one of humankind, to bear an internal relation to all others.)" (*CoR*, p. 376).

Once again, then, *A Doll's House* offers us a political lesson that is rooted in ordinary language philosophy: whatever might be meant by calling Nora a "songbird" or "squirrel," a "doll" or a "fairy," the literal meaning of these terms is not compatible with ordinary behavior toward a human being; and conversely, if the term *wife* designates, and can only designate, a human being, then it is ungrammatical to use this group of terms as a synonym for *wife*. Where Cavell's ordinary language philosophy helps us to see the philosophical emptiness of the terms that are used to exclude certain groups of people from membership in the polis, Rancière's thought highlights the political consequences of said philosophical emptiness. Nora brings politics into *A Doll's House* nowhere more clearly than in the process Rancière calls "subjectivization," whereby she highlights how the terms that are used to designate her are all misnomers and all stand in the way of the equality that is denied her. This is a dispute about the very terms of ordinary language itself. The disagreement in *A Doll's House*, then, is not exactly a disagreement in forms of life; rather, it amounts to a Rancièrean "dispute," because it brings the play's politics into being by introducing a dissensus into *A Doll's House*.

Such an interpretation helps to explain why, as we saw earlier, Cavell's writings on Ibsen have a hard time deciding whether Nora can be considered "representative"—whether her claims speak for others who share her plight or just for herself. That Cavell argues both that she is and that she isn't need not be a contradiction; it is rather that the play itself is proffering a dispute about this very question. Certainly, Nora's voice can be taken to speak on behalf of the "thousands of women" she says are in her condition (*ADH*, p. 230), but for Torvald her speech is empty, because women have an overriding, "most sacred" duty, to their husbands and their children, to religion, to morality, and to public opinion—a duty that deprives them of a voice—and a woman who disputes this is just "talking like a child" (*ADH*, pp. 227–28). If this is what Torvald and the "moral consensus" of his society think, then the women Nora speaks for are what Rancière would term a *demos* to Torvald's *ochlos*. The ochlos seeks to impose a unity on the community, an artificial moral consensus with which it claims to unify society. But each ochlos will find that it ultimately fails to recognize certain groups of people and their claims and thus wrongs them. The claims of a demos for restitution introduce a moment of rupture or fragmentation into the artificial unity of the ochlos, and this is the moment when disagreement, dispute, and dissensus are born. As such, it is the moment of politics. Nora explicitly challenges the artificial consensus of the ochlos when she says, "I know quite well that most people would agree with you, Torvald" (*ADH*, p. 228). Thus, Nora knows that she is in a position where she both is and is not representative: she represents a demos, and so for the ochlos her voice is unrepresentative, inadmissible.

Nora's case is thus a complicated one. On the one hand, she clearly demands what has been denied her—the right to "stand on my own feet" (*ADH*, p. 227) as a member of a polis that has not granted her the capacity of speech or of self-determination. But why does she want this, if, as I have argued, she wishes to repudiate the "we" and leave her polis altogether? Precisely because of the problematic issues that Cavell highlighted regarding withdrawal from the social contract: she needs to have her voice recognized as valid by her community if she is to voice her wish to revoke her membership in that community. She knows she will be marginalized if she does so, no doubt to the point of being politically mute. But Nora gives us to see that there are different kinds of political muteness. At the start of the play, she had virtually no idea of the existence of her polis and its laws, and so in a sense her muteness was indeed that of a songbird, a skylark, or a doll. But by the end of the play, her refusal to participate in the conversation of democracy within her polis is an informed muteness. She has had to convince Torvald that she has a voice precisely so that she can tell him she has nothing more to say to him. As Lyotard puts it, "To be able not to speak is not the same as not to be able to speak."[56] For instance, we should hardly call a government that refused to negotiate with terrorists "mute," and Nora's repudiation of further conversation with Torvald and her polis is of a similar order. Of course, it may turn out that certain "terrorists" (South Africa's ANC would be a good historical example) are, as Nora is, a demos challenging an ochlos. But what this shows us is that true political change takes place outside of the mode of conversation—in what Rancière refers to as disagreement, dispute, and dissensus.

Perhaps it is not possible to draw any proper conclusion to a conversation about the impossibility of conversation. But insofar as it is meaningful to try—which may turn out to be not that far—we might reflect that what Cavell regards as a keyword in *A Doll's House* is, or at any rate ought to be, a keyword in democratic politics too: *change*. This term, so important to politics as to have recently served a successful U.S. presidential candidate as a one-word slogan, is no less important to Cavell: its absence leads to the failure of remarriage in the play, and its presence will be vital to Nora's perfectionist mission to better herself. Certainly, Nora has to leave both her conversation of marriage with Torvald and her conversation of democracy with her polis in order for this change to become possible. But *that* she must do so suggests that these conversations were never really conversations; they were not democratic enough to admit the possibility of meaningful change. So it is, perversely, the *absence* of conversation that becomes the driving force of political change, just as the absence of democracy is something of a precondition for democratic change. Cavell means something along similar lines when he says that

> the inevitability of debased claims to . . . democracy are, so one might put it, not the defeat, not even the bane, of the existence of the genuine article, but part of its inescapable circumstance and motivation. So that the mission of Perfectionism generally, in a world of false (and false calls for) democracy, is the discovery of the possibility of democracy, which to exist has recurrently to be (re)discovered. (*CHU*, pp. 16–17)

A Doll's House dramatizes this process of discovery and rediscovery as Nora's political awakening. But the politics she awakens to is a conversation in which she cannot speak, in which her words seem empty, and in which her voice counts for nothing. What Henrik Ibsen, Nora Helmer, and Jacques Rancière show us is that it is only in bringing an end to the conversation of democracy—only in moments of disagreement and dissensus that fracture it, in the refusal to accept the terms one is given—that change can take place and that a true conversation of democracy becomes possible once again.

CHAPTER SEVEN

Tragedy's Tragedies

Between the Skeptical and the Ethical

Allow me to begin this chapter by asking the reader to visualize a brief yet disturbing scene. Assuming that you are sitting down while reading this, I ask you to imagine, if you will, that about a dozen paces from your seat you see a young couple—an attractive young woman and a well-built young man. They appear to be in love, they are tender enough with each other, and they are engaged in light conversation. Then, all of a sudden—and it is very sudden—the man pins the woman down and starts throttling her. She struggles. She writhes. She tries to scream. They are only a dozen paces from where you are sitting, and you—do nothing. You do not rush to help her, though you could do so in a matter of seconds. You do not call out for help, nor do you look round to see if there are others who could assist or take out your phone and call the police. She gasps in vain for one last breath, and as the life drains out of her body, you have one final chance to get up and save her. A moment later the young woman lies lifeless, and you have not even stirred in your seat.

Presented with such a scenario, I venture the following predictions:

- that most readers would agree that doing nothing in the face of such events would be morally or ethically reprehensible behavior;
- that at least some readers would agree that if we could prove there was a good and valid reason why we were genuinely unable to help the young woman in question, then we would be at least partially exonerated or exculpated from our otherwise deplorable inaction; and
- that almost all readers would agree that a good and valid reason of this kind would be that the seat we were sitting on was in a theater, that the young couple before us were on the stage, that the young man was an actor playing Othello, and the young woman, an actress playing Desdemona.

If I am right in making these predictions, then surely the most intriguing aspect of Stanley Cavell's lifelong and multifaceted philosophical engagements with the problem of tragedy is that for him the excuse of being in a theater turns out to raise more questions than it settles, and it certainly constitutes no reason whatsoever to release us from our ethical obligations toward the people before us.

If this seems to defy common sense, then we should ask what kind of alibi "common sense" affords us for our moral idleness. After all, why should a small detail like the physical position of our chair (i.e., its being in a theater) be an excuse to do nothing in the face of a scene of suffering? There are a number of reasons that common sense might suggest. Some of them hinge on what it means to go to the theater—we might say things like "Because going to a theatrical performance involves certain conventions"; "Because we are part of an audience"; "Because there is an aesthetic context"—and some reasons hinge on the characters we are watching—"Because they are fictional"; "Because they are play-acting"; "Because they are pretending"—but for Cavell none of these is reason enough for doing nothing whatsoever to help another human being who is in need of help and who is right there in front of us. So a good place to start would be to investigate how and why these excuses turn out, in Cavell's view, to be incoherent and hence to offer no excuse at all.

I

Let us take those becauses seriously. What is it that they are really saying? In order to gain a better understanding of them, Cavell moves from tragedy to comedy and turns our attention to "the usual joke . . . about the Southern yokel who rushes to the stage to save Desdemona from the black man" (*MWM*, p. 327).[1] And yet he asks, "What is the joke? . . . what mistake has the yokel in the theater made?" (*MWM*, pp. 327–28). One way of answering this question, as I have just suggested, is to say that going to a theatrical performance is an activity that involves a set of conventions and that our yokel is in breach of some of those conventions. In this respect, his mistake is analogous to "the man lighting a cigarette in church" or "the visitor who drinks from the finger bowl": that is, he has revealed, to his embarrassment and ours, that "he doesn't know how to behave in a theater" (*MWM*, p. 327). But such an answer is itself question-begging, as Cavell points out: "What is it that we then know? What is a theater? Why are we there?" (*MWM*, p. 327). In other words, appealing to the conventions of the theater cannot give a satisfactory explanation unless we first investigate not only those conventions but also the criteria that make for their conditions of possibility.

One way of doing this might be to accentuate the problem slightly differently, by pointing out that going to the theater is tantamount to becoming a member of an audience, and hence to enter into a community (of sorts) with different conventions for behavior than would ordinarily obtain. So can a justification along the lines of "Because he is part of an audience" explain whether the Southern yokel's intervention makes more or less sense than the rest of the audience's inactivity? Discussing Beckett's drama, Cavell asserts that "the first aesthetic fact about performances is that they have audiences" (*MWM*, p. 156). This is what a Wittgensteinian would call a grammatical remark; it describes the very essence of what we understand dramatic theater to be. So it then behooves Cavell to ask, "What is an audience?" (*MWM*, p. 157). His answer—that "'audience' . . . means 'those present whom the actors ignore,' those beyond the fourth wall" (*MWM*, p. 157)—seems reasonable, in that it partially explains the yokel's mistake: it is in the grammar of Shakespearean tragedy (unlike that of, say, Brechtian modernism) that the spectators remain invisible to the play, that Othello is as oblivious to his audience as his audience is extrinsic to *Othello*. "Deny that wall—that is, recognize those in attendance—and the audience vanishes," says Cavell (*MWM*, p. 157). But it is not only the audience that vanishes in these circumstances; it is Othello and the very play itself too. For supposing the yokel persisted in his mistake, what then?

> You may then have to restrain him and remove him from the theater; you may even have to go so far as to stop the play. *That* is something we can do; and its very extremity shows how little is in our power. For that farthest extremity has not touched Othello, he has vanished; it has merely interrupted an evening's work. Quiet the house, pick up the thread again, and Othello will reappear, as near and as deaf to us as ever. (*MWM*, p. 330)[2]

The problem, put simply and roughly, is something like this: if an audience breaks the conventions for spectatorship, then the play immediately vanishes; therefore its spectators cease to be spectators of a play; therefore they are no longer an audience. From this paraphrase we can see, if not a certain circularity, then at least an incompleteness in this view. It explains why the yokel's mistake has no easy remedy without abrogating our very criteria for dramatic theater, but it does not and cannot explain why paralyzed inactivity in the face of violence and murder is the correct thing. Cavell is all too aware of this:

> How do I know I am to *do* nothing, confronted by such events? The answer, "Because it is an aesthetic context" is no answer, partly because no one knows what an aesthetic context is, partly because, if it means anything, a factor of its meaning is "a context in which I am to do nothing"; which is the trouble. (*MWM*, pp. 318–19)

Here the latent circularity in the problem is made manifest. We can indeed argue that there are conventions involved in attending a theatrical performance and in being part of an audience that preclude intervening to stop the suffering we see before us. But what these explanations explain is *that* we do nothing to help the people of a tragedy, not *why* we do nothing. And if we cannot explain that, then we are morally culpable, because we do not have a good or compelling reason not to save the woman before us, and without it, surely we ought at least to try to help her. We could try to ground the conventions of (or, better, conventions for) theatrical performances and audience membership by saying that there is an "aesthetic context" that suspends or abrogates the conventions for ordinary behavior, but, as Cavell demonstrates in the above quotation, this is a circular argument. However, if the case of the yokel has taught us anything, surely it is that the aesthetic context is precisely what makes all the difference: outside a theater, we would no doubt applaud his actions in attempting to save a young lady from murder; we might feel ethically obliged to join in.[3] And so the appeal to aesthetic context, which might have been expected to explain "how the people comprising the audience are different from those same people when they are not an audience" (*MWM*, p. 157), in fact fails to do so, leaving the central question—"What is an audience?"—still unanswered, and the nature of the mistake our yokel has made unexplained.

At this stage we might "take encouragement from remembering that the audience, as we conceive it, is a fairly recent invention in the history of theater" (*MWM*, p. 157).[4] And indeed, the institution is a slightly strange one: "What are we to make of all those people sitting out there in the dark, watching and listening?" (*MWM*, p. 156). We might more profitably turn Cavell's question around and ask what the people sitting out there in the dark are to make of the people stood illuminated by footlights on the stage. Since investigating the institutions of theater and audience has led us to a dead end, a different attempt at accounting for the yokel's mistake would be to treat him "like a child who screams at Red Riding Hood the truth of her situation" (*MWM*, p. 318). We would then end up saying something like "This is only fictional" or "This is just acting" or "They are only pretending." These three are not quite the same thing, though, and ultimately none of them can fully ground or justify the stark discrepancy between the yokel's intervention and the rest of the audience's passivity. The trouble with answers along these lines is that "somehow we had *accepted* its non-factuality, it made it possible for there to have been a play" (*MWM*, pp. 328–29).

If we responded to the yokel along the lines of saying, "You forget this is theater; that they are characters up there, not persons; that their existence is fictional" (*MWM*, pp. 318–19), the yokel might well respond, as Cavell himself does, "The trouble is, there they are" (*MWM*, p. 331).[5] We might explain to him that "we can no more confront a character in a play than we can confront any fictitious being" (*MWM*, p. 331), and this would be true, but why? To the simplistic answer, "Because their existence is fictional," Cavell responds, "Meaning what? That they are not to be met with in space and time?" (*MWM*, p. 331). The same could be said, he points out, of a variety of things—square roots, God, the correct tempo of the Great Fugue, or the spirit of the age—yet we would hardly call those straightforward fictions. Unlike all of these things, Othello and Desdemona are right before our eyes and plain for us to see. Whereas a novel presents us with characters only visible to our imaginations (or perhaps in illustrations), a theater presents us with visible and physically existing characters. Accordingly, "calling the existence of Lear and others 'fictional' is incoherent (if understandable) when used as an explanation of their existence or as a denial of their existence" (*MWM*, p. 332). Cavell's response to our castigating the yokel with the reminder that *Othello* is "only fiction" can be summarized thus: "The trouble with this objection is its assumption that it is obvious what kind of existence characters in a play have, and obvious what our relation to them is" (*MWM*, p. 331).[6]

Telling our yokel that *Othello* is fiction is not quite the same thing, however, as telling him that what he is seeing is playacting. Is this response any more coherent? Cavell conducts a brief Wittgensteinian dialogue to investigate whether the notion of playacting can explain what kind of a mistake the yokel has made:

> He thinks someone is strangling someone.—But that is true; Othello is strangling Desdemona.—Come on, come on; you know, he thinks that very man is putting out the light of that very woman right now.—Yes, and that is exactly what is happening.— . . . The point is that he thinks something is really happening, whereas nothing is really happening. It's play acting. The woman will rise again to die another night. . . . You tell me that that woman will rise again, but I know that she will not, that she is dead and has died and will again die, die dead, die with a lie on her lips, damned with love. (*MWM*, p. 328)

The idea of playacting is presumably meant to draw attention to the presence of actors instead of characters. Presumably, a competent theatergoer can distinguish between them, whereas the Southern yokel cannot. But if Yeats was right to ask us how we can know the dancer from the dance,[7] then Cavell is just as correct to ask competent theatergoers how they make this differentiation and *what* kind of differentiation they think they are making:

> You can say there are two women, Mrs. Siddons and Desdemona, both of whom are mortal, but only one of whom is dying in front of our eyes. But what you have produced is two names. Not all the pointing in the world to *that* woman will distinguish the one woman from the other. The trouble can be put two ways; or, there are two troubles and they pull opposite ways: you can't point to one without pointing to the other; and you can't point to both at the same time. Which just means that *pointing* here has become an incoherent activity. (*MWM*, p. 328)

We could no more show the yokel the difference between Othello and the actor who plays him than the yokel could prevent Othello from murdering Desdemona, and so Cavell concludes of the notion of playacting "that I really do not understand what I am being asked, and of course I am suggesting that you do not know either" (*MWM*, p. 328). We could, perhaps, in our explanation to the yokel, resort to a looser, weaker sense of the term *playacting* in which it doesn't have to mean an actor playing a part, but something along the lines of "pretending." But this suggestion meets with even shorter shrift: "It is an excuse, whistling in the dark; and it is false. Othello is not pretending. Garrick is not pretending, any more than a puppet in that part would be pretending" (*MWM*, p. 330).[8]

Thus far, then, neither the conventions of the theater, nor membership in an audience, nor the appeal to an aesthetic context, nor the notion of fictionality, playacting, or pretending has been able to tell us what kind of a mistake the yokel has made in trying to save Desdemona from Othello or why remaining passive in the face of murder and death should somehow be the right thing to do. So the main questions persist: "Why do I sit there? And the honest answer has to be: There is nothing I can do. Why not?" (*MWM*, p. 330). If, as Wittgenstein has it, "*essence* is expressed by grammar,"[9] then the yokel's attempt to go up to Othello and stop him from murdering Desdemona is a fundamental error of grammar: "We know we cannot approach him, and not because it is not done but because nothing would count as doing it" (*MWM*, p. 334).

Since, according to Wittgenstein, "grammar tells us what kind of object anything is,"[10] we may well ask, "*What* is the existence of a character on the stage, what kind of (grammatical) entity is this?" (*MWM*, p. 332). The most obvious fact of characters' existence is that they are there, *right* there, before us—we see them, we hear them, and, if a tragedy is to count as a tragedy, we feel for them. "They are in our presence," as Cavell bluntly puts it (*MWM*, p. 332). But at the heart of the grammar of tragedy lies a basic asymmetry: "A character is not, and cannot be, aware of us. Darkened, indoor theatres dramatize the fact that the audience is invisible. . . . We are also inaudible to [characters], and immovable (that is, at a *fixed* distance from them). I will say: We are not in their presence" (*MWM*, p. 332). This grammatical asymmetry is as stark as that highlighted by Moore in his famous paradox. To put it succinctly, "Pain and death [are] in our presence when we [are] not in theirs" (*MWM*, p. 346).

This goes some way toward explaining the yokel's mistake, and it also helps explain why the rest of the audience does nothing; it is the nearest Cavell will give us to a coherent account of these questions. Yet this answer itself raises a further problem: in any other situation that involves terrible pain and death, the fact that "there is nothing we can do" normally exculpates us morally and ethically from inactivity. But tragedy makes ethical and moral claims on us nonetheless, in spite of, and perhaps even *because* of, our complete helplessness in its world of pain and death: "There is nothing and we know there is nothing we can do. Tragedy is meant to make sense of that condition" (*MWM*, p. 330). To put it another way, it is a strange fact of the tragic that while there is nothing that we can do or could do to intervene, we may nevertheless feel that there is something that we *should* do. Clearly, this opens up the moral and ethical dimensions of tragic drama. But before exploring what this aspect of tragedy might be, it is worth investigating first *how* its structure invokes an ethical or moral appeal to us.

II

At the center of Cavell's response to this question lies a philosophical theme that has preoccupied him throughout his long career: the problem of skepticism, and specifically the form of skepticism that seeks to query or to doubt the kinds of knowledge we have of, and hence the kinds of relationships we share with, our fellow human beings. For Cavell, "tragedy is the public form of the life of skepticism with respect to other minds" (*CoR*, p. 478).

In each of the seven Shakespearean tragedies scrutinized in *Disowning Knowledge*, Cavell demonstrates that its hero is, or at any rate can be, "characterized as 'living his or her skepticism,' living some inability to acknowledge, I mean accept, the human conditions of knowing" (*CoR*, p. 454). Thus, Hamlet's procrastinations are in large part due to his need to find reasons to doubt the word of his father's ghost; Leontes's jealousy is bound up with his doubting that his children are his own; Lear and Othello go to extraordinary lengths to undermine their own faith in a love that should be a certainty—and so on for Coriolanus, Macbeth, and Antony and Cleopatra. All of these protagonists are caught up in "living one's skepticism, or living the threat of skepticism" (*DK*, p. 26), and in each case this skepticism is the driving motor of the eventual tragedy.

At the risk of a brief excursus, it is worth reminding ourselves what is meant by *skepticism* here. Cavell's contention is that skepticism is not, or not merely, the calling into question of our knowledge of the world or of other people. The reason skepticism is not as simple as this is that our everyday attitude toward the world and toward the other people in it is not ordinarily one of *knowledge* in the first place: nobody would claim, on an everyday basis, to *know* that the people they interact with possess higher levels of consciousness, or (borrowing the example of Lear) to *know* that their daughters love them, any more than they can *know* that whatever place they find themselves in is not a mirage, a dream, or a hallucination. Hence, when the skeptic seeks to call these things into doubt, it avails neither us nor the skeptic to point toward evidence, because for the skeptic the evidence is inevitably incomplete. What differentiates the skeptic from us is not that he doubts something that we know, because the skeptic would claim that we *don't* know it, which suggests that what the skeptic is after is not *knowing* in the sense that *knowledge* is ordinarily conceived. Rather, the difference between the skeptic and us is that we are prepared to *acknowledge* what we know (of other people, of the world itself) *as* knowledge, whereas the skeptic is *forgoing* or *avoiding* that knowledge.[11]

Othello is in this sense the perfect image of the skeptic: according to Cavell's reading, Othello knows that Desdemona loves him and that she is true and faithful to him. But that kind of knowledge is not enough for him; in short, he is forgoing and avoiding his knowledge of Desdemona's love, which is as much as to say that he is forgoing and avoiding her love altogether. There is no shortage of people in the play who assure and reassure him of her love and constancy, but that is not the kind of knowledge Othello is after. He declares, "I'll have some proof" (3.3.392), but this is utterly fruitless, because a skeptic, even when confronted with proof, will merely ask something like, "What proof is there that the proof is proof?"—just as Leontes can bring himself even to doubt the divine word of an oracle. This is because the status of knowledge, proof, and certainty is precisely what skeptics like Othello and Leontes are in flight from. The same can be said of Hamlet's elaborate staging of a play within a play to "prove" that Claudius killed his father and that the ghost he has seen is not the devil tricking him into committing murder. The same can also be said of Lear's need to hear his daughters publicly declare their love for him, and in particular his refusal to acknowledge the love his daughter Cordelia bears him even in the absence of such a declaration. In all these tragic heroes' cases, then, there is "a refusal expressed as a failure to acknowledge. (That this is a refusal, something each character is doing and is going on doing, is what makes these events add up to tragedy . . .)" (*MWM*, p. 313).[12]

This refusal is essentially an unwillingness to acknowledge the truth of what is already known; in this sense the skeptic and the tragic hero doom themselves to failure. Their resulting frustration manifests itself not as a frustration with themselves—perhaps as an exasperation with their own "inner skeptic"—but as a frustration with their loved ones for failing to yield them the kind of certainty they yearn for. This frustration is what drives them to distraction and destruction; it is, as I put it earlier, the motor that drives their tragedy ever onward: "For example, Lear's 'avoidance' of Cordelia is an instance of the annihilation inherent in the skeptical problematic, that skepticism's 'doubt' is motivated not by (not even where it is expressed as) a (misguided) intellectual scrupulousness but by a (displaced) denial, by a self-consuming disappointment that seeks world-consuming revenge" (*DK*, p. 6).

Similarly, Othello chooses to murder Desdemona because his knowledge of her cannot live up to the impossible standards he sets for it, and much the same could be said of Leontes and other Shakespearean tragic heroes. But this is only part of what Cavell means by the tragic avoidance of knowledge. There are also tragedies in which this avoidance is to be found not only in avoiding knowledge of others but also in avoiding being known by them. Once again, *King Lear* is a good example. In it, Edgar refuses to make his true identity known to his blinded father until it is (tragically) too late. Hence, "the tragedy begins because of—the same motivation which manipulates the tragedy throughout its course . . . to the final moments: by the attempt to avoid recognition, the shame of exposure, the threat of self-revelation" (*MWM*, p. 286). So, in summary, both these tendencies of tragedy—the kind that consists in refusing knowledge of the other and the kind that consists in refusing to be known by the other—lead Cavell to conclude that "acknowledgment is to be studied, is what is studied, in the avoidance that tragedy studies" (*CoR*, p. 389). What this means is that Cavell is "taking tragedy as an epistemological problem, a refusal to know or to be known, an avoidance of acknowledgment, an expression (or imitation) of skepticism" (*TOS*, pp. 60–61).

In order to complete this excursus on how Cavell views the deep-seated relationship between tragedy and skepticism, it is worth rounding off the topic with Cavell's observation that "not only [is] tragedy obedient to a skeptical structure but contrariwise, that skepticism already [bears] its own marks of a tragic structure" (*DK*, p. 5). Skepticism can be thought of as the tragedy of knowledge, or as the tragedy to which knowledge falls victim. This is not a statement about the branch of academic philosophy known as skepticism; it is a claim about a stance we might all be tempted to take toward the world and the other people in it, in our everyday lives, at any time. In other words, the claim "that skepticism is the playing out of a tragedy" is simultaneously the claim "that accordingly our ordinary lives partake of tragedy in partaking of skepticism" (*IQO*, pp. 8–9). This is one of the ways, and perhaps the most elemental way, in which we are brought to identify with the characters on stage in a tragedy: Othello, Hamlet, Lear, Leontes, and their like are enacting before us a human possibility that is potentially open to all of us. Their choosing to forgo their everyday knowledge and their refusal of belief in those around them is a path that is potentially open for anyone and everyone to take. And so it is for *us* as well as for them that "tragedy is the working out of a response to skepticism," or to be more precise, "that tragedy is an interpretation of what skepticism is itself an interpretation of" (*DK*, pp. 5–6).

This is a good point at which to turn from questions of skepticism and acknowledgment toward the question I set out at the end of the previous section, namely, how does tragedy establish an ethical and moral appeal that involves its audience? If, as Cavell suggests, tragedy depicts characters who are living out their skepticism before us, and their dramas therefore play out the threat of skepticism for us, then one answer might be that confronting, and being confronted by, the living out of skepticism teaches us how to live our lives ethically. This is indeed a good start, but it is only a start, because there is surely more to the structure of tragedy than bare-faced didacticism, or else it would not be tragic.

Tragedy dramatizes the possibility of skepticism as a possibility that can befall each and every one of us. To the extent of that possibility, a tragic hero is acting out *our* plight as well as his own. In order to investigate exactly what this assertion entails, Cavell embarks upon another of his Wittgensteinian dialogues, which is worth quoting at some length:

> You do not claim, I believe, to go around every day in roughly Othello's frame of mind?—Not exactly. But I claim to see how his life figures mine, how mine has the makings of his, that we bear an internal relation to one another; how my happiness depends upon living touched but not struck by his problems, or struck but not stricken; . . . —If so, isn't this something just about you and about him?—If so, then either *Othello* is no tragedy or I have not seen what it is. I do not claim to have *explained* how one human being's life (fictional or actual) can be representative of human life generally, which would perhaps come to explaining the idea that a human being is something that bears an internal relation to all other human beings, that they are mutually attuned, that they are species-beings. I do claim, for example, that Othello is thus representative, and that to understand that (literary) fact would be the same as to understand what the (philosophical) problem of others is (*CoR*, p. 453)

At this point it becomes clearer how Cavell's literary reflections on the nature and structure of tragedy join hands with his concerns in moral philosophy and ethics. The connection between them is rooted in the same question that was raised by the Southern yokel's intervention at the climax of *Othello*, so that asking "What is the mechanism of our identification with a character?" (*MWM*, p. 334) becomes a way of exploring how we identify with our fellow human beings both inside and outside the theater and how this encounter with others is at root a moral or an ethical moment.

From this point of view, the yokel's attempt to save Desdemona might well appear more morally sound than the rest of the audience's leaving her to her fate. If we add to this perspective the fact that the members of the audience (presumably) *enjoy* watching Desdemona being murdered, that they have chosen and even paid to do so and might well praise the murder scene afterwards, then it isn't hard to see that the spectator at a tragedy takes up a morally questionable position. How is it that witnessing Othello's loss of reason and Desdemona's death could bring us *pleasure*? And to complicate matters further, why is it that certain kinds of pleasure—say, voyeurism, schadenfreude, or just the relief that all this mayhem is happening to some other poor sucker instead of me—would strike us as deeply *un*ethical? This must surely mean that there is a kind of pleasure we can take from being spectators of tragic events that is, in spite of everything, ethically sound.

The trouble with the pleasures of voyeurism, schadenfreude, and so forth, is that they are "irresponsible," in the sense that they do not acknowledge that taking pleasure in the events of a tragedy means that we are implicated ethically in those events. This in turn means that we must take responsibility for what is happening before us: "We are implicated in the failures we are witnessing, we share the responsibility for tragedy" (*MWM*, p. 282). This is not to claim that Othello's mad jealousy is somehow "my fault"; it is to claim that since I watched his mad jealousy unfold, even enjoyed watching it unfold, and yet did nothing (and, as we established earlier, *could* do nothing) to stop it, I am answerable for having taken up, or put myself in, such a morally uncomfortable position. Being part of a tragic audience means that I am to acknowledge this condition, and to acknowledge that it is up to me to do so: "A performance is nothing without our participation in an audience; and this participation is up to each of us" (*TOS*, p. 87). That is what is meant by taking responsibility for the tragic: it involves the necessity of taking an ethical and moral stance in my behavior toward others.

III

As Espen Hammer points out, Cavell's philosophical engagements with questions of morals and ethics can be divided into three distinctive phases that nevertheless share many overlapping concerns and features.[13] Firstly, there are his attempts to establish a dialogue between ordinary language philosophy in the Austinian tradition and questions of moral philosophy, best exemplified by the third part of *The Claim of Reason*. In addition, Cavell's interest in nineteenth-century American thought, specifically in Emerson and Thoreau, leads him to formulate a vision of what he calls Emersonian moral perfectionism, elucidated in *Conditions Handsome and Unhandsome* and elsewhere. And most recently, Cavell has turned to the influential ethical philosophy of Emmanuel Levinas to investigate similarities, differences, and affinities in their thinking.[14] While there are connecting threads linking all of these endeavors, it is with this third, Levinasian strand of Cavell's thought that his work on tragedy can most profitably be compared, and not simply because Levinas has been more central to debates on the ethical dimensions of literature than Austin or Emerson, but because his writings, and Cavell's engagements with them, share with the Cavellian view of tragedy an emphasis on our responsibility toward others.

There is neither the time nor the space here to plot the coordinates of Levinas's compelling philosophy of alterity to anything like its full extent, but at its heart lies an ethical obligation or responsibility that is placed upon us whenever we encounter the face of the Other.[15] This encounter amounts to an ethical appeal to me that "summons me to my obligations and judges me."[16] If I fail to take up this obligation, then I cannot be said truly to encounter the Other, and in thus refusing my responsibility I fail to recognize or to meet the face of the Other as such. A very similar pattern of thought can be detected in what Cavell calls acknowledging the other. Like Levinas's notion of meeting the face, this is not, or not merely, an empirical encounter, nor is it something we can simply decide to do or not to do, on pain of acting "in bad faith." Both Cavell's acknowledging of the other and Levinas's responding to the face of the Other take place on a level that is prior to and even helps ground our own selfhood or subjectivity. Moreover, for both philosophers, to fail in our responsibilities here is directly to do violence to the other. Levinas claims that "to see a face is already to hear: 'Thou shalt not kill,'" because "the principle 'you shall not commit murder'" is "the very signifyingness of the face."[17] Even the violation of this principle cannot destroy or negate the ethical claims of the face, because to take violent aim at the face of the Other with intent to murder it is either to recognize the fact of its presence and its claims or else to miss the face *qua* face altogether.

Cavell's version of this philosophy—his notion of acknowledgment—is described in intriguingly similar terms:

> Whether or not we acknowledge others is not a matter of choice, any more than accepting the presence of the world is a matter of choosing to see or not to see it. Some persons sometimes are capable of certain blindnesses or deafnesses toward others; but . . . avoidance of the presence of others is not blindness or deafness to their claim upon us; it is as conclusive as an acknowledgment that they are present as murdering them would be. (*MWM*, p. 332)

More intriguingly still, Cavell cites the example of watching characters on stage in a tragedy as a particularly revealing example of acknowledgment, because for tragedy to be tragedy, it requires a strong identification with its characters, which entails "not simply that we are seeing and hearing them, but that we are acknowledging them (or specifically failing to)" (*MWM*, p. 332). And if we withhold our acknowledgment, then "tragedy shows us that we are responsible for the death of others even when we have not murdered them, and even when we have not manslaughtered them innocently" (*MWM*, p. 332). A pattern of thought unfolds here that at first blush is nearly identical with Levinas's notion of the appeal of the face, calling me to my responsibility for the Other with its message "Thou shalt not kill." And, crucially, it is the genre of tragedy—specifically, in the acknowledgment of the characters on stage—that highlights the remarkably similar way that Cavell conceives the brutal violence behind failing to respond to the claim of the other:

> Tragedy is the place we are not allowed to escape the consequences, or price, of this cover: that the failure to acknowledge a best case of the other is a denial of that other, presaging the death of the other, say by stoning, or by hanging; and the death of our capacity to acknowledge as such, the turning of our hearts to stone, or their bursting. (*CoR*, p. 493)

For Levinas too, the withholding of our responsibility toward the Other amounts not merely to an attempt to destroy the Other but also to a form of *self*-destruction. As Jill Robbins has it, "The murderer who takes violent aim at the face of the other does not truly *face* the other. He thus loses not only the face of the other but also his own face."[18]

Taken collectively, these tantalizing comparisons would seem to add up to an extraordinarily close family resemblance between Levinas's thought and Cavell's, amounting to an almost perfect coincidence of their philosophical positions in the sphere of ethics. There are, however, crucial differences of emphasis within a remarkably similar orientation, and it is worth stressing them in order that the contrast might delineate each position more sharply. These differences are best encapsulated in the divergent ways these two philosophers respond to the same philosophical text. Remarkably, both Levinas and Cavell set great store by a passage from Descartes's Third Meditation, reading it as a key text in conceptualizing our relationship to the other. As Cavell observes, "The coincidence is striking—I know of no other use of Descartes in this connection. So it is of inevitable interest, not to say concern, for me that I evidently had there derived something like an opposite conclusion, or moral, from the passage in Descartes . . . from the conclusion that Levinas draws" (*PDAT*, p. 145).

The passage in question is Descartes's celebrated proof of the existence of God, which he derives from the fact that he finds within himself the idea of the infinite, that is, God. Descartes argues that a finite being such as himself could not have formulated or fabricated this idea, so it must therefore have been put there by the infinite being that is God, which in turn, for Descartes, proves God's existence. For Levinas, what it proves is that there is an infinite otherness beyond me: it establishes an alterity and, with it, my infinite responsibility toward the Other, thus setting up the foundation of Levinas's ethical philosophy. According to Levinas, this ethical relationship with otherness is more important than the proof of ontological existence derived by Descartes, because as Levinas sees it, ethics, and not ontology, is first philosophy.

Intriguingly, Cavell turns to exactly the same passage in Descartes in order to introduce his interpretation of the nature of tragedy in *Othello*. In doing so, he explicitly seeks to "understand how the other now bears the weight of God, shows me that I am not alone in the universe" (*CoR*, p. 482), an undertaking remarkably close to that of Levinas. But here, for Cavell it is clearly the *other* who establishes and grounds the ethical relationship, and *not* the infinite (or God). Suspicious of Levinas's need to resort to a religious mode of thought in delineating the infinite Other and the ethical claims it makes, Cavell asks, "Why is the existence of a finite other not sufficient to create the reality of such claims upon me?" (*PDAT*, p. 144).[19] It is precisely this relationship with a *finite* other that Cavell locates at the ethical heart of Shakespearean tragedy:

> Levinas's idea is that my openness to the other . . . requires a violence associated with the infinite having been put into me. . . . Now when I say, in response to Descartes's Third Meditation proof, that in Shakespearean tragedy (immediately in connection with *Othello*) this traumatic effect of the recognition of the existence of God is replaced by the idea of a finite other, violence and some sense of an infinite nevertheless remain. But in originating now in the face of a finite other, violence and infinitude cannot be thought to arise from a comparison of myself with the other but from a recognition that this particular other, this creature among all the creatures of the earth similar to me, is also, or rather is therefore, absolutely different, separate from me, I would say, wholly other, endlessly other, the one I single out before whom I am I, eternally singled out. It is the unbearable certainty of this separation to which the torture of skepticism over Desdemona's faithfulness is preferable. . . . I think comparably, beyond Othello in relation to his idea of his bride, of Macbeth in relation to his idea of his wife, of Hamlet in relation to his idea of his mother, of Leontes in relation to his idea of his newborn daughter. The extravagant intimacy at stake in these relations suggests that the "proof" of the other's existence is a problem not of establishing connection with the other, but of achieving, or suffering, separation from the other, individuation with respect to the one upon whom my nature is staked. (*PDAT*, pp. 145–66)

Where Levinas's interpretation of Descartes sees the trace of the infinite Other in the human face, establishing my obligation toward it, Cavell sees the fact of otherness as establishing the fact of my insurmountable separation from the other. If for Levinas the presence of alterity offers the possibility of ethical communion with the Other, for Cavell it torments us with the impossibility of a pure communion, even with those closest to us. Both would concur that my relationship with the other places an ethical claim upon me that calls me to my responsibility. But according to Cavell, the passage in Descartes suggests, not that I bear an overriding infinite responsibility for the other, but that I bear an overriding "infinite responsibility for myself" (*PDAT*, p. 144).

This may sound like narcissism, but it is in fact its antidote. Othello, whom Cavell describes as "the obvious narcissist among Shakespeare's tragic heroes" (*PDAT*, p. 147), is brought to his tragedy precisely because of this failure to acknowledge his responsibility for himself. To simplify Cavell's celebrated interpretation of the play in *The Claim of Reason*, Othello murders Desdemona because the deep love that he has for her, and she for him, establishes her as a being separate from him—his other, whose relationship to him is that of Descartes's God—and this further establishes his emotional dependence on her. He would rather reject this love and murder the other than acknowledge his own incompleteness, which he sees as inadequacy. Levinas is quite right that he has a responsibility to her as the other. This goes without saying: she is his wife. But because "Husband and wife is one flesh" (*Hamlet* 4.3.54), this otherness is precisely what arouses his jealousy; he is not content with the fact of her otherness, because the skeptic in him perceives it as implying his incompleteness. It is only by taking responsibility for *himself* first and foremost, and by acknowledging himself as himself, as who he is, that he can begin to acknowledge Desdemona (and the other in general) aright. Viewed this way, taking responsibility for himself does not imply narcissism or egocentrism but is rather a precondition of the responsibility for the other we call altruism. Conversely, narcissism and its failure to acknowledge the other are precisely what is at stake in the issue of skepticism.[20]

This is an exemplary case of how tragedy dramatizes what skepticism actualizes, and equally of how skepticism builds a royal road straight to tragedy. The structure that is common to both is bound up with doing violence to the other: "Both skepticism and tragedy conclude with the condition of human separation, with a discovering that I am I; and the fact that the alternative to my acknowledgment of the other is not my ignorance of him but my avoidance of him, call it my denial of him" (*CoR*, p. 389). But if the fact of human separation—the fact that I am not and never can be as one with the other—can lead straight to the risk of skepticism and of tragedy, then, as the next section demonstrates, this is a clear and serious threat to the members of the audience at a performance of a tragedy, since they are characterized precisely by their separateness, both from the characters on stage and from their fellow audience members. "Join hands here as we may," says Cavell, "one of the hands is mine and the other yours" (*MWM*, p. 340). And this separation in turn opens up a new dimension to the moral and ethical claims that are placed on us as we participate in the audience of tragedy.

IV

To address this issue is to revisit one of the first questions addressed in this chapter, namely, "What is an audience?" Because "the first task of the dramatist is to gather us and then to silence and immobilize us" (*MWM*, p. 326), to be an audience member in a theater is to adopt a near-Levinasian position of passivity in the face of the Other. This passivity arises from the absolute gulf that lies between me in my seat and Othello on the stage, and from the impossibility of ever bridging that gap. I am therefore obliged, firstly, to recognize or *acknowledge* the separateness of the characters on the stage from me in my seat. This acknowledgment brings with it, not a reciprocity, but instead a moment of *self*-acknowledgment that Michael Fischer explains thus: "I cannot acknowledge their separateness without accepting my own; I cannot coherently declare that they are there without revealing that I am here."[21] But this creates a problem. It is one thing to say, as Cavell does, that "if one is to acknowledge another as one's neighbor, one must acknowledge oneself as his or her neighbor" (*CoR*, p. 434), but quite another to practice this acknowledgment in a theater, where I cannot make myself Othello's neighbor, even though he is physically close enough and has an ethical claim on me that a neighbor might. As Stephen Mulhall explains,

> This suggests a complex relationship between acknowledgement inside and outside the theatre. In a theatre, it is not possible for us to go up to the people who require acknowledgement from us; we can neither declare our presence to them nor hide it, as we must outside the theatre. We might express this difference by saying that, in the theatre, our hiddenness, silence, and isolation are enforced—they are its conditions. But then these conditions can be thought of as literalizing the conditions we enact and exact outside the theatre, the conditions that we so often enforce on ourselves and upon others; so that a failure of acknowledgement outside the theatre can be thought of as a theatricalization of others—leaving ourselves in darkness, converting them into characters on a stage, fictionalizing their existence.[22]

A reasonable response here might be to ask how, if tragic theater *enforces*, or imposes, the conditions of avoidance on its audience, that audience could ever *choose* to acknowledge the characters on stage in the tragedy? That is, how could the audience choose *not* to avoid them if the theater imposes the condition of avoidance upon its audience? Or, better, what is the difference between the *enforced* avoidance imposed by the distance between the darkened auditorium and the illuminated stage and the *chosen* avoidance that each audience member may opt for in letting the tragedies of Othello, Hamlet, Macbeth, Leontes, or Coriolanus pass by before them as they sit unmoved and uninvolved in their seats?

There is something of an ambiguity in Cavell's position here. As Michael Fischer argues, "Avoiding a play presupposes our being able to acknowledge it,"[23] but equally, Mulhall is no less right to point out that since theater prevents us from being present to the characters, it models for us the *failure* of acknowledgment and indeed derives much of its ethical impact from exposing us to failure of this kind: "The conditions of theatre literalize the conditions we create by succumbing to scepticism outside the theatre, and so make the nature of the rest of our existence plain—make it available for us to acknowledge."[24]

One way of resolving this ambiguity might be to claim that theater creates the discrepancy between enforced avoidance (imposed by the theater) and chosen avoidance (for which individual audience members may opt) in order to show us that outside the theater we are free to choose *not* to avoid our fellow men and free to acknowledge them instead. Thus, the enforced avoidance imposed by the theater shows me that I have the power to overcome skepticism and avoidance by choosing to acknowledge the claim of the other (or others) before me on the stage. Conversely, if I choose to avoid a tragedy—if I decide to remain impervious to the plight of the characters and unmoved by the ethical force of the tragic—then I am likely to find it irksome that the conditions of theatrical space have rendered me powerless and immobile before a spectacle that I find unengaging. (Shifting in my seat, whispering my discontent to a neighbor, heckling out loud, or walking out and going home could be seen as ways of choosing to avoid theater's enforced avoidance.)

In this picture of avoidance and its overcoming, the skepticism that tragedy warns us against is the failure to acknowledge our fellow human beings and their claims on us. But there is also a different, perhaps less obvious avoidance that tragedy entails. Cavell defines the skepticism at the heart of tragedy as "a refusal to know *or to be known*" (*TOS*, p. 60, my emphasis), just as Edgar chooses to avoid making himself known to his father in *King Lear*. The enforced avoidance imposed by the theater, whereby I *cannot* make myself known to Othello any more than I can make Edgar known to Gloucester, removes from me the very condition of possibility of making myself known to the other and thus exhibits what the tragedy of skepticism is when I avoid allowing the other a knowledge of me. Cavell describes the epistemological tragedy of this kind of avoidance thus: "My existence is proven, but at the price of not knowing what it is in itself. And the existence of others is proven, but at the price of their being spectators of my existence, not participants in it" (*CoR*, p. 477). It is this sense of participation that is key to the ethical import of tragedy.

In summary, then, the avoidances highlighted by tragedy are of manifold and various kinds. On the one hand, the enforced avoidance the theater imposes on the members of its audience also dramatizes for them the consequences of the avoidance of *being known by* the other; that is, in making us invisible to Othello, the theater shows us the tragedy of refusing others the knowledge of us and of refusing their participation in our lives. On the other hand, the avoidance of our participation in Othello's situation, the making his plight ours, is clearly a different kind of avoidance: it is the avoidance of *knowing* the other. This kind of avoidance is *not* imposed or enforced by the theater; if it were, Othello would surely have to be as invisible to us as we are to him. Instead, this kind of avoidance demonstrates for us the possibility of overcoming it by acknowledging and participating in Othello's tragic life and also demonstrates that it is up to us to take responsibility for doing so. Both these kinds of avoidance make clear to us, in their different ways, that, to use Fischer's apt phrase, "in tragedy we are forced to confront the consequences of our evasions."[25]

Aligning the various kinds of avoidance—enforced and chosen avoidance, avoidance of knowing and of being known—in these ways has the advantage of illustrating how the conditions and conventions of the theater give us a near-perfect mirror image of avoidance outside the theater. Inside the theater, the possibility of making ourselves known to the other is removed from us entirely; outside the theater, it is wholly our responsibility. Inside the theater, the possibility of knowing the other is wholly our responsibility; outside the theater, it can be removed from us by the other's avoidance of being known. But this answer, morally satisfying though it may be, is slightly suspect, because Cavell clearly demonstrates that acknowledging and avoiding are not ordinarily things we *choose* to do and that Shakespearean tragedies demonstrate how skepticism is something that befalls us rather than a choice we opt for.

In comparing Cavell with Levinas, we have already seen that "whether or not we acknowledge others is not a matter of choice" (*MWM*, p. 332), any more than seeing the face of the Other is for Levinas. What is more, Cavell is equally explicit that the condition of separation from a tragedy's characters is not an obstacle the theater places in the way of our acknowledging them, "as if," he writes, "we felt *prevented* from approaching the figures to whom we respond. But we are not prevented; we merely in fact, or in convention, do not" (*MWM*, p. 334). What this means is clear: the distinction I have set up between the "enforced" avoidance imposed by the theater and the "chosen" avoidance for which each member of the audience is responsible is in fact untenable. Equally untenable, therefore, is deriving from this distinction the difference between acknowledgment in the theater and in the outside world:

> But doesn't the fact that we do not or cannot go up to [the characters] just mean that we do not or cannot acknowledge them? One may feel like saying here: The acknowledgment cannot be *completed*. But this does not mean that acknowledging is impossible in a theater. Rather it shows what acknowledging, in a theater, is. And acknowledging in a theater shows what acknowledgment in actuality is. For what is the difference between tragedy in a theater and tragedy in actuality? In both, people in pain are in our presence. But in actuality acknowledgment *is* incomplete, in actuality there is no acknowledgment, unless we put ourselves in their presence, reveal ourselves to them. (*MWM*, pp. 332–33)

What this seems to suggest is that there is no essential difference, not even a sustainable grammatical difference (taking *grammar* in the Wittgensteinian sense) between acknowledgment in theater and acknowledgment in actuality. Another good example is the following passage—and indeed these two passages are only two of several—in which Cavell begins by outlining the special circumstances that obtain in a theater, only to end up arguing that the theater is in some crucial way no different from the world outside it:

> Kant tells us that man lives in two worlds, in one of which he is free and in the other determined. It is as if in a theater these two worlds are faced off against one another, in their intimacy and their mutual inaccessibility. The audience is free—of the circumstance and passion of the characters, but that freedom cannot reach the arena in which it could become effective. The actors are determined—not because their words and actions are dictated and their future sealed, but because, if the dramatist has really peopled a world, his characters are exercising all the freedom at their command, and specifically failing to. . . . They are, in a word, men; and our liabilities in responding to them are nothing other than our liabilities in responding to any man. (*MWM*, p. 317)

It is at this point, if not perhaps before it, that the relationship between tragedy and acknowledgment is apt to appear problematic. If Othello is indeed a man like any other man, then we have effectively vindicated the Southern yokel. A hostile reader of Cavell, or even a casual one, could well object that he seems to argue that there is no substantial ethical difference between acknowledgment inside and outside the theater *and* that such a difference is what his philosophy of tragedy is predicated on, or else the Southern yokel would surely have been in the right. Cavell thus appears, if not quite to contradict himself, at least to want to have his cake and eat it. Accordingly, it is not hard to see how a casual or a critical reader might all too easily misunderstand Cavell here, nor how such misunderstandings might all too easily turn the former kind of reader into the latter.

Such a criticism contains an amount of truth, and more, I think, than just a grain. The root of the problem, I suspect, is what Richard P. Wheeler has diagnosed as a "tension in Cavell's writing between a tendency to see acknowledgment and its failure as the positive and negative poles of a binary opposition and his more technical claim that the failure to acknowledge is one form that acknowledgement can take."[26] Thus, both the path of avoidance, leading to skepticism and to tragedy, and the alternative path of acknowledgment are apt to appear *both* as a choice we each can opt for in our own lives *and* as predicaments that deprive us of our ability to choose, whether for better or for worse. Similarly, as we have just seen, avoidance in the theater can appear both as something the theater imposes and as something each individual audience member chooses. There is at the very least an ambiguity here that ought to be resolved.

The issue of choice (or the lack of it) needs to be highlighted in this way because it is central to so many traditional philosophies of ethics. Cavellian philosophy argues that ordinarily—that is, outside a theater—skepticism and its avoidance of the other is not a choice I would opt for but a threat to which I might succumb. Similarly, inside a theater, I cannot choose to intervene in Othello's and Desdemona's affairs even if I want to, yet nor would we straightforwardly say that I can just choose to ignore or avoid them. If all this is so, it is hard to see how the lesson or the moral of a tragedy could be that once the drama is over and I leave the theater, I must now *choose* to acknowledge the claims of the other and *choose* to cease avoiding them. Yet this appears to be what Cavell claims: "At the close . . . we are cast into the arena of action again. . . . Because the actors have stopped, we are freed to act again, but also compelled to. Our hiddenness, our silence, and our placement are now our choices" (*MWM*, p. 343).

The plus side of this claim is that it gives tragedy a clear ethical, moral, and didactic purpose: tragedy can teach us how to be better people outside the theater. As Espen Hammer summarizes Cavell,

> The conditions of the theater *literalize*, make plain, the hiddenness, silence, and isolation which mark our everyday existence outside the theater. But by taking account of our theatricalizing, theater presents us with an arena within which this fact may be acknowledged. Thus, the theater, by individuating us through its address, exposes us to our own repressions; it puts our self-possession at stake; it unpacks us. And as such, theater may help us, as human beings or as citizens, to stop choosing silence and hiddenness, that is, to see that theatricality must be defeated. By potentially redeeming us from some species of mental bondage, it has, like psychoanalysis or ordinary language philosophy, a therapeutic function. Hence Cavell's ontology of Shakespearean theater might be regarded as an early version of his theory of redemptive reading.[27]

Unfortunately, though, Cavell elsewhere makes it quite clear that "choosing silence and hiddenness" is not in fact a matter of *choosing* at all. I can no more choose whether the tragedy of skepticism will envelop me outside of the theater than I can choose to save Desdemona inside it: neither issue is amenable to solutions based on decision, volition, agency, or choice.

It could no doubt be claimed in Cavell's defense here that I am confusing two branches of philosophy, or rather, that I am conflating two aspects of his thought. The claim would be that avoidance and acknowledgment are matters that pertain to the sphere of epistemology, while the choice to act or not to act is a matter that pertains to ethics. But this would be empty casuistry. That this distinction is porous at best in Cavell's thought can be seen from Michael Fischer's clear and succinct description of the audience's situation in Cavell's philosophy of tragedy: "By not making ourselves present to other people, we theatricalize them, turning their lives into a spectacle and their world into a stage that we (only) view. The physical conditions of the theater thus highlight the hiddenness, isolation, inaction, and silence we can cultivate outside when we watch people instead of taking part in their lives."[28] This summary illustrates that tragic theater is so congenial to Cavell's thought precisely because it offers at least a metaphor, if not an empirical case, of how ethics and epistemology are completely intertwined when it comes to acknowledging the claims of the other. If, as comparing Cavell with Levinas seems to suggest, acknowledging this claim is not simply a choice I can make, that is not because it is a matter for epistemology rather than for ethics, but rather because acknowledgment of the other and of myself is something that comes before, and even helps to ground, the subjectivity of the "I" that knows things (in epistemology) or that chooses things (in ethics).

Does this mean that the Cavellian view of the ethical import of tragedy is incoherent? Not exactly, though it seems at times positively to court such a charge. In fact, distinguishing between ethics and epistemology in the way I have just criticized holds out a clue, but it is only a small clue. The clue is that it is one thing for theater to show us the ramifications of crises in acknowledgment and avoidance, and another thing for it to show us the ramifications of crises in agency and freedom. In the Hegelian view of tragedy, as I put it in the earlier discussion of Ibsen, we are caught between two moral positions, both equally justified yet each overlooking the no less valid claims of the other. Whereas in the (somewhat) Kantian view outlined by Cavell above (see the citation from *MWM*, p. 317), we are caught between two *freedoms*: the audience is free from the constraints and circumstances of tragedy that envelop the characters on the stage but cannot help those characters, while the characters are as free as any other human beings outside the theater are, that is, utterly enveloped by the tragedy of constraints and circumstances, just as *we* are, each and every one of us, when we are not part of an audience in a theater. If Cavell is right that tragedy shows us "*why* we (as audience) are helpless" (*MWM*, p. 346), it does so not by highlighting the fact that we are prisoners of the choices we make and are in principle free to make others. It shows us, rather, that there are no choices ethically available to us unless and until we have first acknowledged that ethical freedom and ethical choices have their limits and that, even when those ethical limits are reached and exceeded, we are still responsible for our actions or inactions toward the other nonetheless.

What, then, becomes of the choice that Cavell suggests is made available to us once we exit the theater after a performance of a tragedy? It is not exactly a chimera nor yet a red herring. Tragedy can indeed "make us practical, capable of acting," but only "by showing us the natural limitations of acting" (*MWM*, p. 347). These limitations are precisely what are shown in the skepticism and avoidance that tragedy exhibits, both in the characters on stage and in the audience seated in the theater: "It is the nature of this tragedy that its actors have to confirm their separateness alone, through isolation, the denial of others. What is purged is my difference from others, in everything but separateness" (*MWM*, p. 338). My separateness and isolation are precisely the limitations on the choices I am free to make. In summary, then, to be a member of an audience of tragedy is to be placed in a position that is stranded between the skeptical and the ethical.

V

In the previous section, certain questions arose about the overall coherence of Cavell's complex and multifaceted engagement with the theme of tragedy. Part of the problem, at least to readers used to dealing with more traditional philosophy, is that Cavell moves from questions of ontology (i.e., what kind of being is a character in a tragedy? what kind of existence do characters on a stage have? why can't the Southern yokel challenge Othello?) to questions of epistemology (i.e., what is the role of knowledge and its avoidance in tragedy? how and why do its characters succumb to skepticism? what are the implications of these questions for the audience?) to questions of ethics (i.e., why is it felt to be a problem that tragedy condemns me to do nothing in the face of the other's suffering? what can tragedy teach me about acknowledging the other? what is the ethical import of tragedy?). It may be asking a lot of the traditional philosopher to take all these issues as interrelated and to explore how they might hang together. Yet equally, it may be asking rather more of a member of an audience at a compelling production of *Othello* to hold them apart, in intellectual and emotional separation from one another.

In this section I hope to demonstrate how the ontological, epistemological, and ethical aspects of tragedy all meet and intertwine in one crucial yet underappreciated facet of Cavell's writings on the tragic. His claim that "in failing to see what the true position of a character is, in a given moment, we are exactly put in his condition, and thereby implicated in the tragedy" (*MWM*, p. 313) may be apt to confuse if taken as a statement simultaneously about the status of fictional characters, the ethical situation of the audience, and the nature of tragedy itself. But these issues might come to seem inseparable if we explore them through the one part of this quotation that is ignored in this potted summary: "in a given moment." The role of time in Cavell's account of tragedy is so central to it that a correct understanding of that account and its manifold implications cannot be grasped without investigating the temporality—or, better, temporalities—of tragedy.

What is this "given moment"? What is the time of tragedy? Firstly, it is the closest Cavell comes to establishing a foundation for "the mechanism of our identification with a character" (*MWM*, p. 334). Summarizing why it is that the Southern yokel's attempt to challenge Othello is inherently futile, Cavell says: "We know we cannot approach [Othello and Desdemona] . . . because . . . they and we do not occupy the same space; there is no path from my location to his. . . . We do, however, occupy the same *time*" (*MWM*, p. 334, my emphasis).

Time therefore underpins the audience's experience of tragedy, and Cavell goes on to claim that it underpins the very nature of tragedy itself:

> And the time is always now; time is measured solely by what is now happening to [the characters on stage], for what they are doing now is all that is happening. The time is of course not necessarily *the* present—that is up to the playwright. But the time presented, whether the present or the past, is this moment, at which an arrival is awaited, in which a decision is made or left unmade, at which the past erupts into the present, in which reason or emotion fail. . . . The novel also comprises these moments, but only as having happened. (*MWM*, p. 334)

And so tragedy, unlike narrative fiction, presents us with things that are happening *right now*, before our eyes. Tragedy is *immediate*—both in the sense that it happens in this instant and in the sense that this instant is right before our eyes, populated by people physically in front of us, whose existence is not diverted away from us through some other medium, like print or film—and it is this property that imparts the sense of urgency to tragedy's ethical claims. It is also this same property that gives it a sense of ontological tangibility, of the "here and now"—not that the action and the characters in it are unproblematically "here" (they are separated from us by being on stage), but they nevertheless have their existence "now." The temporality of the present is therefore fundamental to tragedy itself and also to our experience of it. As Cavell explains, "The perception or attitude demanded in following this drama is one which demands a continuous attention to what is happening at each here and now, as if everything of significance is happening at this moment, while each thing that happens turns a leaf of time. I think of it as an experience of *continuous presentness*" (*MWM*, p. 322). Without this temporality of the continuous present, we are not in the presence of a tragedy. But that is not (merely) because it is an inherent property of the tragic; rather, it is as much up to us, the audience, to enter into this present as it is up to the tragic to impress it upon us. The members of the audience must participate in it, and in order to be able to do so, they must first *acknowledge* that this tragedy they are watching is present to them.

Time, therefore, also plays a central part in demarcating the crucial watershed between acknowledgment and skepticism that is negotiated in a theater, specifically between the audience and the characters on stage acting out their tragedy before us. Cavell suggests that one synonym for the question "what expresses acknowledgment in a theater?" would be "what counts as putting ourselves in a character's presence?" (*MWM*, p. 334). Part of the anguish of helplessness felt by the audience of a tragedy comes from the fact that "pain and death [are] in our presence when we [are] not in theirs" (*MWM*, p. 346). But Cavell argues that time offers us a way, indeed the only way, of acknowledging the claims of the other even when there is no possibility of being physically present to them: "We are not in, and cannot put ourselves in, the presence of the characters; but we are in, or can put ourselves in, their *present*. It is in making their present ours, their moments as they occur, that we complete our acknowledgment of them. But this requires making their present *theirs*" (*MWM*, p. 337).

One of the main roles that time therefore plays in the Cavellian account of tragedy, then, is to help explain how the claim of the other upon me—the claim of Lear, of Othello, of Hamlet, and of their tragic brethren—is binding upon me even though we cannot acknowledge one another in any traditional sense. As Cavell has it, "What is revealed is my separateness from what is happening to them; that I am I, and here. It is only in this perception of them as separate from me that I make them *present*" (*MWM*, p. 338, my emphasis). I take this to mean that time—specifically, entering into tragedy's temporality of the "continuous present"—is the only bridge that can cross the ontological gulf that otherwise separates what happens on stage from the rest of the auditorium, or from the outside world. But it does so not by establishing some kind of higher unity into which the audience members can enter that somehow makes them "as one with" the characters and actions of the tragedy and thereby empathize with them in some mystical or metaphysical way; rather, it establishes the basis for both ethics and acknowledgment because it does the very opposite: it enables us to "make them *other*, and face them" (*MWM*, p. 338).

It is here that the tragic temporality of the continuous present brings together the epistemological question of acknowledging the other with the ethical claim of the other that, for tragedy to be tragic, accompanies it. Relatedly, this temporality can also explain why it is that in the instant in which Desdemona is about to be strangled or Duncan stabbed or Cordelia disowned, I sit still and quiet and do nothing. "It is not that my time is different from theirs but that I have no present apart from theirs. The time in which that hint is laid, in which that knowledge is fixed, in which those fingers grip that throat, is all the time I have. There is no time in which to stop it" (*MWM*, p. 338). Sharing a temporality of continuous presentness with the characters of a tragedy means that what is happening to them right now is also happening before me right now, and yet that same temporality also means that all I can do right now is acknowledge what is happening. "The present in which action is alone possible is fully occupied" by my acknowledgment of the other, which means that from the audience member's perspective, "everything which can be done is being done" (*MWM*, p. 338). And so, *pace* our long-suffering Southern yokel, Cavell explains:

> Now I can give one answer to the question: Why do I do nothing, faced with tragic events? If I do nothing because I am distracted by the pleasures of witnessing this folly, or out of my knowledge of the proprieties of the place I am in, or because I think there will be some more appropriate time in which to act, or because I feel helpless to un-do events of such proportion, then I continue my sponsorship of evil in the world, its sway waiting upon these forms of inaction. I exit running. But if I do nothing because there is nothing to do, where that means that I have given over the time and the space in which action is mine and consequently that I am in awe before the fact that I cannot do and suffer what it is another's to do and suffer, then I confirm the final fact of our separateness. And that is the unity of our condition. (*MWM*, p. 339)

What all this suggests is that the temporality of tragedy—its time of the continuous present—is a crucial feature of it that binds together our ontological understanding of the tragic (i.e., the kind of existence its characters and their actions have is one that involves a special form of temporality); our epistemological relation to it (i.e., acknowledging these characters and avoiding the skepticism to which they fall prey involves first and foremost understanding and entering into this temporality); and the ethical claims of tragedy. But the time of tragedy, this temporality of continuous presentness, does not reveal to its audience members any positivistic message of what *should be done* in the name of ethics. In fact, it does quite the opposite.

> Then what is revealed? . . . what I share with everyone else present with me at what is happening: that I am hidden and silent and fixed. In a word, that there is a point at which I am helpless before the acting and the suffering of others. But I know the true point of my helplessness only if I have acknowledged totally the fact and the true cause of their suffering. Otherwise I am not emptied of help, but withholding of it. Tragedy arises from the confusion of these states. (*MWM*, pp. 338–39)

The time of tragedy, then, is what puts us in a near-Levinasian position of passivity in the face of the Other. It creates the condition of possibility for the kind of acknowledgment of the other that constitutes the ethical dimension of tragedy itself.

Whether this outline of temporality and its role in tragedy strikes one as complex or as facile, it is likely to have its opponents. Perhaps the most commonsensical objection to it arises from the way Cavell describes the "experience of *continuous presentness*" by saying, "Not that anything is possible (though it is) but that we do not know what is, and is not, next" (*MWM*, p. 322). Now, this is likely to be palpably untrue for many members of Hamlet's, Othello's, and Macbeth's audiences, who are likely to know exactly what is next, because many are likely to be familiar with the plot in advance, and many more are likely to find it utterly predictable. Surely a key problem with describing tragedies as rooted in a "continuous present" is that so many of them are just as rooted in something that happened in the past, before the curtain was raised (one thinks of Oedipus slaying his father at the crossroads, or of Claudius murdering Hamlet's father), or else are oriented toward the future in their inexorable buildup to the denouement (one thinks of Othello's implacable descent to murderous jealousy, or Hamlet's procrastination leading his revenge awry), or, as the example of Hamlet demonstrates, oriented in both directions at once. How, then, can it make sense to locate the basis of tragedy in a temporality that consists solely in an ongoing present? Stephen Mulhall explains things thus:

> The characters in the play live through a sequence of moments each of which constitutes the present for them, and if the audience is genuinely to confront those characters, it must confront each presented moment of the play's events as the present moment of its characters. If, for example, I import my knowledge of the play's ending into my judgement of a character's motives at its outset; or if I regard events already presented as determining present and future events so that I completely expunge the character's freedom to have chosen differently at each moment of decision and action . . . then I fail to acknowledge her and her fellows as particular individuals located but not locked in time and space; I fail to acknowledge them as people.[29]

Viewing a tragedy by stepping outside of the perpetually unfolding present—whether by viewing it as the atemporal "verbal icon" of the New Critics or as some prescripted, predestined sequence of cause and effect ordained by the fates—is simultaneously to change the ontological status of the characters in it, our epistemological apprehension of them, and our ethical relation to them, in that we are avoiding their plight as the plight of a fellow human being.

Such an avoidance is all too common in traditional writings on tragedy, and perhaps regrettably common among theatergoers as well. Wittgenstein paraphrases a typical view common to critics, students, and audience members who find themselves moved by a tragedy: "Every tragedy could really start with the words: 'Nothing would have happened had it not been that. . . .' "[30]

There is some deep-seated human need to understand how things could have come to such a tragic end. But the mistake that we make here is to assume that we could understand things by *explaining* them, by tracing and retracing their origins and outcomes, in short, to view tragedy in terms of its past and its (eventual) future.[31] Such a view, for Cavell,[32] contains a grain of truth, but only a grain:

> Many critics seem to know quite well what is good for Lear and what he ought not to have done. . . . Here the well-known experience of *inevitability* in a tragic sequence comes to attention. But to what shall we attribute it? It [is] not wrong to read the sense of inevitability in terms of a chain of cause and effect; what [is] wrong . . . [is] to read this chain as if its first link lay in the past, and hence as if the present were the scene of its ineluctable effects, in the face of which we must learn suffering. (*MWM*, pp. 317–18)

For Cavell, this notion is problematic because each present moment of tragedy as it becomes present (to the characters and the audience) contains within it the possibility of an end to the skepticism and the avoidance of the other that could halt the tragedy in its tracks. Not that this possibility will strike us as a very live possibility for Macbeth, Hamlet, Lear, or Othello (and least of all for Coriolanus); "if one is assured they could" put a stop to their avoidances, Cavell writes, "one is forgetting who these characters are" (*MWM*, p. 341). But the ethical power of tragedy resides in the fact that acknowledging the plight of the other remains a live possibility for us in the audience, whom these characters ignore. This possibility is removed from us the moment we succumb to the temptation to explain tragedy away by enshrining past origins (as causes) and inevitable outcomes (as effects) in what is a very different form of tragic temporality. The temporality of past cause and eventual effect removes from us the possibility of making the plight of the characters present to us—we can no longer *acknowledge* them aright. Ontologically, they become mere products of their histories; epistemologically, they become puppets rather than people; ethically, their claims are prescripted and no longer the claims of a genuine "other."

And so, while there is, as I mentioned earlier, a grain of truth in statements like "At the beginning there is no reason why things have come to this pass, nothing an exposition could clarify. It is a crossroads, they are there" (*MWM*, p. 342), Cavell is nonetheless right to warn us that "there is danger in the truth that everything which happens is 'contained' in these openings" (*MWM*, p. 342). The danger is that in containing the tragic within a dead, mechanical temporality of past causes and eventual outcomes, we underestimate the threat of skepticism as a live, human possibility. The grain of truth, as I see it, is that such a temporality does indeed exist as a possibility for each and every audience member. This temporality provides all of us with a temptation from within tragedy itself, a temptation, perhaps *the* temptation, toward skepticism and avoidance of the claims of tragedy as tragedy, because nothing could be more simple, or more simplistic, than a member of an audience explaining tragedy away in terms of cause and effect and so remaining unmoved by it. But I want to argue that this temptation is also something of an opportunity. The mechanical temporality that sees tragedy as deriving from causes in the past leading eventually to an inevitable outcome gives us, alongside its temptation to skepticism and avoidance, a chance to see this very kind of temporality as something from which we can reclaim—even, perhaps, liberate—our understanding of time itself. Tragedy thought of this way can give us the vision to redeem time, both the time of the tragedy and *our* time, by bringing it out of a mechanical past and into a free present: "We have, as tragic figures do, to go back to beginnings, either to un-do or to be undone, or to do again the thing which has caused tragedy, as though at some point in the past history is stuck, and time marks time there waiting to be released" (*MWM*, p. 349).

That, at any rate, is how I understand Cavell's assigning a crucial role to the temporality of the present in the power of tragedy to move us and to speak to us. Reframing the classic Aristotelian account of catharsis, he claims: "Catharsis, if that is the question, is a matter of purging attachment from everything but the present, from pity for the past and terror of the future" (*MWM*, p. 338). And if I am right about this reframing, then unlike traditional Aristotelian catharsis, which seeks to demonstrate what tragedy can do for me, Cavell's version of catharsis seeks also to suggest what I can do for tragedy.

VI

This emphasis on the continuous presentness of tragic drama opens the door to what many will doubtless find the most problematic aspect of the Cavellian account of tragedy. Surely, after all, philosophers have known since at least the *Confessions* of Saint Augustine that there is no aspect of time more elusive or thorny than the present moment; since Heidegger's descriptions of *Dasein* that the present, and presence itself, involves an experience of incompleteness; and since Derrida's critique of the metaphysics of presence that all this is a very good thing too. True as it may be that what Cavell means by *the present* is not quite what Derrida means by *presence*, neither is it an entirely different thing altogether. In his essay "Macbeth Appalled," Cavell adduces a passage from Emerson's essay "History" that he is fond of quoting: "When a thought of Plato becomes a thought to me—when a truth that fired the soul of Pindar fires mine, time is no more" (*DK*, p. 226). This, it seems, is simultaneously a description of what is involved in entering into the present of a tragedy and its characters—what Cavell calls "making their present ours"—and just as clearly a textbook instance of the illusory myth of pure communion that Derrida critiques as the metaphysics of presence.

If contemporary critics' and philosophers' engagement with deconstruction is likely to make them suspicious of Cavell's temporality of tragedy, it is unlikely to appear any more satisfactory to traditionalists. Notwithstanding the disclaimer that "my object here is not a theory of tragedy" (*MWM*, p. 320), the experience of time Cavell diagnoses as fundamental to the genre seems at odds with the traditional cliché that Shakespeare's tragedies are "timeless." Going back to the earliest engagement with tragedy in Aristotle's *Poetics*, we find in the call for tragedy to observe the unity of time a nod to the importance of maintaining a coherent sense of the "now" (something Shakespeare was notoriously bad at, as in, most obviously among the plays Cavell studies, *The Winter's Tale*), but we also find that Aristotle differentiates tragedy from history on the basis that where history deals with particular people in a particular time, tragedy has the ability to speak to the universal. Tragedy shares this property with philosophy, meaning that, for Aristotle, it is to be valorized above history. On the one hand, this offers a partial confirmation of Cavell's thesis: if history deals with the "then," then tragedy's unity of time implies that it deals with the "now." But from an Aristotelian point of view, this immediacy is not enough: granted, *that* man, Othello, is about to strangle *that* woman, Desdemona, and is doing so *right now*, but this temporality of the present is not enough to make the event tragic. Tragedy would not have the ability to speak to our lives, our futurity, and our culture—in short, it would not be seen as *tragic*—if the present were its only form of temporality. What I mean is, tragedy would not be able to convey any of its powerful sense of the redemptive, nor would it retain its cathartic ability to move us once we have left the theater, nor, most importantly, would it exert an ethical power to direct our actions and sympathies throughout our lives if it were not able to address itself in some way to a futurity beyond the now.

A rather stronger articulation of this kind of future-oriented tragic temporality is to be found in the early Nietzsche. To paraphrase (roughly) the position of *Untimely Meditations*, tragedy, like art itself, is neither on time nor in time. It is against time, in favor of times to come. Since Cavell reveals himself to be an astute reader of Nietzsche's *Birth of Tragedy*, there is no need to conduct a survey of relationships between Nietzschean and Cavellian views on the subject of tragedy. But it is worth drawing attention to some of Nietzsche's comments in *Untimely Meditations* that ascribe a power to tragedy that is not merely redemptive but sounds almost messianic. He claims that "there is only one hope and one guarantee for the future of humanity: it consists in his *retention of the sense for the tragic*." He further claims that tragedy makes us "free of the terrible anxiety which death and time evoke."[33] Here we find a concise declaration of tragedy's orientation toward futurity, its redemptive properties in the face of death, and its ability to liberate us from time itself—all messianic properties. This would seem to fly in the face of the Cavellian emphasis on tragedy's power as rooted in a continuous present. But I owe to Giorgio Agamben's recent essay "What is the Contemporary?" an insight that provides a way out of this impasse, and that is his observation that "contemporariness par excellence" is to be found in Saint Paul's description of messianic time as *ho nyn kairos*, "the time of the now."[34]

Indeed, it is precisely this conception of messianic time as "the time of the now" that lies at the heart of what Agamben calls "the contemporary." At the start of his essay, Agamben invokes Nietzsche by approvingly citing a remark of Roland Barthes's that "the contemporary is the untimely."[35] He further notes that Nietzsche turned to philosophizing untimeliness immediately after his writings on tragedy, and Cavell makes the very same connection: "Nietzsche's formulations will have helped produce some of mine, but a more interesting matter would be to understand what helped produce some of his—doubtless his work on tragedy went into it" (*DK*, p. 211). If, as I am about to argue, there is a potentially fruitful relationship between the "contemporary" temporality of Agamben's messianic time and the "continuous present" of Cavell's tragic temporality, then a good starting point from which to explore it would be the observation that all seven of Cavell's readings of Shakespeare's tragedies hinge on ways in which the present is avoided, forgone, forfeited, and so on, leading him to suggest that "the loss of presentness . . . seems to be the message . . . of Shakespeare's tragedies themselves" (*MWM*, pp. 322–23). Agamben's messianic view of the contemporary might help address this loss, in that for him, "the messianic now . . . is not the chronological end of time, but the present as the exigency of fulfillment."[36] As such, the messianic now recalls the sense of eternity found in the present moment that Wittgenstein describes in the *Tractatus* 6.4311.

According to Agamben, "The widespread view of messianic time as oriented solely toward the future is fallacious"[37] and is responsible for a pervasive confusion between messianic time and the more straightforwardly future-oriented temporalities of the apocalyptic, the eschatological, and the prophetic conceptions of time. And yet, while the messianic *kairos* is best understood as the Pauline "time of the now," it nevertheless retains a vestigial or gestural relationship with the future—an aporetic temporality that Agamben describes in terms of a "paradoxical tension between an *already* and a *not yet*," because "for Paul, the messianic . . . is a caesura that divides the division between times, . . . a zone of undecidability. . . . Messianic time is neither the complete nor the incomplete, neither the past nor the future, but the inversion of both."[38]

When Agamben's messianic time is described in these highly deconstructive terms, it might well be hard to see how it could have anything whatever to do with Cavellian tragic time. They emerge from such utterly divergent subdisciplines of philosophy and set out their temporalities in terminology so different that it is far from easy to compare them or to place them in any meaningful relation to each other. However, both Agamben's messianic sense of the contemporary and Cavell's tragic sense of the continuous present are faced with a similar challenge: how can a temporality that is rooted in the "now" speak toward a futurity, let alone redeem it? If what is required of the members of an audience of a tragedy is to acknowledge what is before them now, then how can tragedy deliver an ethical message that they are to know will hold good once they have left the theater? Similarly, if to be a true apostle or a true disciple is to dwell in "the time of the now," how can the messianic promise of a redemption that is yet to come retain its meaning? T. S. Eliot puts the problem neatly and succinctly: "If all time is eternally present / All time is unredeemable."[39] For Cavell's tragic continuous present and for Agamben's messianic time of the contemporary to hold any water, this seemingly intuitive statement will have to prove false.

I want to suggest that at least in Cavell's case the key to finding a way of experiencing time such that one's complete involvement in the present is not undermined by attending simultaneously to the redemptive demands of a yet-to-come future can be found in the very place that we began this chapter by problematizing: the space of the theater itself. Cavell asks of those who upbraid the Southern yokel by enjoining him to "remember that he is in a theater":

"How do I remember something there is no obvious way for me to forget?" (*MWM*, p. 319). It can be inferred from this that however fully we immerse ourselves in the present of the characters on stage before us, we do not—cannot—lose sight of the fact that our presents cannot coincide forever: the denouement will play itself out to a tragic end, the curtains will come down, the house lights will illuminate, and the audience will eventually leave the theater. This much is obvious. In discussing the problem of how acknowledgment of the characters on stage can ever be complete, Mulhall says that "in a theatre something is omitted which must be made good outside."[40] This statement is suggestive for two reasons. Firstly, if the audience is aware that different conventions pertain outside the theater and inside it, then they must be aware that the continuous present of the theater is not a permanent temporality and that it will end once the play they are watching ends, but the awareness that they are in what can only be called a "temporary temporality" does not appear to interfere with or detract from their involvement in acknowledgment of the tragic present in any way. Secondly, Mulhall's phrase "made good" suggests that there is something redemptive, perhaps even messianic, about the ending of tragic temporality and the leaving of a theater to enter into a space where we can at last make good on the ethical demands that tragedy makes on us. It is in the possibility of a connection between these two implications of Mulhall's statement that I sense a strong family resemblance with Agamben's messianic conception of the contemporary.

For Agamben, the definition of messianic time is "*the time that time takes to come to an end.*"[41] That is, "the messianic is not the end of time, but the time of the end. . . . It is not the instant in which time ends, but . . . the time that remains between time and its end."[42] It seems to me that this would also be a good description of the time of tragedy as experienced by its audience. The members of an audience at a tragedy will no doubt be aware that what they are watching takes place in "the time of the now," but this is accompanied by an awareness that precisely because of the impending denouement that will end the drama and the curtains that are waiting to come down, the time of what we are watching is also "a time that begins to end," which is precisely how Agamben, drawing on Pauline formulations of "the time that remains" and "the time that is left us [*il tempo che ci resta*]," characterizes messianic time.[43] However invested in the present plight of Othello or Hamlet one may be, one nevertheless cannot avoid a growing awareness that their stories will inevitably reach their denouement and draw to an end, and one cannot avoid the knowledge that the curtain will then fall and we will rise from our seats to leave the theater and rejoin the outside world. In other words, tragedy's time of the now must and will come to an end; it is, in fact, a time that is inexorably ending itself, and its audience knows this.

Now, if it is true that we cannot avoid this knowledge, then at least from a Cavellian point of view it must also be true that we cannot exactly acknowledge it either. Instead, the audience's experience is not unlike that of Agamben's messianic time—experiencing the time that is left us (in which the "us" also includes Othello or Hamlet or the characters on stage) as a time that is made urgent and aporetic by our knowledge that it is coming to an end. As if to prove this point, Agamben himself uses the experience of being "spectators" to differentiate messianic time from chronological time:

> Whereas our representation of chronological time, as the time *in which* we are, separates us from ourselves and transforms us into impotent spectators of ourselves—spectators who look at the time that flies without any time left, continually missing themselves—messianic time, an operational time in which we take hold of and achieve our representations of time, is the time *that* we ourselves are, and for this very reason, it is the only real time, the only time we have.[44]

It should be clear from this that rather than blinding us with a redemptive futurity that condemns us to an avoidance of the present, messianic time is on the contrary geared principally toward an acknowledgment of the now, and that entering into it is in essence a very similar thing to a Cavellian acknowledging of the present and the presence of the other and of myself. It too puts an end to the experience of (mere) spectatorship that Cavell calls theatricalization.

When Agamben characterizes the contemporary as "that part within the present that we are absolutely incapable of living,"[45] he is describing precisely the experience of time that Cavell envisages an audience member's undergoing in entering into the present of characters who are enacting their tragedy before us in the now, but separated from us by their being on stage: we cannot live the experience of time we see before us. To be a spectator of tragedy as Cavell understands it, then, is to be what Agamben describes as contemporary: "And to be contemporary means in this sense to return to a present where we have never been."[46] There would be no point in pursuing this train of thought any further if it were simply a claim that both Agamben's contemporary and Cavell's tragedy entailed a sense of disjuncture or rupture in the moment of the present—that would hardly differentiate them from Saint Augustine or Bergson. What is suggestive here is Agamben's assertion that a contemporary is one who "is capable of transforming [the present] and putting it in relation with other times."[47] An audience member, then, becomes what Agamben calls a contemporary not merely by bridging the gulf between his or her own present and that of the characters on the stage but, further, in perceiving and building relations between his or her present and other times or temporalities that can transform the present itself. This offers us a way of understanding how our experience of tragedy, so deeply rooted in an experience of presentness, can nevertheless address itself toward a futurity in a redemptive, even messianic sense. As Agamben puts it, "Messianic time aims toward the fulfillment of time."[48]

What is so congenial about reading this insight alongside Cavell's view of tragedy is that it welds tragedy's ethical orientation toward futurity and redemption with its rootedness in the moment of the present. In order to demonstrate how it does this, I turn now to Cavell's interpretation of *The Winter's Tale*, partly because the play abounds with different conceptions of the role of time and temporality and partly because this interpretation is singled out by commentators, including Stephen Mulhall and Lawrence Rhu, as the most significant of Cavell's readings of Shakespeare.[49] Fortuitously, it is also easy to establish a direct connection between Cavell's view of *The Winter's Tale* and Agamben's idea of the messianic, in that the play moves away from its tragic first half toward a redemptive second half, which, according to Mulhall, exemplifies Cavell's "understanding of the process of redemption or recovery that the plays themselves work to achieve in their audience."[50] What is more, this redemption is owing in large measure to the agency of the character Paulina, whom Cavell sees as "a figure for St. Paul" (*DK*, p. 218),[51] for it is Paul's writings that form the very basis of Agamben's messianic temporality.

To diagnose a messianic dimension to *The Winter's Tale* is, importantly, not to ascribe to it a religious meaning or message. Rhu correctly points out that "Cavell balks at a Christian interpretation of *The Winter's Tale*."[52] His reason for doing so is "a sense of this theater as in competition with religion, as if declaring itself religion's successor" (*DK*, p. 218), and it is of course the play's offering of a vision of redemption that is largely responsible for this. For some, this may offer confirmation of "the hypothesis of the origin of tragedy in religious ritual," but for Cavell, "whether the hypothesis is true depends on what is meant by 'tragedy,' what by 'origin,' and which ritual is in mind" (*DK*, p. 167). The question is problematized in *The Winter's Tale* because, as Cavell observes, the play's apparent happy ending is incomplete: the young prince Mamillius, son of Leontes and Hermione, is left unaccounted for, dead but not resurrected along with Hermione or found along with Perdita. If this implies that his sacrifice is necessary to bring the play to its conclusion, then the sacrifice of an only begotten son might make of the young Mamillius a messianic figure. But what is troublesome about this is that, firstly, this messiah does not return after his sacrifice to bring redemption and, secondly, the play itself lacks the terms on which religion might offer such redemption:

> When the sharing of a sacrifice is held on religious ground, the ritual itself assures its effectiveness. When it is shifted to aesthetic ground, in a theater, there is no such preexisting assurance; the work of art has to handle everything itself. You might think of this as the rebirth of religion from the spirit of tragedy. (*DK*, p. 168)

If there is indeed a messianic dimension to *The Winter's Tale*, then something more will be needed to establish its basis than the ambiguous sacrifice of an ambiguously messianic figure.

Perhaps a better place to start would be with a remarkable speech that plays a crucial role in Cavell's reading of the play. It begins with Leontes's question, "Is whispering nothing?" (1.2.284) and ends with him concluding:

> Why then the world and all that's in't is nothing,
> The covering sky is nothing, Bohemia nothing,
> My wife is nothing, nor nothing have these nothings
> If this be nothing. (1.2.293–96)

Cavell draws our attention to this extraordinary passage because in it "Leontes has manifested the collapse of the power of human knowing" (*DK*, p. 197), leading, perhaps predictably, to the very Cavellian claim that the play begins as a tragedy, with "a study of skepticism," from which "its second half must be understandable as a study of its search for recovery" (*DK*, p. 198). I do not wish for a moment to dispute that this speech expresses what Mulhall calls "the sceptical impulse, an inability to say whether language applies to anything—an inability to say what exists."[53] Rather, what both Cavell and Mulhall seem to miss is that Leontes's skepticism explicitly takes in time, or, more specifically, the chronological measurement of it: he accuses Hermione and Polyxenes of "wishing clocks more swift," "Hours, minutes," and "noon, midnight" (1.2.289–90). This is not a claim that Leontes's skepticism includes the ontological existence of time or even the epistemological accuracy of its measurement. To the contrary, he can recall with accuracy the "Three crabbed months" it took him to woo Hermione (1.2.102) and the "Twenty-three years" since he was his son's age (1.2.155). This may bear a significant relation to the "Twenty-three days" (2.3.196) he calculates Cleomenes and Dion to have taken in consulting the oracle, which is "speed . . . beyond account" (2.3.195–96), and perhaps also a relation to the Shepherd's wish that "there were no age between ten and three-and-twenty, or that youth would sleep out the rest" (3.3.59), which may in turn be significant because since Florizel, son of Polyxenes and prospective son-in-law to Leontes, is the same age as Leontes's son Mamillius, after the sixteen years it takes to find Perdita he is likely to be in his twenty-third year.

Whatever these numerical relations may suggest, they show that Leontes cannot be understood as failing to acknowledge the existence of time or objecting to the conventional way of counting it. Rather, his skepticism extends toward the significance behind failing to count it properly—the significance of wishing the hours and minutes of the clock to hasten. Well may Cavell ask, "Of all the reasons not to wish to count time, what is Leontes' reason?" (*DK*, p. 209). The closest he comes to answering this question is the following passage:

> Nietzsche spotted us as taking revenge on Time, Time and its "It was." . . . Leontes seems rather to want revenge on Time and its "It will be," not because of its threat of mutability, bringing change to present happiness, but for something like the reverse reason, that its change perpetuates the nightmare of the present, its changes, its issuing, the very fact of more time. This may mean that Leontes' case is hopeless, whereas Nietzsche is led to a proposal for reconceiving time; but then this also meant reconceiving human existence. (*DK*, p. 211)

This observation is an interesting one and deserves more following up than Cavell finds space for. Leontes's "nightmare of the present" contrasts starkly with an early reminiscence of Polyxenes, in which he recalls to Hermione a time when he and Leontes were

> Two lads, that thought there was no more behind,
> But such a day tomorrow as today,
> And to be boy eternal. (1.2.63–65)

This is, of course, a description of one way of experiencing time as a continuous present, but it seems to involve an illusion of eternity brought about by obliviousness to the passage of time, which is hardly what Cavell means by describing the temporality of tragedy in these terms. Could it be that Leontes, whose lost boyhood seemed to involve this rather distorted sense of continuous presentness, is somehow playing out the temporal criteria for tragedy before us? Could his dread of passing time—of wishing hours minutes—owe something to the tragic loss of this youthful experience of eternal presentness? If we grant the central insight of Cavell's reading of *The Winter's Tale*, namely, that at its conclusion a young boy remains unaccounted for, then could it not be said that the two young boys Leontes and Polyxenes, who are Mamillius's age at the time recalled by Polyxenes, are also unaccounted for, in the sense that their boyhoods have unaccountably vanished, and with them their carefree illusions of eternity? (This sense of loss, incidentally, recalls our earlier discussion of Wordsworth's "Intimations" Ode, which shares with this play the theme of meditation on a childhood now vanished.) And what is the relation of these vanished boyhoods to the vanished childhood of Perdita, whose sixteen lost years, Cavell observes, are not recovered?[54]

Cavell suggests that Leontes is perturbed by "the time of breeding, the fact of life that time is a father, that it has issue, even, as Time, the Chorus, says in this play, that it 'brings forth' its issue, which suggests that time may also be, like nature, a mother" (*DK*, pp. 208–9).[55] This might suggest that Leontes's resentment of time has to do with children, but not, or not directly, with childhood. Cavell observes that "Time may present itself as a good-humored old man, but what he speaks about in his appearance as Chorus in this play is his lapse, his being spent, as if behind our backs" (*DK*, p. 193), which recalls how Polyxenes describes the loss of his and Leontes's childhood: they "thought there was no more behind, / But such a day tomorrow as today" (1.2.63–64). In light of this experience of time without measure, it is interesting that the first words spoken by the adult Polyxenes to the adult Leontes are, precisely, a measurement of time: "Nine changes of the watery star have been / The shepherd's note" (1.2.1–2).

Leontes, we have observed, has grown into a strict timekeeper who demands that his orders be carried out punctually: "Within this hour bring me word 'tis done," he says (2.3.134). He similarly barters with Polyxenes to "part the time between's" (1.2.18) after asking him to stay "One seven-night longer" (1.2.17), trading in measured units of time as if it were a commodity. As we have seen, he is perturbed at the idea of lovers wishing time to pass more swiftly, as does the young lover Florizel, who voices his cavalier resolve to "let myself and fortune / Tug for the time to come" (4.3.501–2). This contrasts with Leontes's "Three crabbed months" of courtship, at the end of which, he recalls, Hermione said, "I am yours for ever" (1.2.104). To my ear, the exactitude with which Leontes insists on time in small, measurable units (here, three months) is strongly, even perversely, at odds with the sense of eternity of Hermione's "for ever." Leontes's loss of the present, I contend, is a matter of losing touch with it through his constant attempts to measure it and define it. That is, in a play that focuses on the loss of childhood, Leontes seeks to compensate for losing the sense of the present in his once-eternal boyhood with a true skeptic's insistence on the knowability and measurability of time, to which all the experiences of time that really matter—the time of love, the time of breeding, the time to come—fail to compare. By referring to time in its chronological units, he hopes to reconnect with the present, when it is precisely this tendency of his that prevents him from doing so. This temporal version of the uncertainty principle explains his skepticism toward time in the "Is whispering nothing?" speech *and* his fear of the "It will be" diagnosed by Cavell.

His punishment fits the crime, in that he must do penance for a period of time that Apollo's oracle leaves unspecified and undefined: "the king shall live without an heir, if that which is lost be not found" (3.2.134–35). His (self-)punishment is described by Camillo as bearing an unnatural relation to time, in that his is a sorrow:

> Which sixteen winters cannot blow away,
> So many summers dry: scarce any joy
> Did ever so long live; no sorrow
> But kill'd itself much sooner. (5.3.50–53)

That this penance's relation to time is unnatural can be inferred from the accusation of untimeliness leveled at Paulina when she seeks to prolong it: she is told by Cleomenes that she could "Have done the time more benefit" by saying almost anything else instead (5.1.22). Indeed, the temporality of Leontes's punishment is so different from that of the first half of the play that it needs the figure of Time himself as a chorus to provide a gloss to it.[56]

One way of understanding this change of temporality in the play—which tellingly coincides with the change of gear between its tragic first half and its redemptive second half—is to borrow an insight from Cavell's essay on Eric Rohmer's adaptation of *The Winter's Tale* into the film *Conte d'Hiver*.[57] In "Shakespeare and Rohmer: Two Tales of Winter," Cavell claims that *Conte d'Hiver* opens up a contrast of temporalities that obliges us to "consider two kinds of time—a time of the experience of transcendence . . . and a time of articulation or understanding of this experience" (*CoW*, p. 428). That, I wish to claim, is also the case in the film's Shakespearean prototype, and it is not the time that Leontes needs to atone for his jealousy that shows us this, but rather the time it takes for that atonement to come to an end, in the closing scene of the play. Furthermore, as I hope now to demonstrate, this scene, which brings the play its messianic resurrection and redemption, also involves an example of Agamben's messianic time.

Agamben avers that "the messianic *ho nyn kairos* can never fully coincide with a chronological moment,"[58] and this is why Leontes's hope to reconnect with his boyhood sense of the eternal in the present through measuring time in chronological units is doomed. Interestingly, the play's climax is as much as anything a climax of chronologies, which need ironing out. That is why Leontes ends the play with his order

> Good Paulina,
> Lead us from hence, where we may leisurely
> Each one demand, and answer to his part
> Perform'd in this wide gap of time, since first
> We were dissever'd. (5.3.151–55)

In doing so, he is finally able to acknowledge what Agamben would call a "messianic *kairos* between present and past."[59] That is, for each character on the stage at this moment, "the past (the complete) rediscovers actuality and becomes unfulfilled, and the present (the incomplete) acquires a kind of fulfillment."[60] In the reunion offered by the final scene, the characters each become aware (and, I take it, acknowledge) that the present moment is a moment of plenitude and simultaneously that the past as they knew it is not the whole picture. It is thus that a transition is made into Agamben's messianic "time of the now," with the moment of Hermione's redemptive resurrection as catalyst for it—unleashed, appropriately, at the command of Paulina, the play's surrogate Saint Paul, with the phrase " 'Tis time" (5.3.99).

Leontes's closing speech draws attention to one of the themes consistently stressed in Cavell's reading of the play: the importance of recounting. But it is worthy of note that his order for everyone to fill in "this wide gap of time" with their stories is preempted by Paulina. When Hermione asks of her rediscovered daughter, "Where hast thou been preserv'd? where liv'd? how found / Thy father's court? For thou shalt hear, that I, / . . . / . . . have preserv'd / Myself to see the issue" (5.3.124–28), Paulina replies:

> There's time enough for that,
> Lest they desire . . . to trouble
> Your joys with like relation.—Go together,
> You precious winners all: your exultation
> Partake to every one. (5.3.128–32)

What Paulina is saying is that there is "time enough" to fill up the "wide gap of time" by relating it and exulting in it. That it is necessary to redeem the present not by speaking of the future but by recounting the past is one of the more intriguing upshots of Agamben's perspective on messianic time. The play seems to offer support to his view that "the widespread view of messianic time as oriented solely toward the future is fallacious. . . . To the contrary, for Paul . . . *ho nyn kairos* is a contraction of past and present, that we will have to settle our debts, at the decisive moment, first and foremost with the past."[61] Cavell's reading of the play places a strong emphasis on recounting as counting and as the settling of accounts and debts (see *DK*, p. 200), which seems to point toward the very same conclusion as Agamben does on this issue.

But what exactly is "this wide gap of time"? Astutely, Cavell asks, "How are we to understand the range of Leontes', and the play's, final words? . . . When were we first dissevered?" (*DK*, p. 207). Depending on "Who is we?" (*DK*, p. 207), this dissevering might mean Hermione from Leontes, Hermione from Perdita, Leontes from Perdita, Leontes from Polyxenes as a result of his jealousy, or, significantly, Leontes from Polyxenes at the end of their boyhood together. Another possibility, which Cavell does not raise, is that, given Shakespearean royalty's predilection for speaking of themselves in the first-person plural, it *could* mean Leontes's dissevering from himself, the loss of himself to skepticism, or perhaps the loss of his youthful, boyhood self, or perhaps even both. If we are to conclude from these competing possibilities that we cannot say when first "we" were dissevered, then we cannot say just how wide this wide gap of time is. Nor can we say what precisely would fill it, except, perhaps, for Paulina's suggestion of more time. In making these observations, I am not trying to tear open the play's closing lines in aporetic fashion. Rather, what strikes me as interesting is that Leontes is finally prepared to acknowledge time as an unknown quantity and to forgo the exactitude he demanded of time throughout the play. This is Leontes's only reference to time in *The Winter's Tale* that does not involve quantifying it. Furthermore, even though he is in a position to declare his story at an end, he does so only by calling for more stories—he does not seek closure to this episode. Agamben's description of messianic time seems once again to apply here:

> This is not the line of chronological time (which was representable but unthinkable), nor the instant of its end (which was just as unthinkable); nor is it a segment cut from chronological time; . . . it is the time we need to make time end: *the time that is left us* [*il tempo che ci resta*]. . . . For this very reason, messianic time is the time we have, par excellence.[62]

Leontes orders Paulina to "hastily lead away" into a temporality where the characters are finally present to one another again, across space and time, where they will redeem the time that is left them by recounting and accounting for their past.

How, though, does this reading connect with the play's audience and provide a redemptive ethical experience for them? If what I have said of the role of time and temporality in Cavell's understanding of tragedy is correct, then any reading that does not take steps in this direction is not exemplifying the full reach or import of his views on the subject. Leontes's closing speech is crucial here too. His vocabulary is explicitly theatrical, in that each one must "answer to his part / Perform'd" (5.3.153–54). Cavell rightly draws our attention to the play's metafictional moments, as when Mamillius tells his mother a sad tale for winter, or when various moments in the plot are likened to an old tale (see *DK*, pp. 198–99). Similarly, there are several moments that draw attention to the play's own theatricality, such as Hermione's assertion that she has been continent, chaste, and true "more / Than history can pattern, though devis'd / And play'd to take spectators" (3.2.35–37), and Leontes, in what is in effect a soliloquy, declares:

> many a man there is, (even at this present,
> Now, while I speak this) holds his wife by the arm,
> That little thinks she has been sluic'd in's absence (1.2.192–94)

Obviously, "at this present" could mean both "at this moment in time" and "present at this performance," and so the play calls out to the members of its audience directly to involve them in its thematic of temporality and the present. Most interestingly of all, though, is Time's direct appeal to the audience at the start of act 4, where, as chorus, he requests the audience:

> Of this allow,
> If ever you have spent time worse ere now:
> If never, yet that Time himself doth say,
> He wishes earnestly you never may. (4.1.29–32)

This explicit reference to the time of the theater, and the time the audience spends in it, calls to mind a pair of questions Cavell addresses to the film *Letter from an Unknown Woman*, in which the male lead squanders the time that is his only opportunity to escape death in a duel by reading a letter that informs him fully of the circumstances leading up to it. Faced with a film in which the passage of diegetic time plays such a role, Cavell asks, "What time has it used of ours, what time does art take?" (*CoW*, p. 388). These questions are just as pressing when asked of *The Winter's Tale*, even though (and perhaps because) its handling of diegetic time is so completely different. But if we bear in mind the play's propensity to address itself toward its audience in the ways I have just cited, then it is entirely plausible that the play itself is asking us these very questions at its end. When Leontes asks that we "Each one demand, and answer to his part, / Perform'd in this wide gap of time, since first / We were dissever'd: hastily lead away" (5.3.153–55), he may well be understood as including the audience in this "we"—that we too must answer for the part we have played in the gap of time that Time himself reminded us we are spending, pleasurably or otherwise, in a theater. The command to "hastily lead away" makes as much sense when addressed to the members of an audience, who must now make ready to rise from their seats and leave the auditorium, as it does when addressed to the characters on stage, who have no particular reason to go anywhere else. Thus, the "we" who have been dissevered could well imply the audience's dissevering from the characters on stage that necessarily happens during the gap of time spent in a theater.

How, though, does this calling attention to the play's theatricality offer an ethical message or position? It is certainly qualitatively different from Brecht's political use of similar devices. Tellingly, each of the moments that can be read as audience-directed involve some invocation of time, and they thus call our attention to what I earlier described as the "temporary temporality" of the theater—the audience's awareness of being in a theater, at a performance, which will inevitably come to an end. Connecting this with Agamben's idea that messianic time is the time that time takes to come to an end, it seems that *The Winter's Tale* uses this temporary temporality to draw attention to the importance of the time of the now, the continuous present. Agamben states that messianic time "is not other to chronological time or eternity, but is the transformation that time undergoes when it is taken for a remnant,"[63] and that is precisely what happens in *The Winter's Tale*. Firstly, it presents itself to its audience as an experience of time as a "wide gap" that is nevertheless to be closed. Secondly, this gap of time can be spent, as Time's chorus reminds us, for better or for worse. And thirdly, as Leontes reminds us, we are all answerable for how the remnant of time that is left us is spent and the part we have performed in spending it. There is a merging of temporalities as audience and characters are both included in the "us" of the messianic phrase "the time that is left us." To borrow a phrase from Lawrence Rhu, "Such a moment happens in time, but it can also alter time."[64] And that is how this theater does its ethical work on its audience. Elsewhere Cavell asks, admittedly in a different context and of a very different Shakespearean tragedy: "And what is wrong with strutting and fretting for an 'hour on the stage' that is not wrong with time altogether?" (*DK*, p. 236). Cavell's writings on tragedy, like Shakespearean drama in general and *The Winter's Tale* in particular, are of a special urgency because they demonstrate that when it comes to questions of ethics, there is no time like the present.

Just An Ordinary American Tragedy

By way of a conclusion, I turn now to an attempt at a Cavellian reading of a modern classic, Arthur Miller's *Death of a Salesman*. This may seem a strange move, given that Cavell himself has never written on Miller's work, but in making it I hope to demonstrate, among other things, that Cavell's philosophical approaches to literature have a wider degree of applicability than just to the texts he discusses in his *oeuvre*, and that his ideas have much to bring to debates about, and interpretations of, particular works of literature that do not feature in the indexes of Cavell's books. Miller's well-known play is particularly suited to the task because it is remarkable for the way it dramatizes the interrelation of three of the principal themes in Cavell's thought: the "ordinary," the "American," and the "tragic." Offering a reading of this play, then, should involve highlighting the way these issues overlap and scrutinizing the complex interrelatedness of the ordinariness, the unapproachability, and the tragic nature of Willy Loman's America; that, if achieved, would surely be enough to justify calling my reading of the play "Cavellian."

I

Let us begin by establishing some continuity with the previous chapter. In "The Avoidance of Love," Cavell's first essay on Shakespeare and arguably his most suggestive as regards the nature of tragedy itself, there is a strong suggestion that tragedy is now outmoded as a literary genre and that the advent of modernity and democracy have removed the conditions that once made it such a uniquely powerful form of art:

> Why are princes (or the high born) the subjects of tragedy? Why is high tragedy no longer, apparently, an available artistic option? Everything said, in my hearing, about the appropriateness of the high born is right enough: they show most dramatically a downfall, which tragedy comments upon; the life of an entire community is staked in their fortunes; they rationalize the use of elevated style, in particular, of poetry. To this list I would add two simple, or geometrical, features of the prince: (1) The state of which he is head, as befits the medieval universe, is closed. The extremest consequences attending on his life and death, however extensive and however high their cost, are finite, run a certain course—so long, that is, as the state survives. However far his life and death have entered his subjects, each has a position from which to assess its effects, and pay for them. (2) His life and death are the largest in his state, hence easiest to see matched or lost to one another; and since his legitimate succession is the only promise of continued life to his state, his death has to be accounted for. When the closed world burst into the infinite universe, consequences became fully unlimited and untraceable. . . . Tragedy was the price of justice, in a disordered world. In a world without the hope of justice, no price is right. (*MWM*, p. 343)

What is remarkable about this passage, and indeed about the discussion from which it is drawn, is that its terms and its ideas are strikingly consonant with an essay by Arthur Miller entitled "Tragedy and the Common Man," published in the *New York Times* some two decades before the appearance of *Must We Mean What We Say?* What is more remarkable yet is that Miller, while using terms that distinctly anticipate Cavell's, appears to come to something like the very opposite conclusion.

Miller certainly agrees with Cavell that tragedy is widely considered to be a thing of the past and that the advent of modernity, bringing with it the skeptical world-view of the scientist—one recalls Cavell's observation that tragedy culminates in Shakespeare partly because of his contemporaneity with Bacon and Galileo[1]—is in part to blame: "In this age few tragedies are written," he begins. "It has often been held that the lack is due to a paucity of heroes among us, or else that modern man has had the blood drawn out of his organs of belief by the skepticism of science."[2] Miller also agrees with Cavell that "tragedy . . . is the consequence of a man's total compulsion to evaluate himself justly."[3] Where he departs from Cavell is in the suggestion that the demise of the closed, hierarchical, ordered state, and the coming of modern democracy that succeeded it,[4] should imply a situation in which "we are often held to be below tragedy—or tragedy above us." Miller, *pace* Cavell, states, "I believe that the common man is as apt a subject for tragedy in its highest sense as kings were."[5] What is more, he briefly uses a strategy remarkably close to that of Cavell's ordinary language philosophy—clarifying "what we say when"—in defense of his argument. As regards the ordinary use of the word *tragic*, Miller argues, "When the question of tragedy in art is not at issue, we never hesitate to attribute to the well-placed and the exalted the very same mental processes as the lowly."[6] Indeed, an implicit appeal to the ordinary can be used to challenge the very idea that tragedy is preeminently the territory of princes, because "if the exaltation of tragic action were truly a property of the high-bred character alone, it is inconceivable that the mass of mankind should cherish tragedy above all other forms, let alone be capable of understanding it."[7]

Having thus highlighted the important differences between Cavell's and Miller's positions, I find it no less important to stress that these differences are as likely to amount to a *divergence* as to a *disagreement* and that it is highly probably that Cavell and Miller only *appear* to come to opposite conclusions. Part of the reason for this is that Cavell is by no means as willing as some critics and theorists have been to consign the genre of tragedy to the reliquaries of literary history. At times he is ready to speculate on the possibilities of a genre of tragedy to come, a tragedy that would once again be a tragedy of the present:

> Tragedy, could it now be written, would not show us that we *are* helpless—it never did, and we are not. It would show us, what it always did, *why* we (as audience) are helpless. Classically, the reason was that pain and death were in our presence when we were not in theirs. Now the reason is that we absent ourselves from them. Earlier, the members of the audience revealed only their common difference from the actors. Now each man is revealed privately, for there is no audience, apart from each man's making himself an audience; what is revealed is that there is no community, no identity of condition, but that each man has his reasons, good or bad, for choosing not to act. After a tragedy now, should one be written, the members of the audience would not see one another measured against nature again, but ranged against it, as if nature has been wiped out and the circle of social and historical arbitrariness is now complete. (*MWM*, p. 346)

If the aesthetic of separation once dramatized in classical tragedy has now, through the social isolation of modernity, become an established, everyday fact, then the very criteria for tragedy have changed, and so too then must tragedy itself if it is to be written in this age. In another essay, written just one year after "Tragedy and the Common Man," Miller seems to concur with Cavell's diagnosis of the sea change in the tragic audience. *Death of a Salesman*, in subject, theme, and form, is predicated upon an audience that Miller describes as "a terribly lonely people, cut off from each other by such massive pretense of self-sufficiency, machined down so finely we hardly touch any more. We are trying to save ourselves separately, and that is immoral, that is the corrosive among us."[8] Nevertheless, he believes that tragedy shows us "a way beyond fear of each other, beyond bellicosity, a way into our humanity."[9] In another essay dating from this time, he echoes the Cavellian position on tragedy sketched out in the previous chapter by arguing that tragedy, in direct contrast to melodrama, offers us an "illumination of the ethical."[10]

So far, it might perhaps be asked, so what? After all, the suggestion that social isolation is one of the conditions of reception criterial to the modern artwork does not point to anything that would link Miller's work closer to Cavell's than to that of any number of other twentieth-century philosophers of art (Theodor Adorno, for example). Moreover, the suggestion that tragedy has an ethical mission to its audience would scarcely have struck Aristotle as news, and in some contemporary philosophers writing on tragedy (Martha Nussbaum, for example), it risks becoming something of a platitude. Indeed, in a slightly later essay Miller seems to edge toward a position that chimes more closely with that of Nussbaum, or perhaps that of Alasdair MacIntyre, than it does with that of Cavell in plotting the central role of tragedy in the ancient Greek polis. Writing on the genre of the "social play" à la Shaw, Miller observes that "a Greek living in the classical period would be bewildered by the dichotomy implied in the very term 'social play.' Especially for the Greek, a drama created for public performance had to be 'social.' . . . That is, the relations of man as a social animal, rather than his definition as a separated entity, was the dramatic goal."[11] The decline of Greek tragedy, according to Miller (again suggesting much common ground with Nussbaum and MacIntyre), is linked with the decline of the social—the demise of the polis and the rise of the "cosmopolitan" in its place.[12]

Nevertheless, Miller's rapport with the philosophies of Nussbaum and MacIntyre is underpinned by an insight that can only be called Cavellian *avant la lettre*: that the sea change in the status of tragedy is bound up with a sea change in its audience, principally because the cosmopolitan's position entails an avoidance of his involvement in the polis and its claims upon him, and so he anticipates the avoidances practiced by the Cavellian skeptic. Miller uncannily anticipates Cavell's vocabulary in describing this "intimation—or more—of skepticism, of self-removal, that presages the radical separation of man from society which the American drama expresses."[13] This skepticism, this self-removal (Cavell would call it "avoidance"), and this radical separation have left their mark on the audience of the contemporary American play: "For deep down we no longer believe in the rules of the tragic contest; we no longer believe that some ultimate sense can in fact be made of social causation, or in the possibility that any individual can, by a heroic effort, make sense of it."[14] Is the "social play," then, the modern successor of, or, as it were, the replacement for, the tragedy? For Miller the answer is a resounding no. On the contrary, the seeming impossibility of a contemporary tragedy is precisely what points to the necessity for it.

For Miller, the very skepticism that would seem to vitiate the possibility of tragedy as an art form holds the key to its reinvigoration. That there is such a lack of belief, and especially a lack of belief in answers, may in fact provide the conditions needed for a spirit of wholesale questioning that ought to be highly conducive to tragedy. According to Cavell, it is simply not the case that "our trouble is that there used to be answers and now there are not. The case is rather that there used not to be an unlimited question and now there is" (*MWM*, p. 352). Miller seems to agree, but for him, this is good news, because "no tragedy can . . . come about when its author fears to question absolutely everything, when he regards any institution, habit or custom as being either everlasting, immutable, or inevitable."[15] Miller is clear that his argument "is not to say that tragedy must preach revolution,"[16] but that there is, necessarily, a politics to tragedy. It is here that a close rapprochement develops between his views and Cavell's:

> In such circumstances, a purpose of tragedy remains unchanged: to make us practical, capable of acting. It used to do that by showing us the natural limitations of acting. Now its work is not to purge us of pity and terror, but to make us capable of feeling them again, and this means showing us that there is a place to act upon them. This does not mean that tragedy now must become political. Because first, it was always political, always about the incompatibility between a particular love and a particular social arrangement for love. Because second, and more specifically, we no longer know what is and is not a political act, what may or may not have recognizable political consequences. (*MWM*, p. 347)

To become a live possibility, tragedy, under the conditions of modernity, can no longer count on a model of consensus to provide a foundation to its political and ethical teachings. Instead, it has to create these foundations for itself, as part of its drama. Both Cavell and Miller seem to share this view: a tragedy is not so much a political art form or a political act as an art of creating the conditions of possibility for a politics. Perhaps, then, the divergence between them amounts to an agreement about the diagnosis, but a disagreement as to the prognosis: Miller, for obvious reasons, places a great deal of faith in the possibilities for tragedy as a contemporary art form, while Cavell appears to be more tentative, more speculative about those possibilities.

In what follows, I regard Miller's *Death of a Salesman* as a contemporary tragedy, one that is fully responsive to the conditions of modernity. Given Cavell's relative pessimism about such a genre, though, it may seem that I am begging the question by considering this play an example of it in the first place. For it is indeed a moot point whether this tragedy succeeds *qua* tragedy. The play itself seems eager to voice its own doubts. For example, when his friend, Charley, gives Willy Loman the money with which to pay the premium on the $20,000 insurance policy he intends his son Biff to collect after his death, Willy observes, "After all the highways, and the trains, and the appointments, and the years, you end up worth more dead than alive," to which Charley replies, "Willy, nobody's worth nothin' dead."[17] Moments before the salesman's death, Biff attempts to deter his father from suicide by warning him, "There'll be no pity for you, you hear it? No pity!" (*DoS*, p. 130). And indeed, as the "Requiem" scene makes clear, Willy's death is not a solution of any kind. If, according to Charley, Willy Loman ends up "worth nothin'" and, as Biff says, without pity—the emotion pertaining, after all, to Aristotelian catharsis—then are we really in the presence of tragedy at the end of *Death of a Salesman*?

Cavell's essay on Shakespeare's *Coriolanus* offers a couple of hints that might help to steer us here. He says of Coriolanus that "his sacrifice will not be redemptive, hence one may say his tragedy is that he cannot achieve tragedy" (*DK*, p. 161), and while the fate of this heroic Roman general clearly could not be more different from that of Willy Loman, there is nevertheless a certain applicability here. The death of our salesman does not bring with it any form of redemption: his elder son returns to a life that Willy hoped his death would change; his younger son remains as self-deluded as was Willy himself; there is no indication that his insurance company has paid out; and the sobs of his widow with which the play closes ring utterly hollow ("We're free . . . We're free . . ." [*DoS*, p. 139]). All in all, we may well ask whether the failures of Willy Loman can be said to add up to tragedy. That we can ask this question, however, is precisely the point: it means that, as with artworks in general under the conditions of modernity, we are in the presence of self-consciousness, dealing with a tragedy that is asking whether it is in fact a tragedy. That is how I read Biff's and Charley's comments—as invitations to question what it is that we are watching and how we are to respond to it. That we ask these questions does not, in the Cavellian view, invalidate the status of *Death of a Salesman* as a tragedy, because Cavell himself asks similar questions of *Coriolanus* ("What is the good of such a tragedy of failed tragedy? Which is to ask: What is this play to us? How is it to do its work?" [*DK*, p. 162]). Asking such questions does not compromise a play's status *qua* tragedy; rather, it foregrounds the problematic lack of a foundation on which such a tragedy of failed tragedy could ultimately come to rest.[18] It is, in part, this lack of foundation that I intend to address in offering a Cavellian reading of *Death of a Salesman*.

II

Miller's essay "Tragedy and the Common Man," published in 1949, amounts in more or less equal measure to a manifesto for and an explanatory gloss on his highly successful play *Death of a Salesman*, in which he apparently succeeds in creating a contemporary tragic hero named Willy Loman. Forty years later, when Cavell takes us on his journey "in quest of the ordinary," he sets out by stating his "interest in putting Wittgenstein's and Austin's preoccupation with the ordinary and the everyday together with Emerson's and Thoreau's emphasis on the common, the near, and the low" (*IQO*, p. 6). Strikingly, the title of Miller's essay and the surname of his protagonist anticipate two of the three American synonyms Cavell proposes for the ordinary and the everyday. While this is surely no more than coincidence, it is nevertheless a very enlightening one: if Willy Loman's is a tragedy of the common man, then could one call it, at the risk of oxymoron, an ordinary or an everyday tragedy?

It has long been a critical commonplace that Miller's salesman is a very different kind of tragic hero from a Hamlet, a Macbeth, a Lear, or an Othello precisely because his is not a fall from lofty, elevated heights; he is an everyman. His wife describes him in these terms: "I don't say he's a great man. Willy Loman never made a lot of money. His name was never in the paper. He's not the finest character that ever lived. But he's a human being. . . . So attention must be paid" (*DoS*, p. 56). It is just this kind of ordinariness that, for those who locate tragedy within the territory of the high-born, problematizes Willy Loman's tragic status. Miller's response to this problematization is worth quoting:

> The play was always heroic to me, and in later years the academy's charge that Willy lacked the "stature" for the tragic hero seemed incredible to me. I had not understood that these matters are measured by Greco-Elizabethan paragraphs

> which hold no mention of insurance payments, front porches, refrigerator fan belts, steering knuckles, Chevrolets, and visions not seen through the portals of Delphi but in the blue flame of the hot-water heater.[19]

And so Miller is well aware that, paradoxically, it is Willy Loman's ordinariness, his proximity to the everyday, the common, and the low, that makes him so very *extra*ordinary as a tragic hero.

It is worth spending a short while recapping what *ordinary* might be taken to mean here, because, for Cavell in particular, it has a very specific and complex meaning. Strikingly, though, a good part of this conception of the ordinary appears to be shared by Miller. Miller is well aware that "inevitably, people are going to say that Willy Loman is not a typical salesman," and he freely concedes, "It is obvious that Willy *can't* be an average American man, at least from one point of view; he kills himself. That's a rare thing."[20] However, this frames the ground of the ordinary in the wrong terms; "typical" or "average" implies something that is statistically normal, and that is not what either Cavell or Miller is in quest of in his writings. As Miller puts it:

> As a matter of fact, that standard of "averageness" is not valid. It neither tells whether the character is a truthful character as a character, or a valid one. I can't help adding that that is the standard of socialist realism—which of course wasn't invented by socialists. It is the idea that a character in a play or in a book cannot be taken seriously unless he reflects some statistical average, plus his ability to announce the official aims of the society; and it is ridiculous. Hamlet isn't a typical Elizabethan. . . . Willy Loman is, I think, a person who embodies in himself some of the most terrible conflicts running through the streets of America today. A Gallup Poll might indicate that they are not the majority conflicts; I think they are.[21]

For Cavell as for Miller, the ordinary is not to be accessed through statistical trends telling us what the average or the typical is. Early in his career, Cavell maintained, in defense of the (then) relatively new practices of ordinary language philosophy, that the philosopher need not conduct the kind of surveys and data gathering associated with the science of linguistics in order to enter claims about what is and what is not ordinary in the language.[22] (The ordinary, for Cavell, cannot be counted, although it can be recounted.) Instead, it is enough that the philosopher, or any competent speaker of the language, after due reflection, is prepared to take responsibility for the claim he stakes as to what is ordinary. Thought of this way, a philosophical statement about what is ordinary in our language conveys the same information, carries the same risks, and makes a similar truth claim as do philosophical statements about what is good in the areas of human activity surveyed by ethics, politics, and aesthetics. All are attempts, not to arrive at an absolute fact or ground (which does not exist), but "to confront the culture with itself along the lines in which it meets in me" (*CoR*, p. 125). And it is this that, according to Cavell, affords such claims the status and the name of philosophy.

Accordingly, when Cavell makes a claim along the lines of "the everyday is everyday, the ordinary is ordinary, or you haven't found it" (*CoR*, p. 463), he is to be understood not, as Richard Rorty and certain other critics would have it, as seeking to derive from the idea of the ordinary a grounding, a foundation, or, as Rorty puts it, "the latest disguise of the *ontos on*."[23] The ordinary does not, and cannot, provide any foundation or grounding for anything, and not simply because it lacks any foundation and grounding itself (lack them though it does), but because the ordinary as Cavell understands it is not ordinarily available to us in a readily apprehensible or tangible form. Hence, as Sandra Laugier observes, "To think the ordinary we must pose the question: do we really know what is ordinary, what is ordinary for us?"[24] And the answer is most likely to be in the negative, since, for Cavell, the ordinary is to be grasped only once it is already lost—grasped, perhaps, in or through the experience of losing it. Rather than casting the ordinary as a foundational *ontos on*, then, some of Cavell's work tends rather to the conclusion that, as Laugier has it, "the ordinary itself is a myth and an illusion."[25]

If the ordinary is more satisfactorily to be apprehended through losing touch with it rather than through grasping it, then this straightaway gives us an angle from which to consider Willy Loman, who, while Biff and Happy have "left him babbling in a toilet" (*DoS*, p. 124), where he relives the traumatic experience of being detected in adultery by his own son, is described by the stage directions as "suddenly striving for the ordinary" (*DoS*, p. 119)—a quintessentially Cavellian quest. If, as I have suggested, Willy's tragedy is an extraordinarily ordinary one, then it will be important to establish exactly what understanding it has of its own connection with the ordinary, that is, how *Death of a Salesman* presents or pictures the relationship between Willy's tragedy and the ordinary. And doing this will first necessitate a few words on the relationship between tragedy and the ordinary in order the better to appreciate what is so unique and important about Miller's play.

For both Miller and Cavell, tragedy necessarily involves a departure from the ordinary. Speaking as a playwright, Miller is well aware that "it is more likely to be typical of people to be humdrum and indifferent and without superb conflicts. When a writer sets out to create high climaxes, he automatically is going to depart from the typical, the ordinary, and the representative."[26] And so tragedy, if it is to be tragedy, is of necessity going to entail something out of the ordinary; this has been true from ancient Greece onwards. Accordingly, if it is in the nature of traditional tragedy to depart from the ordinary, then what kind of relationship with the ordinary would be envisaged in a nontraditional tragedy? On the one hand, it would seem quite experimental and contemporary—Cavell would say "modern"—for a tragedy to remain in touch with the ordinary and the everyday, and according to his "Tragedy and the Common Man" this is partly Miller's goal in *Death of a Salesman*. On the other hand, surely no play that fails to depart from the ordinary or the everyday could ever be described as a tragedy. Cavell sums up the problem thus:

> The classical environment of tragedy was the extraordinary and the unnatural, and it is tempting, now that things have changed, to say that the environment of tragedy has become the ordinary and the natural. Except that we no longer know what is ordinary and natural, and hence no longer know what is tragic and what is not (so it is not surprising that tragedies are not written). We could say that just this amnesia is our tragedy. Except that it is not amnesia and it is not necessarily bad—for it is not as if we knew or could remember a state of society in which the ordinary was the natural state of affairs. (*MWM*, p. 350)

If we seemed to be heading for a paradox—roughly, that a modern and contemporary tragedy had to adhere to the ordinary for it to be modern and contemporary, but had to depart from it in order to be a tragedy—then this paragraph helps resolve it. A picture of the ordinary as a tangible environment or context for tragedy is flawed, as is a picture of tragedy as a definable, readily identifiable art form. For Cavell, the lines that demarcate the ordinary and the tragic are not just hard to draw, they are in fact interpermeable, and the reason for this has to do with the rise of skepticism in the modern world: "Skepticism is the playing out of a tragedy, that accordingly our ordinary lives partake of tragedy in partaking of skepticism" (*IQO*, p. 8).

We saw in the previous chapter how central the issue of skepticism is to Cavell's view of tragedy. Skepticism is highly relevant here because it is through skepticism that the doorway between the ordinary and the tragic is opened, and the traffic flows in both directions through it. The doubts that plague Othello and Hamlet, Lear and Leontes, are leaps into the tragic at the same time as they are—and *because* they are—departures from the ordinary. "The concept of belief is turned from its common course" (*DK*, p. 7), as Cavell says. Miller seems to agree with Cavell that skepticism is of the essence in tragedy, because it is important to him, as we have seen, that tragedy question absolutely everything. The trouble here is that skepticism, while it seems to describe Othello and Hamlet well enough, equally seems a shabby fit for Willy Loman. He simply cannot view his son's potential or his own (highly questionable) success with any degree of skepticism whatsoever: they are inviolable, beyond question, and that is precisely the driving force of his tragedy. He recalls, in fact, Cavell's observation that "not finitude, but the denial of finitude, is the mark of tragedy" (*CoR*, p. 455). Willy will go to tragic lengths to deny the finitude, or, better, the ordinariness, of his own achievements and of Biff's promise: "I am not a dime a dozen!" he thunders "in an uncontrolled outburst." "I am Willy Loman, and you are Biff Loman!" (*DoS*, p. 132). He is very much the kind of tragic hero Miller describes, who, rather than questioning everything, discovers, in the course of the play, something unquestionable—"some conflict, some value, some challenge, however minor or major, which he cannot find it in himself to walk away from or turn his back on"—and he sticks to it.[27] This does not sound like a description of a traditional skeptic; it is a portrait of a tragic hero made from a different isotope of the crisis of knowledge. Willy Loman, says Miller, is a man of "tremendously powerful ideals,"[28] "a very brave spirit who cannot settle for half but must pursue his dream of himself to the end."[29] In a single word, he is—and Miller refers to him as—a "fanatic."[30]

One might think of fanaticism as the very opposite of skepticism, but both entail ways in which we forgo or avoid our acknowledgment of the ordinary. What is more, Cavell, via Immanuel Kant's chapters of "General Observations" in his *Religion Within the Limits of Reason Alone*, sees a great deal of affinity between skepticism and fanaticism. Kant identifies fanaticism (together with superstition, delusion, and sorcery) as what Cavell calls "a particular distortion of human reason" (*CoR*, p. 455), one of "philosophy's irrational competitors" (*PDAT*, p. 13). Indeed, so much common ground does Cavell see between Kant's description of fanaticism and his own understanding of skepticism that he is prepared to consider certain Shakespearean tragedies—principally *The Winter's Tale* but to a lesser extent *Othello* and *Macbeth*—as driven as much by fanaticism as they are by skepticism: "Fanaticism is explicitly one of Kant's names for a distorted expectation of reason, one form taken by the desire to refuse human limitation, the limitation of finitude; hence it is exactly measurable with skepticism. This affinity is what permits me to describe Leontes as a portrait of the skeptic as fanatic" (*DK*, p. 17). If I am right that Willy's "denial of finitude"—his and his son's—is the driving force of his tragedy, then we are clearly in the presence of a tragedy driven by fanaticism rather than skepticism, where both these diseases are seen to culminate in what Cavell calls "a refusal expressed as a failure to acknowledge. (That this is a refusal, something each character is doing and is going on doing, is what makes these events add up to tragedy rather than to melodrama)" (*MWM*, p. 313). And so in *Death of a Salesman* the ordinary is forgone, knowledge is disowned, and love is avoided—but for different reasons and in different ways from those envisaged by some of the classical, skepticism-driven Shakespearean tragedies Cavell analyzes.

Willy Loman is a fanatic insofar as he cannot help but reject the ordinary in favor of the ideal. He *must* succeed, and so must his son Biff, not just in financial terms but also in being admired and "well-liked." In the final scene, Biff constantly cajoles his father to understand that "I'm nothing!," "a buck an hour" (*DoS*, p. 132), "a bum" (*DoS*, p. 128), "a dime a dozen" (*DoS*, p. 132). In spite of Biff's emotive insistence on his ordinariness, Willy cannot acknowledge this finitude and pronounces what is virtually his own death sentence: "That boy is going to be magnificent!" (*DoS*, p. 133). This is merely the most climactic of his retreats from the ordinary in his fanatical pursuit of what Biff (rightly) calls "that phony dream" (*DoS*, p. 133). Other examples abound. It is not out of arrogance that Willy declares, "Call out the name Willy Loman and see what happens! Big shot!" (*DoS*, p. 62). It is that he has set up a dream of greatness with which he and Biff must but cannot coincide. "You got a greatness in you, Biff, remember that. You got all kinds a greatness" (*DoS*, p. 67), Willy declares, and he predicts that "when he walks into a business office his name will sound out like a bell and all the doors will open to him!" (*DoS*, p. 86). Yet when asked by Biff to "hold on to the facts" (*DoS*, p. 106), namely, the fact that Biff was never a successful salesman for Bill Oliver but rather a lowly shipping clerk, Willy says he is "not interested in stories about the past" (*DoS*, p. 107). Instead, he concocts his own version of Biff's meeting with Oliver and says of it, "It's great news, Biff" (*DoS*, p. 108); and when the reality of the situation is forced upon him, he declares, "You're no good, you're no good for anything" (*DoS*, p. 111). Willy gives us ample evidence throughout the play that he is not capable of viewing the world in terms other than those of his all-or-nothing visions of success. It is precisely this kind of fanaticism that blinds Willy to the ordinary, for example, to the love his wife and son bear him, in spite of his apparent failure to fulfil his own unattainable ideal. Indeed, in his case a healthy dose of skepticism would not go amiss; directed towards himself and his outlook on life, a certain amount of skepticism might even avert the tragedy toward which his fanaticism propels him.

Cavell gives us a good way of framing Willy's fanaticism when he argues, in the context of his reading of *King Lear*, that tragedy shows us that "the *reason* consequences furiously hunt us down is not merely that we are half-blind, and unfortunate, but that we go on doing the things which produced these consequences in the first place. What we need is not rebirth, or salvation, but the courage, or plain prudence, to see and to stop" (*MWM*, p. 309). Willy Loman is indeed surrounded by people who are urging and even begging him to stop—particularly, to stop holding onto his vision of Biff's future greatness. "Let him go," advises Charley. "When a deposit bottle is broken you don't get your nickel back" (*DoS*, pp. 43–44). His advice anticipates Biff's "crying, broken" plea in the final scene: "Will you let me go, for Christ's sake?" (*DoS*, p. 133). "I'm not bringing home any prizes any more," he says, "and you're going to stop waiting for me to bring them home!" (*DoS*, p. 132). But Willy cannot stop.

It is to Cavell's credit that he sees tragedy as not merely showing us that we should stop our destructive behaviors but simultaneously showing the tragic impossibility of certain people's doing this: "But how do we stop?" (*MWM*, p. 324). Willy Loman is a fanatic precisely because he cannot stop his idolatry of his son's future. "Sometimes, Willy, it's better for a man just to walk away," advises Biff's childhood friend Bernard. Willy returns: "But if you can't walk away?" (*DoS*, p. 95).[31] This inability is what makes Willy a fanatic rather than a skeptic: the skeptic not only walks away from knowledge, he turns his back on it. Willy cannot forgo his certainty of a golden future for Biff, and though Biff, after his moment of self-realization in act 2, wants to "just wrap it up" (*DoS*, p. 128) and say good-bye to his father, his father cannot bring himself to say good-bye to him. Nor is Willy alone in his inability to stop himself. Biff himself reveals to Happy that every springtime he has left the farms on which he works because he is "not gettin' anywhere" (*DoS*, p. 22), but on his return to the city he doesn't know what to do with himself. The difference is that Biff, after his abortive meeting with Bill Oliver, finds it within himself to stop:

> Suddenly I stopped, you hear me? . . . I stopped in the middle of that office building and I saw—the sky. I saw the things that I love in this world. The work and the food and time to sit and smoke. And I looked at the pen and said to myself, what the hell am I grabbing this for? Why am I trying to become what I don't want to be? What am I doing in an office, making a contemptuous, begging fool

of myself, when all I want is out there, waiting for me the minute I say I know who I am! (*DoS*, p. 132)

Biff is able to forgo the fanaticism of his father and see that, as Cavell puts it, "the cause of tragedy is that we would rather murder the world than permit it to expose us to change" (*MWM*, p. 351). And it is instructive that it is a vision of the ordinary things in his life—the very things he is attempting to repudiate and leave behind, the ordinary commonplace things, like manual work, open air, eating, and smoking—that inspires the revelation that leads him beyond fanaticism and idolatry and toward a form of self-knowledge that is rooted in the ordinary.

III

The kernel of *Death of a Salesman*, then, lies in Biff's redemptive moments of self-acknowledgment and the contrast between these and Willy's ongoing delusions. Miller once observed, "I am sorry the self-realization of the older son, Biff, is not a weightier counterbalance to Willy's disaster,"[32] but I see no need for such an apology. After he has "realized what a ridiculous lie [his] whole life has been" (*DoS*, p. 104), he tries to reveal this lie to his father by communicating the truth to him instead: "You're going to hear the truth—what you are and what I am" (*DoS*, p. 130). Because "we never told the truth for ten minutes in this house" (*DoS*, p. 131), Biff sees that "the man don't know who we are! The man is gonna know!" (*DoS*, p. 131). The effort is, tragically, entirely in vain—"you're never going to see what I am" (*DoS*, p. 129)—and so Biff's fitting epitaph for his father is, "He never knew who he was" (*DoS*, p. 138). Unlike Willy, and unlike Happy, who persists in his father's delusions, Biff is able to say, "I know who I am" (*DoS*, p. 138). Clearly, then, issues of self-discovery, self-realization, self-knowledge, and self-acknowledgment lie at the very heart of *Death of a Salesman*. It is hardly surprising that, in "Tragedy and the Common Man," Miller suggests that the play depicts "the disaster inherent in being torn away from our chosen image of what and who we are in this world" and, further, that "it is the common man who knows this fear best."[33]

Cavell has written at great length about a tragedy in which what he calls "the old tragic question" (*MWM*, p. 307) features prominently—the question being asked in more or less the exact terms Biff uses: "Who is it that can tell me who I am?" The play under discussion is, of course, *King Lear* (1.4.238). Cavell says of Lear that "his tragedy is that he has to find out too, and that he cannot rest with less than an answer" (*MWM*, p. 307), and in this, I contend, he resembles Willy Loman. According to Cavell, Lear is "everyman who has gone to every length to avoid himself" (*MWM*, p. 280), but a more fitting description of Willy Loman is harder to imagine: certainly Willy, because of his "common man" status, is more obviously an everyman figure than is a king of England. There is in many respects a clear family resemblance between Lear and Loman:[34] both are older men, driven to the very brink of their sanity by their fraught relationships with their offspring. Like Lear's fanatical need to have his daughters voice the love and pay him the respect he feels he deserves, Loman's self-image also requires the devotion and admiration of his sons. Like Regan and Goneril, Happy is prepared to pay lip service to his father, promising him that "I'm gonna retire you for life" (*DoS*, p. 41), yet we learn from his mother, Linda, that he has given his parents no money since the previous Christmas (*DoS*, p. 57), and he has no riposte to Biff's charge that "you don't give a good goddam about him . . . he doesn't mean anything to you. You could help him—I can't!" (*DoS*, p. 115). Like Cordelia, Biff is as sincere as Happy, Regan, and Goneril are insincere; like Cordelia, he is unable to tell his father of the love he still clearly bears him, and he cannot follow Happy's advice to just lie and "tell him something nice" (*DoS*, p. 105). Before their tragic deaths, both Lear and Loman are granted a glimpse of redemption that makes their end even harder to bear: they finally attain the love and the forgiveness of their favorite child, the very love they have avoided and squandered throughout. As Miller puts it:

> Willy Loman is filled with a joy, however broken-hearted, as he approaches his end. . . . In terms of his character, he has achieved a very powerful piece of knowledge, which is that he is loved by his son and has been embraced by him and forgiven. In this he is given his existence, so to speak—his fatherhood, for which he has always striven and which until now he could not achieve.[35]

This description of Willy Loman fits Lear as closely as Cavell's description of Lear fits Willy Loman.

There is, however, one crucial difference between them: once Lear is able to cease avoiding his love for Cordelia, he is able briefly to regain his self-knowledge and his sanity. The Lear that dies at the end of the play is not the same Lear that ran about mad in a storm upon the heath. Willy Loman is given no such respite:

> That he is unable to take this victory thoroughly to his heart, that it closes the circle for him and propels him to his death, is the wage of his sin, which was to

> have committed himself so completely to the counterfeits of dignity and the false coinage embodied in his idea of success that he can prove his existence only by bestowing power on his posterity, a power deriving from the sale of his last asset, himself, for the price of his insurance policy.[36]

Why does he do this? His own wife, who says she "know[s] every thought in his mind" (*DoS*, p. 60), asks this very question. Once Willy understands, as clearly he does, that Biff indeed "always loved [him]" (*DoS*, p. 135), the knowledge does not bring him any closer to sanity. Instead, while recalling the two great anticlimaxes of his life—Biff's Ebbets Field game and Ben's invitation to Alaska—he becomes frantic, "almost dancing. . . . He turns around as if to find his way; sounds, faces, voices, seem to be swarming in upon him and he flicks at them, crying, Sh! Sh! . . . He goes up and down on his toes, and rushes off around the house. Shhh!" (*DoS*, pp. 135–36). Willy, like Lear, is on the verge of madness here, but unlike Lear, who runs mad midway through his tragedy, in time to recover his wits later, Willy is at the very end of his.[37] The reason, I think, can be found in one of Cavell's descriptions of Lear, which suggests that "Lear runs not because in his madness he cannot distinguish friends from enemies but because he knows that recognition of himself is imminent. Even madness is no rescue" (*MWM*, p. 280). Willy has just had the following recognition of himself thrust upon him by Biff: "You were never anything but a hard-working drummer who landed in the ash can like all the rest of them!" (*DoS*, p. 132). This is the "truth" about "who we are" with which Biff confronts him. Willy's tragedy is that he cannot face this truth. He kills himself because the $20,000 insurance payoff is not just a way of making *Biff* magnificent; it is also Willy's way of deserving or even requiting Biff's love by making *himself* magnificent in Biff's eyes. He even boasts of this to his brother, Ben: "He'll see what I am, Ben! He's in for a shock, that boy!" (*DoS*, p. 126).

This theme of the quest for identity, together with the inevitable acknowledgments or avoidances of it, constitutes, in Cavell's view, one of the most central and elemental themes of tragedy since classical times:

> The recognition of the other takes the form of an acknowledgment of oneself, one's own identity. This need not be a case, as with Oedipus, in which the hero had before the learning not been cognizant of his identity. It can be a case, as with Antigone, in which everything is known but in which the logic of recognition (viz., that it demands acknowledgment) is itself the drama. Here the tragedy is that the cost of claiming one's identity may claim one's life. (*CoR*, p. 389)

What makes *Death of a Salesman* such a quintessentially Cavellian tragedy is that this quest for an acknowledgment of an identity—especially Biff's struggle for his father's acknowledgment—is bound up with Biff's quest for the ordinary. Perhaps this is nothing remarkable; perhaps some sense of the ordinary is needed in order to ground anyone's understanding of who he or she is. But what makes *Death of a Salesman* so very apposite is that Biff's quest for his identity simply *is* his quest for the ordinary, and conversely Willy's flight from his identity simply *is* his flight from the ordinary.

In several complex ways, the play is structured by these stark contrasts between father and son, especially with their different attitudes toward the ordinary and toward their own and each other's identities. To complicate matters further, however, the issues of identity or selfhood and the ordinary or everyday seem to meet in the contrasting visions these two men have of another term central to Cavell's thought, *America*.[38] Willy describes himself as "the New England man. I'm vital in New England" (*DoS*, p. 14), while Biff is drifting around "out West," specifically in Texas (*DoS*, p. 23). Geographically as well as in terms of the place they occupy in America's historical and cultural conception of itself, these places could scarcely be further apart. Neither could Biff's and Willy's visions of America. Willy, who regularly travels to "the cradle of the Revolution" (*DoS*, p. 31), voices the view of the patriot: America is "the greatest country in the world" (*DoS*, p. 16), "full of beautiful towns and fine, upstanding people" (*DoS*, p. 31). Biff rejects his father's America, declaring that "we don't belong in this nuthouse of a city! We should be mixing cement on some open plain, or—or carpenters" (*DoS*, p. 61).[39] It is telling that he is regarded by his mother and father as "very lost" and consequently as "finding himself" (*DoS*, p. 16).

That Biff is finding himself in the West of America instantly recalls a passage from Emerson's essay "Experience" that gives one of Cavell's books its very name: one of Emerson's responses to the condition of finding himself lost to himself is to declare, "I am ready to die out of nature and be born again into this new yet unapproachable America I have found in the West." Furthermore, as Cavell observes, "finding a new America in the West while being, or because, lost, is remembering or repeating something Columbus did" (*IQO*, pp. 90–91), which connects the idea of finding a New World with founding it. Consequently, if one is lucky enough to find a new identity in, and thanks to, America, it can be said that, however provisionally or imperfectly, one has founded a new American identity (which has indeed been the experience of the many peoples who have been described as "new" Americans). To return this discussion toward *Death of a Salesman*, Cavell remarks:

> What seems to me evident is that Emerson's finding of founding as finding, say the transfiguration of philosophical grounding as lasting, could not have presented itself as a stable philosophical proposal before the configuration of philosophy established by the work of the later Heidegger and the later Wittgenstein, call this the establishing of thinking as knowing how to go on, being on the way, onward and onward. At each step, or level, explanation comes to an end; there is no level to which all explanations come, at which all end. All America might see this as taking the open road. The philosopher as the hobo of thought. (*TNYUA*, p. 116)

In some ways, I would suggest, this passage describes Biff's vision of America. It is a vision that his brother, Happy, sees as that of "a poet" or "an idealist" (*DoS*, p. 23), but I intend to argue that it is also that of a certain kind of philosopher, understanding the picture of the philosopher in America, as Cavell demonstrates in his various readings of Emerson's "The American Scholar," to be a highly ambiguous and contested one.[40]

Biff's clearest articulation of his vision comes toward the start of the play and is worth quoting in full:

> I've had twenty or thirty different kinds of jobs since I left home before the war, and it always turns out the same. I just realized it lately. In Nebraska when I herded cattle, and the Dakotas, and Arizona, and now in Texas. It's why I came home now, I guess, because I realized it. This farm I work on, it's spring there now, see? And they've got about fifteen new colts. There's nothing more inspiring or—beautiful than the sight of a mare and a new colt. And it's cool there now, see? Texas is cool now, and it's spring. And whenever spring comes to where I am, I suddenly get the feeling, my God, I'm not gettin' anywhere! What the hell am I doing, playing around with horses, twenty-eight dollars a week! I'm thirty-four years old, I oughta be makin' my future. That's when I come running home. And now, I get here, and I don't know what to do with myself. [*After a pause*] I've always made a point of not wasting my life, and everytime I come back here I know that all I've done is to waste my life. (*DoS*, pp. 22–23)

One could scarcely hope for a clearer exemplification of Cavell's answer to the question he asks of Emerson: "Why is this new America said to be yet unapproachable?" (*IQO*, p. 91). The first and most obvious answer to this question is, according to Cavell, that "it is unapproachable if he (or whoever belongs there) is already there (always already), but unable to experience it, hence to know or tell it; or unable to tell it, hence to experience it" (*IQO*, p. 91). Biff, as this speech makes clear, is simultaneously the hobo and the philosopher, the drifter and the poet, lost precisely because he is already where he wants to be. Since he is unable to recognize his destination and therefore to arrive at it, his quest for America is his quest for the ordinary, a quest in which, as Sandra Laugier puts it, "finding . . . is not the same thing as discovery," because it is in the nature of the ordinary, like Biff's experience of the unapproachable America he has found in the West, "that it is already there, that there is in a sense nothing for us to discover."[41] This, no doubt, is why the solution Biff finds to his and his father's problems is not a found solution (an answer) at all. As we have seen, it is simply to *stop*, to stop his questing, to realize his identity, to acknowledge—as Biff does and Willy tragically cannot—that he is just an ordinary American.

IV

If Biff's experience of America bears some passing affinities with Emerson's sketch of its unapproachability, then Willy's vision of America is, at least on one occasion, even more explicitly Emersonian.[42] The tragedy is that Willy too finds this Emersonian vision of America unapproachable. When telling his boss, Howard, of a long-missed opportunity to work with his brother, Ben, in the wilderness of Alaska, he boasts, "We've got quite a little streak of self-reliance in our family" (*DoS*, p. 81), and thereby name-checks what is probably Emerson's best-known discussion of America and the American identity. It is in this speech that he reveals that he has chosen to die the "death of a salesman" instead of following his "yearning to go to Alaska. . . . Just for the ride, you might say" (see *DoS*, pp. 80–81). Accordingly, his opting to ignore his roaming heart and remain in New York to pursue what he calls, ironically, "the greatest career a man could want" (*DoS*, p. 81) sets him up yet again as Biff's structural opposite, because Alaska is to Willy the very mirror image of what Texas is to Biff: Biff goes to Texas but cannot locate the solution to his problems there; Willy does not go to Alaska but locates the solution to his problems there nevertheless. "If I'd gone with [Ben] to Alaska that time, everything would've been totally different," he says (*DoS*, p. 45), and he is not deterred by the pragmatism of Charley's reply ("Go on, you'd froze to death up there" [*DoS*, p. 45]).

Before exploring exactly how Willy's sense of "self-reliance" relates to the vision of America he locates in Alaska, it is worth unpacking what exactly that vision entails. Alaska is described largely by Willy's recollections—or, perhaps, hallucinations?[43]—of his brother, Ben, who uses terms that describe the Great Outdoors in a very different way from Biff's portrait of the ordinary as a young colt. "Opportunity is tremendous in Alaska," he says (*DoS*, p. 45), and later he adds, "You've a new continent at your doorstep, William. Get out of these cities, they're full of talk and time payments and courts of law. Screw on your fists and you can fight for a fortune up there" (*DoS*, p. 85). Ben does not invite Willy to Alaska to go in quest of the ordinary; he invites him there in order to "walk out rich. Rich!" (*DoS*, p. 87). He shares Biff's contempt for the city and would no doubt endorse Biff's exclamation "Screw the business world!" (*DoS*, p. 61), but probably more because of his refusal to "fight fair" (*DoS*, p. 49) than because of a need to find himself. Ben describes Alaska in classically American terms, as a land of "opportunity," but the opportunities he offers Willy are not the opportunities Willy really needs. It is to Ben, and to Ben alone, that Willy is prepared to confide to a certain incompleteness in his sense of self and identity: "I still feel—kind of temporary about myself," he admits (*DoS*, p. 51). Thus, Biff and Happy are not the only pair of brothers in the play who fail to realize that their dream of wealth and success together as "the Loman Brothers" is in fact a front for an underdeveloped sense of security and identity. For Willy, Alaska is, to paraphrase a certain song, the land where my father died, and the sense of stability and identity articulated in that song is no doubt a large part of what attracts him to it, attracting him there because of his lack of it.[44] But so fanatical is Willy in his pursuit of Ben's ideals—he sees Ben as "the only man I ever met who knew the answers" (*DoS*, p. 45), "a genius . . . success incarnate" (*DoS*, p. 41)—that he cannot acknowledge his incomplete sense of self and thus avoids attaining it by opting for the pursuit of material success instead.

In summary, what this vision of Alaska suggests is that Willy's little streak of self-reliance is indeed *very* little and that his locating it in his *family* (and *not* in himself) points more convincingly to Biff than to himself as realizing that streak. In order to explain this, it is important to understand first that, for Cavell, self-reliance is to an extent synonymous with the idea of Emersonian moral perfectionism. To be self-reliant in this sense is to acknowledge one's ordinary self as a self one has attained and simultaneously to acknowledge its limits, its incompleteness, as a precondition for attaining a "further" or "higher" state of self. This means that selfhood becomes a series of attained selves, each en route to a series of unattained but attainable selves. "That the self is always attained, as well as *to be* attained, creates the problem in Emerson's concept of self-reliance . . . —that unless you manage the reliance of the attained on the unattained/attainable . . . you are left in precisely the negation of the position he calls for, left in conformity" (*CHU*, p. 12). It is quite correct to say of Willy that the self he has not yet attained but desperately wishes to attain underpins the sense of self he has attained. His tragedy is that that self he aspires to attain is the product of "false or debased perfectionisms" (*CHU*, p. 16), the pursuit of which inspires a fanaticism so self-consuming that it undermines and ultimately destroys his sense of the self he *has* attained. How can it be that in a figure so quintessentially American as Willy Loman the quintessentially American ideal of self-reliance has become so pernicious, so twisted?

Answering this question will take us right to the heart of Cavell's conception of America. If "a new America is said to be unapproachable" (*IQO*, p. 79), then we must surely ask, as Simon Critchley does, "Does one approach the unapproachable America?"[45] His conclusion is that Cavell's America is preeminently approachable because it is only and no more than approachable: it is never actually arrived at, and is to be discovered only in the process of approaching it, much as happiness is to be discovered only in its pursuit. "We arrive and it is too late. There is only the approach," Critchley says.[46] This is not, however, to say that Cavell's America is a unitary unattainable entity. Considering the analogy with the self of Emersonian moral perfectionism, Cavell denies "that there is one unattained/attainable self we repetitively never arrive at, but rather that 'having' 'a' self is a process of moving to, and from, nexts" (*CHU*, p. 12). Similarly, the Cavellian unapproachable America is a series of unattained but attainable states, "a kind of perfectionist *Amerique a venir*," as Critchley calls it.[47] It is telling, for Critchley and for other commentators, that Cavell's unattainable America "is never quite there, is always on the way, always to come."[48] Hence Critchley asks, "What is the time of America? Philosophically and politically, America is the thought and the land of the *future*."[49] Cavell does not deny this; to the contrary, in elucidating this perfectionist vision of an unattainable America, he argues that "what is under attack is, one might say, a way of arriving at the future (a way of discovering America), pictures of progress and of piety that deny that the conditions of a society of undenied human beings remain to be realized" (*TNYUA*, p. 45).

Now, if Stanley Cavell's vision of America is oriented toward a futurity, it is surely noteworthy that Willy Loman's is too. His wife, Linda, says that when he "talks about the future . . . he's just wonderful" (*DoS*, p. 54), and his younger son agrees that "Dad is never so happy as when he's looking forward to something" (*DoS*, p. 105). Willy himself recalls the happiness of the days when there was "always some kind of good news coming up, always something nice coming up ahead" (*DoS*, p. 127). Why, then, does his vision of America culminate in tragedy? The answer, I think, has to do with the temporality of tragedy as discussed in the previous chapter. There I explored a certain tension between the redemptive power of tragedy that is oriented toward a futurity and Cavell's observation that tragic heroes generally avoid or forgo the present (and presentness itself), so that avoiding tragedy requires acknowledging the present. Willy is, at least in part, a tragic hero because the form of refusal his avoidance of the ordinary takes is to live his life out of time with it. His fanatical adherence to ever fantastical hopes of future success and greatness is better understood not as a perfectionist orientation toward a future self but as a tragic avoidance of his present state of self. (Indeed, Willy spends far more time losing himself in nostalgia and reliving his past than he does anticipating the future.)

Miller himself declares that "*Death of a Salesman* explodes the watch and the calendar"[50] for reasons that have to do with Willy's highly tenuous grasp of the present and, interestingly, the relationship between Willy's grasp of time and his own identity and sense of self:

> The past and the present are so openly and vocally intertwined in his [Loman's] mind. . . . There are no flashbacks in this play but only a mobile concurrency of past and present, and this, again, because in his desperation to justify his life Willy Loman has destroyed the boundaries between now and then.[51]

And so Willy's dreams of a magnificent future for himself and especially for Biff are not enough for us to view him as a self-reliant moral perfectionist in the Emersonian mold, oriented on the nextness of his next self. Rather, the fact that these dreams are concocted out of a fanatical need to escape the past and the present, together with the fact that the unattained self Willy wishes to attain in these dreams measures its self-worth only financially, means that his America remains unapproachable, because, in the epitaph Biff provides for his father, "He had the wrong dreams. All, all, wrong" (*DoS*, p. 138). If the idea of America is to be conceived of as a dream rooted in futurity, then one had better dream that futurity aright.

Perhaps, however, this verdict does not really accord with the truth, or at any rate, not the *whole* truth. Looking more closely at the scene in which Willy decides not to yield to the alluring false promises of Ben's Alaska, it might perhaps seem as if here is a man reaching a fair settlement with the ordinary and the present. The principal voice of dissuasion in his decision comes from Willy's wife, Linda. "You're doing well enough, Willy!" she protests (*DoS*, p. 85). When challenged by Ben's asking, "Enough for what, my dear?" her telling reply is, "Enough to be happy right here, right now" (*DoS*, p. 85). Linda seems to be advising Willy to make a fair settlement with the ordinary and to seek his identity and his happiness in that instead of in Alaska. "Why must everybody conquer the world?" she asks him (*DoS*, p. 85). (Her question, incidentally, could be taken to imply that Cavell's suggestion about women being less susceptible than men when it comes to skepticism is a suggestion that might also prove true when it comes to fanaticism.)[52] The fact that Willy follows her advice and stays in Brooklyn could be read as suggesting that Willy is, after all, prepared to renounce his fanaticism rather than the ordinary and the present.

This reading, however, mistakes Willy's motivations in staying in Brooklyn. The fact is that he does *not* follow his wife's advice: he does *not* embrace the ordinary or the present. His decision does not in any way constitute a renunciation of his false view of America and the false aspirations it holds for his unattained self. "That's the wonder, that's the wonder of this country, that a man can end with diamonds here on the basis of being liked!" he exclaims (*DoS*, p. 86). So it is not Ben's vision of success or of America that he is rejecting, but merely the geography of it: "We'll do it here, Ben! You hear me? We're gonna do it here!" (*DoS*, p. 87). And in a certain sense there is a Cavellian motivation behind his reasoning. If we take Linda's advice to constitute an appeal to the ordinary and to the present, then Willy's refusing to attend to such advice is indeed a tragic move. But there is another way of taking Linda's advice, and that is as suggesting that he give up his aspirations to a better self and simply settle for what he has and what he is. If that is what Linda means when she says, "Enough to be happy right here, right now," then this advice resembles the kind of caricature that is often given out as a simplistic summary of a certain branch of philosophy that, for good or ill, has come to be synonymous with American thought. That branch, of course, is pragmatism. From a Cavellian point of view, pragmatism is innately at odds with perfectionism, because the perfectionist cannot, by definition, settle for the present state of affairs as final or even as "good enough." That is what a commitment to perfectionism entails. If one embraces this commitment, one is embracing not just a vision of one's self and one's identity but also a certain vision of America and its legendary promise. It is a vision that, according to most readings, is fundamentally at odds with the territory pragmatism has staked out as "American."[53]

This, then, is how I read Willy's dilemma. To go to Alaska would be to take flight from the ordinary in quest of a self that is as unattainable as the success by which Willy defines it. To remain in Brooklyn would be to enter into a pragmatist accommodation of the ordinary, which holds no promise for, or even of, an unattained, further self to come. To take Biff's route—to attain a knowledge of who he is and a vision of selfhood that is rooted in the ordinariness and presentness of America—is not an option that is open to Willy, for his dreams are of a futurity that is in flight from the present, and of a greatness that is in flight from the ordinary. His tragedy is that his vision of America is unapproachable because the sense of futurity that is essential to perfectionism is out of time with the sense of the present that is simultaneously the key to the ordinary and the antidote to tragedy.

That is not to suggest, for a moment, that the present is synonymous with the ordinary. On the contrary, that—at least, from a perfectionist point of view—is the basic mistake driving pragmatism. Pragmatism conceives the ground of the ordinary as what there is here and now; Cavell's perfectionism sees the ordinary as something to be achieved or attained, turned to or returned to. It is, as it were, an *eventual* ordinary, in a sense new and in a sense unapproachable. By contrast, at its crudest level American pragmatism is apt to strike the Cavellian commentator as a manifesto for conformity, and it is telling that this is precisely the bugbear Emerson sets up as the opposite to his vision of self-reliance. Conformity of this kind is a false settlement with the ordinary and simultaneously a false picture of the kind of society and politics that America embodies. Cavell points out that in repudiating the ground of what is ordinarily called American philosophy, one is not dismissing American thought but gesturing instead toward an alternative possibility for American thought that in turn grounds a new thought of America:

> When "Self-Reliance" says "Self-reliance is the aversion of conformity" it means that this writing finds America, as it stands, or presents itself, to be repellent, or say unattractive; and it means that America so finds this writing. Emerson by no means, however, just shrinks from America, because this "aversion" turns not just away, but at the same time, and always, toward America. (*IQO*, p. 92)

Turning away from America in order to turn toward it is a way of achieving or attaining its ordinariness, and it is also a good description of Biff's perfectionist journey of self-discovery. Why is his quest for the ordinary apparently successful, while his father's is a failure? Why, if his solution is simply to abandon the quest for a further self and to settle for what he is in the here and now ("Why am I trying to become what I don't want to be . . . when all I want is out there, waiting for me the minute I say I know who I am!" [*DoS*, p. 132]), is Biff any different from a pragmatist?

The difference is that Biff's is not a straightforward acceptance of the present à la pragmatism; otherwise he would not struggle so much to find his place in it. (As it is, he says, "I don't know—what I'm supposed to want. . . . Maybe I oughta get stuck into something" [*DoS*, pp. 22–33].) Rather, it is a question of making himself present to the present and allowing its presentness to be present to him. For Biff, the everyday remains something to be achieved, attained, or perfected, and not, as Heidegger might put it, something present-at-hand. His vision of the ordinary and the everyday is thus in line with Cavell's perfectionist vision of America. As Critchley puts it, "For Cavell . . . America is always linked to the perfectionist hope for a redemption of culture through a recovery of the everyday, the demand for a sky under which philosophy might be possible."[54] Critchley is here paraphrasing an early passage in *This New Yet Unapproachable America* in which Cavell, responding to some thoughts of Santayana, ponders whether the sky remains a suitable canopy for philosophy. Interestingly, it is precisely the thought of the sky in Bill Oliver's New York office that provides Biff with his insight into himself. Biff's longing to spend his time dwelling, working, and building under the sky[55] suggests that my earlier allusion to Heidegger might not be as out of place as it may seem: what he values about this mode of being in the world is the relationship between "the work and the . . . time to sit and smoke" (*DoS*, p. 132), which suggests that his sense of being and time and their interrelatedness has allowed him to attain a heightened sense of the present as present and the ordinary as ordinary.

By contrast, Willy's alienated existence has no room for this relationship: he is "always in a race with the junkyard" (*DoS*, p. 73). Although he feels that "a man who can't handle tools is not a man" (*DoS*, p. 44) and dreams of building houses for his sons and their families (*DoS*, p. 72), Ben points out to him, again in somewhat Heideggerian terms, that he cannot lay his hands on what he is building in his career as a salesman (*DoS*, p. 86). Charley, the only friend Willy has (*DoS*, p. 98), emphasizes this in another fitting epitaph for our dead salesman: "Willy was a salesman. And for a salesman, there is no rock bottom to the life. He don't put a bolt to a nut, he don't tell you the law or give you medicine. He's a man way out there in the blue, riding on a smile and a shoeshine" (*DoS*, p. 138). Coincidental as this may be, Cavell attaches a significance to the idea of a shoeshine in an essay on a Fred Astaire song-and-dance sequence in which Astaire's encounter with a shoeshine man "inspires him to stop and think," and a great deal of what he thinks about involves "the question of America" (*PDAT*, p. 73). Willy, unlike Biff, does not find the time to stop and think. His pursuit of a better future is precisely what prevents him from doing so. That this future will be better is simply taken for granted by Willy—accepted as simply the way things will be. He never questions *how* things will be better and thus merely settles for the dream without reorientating himself toward a new ground that could picture its attainability. Thus, Willy is a perfectionist who measures his attainment of perfectionism in pragmatist terms.

V

Death of a Salesman, in its stark contrast between father and son, between tragic failure of and successful insight into the attainment of a further self, offers its audience a therapeutic intervention that matches that on offer in Cavell's unique brand of ordinary language philosophy. This intervention consists of "*returning* us to the ordinary, a place we have never been" (*PDAT*, pp. 9–10). The deadness to us of Willy's actual ordinary is revealed to us by Biff's attainment of an eventual ordinary, thus showing that just as in turning from one version of America one turns toward another, so too the ordinary is to be redeemed in, by, and through the ordinary. For Cavell, "Wittgenstein's insight is that the ordinary has, and alone has, the power to move the ordinary, to leave the human habitat habitable, the same transfigured. The practice of the ordinary may be thought of as the overcoming of iteration or replication or imitation" (*IQO*, p. 47). That the ordinary can redeem the ordinary from the ordinary may seem contradictory, tautological, or both, but *Death of a Salesman* shows us that it is neither: Biff's redemptive vision of the ordinary reframes the audience's grasp of the ordinary from Willy's tragic avoidance of the ordinary. It makes the ordinary available to us in order for us to change our relationship toward it, to attain, in a perfectionist fashion, a new state of the ordinary. It is for this reason that appealing to the ordinary, as Wittgenstein, Austin, and Cavell do, is anything but appealing to political and social conservatism. As Stephen Mulhall explains:

> When Wittgenstein talks of grammatical investigations as returning us to the ordinary or the everyday, or as requiring that we accept forms of life as given, he need not be counselling an acceptance of the particular inflection of our interests, capacities, and needs that prevails at a given historical juncture. On the contrary: the actual everyday may have to be overthrown if the eventual everyday—the real possibilities of the distinctively human life form that are covered over by particular cultural formations as well as by enactments of skeptical thinking—are to be realized. The form of philosophical practice that is required to oppose skepticism therefore need not be a reactionary reiteration of whatever happens to be the case, but might rather revolutionize our ordinary life with language. . . .

> It asks us to let our words teach us the present and possible configurations of our life form; and then it calls us actively to maintain or enact the best of those possibilities, in the name of a world worthy of the investment of our interest and desire.[56]

Death of a Salesman dramatizes the way that the ordinary can be remade if the pragmatist impulse to settle for it or to accommodate it is resisted, and in dramatizing this realization, it sets its audience free from the confines of the actual everyday and on the path to a perfectionist, eventual everyday.[57] Miller, in reflecting on his play, does not use these exact terms, but he certainly sees his play as inviting his audience to embark on a quest for a higher state of morals, and this implies some kind of perfectionist journey similar to that described by Cavell. Miller writes: "In *Death of a Salesman*, we are shown a man who dies for the want of some positive, viable human value. . . . In other words, by showing what happens when there are no values, I, at least, assume that the audience will be compelled and propelled toward a more intense quest for values that are missing."[58]

Interestingly, even a casual reading of Miller's theater essays, especially those written at the same time as *Death of a Salesman*, reveals that Miller shares Cavell's enthusiasm for a certain idea of moral perfectionism and, moreover, sees tragedy itself as a genre that tends inherently toward a moral perfectionism of sorts. The great tragedies, Miller says, take root from a "vision of man's great possibilities" and are thus "the perfect means we have of showing us who and what we are, and what we must be—or should strive to become,"[59] because "in them, and in them alone, lies the belief—optimistic, if you will, in the perfectibility of man."[60] The typical tragic plot, Miller suggests, exemplifies the journey of a moral perfectionist toward the attainment of a higher state of self—or at least that is how I interpret his contention that "if it is true to say that in essence the tragic hero is intent upon claiming his whole due as a personality, and if this struggle must be total and without reservation, then it automatically demonstrates the indestructible will of man to achieve his humanity."[61] Though describing this achievement makes it sound grandiose, nevertheless, as in Cavell's Emersonian moral perfectionism, its parting company with the ordinary is a false departure, and, as Miller says, "in no way is the common man debarred from such thoughts or such actions."[62]

Thus, it is unsurprising to find Cavell describing the tragedy of *King Lear* in more or less the exact terms I would use to describe that of *Death of a Salesman*: "The cost of an ordinary life and death, of insisting upon one's own life, and avoiding one's own cares, has become the same as the cost of the old large lives and deaths, requires the same lucidity and exacts the same obscurity and suffering" (*MWM*, p. 351). If, for Cavell, the way we imagine the attainability of the ordinary and the everyday is, philosophically, analogous to the way we imagine the attainability of America, and if the question of tragedy is bound up with the avoidance of the ordinary, then Willy's tragedy is also an avoidance of (a certain vision of) America. What *Death of a Salesman* shows us, simultaneously and synonymously with Willy's tragic flight from the ordinary and his failure to realize an attainable self, is, in a sense, a tragedy of America.[63] Cavell points out that classically, tragedies were often centered around the fate of a state and hence formed a crucial part of a nation's culture, mythology, and identity. Although America was founded after the era of national tragedies had come to an end, Miller's resurrection of tragedy as a genre provides a preemptive counterpoint to a passage Cavell wrote some twenty years later in "The Avoidance of Love," published at the height of the Vietnam War. This passage, in which Cavell meditates on the relationship between tragedy and the American identity itself, is worth quoting at some length:

> Classical tragedies were always national, so perhaps it is not surprising that nations have become tragic. And of the great modern nations which have undergone tragedy, through inexplicable loss of past or loss of future or self-defeat of promise, in none is tragedy so intertwined with its history and its identity as in America. It is cast with uncanny perfection for its role, partly because its power is so awe-inspiring, partly because its self-destruction is so heartbreaking. It had a mythical beginning, still visible, if ambiguous, to itself and to its audience: before there was Russia, there was Russia; before there was France and England, there was France and England; but before there was America there was no America. America was *discovered*, and what was discovered was not a place, one among others, but a setting, the backdrop of a destiny. It began as theater. Its Revolution, unlike the English and French and Russian Revolutions, was not a civil war; it was fought against outsiders, its point was not reform but independence. And its Civil War was not a revolution; the oppressed did not rise, and the point was not the overthrow of a form of government but secession and union, the point was its identity. And neither of these points was settled, nor has either been lost, through defeat or through loss of empire or change of political constitution. So its knowledge is of indefeasible power and constancy. But its fantasies are those of impotence, because it remains at the mercy of its past, because its present is continuously ridiculed by the fantastic promise of its origins and its possibility, and

> because it has never been assured that it will survive. Since it had a birth, it may die. It feels mortal. And it wishes proof not merely of its continuance but of its existence, a fact it has never been able to take for granted. Therefore its need for love is insatiable. It has surely been given more love than any other nation: its history, until yesterday, is one in which outsiders have been drawn to it and in which insiders are hoarse from their expressions of devotion to it. Those who voice politically radical wishes for this country may forget the radical hopes it holds for itself, and not know that the hatred of America by its intellectuals is only their own version of patriotism. It is the need for love as proof of its existence which makes it so frighteningly destructive, enraged by ingratitude and by attention to its promises rather than to its promise, and which makes it incapable of seeing that it is destructive and frightening. (*MWM*, pp. 344–45)

Miller seems to agree wholeheartedly with the basis of Cavell's diagnosis—that America's tragedy is the love inspired by its idealism, squandered in the twentieth century by increasingly destructive posturing at home and abroad.

> In the period of her so-called naiveté, America held the allegiance of people precisely because she was not cynical, because her name implied love and faith in people, and because she was the common man's country. In later years we have gone about forgetting our simplicity while a new ideology has risen to call for justice, however cynically, and imparting the idea that Russia stood for the working man. Meanwhile in a small voice we have spoken of justice and in a big voice of arms and armaments, wars and the rumors of wars. Now we must face ourselves and ask . . . What is in us that the world must know of? When we find this, the essence of America, we shall be able to forge a foreign policy capable of arousing the hopes and the love of the only force that matters any more, the force that is neither in governments nor armies nor banks nor institutions, the force that rests in the heart of man. When we come to address ourselves to this vessel of eternal unrest and eternal hope, we shall once again be on our way.[64]

Is the phrase "this vessel of eternal unrest and eternal hope" a description of "the force that rests in the heart of man," or does it refer to "the essence of America"? That it might potentially be read both ways illustrates how deep the streak of moral perfectionism runs in this vision of America and how this vision shows us once again that love and its avoidance run in parallel to the destructive avoidance of the ordinary in tragedy. And if this is so, then perhaps the perfectionist hope that this love of America, like Willy's love of Biff, might one day find an object worthy of it can enable us to understand how those who make up the audience of this ordinary American tragedy, themselves ordinary citizens watching a cast of ordinary Americans, become ready to die out of themselves and be born again into a new yet unapproachable Willy Loman.

VI

As we saw earlier, one of the common strands that binds skepticism, fanaticism, and tragedy together is that each of them is driven by an incapacity to stop. This incapacity can, of course, take many forms: an inability to let go (Willy Loman), a fixation with endlessness or the infinite (Leontes), or the need to just keep on going until the end—an inevitably bitter end—is reached (Coriolanus, perhaps, or maybe Othello). If these three propensities toward destruction—skepticism, fanaticism, tragedy—are hallmarked by their failure to stop, then surely one of the lessons to be learned from this is the importance of making an end, of drawing to a conclusion.

I have argued, both in the previous section and in the previous chapter, that tragedy evokes, or, better, *con*vokes, a response from its audience. I have also made some suggestions as to how it does this: as the previous chapter established, this response is something predicated on the sense that tragedy is coming to an end, and bringing its time to an end, with the ethical dimension of tragedy being projected into the time to come, after this end. So perhaps it makes sense to conclude by asking, if tragedy shows us the importance of coming to a stop, then when and where does our response to tragedy come to a stop?

Two answers to this question seem possible. The first, and more straightforward, would be that it doesn't. The analogy between Cavell and Levinas would suggest that our ethical response to and responsibility for tragedy is infinite, hence without end. So if *Death of a Salesman* is, to adapt Cavell's terms, a national tragedy for a tragic nation, then its audience, as citizens, is endlessly implicated in its tragedy. This is certainly a view one could take, and, as explored in the previous chapter, there is much about Cavell's position to suggest that he does indeed take it. But its sense of infinity is redolent of the impulse toward skepticism rather than of the equally Cavellian emphasis on finitude and limits. So a second possible answer would go something like this: "When [tragedy] . . . is brought to a close its content is not exhausted. We could say, it has infinite content: but what this comes to is that we have stopped pursuing it (or it us), that we have been shown that a stop can be *made*" (*MWM*, p. 342).

So tragedy shows us—Biff Loman shows us—that we can and must stop ourselves. Cavell likewise says that his "aim in reading is to follow out in each case the complete tuition for a given intuition (tuition comes to an end somewhere)" (*DK*, p. 5). But where and how does it come to an end? Answering this question would be a good way to bring this study to a close, not just because it would show us that making an end is indeed possible, not to mention important or even downright necessary, but because the answer will help encapsulate the relationship between the philosophical and literary enterprises in Cavell's work.

Back in the introduction, I asked, "What is the 'other' of philosophy?" I asked this question so as to reject those philosophers who cast literature in this role, but although literature has been duly discounted as an answer, I have not yet supplied an alternative. Hopefully, it is clear enough that just as failed tragedy is melodrama and failed music is noise, so too failed philosophy is skepticism. And if what characterizes skepticism is its inability to end its (bogus) questioning, then it is part of the task of philosophy to set a bound to skepticism. As Cavell puts it, "Until the passing of skepticism there is no better alternative for the mind . . . than procedures of philosophy that wish to end philosophy" (*DK*, p. 30).

This means that for Cavell the structure of philosophical investigation is the same as the structure of critical reading: both are enterprises that must ultimately seek to bring themselves to an end. Both philosophy and reading are troubled by skepticism because "there is no assignable end to the depth of us to which language reaches" (*CoR*, p. 369). Both must therefore *find* an end to it. The end is not, however, a pragmatist end—a shrugging of the shoulders while huffing something like, "This is simply what I do"—nor a deconstructive end that culminates in aporia and impossibility, which masquerades as endless and hence as providing no end at all. Instead, the Cavellian end is simultaneously less simple and less grandiose. As we saw earlier, in the passage that described the philosopher (and, in my reading, Biff Loman) as "the hobo of thought," there is no ultimate destination to the philosophical journey—not simply because there is no final position or truth to be finally arrived at but, more importantly, because philosophy is *perpetually* arriving at it. "At each step, or level, explanation comes to an end; there is no level to which all explanations come, at which all end" (*TNYUA*, p. 116). The same is, of course, true of how we read, whether what we read is philosophy or literature.

Cavell observes that "philosophical books are forever postponing their conclusions" (*IQO*, p. 18), which seems to allude to Wittgenstein, who held that "in philosophy we do not draw conclusions."[65] If this is so, then what is there to differentiate philosophy from skepticism? Wittgenstein's answer, according to

Cavell's reading, would be that "it is not that philosophy ought to be brought as such to an end, but that in each case of its being called for, it brings itself to an end" (*TNYUA*, p. 74).

This position should not be mistaken for a proclamation of the end of philosophy itself, whether that is to be understood as a call to give up the enterprise as fruitless or else as a triumphant declaration that philosophy's success has rendered it redundant. Cavell contrasts Wittgenstein with Heidegger on this point:

> Heidegger sees [philosophy] as having some place and time at which it will end, while for Wittgenstein the end of philosophy is not something that happens in the future, or elsewhere. It is . . . a way in which philosophy directs itself, motivates itself, in every given instant in which it has its origination. So that philosophy originates and comes to an end in every moment of genuine philosophical conversation.[66]

Thus, as opposed on the one hand to the view of philosophy *qua* philosophy coming to an end and on the other hand to the view of skepticism's posing of (and hence posing as) an infinite questioning, the view Cavell finds in Wittgenstein is that "there is a sense of philosophy as unending, and as falsely ending, that Wittgenstein is prepared, unendingly, to bring to an end."[67]

So there is no such thing as a final destination in philosophy if what we mean by such a thing is a position from which we could pronounce the End of Philosophy. Instead of such an end—whether it is pictured as a bang or a whimper, as philosophy's failure, its success, or its redundancy—philosophy has rather *endings* that it endlessly arrives at. And in this respect, as is perhaps unsurprising given Cavell's insistence on the textual character of philosophy, it approximates the condition of reading. For it would be quixotic, to say the very least, to declare the End of Reading, partly because each reading aspires to constitute an end in itself (and so to put an end to itself) and partly because that this is so makes the very idea of an end to reading per se ungrammatical, even absurd.

What would *the* End of Reading look like? Might it mean that we had found a way to achieve pure communion with the mind of an author, making reading superfluous? Or that we had found an infallible literary theory that yielded, unfailingly, the key that unlocked each and every text, so that all that remained to us was not to read texts but to apply the theory? These are of course metaphysical pictures, fantasies. But it is no less metaphysical, no less fantastical, to suggest that in the absence of these solutions we should either abandon reading (where *reading* means roughly a search for coherent meanings) or else recognize that all that is left to us is an infinite number of incompatible yet equally plausible readings.

Like philosophy, each reading is, among other things, a search for the grounds that justify the reading—a search carried out in acceptance of the lack of ultimate grounds. "How far off a final reading is, is something I hope I have already suggested," Cavell observes (*SoW*, p. 12). That any final reading still lies thus far off suggests that the journey of reading, understood this way, resembles in its structure and its nature the journey of perfectionism discussed earlier. Reading is thus a quest, but not in the treasure-hunt sense that old-fashioned hermeneutics understands this term. Any reading we might advance is an attempt to approach an unapproachable final reading, made in the knowledge that a final reading is as yet unattained, if in principle attainable. Because unlike the quest for a perfectionist self, in which the questing self is answerable essentially to itself, the quest of reading is attained through the uptake of other readers. So however satisfactory our readings may seem to ourselves, attaining a final reading would inevitably entail a need for further elucidation, further insight, and, more plainly, further reading. The attainability of a final reading—the perfectibility of reading, if you will—is a matter settled by the claims and the counterclaims readers make for or about the texts they read. Yet what is adduced as grounds for and against these claims and counterclaims is generally the very same body of evidence—the text under discussion. We seem to have reached a paradox.

How, then, are we to understand this Janus-faced characteristic of reading, whereby a final reading is, from a perfectionist viewpoint, attainable, though never in practice attained? Is it a meaningless, contradictory formulation? Is it born of empty theorizing, not sustained by critical practice? On the contrary. If a reading attempts to ground an intuition with tuition, then a successful reading, whether of a literary text or of a philosophical one, will find a ground upon which it comes to rest. Such a ground will be where each reader rests his or her case. Whatever skepticisms a reading is intended to assuage, to forestall, or to refute, this ground will be what the reader and the reading advance in order to do so. Since such a ground is meant to provide the reading's final justification and to end further skepticism, it makes sense to call that ground the *end* of each reading, where *end* can also be understood in the sense of a goal, aim, or purpose. But there is no end to the claims we make on literature and to the claims it makes on us. Readings, like philosophies, are to be debated in the public sphere.

And here there *are* no foundations—any more than there are to ordinary language or democratic conversation. That is why literary criticism finds it as hard as philosophy to reach a conclusion. Readings, like philosophies, come to an end, but the claim of literature, like the claim of reason, does not. Can literature become philosophy, or philosophy literature, and still know itself? How could either know itself, let alone the other, if not through reading?

Notes

Introduction: Approaching the Unapproachable

1. Fischer, *Stanley Cavell and Literary Skepticism*, p. 4.

2. Cavell, "*Investigations*' Everyday Aesthetics of Itself," p. 373.

3. Stanley Bates puts this matter well in his observation that "supposedly, literature particularizes and philosophy generalizes; hence, no account of the relationship of their texts can profitably be theorized. It isn't exactly that Cavell has a theory about the relationship of philosophy to literature, but the question of that relationship is central to all of his writing." Bates, "Stanley Cavell and Ethics," p. 39.

4. Fischer, *Stanley Cavell and Literary Skepticism*, p. 7.

5. Cavell, "Interview with Stanley Cavell," p. 66.

6. Mulhall, "On Refusing to Begin," p. 36. For a fuller discussion of the idea of the "paradox of reading," see chapter 1.

7. Stewart, "Avoidance of Stanley Cavell," p. 140.

8. Stewart, "Avoidance of Stanley Cavell," pp. 140–41.

9. Fischer, *Stanley Cavell and Literary Skepticism*, p. 2.

10. For a more substantial discussion of the rise and fall of the theoretical "detour," see my "Literature and Philosophy: The Contemporary Interface," in Rudrum, *Literature and Philosophy*.

11. Cavell, foreword to *Philosophical Shakespeares*, p. x.

12. But not entirely unheard of: "What is the Scandal of Skepticism?," discussed in chapter 7, is one question to which Cavell *does* provide a neat answer.

13. Mulhall, *Stanley Cavell*, p. 187.

14. See the beginning of chapter 5, "What Did Cavell Want of Poe?," for a brief taster of how extensively and consistently some of Cavell's essays on literature withhold the answers to the questions they ask.

15. See Payne and Fleming, "Conversation with Stanley Cavell," p. 313.

16. Mulhall, *Stanley Cavell*, p. 187.

17. Kenny remarked that the very first sentence of the book would be enough to make some readers put it down and never take it up again. See Kenny, review of *The Claim of Reason*.

18. Fischer, *Stanley Cavell and Literary Skepticism*, p. 4.

19. Fleming, "Literary Understanding of Philosophy," p. 289–90.

20. Stewart, "Avoidance of Stanley Cavell," pp. 152, 153. Stewart goes on to suggest that "philosophy as criticism as poetry" might be a better description of Cavell's writing (p. 153).

21. A good discussion of, and challenge to, Cavell's notion of the modern is to be found in Bernstein, "Aesthetics, Modernism, Literature."

22. See, for example, *IQO*, p. 12.
23. Bernstein, "Aesthetics, Modernism, Literature," p. 124.
24. Laugier, "Rethinking the Ordinary," p. 92.
25. Eldridge, "Introduction," p. 6.
26. Obviously, it is more common for analytic philosophy to be taught to students in forms like "This is what we would ordinarily call a justification"; "This is how we would ordinarily tell whether a statement was true"; "This is when we would ordinarily say an argument was coherent," and so on.
27. Critchley, "Cavell's 'Romanticism' and Cavell's Romanticism," p. 42.

Chapter 1: Making Sense(s) of *Walden*

1. Hammer, *Stanley Cavell*, pp. 30–31.
2. In this particular quotation, the pronouns refer to Emerson rather than to Thoreau, but the point still stands.
3. Thoreau, *Walden*, p. 39 (hereafter *W*).
4. For Cavell's critique of Paul de Man, see the essay "Politics as Opposed to What?," in *TOS*, pp. 27–59. Aspects of de Man's work feature in discussions in chapter 5.
5. Bloom, *How To Read and Why*, p. 28.
6. Hammer, *Stanley Cavell*, p. 137.
7. Rhu, *Stanley Cavell's American Dream*, p. 110.
8. Melville, "Oblique and Ordinary," p. 188.
9. Bloom, *How To Read and Why*, p. 21.
10. Bloom, *Western Canon*, pp. 519, 524.
11. Bloom, *Western Canon*, p. 31.
12. Iser, *Implied Reader*, p. 282.
13. Iser's essay was originally published in the journal *New Literary History* in 1972, the same year that Cavell's *Senses of Walden* first came out.
14. Garrett Stewart draws a brief contrast between Iser's literary phenomenology and Cavell's take on Thoreau and reading and suggests that "the invitation remains ripe" for further comparison. See Stewart, "Avoidance of Stanley Cavell," p. 151.
15. Cavell identifies the skeptic as a narcissist in his essays on *Othello* and *Coriolanus* in *Disowning Knowledge*, and more generally in part 4 of *The Claim of Reason*, esp. pp. 463–65. What is meant by *skepticism* here is discussed in chapter 7.
16. Mulhall, introduction to *Cavell Reader*, p. 18. Mulhall here explicates Cavell's comparison of the reading process and the psychoanalytic process more effectively and concisely than I could.
17. See Mulhall, *Stanley Cavell*, esp. the chapters "Writing, Reading, and Being Read," pp. 171–81, and "Redemptive Reading: Refractions and Reflexivities," pp. 185–95.
18. Mulhall, *Stanley Cavell*, p. 255.
19. Mulhall, *Stanley Cavell*, p. 177. For the record, I am not altogether convinced that *Walden* envisages its readers as exactly "passive."
20. "Of what use this measuring of me if she does not measure my character, but only the breadth of my shoulders, as it were a peg to hang the coat on?" the passage continues (*W*, p. 24).
21. On this point, we could indeed say of Cavell what Borges says of Kafka: that his novelty is of a kind that creates its own predecessors.
22. Mulhall, introduction to *Cavell Reader*, pp. 18–19.

23. Ralph Waldo Emerson, "Self-Reliance," in Emerson, *Selected Writings*, p. 145. It is worth pointing out that Harold Bloom is also fond of this quotation and uses it as a description for what is involved in reading.

24. To sound a note of caution: such successful experiences can be painfully rare in psychotherapy. They may be rare in reading too, but perhaps less painfully so.

25. Stewart, "Avoidance of Stanley Cavell," p. 151.

26. Davis, *Critical Excess*, p. 139.

27. Davis, *Critical Excess*, pp. xii, ix.

28. Davis, *Critical Excess*, p. 180.

29. See Davis, *Critical Excess*, pp. 140, 187.

30. For an insightful discussion of this aspect of Cavell's reading, see Davis, *Critical Excess*, pp. 150–63.

31. Davis, *Critical Excess*, p. 135.

Chapter 2: The Avoidance of Shakespeare

1. I realize I am raising or begging at least two questions in this sentence: Firstly, both Emerson and Thoreau are writers who have preoccupied Cavell to an extent as great as Shakespeare, but since a great many of Cavell's efforts have been to correct those who too readily identify what they write as "literature" (rather than "philosophy"), it would run counter to the thrust of his work to make that mistake here. Secondly—and conversely—if we are too ready to identify Shakespeare's plays as literature, Cavell's work upbraids us for not responding to them philosophically. I shall return to this point shortly.

2. Rhu, *Stanley Cavell's American Dream*, pp. 113–14.

3. The following is a good example: "By instinct and training my mode has been that of careful ignorance, but nowhere more than in my reading of Shakespeare have I been more aware of the liabilities and hazards of this course, hence nowhere more needful of timely aid and encouragement." *DK*, p. ix.

4. Fischer, *Stanley Cavell and Literary Skepticism*, pp. 80–81.

5. Cavell's answer to this question, insofar as he has one, would go like this: "Theoretically . . . I claim my text on Shakespeare's text as an enactment of (illustration of? evidence for? instance of? model for? image of? allegory of?) the theoretical movement of *The Claim of Reason* at large, but to no greater extent, and to no smaller, than the convincingness of the reading of *Othello* in its own terms; I mean to no greater extent than the capacity of the terms thus brought to the play to sustain themselves under pressure from alternative, competing readings of the play." *DK*, p. 12.

6. Bruns, "Stanley Cavell's Shakespeare," p. 612.

7. See Foucault, "What Is an Author?," esp. pp. 113–17.

8. Wheeler, "Acknowledging Shakespeare," p. 138.

9. See Stewart, "Avoidance of Stanley Cavell." Stewart's and Wheeler's essays are the best discussions of the relationship between Cavell's work and the New Historicism.

10. Fischer, *Stanley Cavell and Literary Skepticism*, pp. 84–85.

11. For a discussion of the skepticism involved in Cavell's readings of Shakespeare, see chapter 7.

12. See, for instance, Graham Bradshaw's now rather dated *Shakespeare's Scepticism* (1987). Surprisingly, given that this book was published in the years immediately following *The Claim of Reason*, Cavell gets little more than a name-check in it. More recently, see Millicent Bell's *Shakespeare's Tragic Skepticism* (2002).

13. Mulhall, *Stanley Cavell*, p. 189.

14. Admittedly, Cavell qualifies this immediately by specifying that "the formulation of uniqueness is not quite right." He discusses the question of Shakespeare's "uniqueness" in more detail in his foreword to John Joughin's *Philosophical Shakespeares*.

15. For example, "When we are made to know that Shakespeare lived in Shakespeare's age and so dealt in his age's understandings and conventions, we can forget that it is Shakespeare demanding of us; and so *his* Bastard slumps back into 'the' Bastard of his age, from which he had pointedly lifted it . . . the drama is missed, our perception of it blanked." *DK*, p. 82.

16. For example, "A work such as a play of Shakespeare's cannot contribute to the help I want from it for the philosophical issues I mention, unless the play is granted the autonomy it is in one's power to grant, which means, seen in its own terms." *DK*, p. 144.

17. For Cavell, "the issue of Shakespeare's identity, serves to blunt this wonder, namely that *anyone* can have been responsible for these texts." *PDAT*, p. 36.

18. Rhu, *Stanley Cavell's American Dream*, p. 24.

19. "A full description, let alone explanation, of the history of Shakespearean criticism would be part of a full description of Western cultural history since the Renaissance." *DK*, p. 39.

20. Rhu, *Stanley Cavell's American Dream*, p. 24.

21. The conventions for dramatic performances involve the audience and the theater as much as they do the playwright and the text. Cavell's analysis of these conventions is discussed in chapter 7.

22. See also *DK*, p. 181, where Cavell asks why, among critics of *Hamlet*, it is assumed without question that the ghost of Hamlet's father is telling the truth about his murder: "Must the Ghost's word be preserved because of some dramatic convention concerning ghosts, or because of some theories contemporary with the play concerning the walking of ghosts—conventions or theories that Shakespeare is presumably incapable of challenging? You might as well say that in writing the revenge play to end revenge plays, Shakespeare had nothing new of interest to offer concerning the idea of revenge."

23. Wittgenstein, *Zettel*, §302.

24. "How may we understand the dumb-show, so construed, to work at the heart of *Hamlet*? How does it figure the body of the play? Of course I am using it, in such a question, as an image of what Shakespeare thinks a play is; that is, to interrogate *Hamlet* for its testimony as to the work of theater." *DK*, p. 186.

25. "I take the telling of the parable of the belly as a sort of play-within-the-play, a demonstration of what Shakespeare takes his play—named for Coriolanus—to be, for *Coriolanus* too is a tale about food." *DK*, p. 163.

26. "The resurrection of the woman is, theatrically, a claim that the composer of this play is in command of an art that brings words to life, or vice versa, and since the condition of this life is that her spectators awake their faith, we, as well as Leontes, awake, as it were, with her. A transformation is being asked of our conception of the audience of a play." *DK*, p. 218.

27. "Cleopatra's specification of her consciousness of herself as actress shows Shakespeare at I imagine his most daring in his always daring us to become conscious of his theatre . . . daring us to see the boy here and now squeaking *this* Cleopatra, in *that* line, to challenge us to ask and specify in what (other) position she is here and now presented, presents herself." *DK*, pp. 30–31.

28. Cleopatra's self-referential theatricalization can be read in a similar way: "To see the theatricality of the boy in the woman" is, Cavell suggests, a "dare" to the audience that "show[s], and allows us to choose not to see, the theatricality of the woman, Cleopatra's theater; to show her sense that in playing her last in Egypt, in refusing to be cast as 'an Egyptian puppet [to] be shown / In Rome' (V, ii, 207–8) she is not avoiding her theatricalization—her story will publicly be

burlesqued and debased in Rome with or without her—but rather producing, as if in competition, her own theatre, womaning herself, queening, divining, childing, mothering, nursing, enacting, creating herself." *DK*, p. 31.

29. Cavell, "*Investigations*' Everyday Aesthetics of Itself."

30. See Cavell, "*Investigations*' Everyday Aesthetics of Itself," pp. 376–77.

31. "*Investigations*' Everyday Aesthetics of Itself," p. 373. Cavell immediately qualifies this statement thus: "It does not follow that the distinction between philosophy and literature is thereby meant to be levelled, but rather that the genres occur simultaneously, and perhaps work to deepen their differences, even to bring them to a crisis" (p. 373).

32. Cavell, foreword to *Philosophical Shakespeares*, p. xii.

33. "The original essay on *Lear* concludes my first book, *Must We Mean What We Say?* What it follows is a philosophically determined essay entitled 'Knowing and Acknowledging,' on overcoming, or reconceiving, skepticism with respect to the existence of others, and it in effect concludes the analysis of acknowledgement presented in that preceding essay by making visible . . . the fantastic consequences of the avoidance of acknowledgement." *DK*, p. xiv.

34. See, as one example among many, *DK*, p. 206: "Shakespeare's portrait indicates what the intimation is of, of which the philosopher's portrait is the intellectualization. It is an intimation, as I keep coming back to putting it, of the failure of knowledge as a failure of acknowledgment, which means, whatever else it means, that the result of the failure is not an ignorance but an ignoring, not an opposable doubt but an unappeasable denial, a willful uncertainty that constitutes an annihilation."

35. Since the relationship between skepticism and tragedy is dealt with at length in chapter 7, there is good reason to dispatch this discussion quickly here.

36. Cascardi, "Disowning Knowledge," pp. 190–91.

37. Lawrence Rhu also sees a link between Cavell's investigations of Shakespeare and his investigations of ordinary language, albeit a slightly different one: "Shakespeare's words can be used to impart unjustifiably high value to humdrum occasions otherwise deemed unworthy of eloquence. But such an argument can be turned upside down. The very occasions that we consider routine and prosaic may hide in plain sight nothing less than the significance of our lives. Cavell characterizes the adventure that his philosophy undertakes as a quest whose object is the ordinary, the everyday, whose capacity to disappoint us remains withering." Rhu, *Stanley Cavell's American Dream*, p. 113.

38. Asking about the difference between the textualities of Shakespeare, pulp fiction, and song lyrics is basically to ask about the relation of the poetic or the aesthetic to the ordinary. Elsewhere, Cavell remarks that "a theory of . . . textuality designed to explain, say, our relation to Wallace Stevens's jar in Tennessee or to Heidegger's jug in the Black Forest is of no use to me if it fails to explain my relation to the chipped mug from which I drank my coffee this morning." *TOS*, pp. 47–48.

39. *Pace* Cavell, "Dancing Cheek to Cheek" is an Irving Berlin number, and not a Kern/Fields composition.

40. For the entirety of this anecdote and its significance for Cavell, see *PoP*, pp. 48–50.

41. See Cavell, "Shakespeare and Rohmer: Two Tales of Winter," in *CoW*, pp. 421–43.

42. Cascardi, "Disowning Knowledge," p. 194.

43. Cascardi, "Disowning Knowledge," pp. 195–96.

44. Bruns, "Stanley Cavell's Shakespeare," p. 617.

45. Richard Wheeler, A. J. Cascardi, and Garrett Stewart have all explored the discrepancy between Cavell's approach to the question of character and that of current literary criticism, particularly the New Historicism. Cascardi rightly observes that whereas "recent Shakespearean criticism

raises the possibility that historical context, repressed desires, ideological structures, and the like might account for the meaningfulness of what Shakespeare's characters say" ("Disowning Knowledge," p. 193), Cavell engages with Shakespeare's characters and their words as if they were speaking human subjects and agents, and not mere exercises in Renaissance self-fashioning. Stewart's discussion of the contrasts involved here is probably the most rigorous of the three.

46. See Bruns, "Stanley Cavell's Shakespeare," p. 617, for a gloss on Cavell's position here.

47. Bruns, "Stanley Cavell's Shakespeare," p. 617.

48. See the beginning of chapter 7.

49. Rhu, *Stanley Cavell's American Dream*, p. 14. As Rhu points out, this is a criticism made not only of Cavell's work on Shakespeare but also of his work on film. He cites E. Ann Kaplan's review of *Contesting Tears*, which considers the book naive because, says Rhu, "Cavell treats movie characters as if they were real people" (p. 168).

50. Bruns, "Stanley Cavell's Shakespeare," p. 617.

51. Cascardi, "Disowning Knowledge," p. 192.

52. See Mulhall, introduction to *Cavell Reader*, p. 17.

53. In this respect, it is instructive to contrast Cavell's essays on Shakespeare with his essay on Beckett, in whose plays Cavell sees a nuanced and problematic relationship to ordinary language that forms the subject of the next chapter.

54. Mulhall, introduction to *Cavell Reader*, p. 17.

55. See Bakhtin, *Problems of Dostoevsky's Poetics*. A commendable but ultimately unsatisfactory attempt to read Bakhtinian and Cavellian approaches to literature alongside each other can be found in Newton, *Narrative Ethics*.

56. Cascardi, "Disowning Knowledge," p. 193.

57. Cavell's engagement with the "obvious warhorses" of Barthes and Foucault is admittedly rather too abortive. See *PDAT*, p. 66.

58. Mulhall, *Stanley Cavell*, pp. 188–89.

59. Mulhall, *Stanley Cavell*, p. 190.

60. Wittgenstein, *Philosophical Investigations*, §337.

61. Mulhall, introduction to *Cavell Reader*, p. 17.

62. Hammer, *Stanley Cavell*, p. 101.

63. "The Intentional Fallacy is a confusion between the poem and its origins, a special case of what is known to philosophers as the Genetic Fallacy. It begins by trying to derive the standard of criticism from the psychological *causes* of the poem, and ends in biography and relativism. The Affective Fallacy is a confusion between the poem and its *results* (what it *is* and what it *does*). . . . It begins by trying to derive the standard of criticism from the psychological effects of the poem and ends in impressionism and relativism." Wimsatt and Beardsley, "Affective Fallacy," p. 345. See also their "The Intentional Fallacy," pp. 333–45.

64. "It is one irony of recent literary history that the New Criticism, with one motive fixed on preserving poetry from what it felt as the encroachment of science and logical positivism (repeating as an academic farce what the nineteenth century went through as a cultural tragedy), accepted undemurringly a view of intention established, or pictured in that same philosophy—according to which an intention is some internal, prior mental event causally connected with outward effects, which remain the sole evidence for its having occurred." *MWM*, p. 226.

65. Mulhall, introduction to *Cavell Reader*, p. 17.

66. Mulhall, introduction to *Cavell Reader*, p. 17.

67. "The usual interpretations follow one of three main lines: Lear is senile; Lear is puerile; Lear is not to be understood in natural terms, for the whole scene has a fairy-tale or ritualistic character." *DK*, p. 57.

68. Later in the same essay, Cavell accuses the traditional anti-intention positions of "imagining that to claim that an author means what he or she says is to claim that his or her intention has created all the conditions in conjunction with which intention does what it does, as if the striking match creates the fuse it lights, together with the anger and the enemy and the opportunity in and for and from which it is struck. (In a sense, no doubt, it does. What sense?)." *DK*, p. 243.

69. Mulhall, *Stanley Cavell*, p. 190.

70. The best exploration of Cavell's critique of this aspect of New Criticism is Fischer, *Stanley Cavell and Literary Skepticism*, which compares his views in this area to his critique of skepticism toward the external world.

71. Mulhall, *Stanley Cavell*, p. 190.

72. Wittgenstein, *Culture and Value*, p. 84.

73. See Wittgenstein, *Culture and Value*, pp. 48, 84.

74. Wittgenstein, *Culture and Value*, p. 86.

75. Wittgenstein, *Culture and Value*, p. 49.

76. See Wittgenstein's preface to his *Philosophical Investigations*, pp. vii–viii.

Chapter 3: From the Sublime to the Ordinary

1. Theodor Adorno, "Trying to Understand *Endgame*," p. 284.

2. For Deleuze on Beckett, see Deleuze, "He Stuttered," as well as Deleuze, "The Greatest Irish Film (Beckett's 'Film')" and "The Exhausted," in Deleuze, *Gilles Deleuze: Essays Critical and Clinical*, pp. 23–29, 152–74; for Blanchot on Beckett, see Blanchot, "Where Now? Who Now?"; for Badiou on Beckett, see Badiou, *On Beckett*. A good account of these positions is Tubridy, "Absence of Origin."

3. Stanley Cavell, "Ending the Waiting Game: A Reading of Beckett's *Endgame*," in *MWM*, pp. 115–62; Nussbaum, "Narrative Emotions."

4. Critchley, "Know Happiness—On Beckett," pp. 141–42.

5. Critchley, "Know Happiness—On Beckett," p. 144.

6. It is precisely this aspect of Cavell's approach to which Benjamin Ogden objects. He asks, not unreasonably, "What does it mean, ultimately, for a line in *Endgame* to be read literally?" See Ogden, "What Philosophy Can't Say About Literature," p. 137.

7. Beckett, *Endgame*, pp. 111, 116 (hereafter *EG*).

8. See Bernstein, "Philosophy's Refuge."

9. Critchley, "Know Happiness—On Beckett," pp. 178, 179.

10. It is for this reason that I find the main thrust of Ogden's critique of Cavell's interpretation unconvincing. Ogden says of Cavell: "His work of criticism is in search of something that it *must* find (that is, something that it claims to have found even when it may not have); what it must find is a work of literature that demonstrates the utility and validity of ordinary language philosophy." Ogden, "What Philosophy Can't Say About Literature," p. 126. On the contrary, Cavell's reading of Beckett, and indeed a large component of his broader philosophical project, tends rather to problematize what the ordinary might mean or might be, in ways not always as congenial to mainstream ordinary language philosophy as Ogden makes out.

11. Wittgenstein, *Philosophical Investigations*, §304.

12. See Wittgenstein, *Philosophical Investigations*, §§38, 94, 89.

13. Noggle, "Wittgensteinian Sublime," p. 610 (hereafter "WS").

14. Wittgenstein, *Philosophical Investigations*, §119.

15. This compulsion is, of course, described in much detail in Wittgenstein's *Philosophical Investigations*, where it forms one of the principal kinds of philosophical "illness" or "disease" that Wittgenstein's therapeutic approach seeks to address. In philosophy, we are told, "it is difficult as it were to keep our heads up,—to see that we must stick to the subjects of our every-day thinking, and not go astray and imagine that we have to describe extreme subtleties which in turn we are after all quite unable to describe with the means at our disposal. We feel as if we had to repair a torn spider's web with our fingers" (§106).

Yet it is no less difficult to escape from the grip of metaphysical ideals once they have us in thrall: "The ideal, as we think of it, is unshakable. You can never get outside it; you must always turn back. There is no outside; outside you cannot breathe.—Where does this idea come from? It is like a pair of glasses on our nose through which we see whatever we look at. It never occurs to us to take them off" (§103).

The Wittgensteinian project of philosophy as a form of therapeutic intervention would, on the evidence of these quotations, appear at least in part to take its cue from the richly problematic interrelation of ordinary, everyday language, as well as the metaphysical emptiness of the Wittgensteinian sublime, though that must form the subject for a more ambitious discussion than this one.

(Incidentally, it might be of passing and coincidental interest that the vocabulary Wittgenstein uses in *Philosophical Investigations*, §103, is highly reminiscent of Hamm and Clov's, particularly of Hamm's blindness and Clov's inability to leave their shelter.)

16. *TNYUA*, p. 54, quoted by Noggle in "WS," p. 607. It is worth pointing out that the idea of the sublime and its relation to Wittgenstein's thought crops up throughout *This New Yet Unapproachable America*. On the very first page, Cavell asserts, "I specify as philosophical work what Wittgenstein means by 'leading words home,' back from the sublime into our poverty" (p. 1), and elsewhere he admires Wittgenstein's "relentless project to, perhaps we can say, desublimize thought" (p. 71). More importantly, in an argument that closely anticipates Noggle's, he implicitly opposes the "ordinary" with what he calls "this frozen emptiness of sublimity" (p. 56). See also the brief discussion of "the perception of the sublime in the everyday" in *PoH*, pp. 14–15.

17. See Perloff, "Witt-Watt."

18. Perloff, "Witt-Watt," p. 22.

19. Wittgenstein, *Philosophical Investigations*, §524.

20. Wittgenstein, *Culture and Value*, p. 52e.

21. Cavell has pointed out to me that for this reason the cited passage neatly demonstrates that the literal can *not* be equated with the ordinary or the everyday: the ordinary and the literal meanings are divergent here. By the same token, we should avoid equating the literary with the metaphysical, or with some other "extra-ordinary" term.

22. Wittgenstein, *Tractatus Logico-Philosophicus*, 6.51.

Chapter 4: How to Do Things with Wordsworth

1. For a discussion of Cavell's reading of Wordsworth that takes a different tack from my own, see Fischer, *Stanley Cavell and Literary Skepticism*, pp. 44–45, 110–11.

2. Quotations from the "Intimations" Ode are taken from Wordsworth's *Poetical Works*, pp. 460–62.

3. Angela Esterhammer, *Romantic Performative*, p. 135 (hereafter *RP*).

4. Wordsworth, Preface to *Lyrical Ballads*, 1:140 (hereafter Preface).

5. This is the principal difference between the Austinian performative, where the "I" that says "I promise" is an established subject, and the Romantic performative, where it need not be. "[The] concept of identity . . . emblematizes the difference between the Romantic performative and the speech act of modern analytic philosophy. Austin and Searle analyze performatives such as oaths and promises based on the heuristic assumption of a stable, unified speaker. But the notion of speech acts that arose among Romantic writers, particularly in response to Kant's First *Critique*, is predicated on an I that is in the process of becoming. This processive—and therefore also unstable—status of the I is reflected in . . . eighteenth-century moral philosophers [who] recognize that the uniqueness of individual identity is crucial to commissive speech acts, for individual volition is the basis of moral responsibility." *RP*, p. 257.

6. Esterhammer's study is more ambitious than this description implies. She claims that "rather than assimilate Romantic philosophy of language to speech-act theory, I maintain that Romantic theory can provide a necessary critique of speech-act theory as it has been formulated by twentieth-century analytic philosophers. It does this because of its greater and, in the literal sense of the word, wonderful attention to the speaking subject as a subject-in-process." *RP*, p. 19.

7. "I understand Wordsworth's *Prelude* to be simultaneously about being born in 1770 (hence, being nineteen in 1789) and about accepting the ambition to be a writer in those years of English writing." *TOS*, p. 146.

8. That said, the struggle between philosophy and literature over the terrain of skepticism is not confined to romanticism *strictu sensu*; it is a tendency that Cavell sees at work in literature ranging from Shakespeare to Poe:

> My idea is that what in philosophy is known as skepticism . . . is a relation to the world, and to others, and to myself, and to language, that is known to what you might call literature, or anyway responded to in literature, in uncounted other guises—in Shakespeare's tragic heroes, in Emerson and Thoreau's "silent melancholy" and "quiet desperation," in Wordsworth's perception of us as without "interest," in Poe's "perverseness." Why philosophy and literature do not know this about one another—and to that extent remain unknown to themselves—has been my theme it seems to me forever. (*IQO*, pp. 154–55)

9. For a brief discussion of the relationship between Kant and romanticism in Cavell's thought that takes a different tack from mine, see Desmond, "Second *Primavera*," esp. pp. 146–47. A more probing critique of Cavell's conception of romanticism in general is Critchley, "Cavell's 'Romanticism' and Cavell's Romanticism," which is probably the best discussion of this topic.

10. "For philosophers of language, Humboldt and Coleridge especially, Kant's concept of synthesis will serve to redefine . . . the relationship between subject and predicate in a sentence." *RP*, p. 75.

11. This quotation points to a significant difference between the Austinian and Wittgensteinian influences on Cavell's thought. For the Wittgensteinian, the idea that a statement can be preceded by a phrase like "It is asserted that" recalls the critique of Frege's assertion sign made in Wittgenstein's *Philosophical Investigations*, §22.

12. There are at least two good reasons why Wordsworth's use of the Romantic performative cannot be a stable antidote to skepticism. Firstly, and most obviously, one is no more likely to refute one's skepticism regarding the external world simply by *talking* to that world than Dr. Johnson was likely to refute Berkeley by kicking a stone. Secondly, by talking to the world, Wordsworth treats it as another speaking subject and thereby surely courts other-minds skepticism. Rather than vanquishing skepticism, this merely replaces it with another isotope of skepticism.

Chapter 5: What Did Cavell Want of Poe?

1. For Cavell's reading, see "Being Odd, Getting Even (Descartes, Emerson, Poe)" and its three "Postscripts," in *IQO*, pp. 105–49. For readings by Derrida, Johnson, and Lacan, see John Muller and William Richardson's useful anthology *The Purloined Poe*, which, interestingly, appeared at the same time as Cavell's reading.

2. See Poe, *Selected Tales*, pp. 283–88 (hereafter "Imp").

3. For the directions, see *IQO*, pp. 123–25; for the questions, see pp. 126–29.

4. See *PP*, pp. 42–65. See also "Seminar on 'What Did Derrida Want of Austin?,'" *PP*, pp. 66–90. Since the postscripts to "Being Odd, Getting Even" are mostly discussions of deconstruction, there is an important link between Cavell's readings of Poe and of Derrida: both involve his ambivalent response to the deconstructive movement, as discussed in the introduction.

5. Cavell refers to the tale as "a fictional confession" on *IQO*, p. 126.

6. Elsewhere (in the context of his reading of *King Lear*) Cavell asserts, "As long as no one *knows* what you have done, you are safe; or your conscience will press you to confess it and accept the punishment" (*MWM*, p. 278). But that is not what happens in "The Imp of the Perverse," where the conscience has nothing to do with it: no one knows what the narrator has done, but, perversely, the utterance "I am safe" leads directly to the confession.

7. See Poe, *Selected Tales*, pp. 92–94, 261–65, and 13, respectively.

8. See *IQO*, p. 137.

9. Poe, *Selected Tales*, p. 232.

10. Cavell has taken de Man to task for misunderstanding the nature of performative language. See "Politics as Opposed to What?," in *TOS*, pp. 27–59.

11. De Man, *Allegories of Reading*, p. 281.

12. For Cavell's discussion of this phrase, see "Must We Mean What We Say?," in *MWM*, pp. 1–43.

13. De Man, *Allegories of Reading*, p. 280.

14. De Man, *Allegories of Reading*, p. 281.

15. De Man, *Allegories of Reading*, p. 280.

16. J. L. Austin, "A Plea for Excuses," in Austin, *Philosophical Papers*, pp. 175–204. For Cavell's critique of Derrida's oversight, see *PP*, pp. 52, 71–73.

17. For Cavell's discussion of this issue, see *PP*, pp. 74–77.

18. See *MWM*, pp. 1–43, esp. pp. 2–12.

19. Poe, *Selected Tales*, p. 232. For Cavell's discussion of the passage, see *IQO*, pp. 137–38.

Chapter 6: "Politics as Opposed to What?"

1. Ibsen, *A Doll's House*, p. 228 (hereafter *ADH*).

2. Immanuel Kant, *Groundwork of the Metaphysics of Morals*, Ak. 421, as quoted by Cavell in *CoW*, p. 250.

3. Bernstein, "Aesthetics, Modernism, Literature," p. 123.

4. See, for example, Andrew Norris's recent collection of essays, *The Claim to Community: Essays on Stanley Cavell and Political Philosophy*.

5. There is, incidentally, a more direct linkage between the essay and the previous chapter, in that it is where Cavell takes Paul de Man to task quite rigorously for carelessness in his interpretation of J. L. Austin and performative language outlined in *Allegories of Reading*.

6. Hammer, *Stanley Cavell*, p. 138.

7. See Moi, *Henrik Ibsen and the Birth of Modernism*, esp. p. 10: "My understanding of Ibsen is inspired by the profound and original work of Stanley Cavell."

8. See Toril Moi, "Wife, Daughter, Mother: Hegel Rebuffed," in Moi, *Henrik Ibsen and the Birth of Modernism*, pp. 242–47.

9. For example, "Ibsen considers skepticism as perhaps the most important existential and philosophical problem of modern life . . . and tries to find non-idealist ways to overcome it." Moi, *Henrik Ibsen and the Birth of Modernism*, p. 5. Moreover, "Ibsen's relation to the everyday" (p. 11) is such that "the everyday is represented as a possible alternative to skepticism"; "self-theatricalization in everyday life is a central theme"; "love is shown to be destroyed by theatricality and skepticism"; and furthermore "marriage is a central theme, often used as a figure for the everyday" (p. 10).

10. In describing the Hegelian view of tragedy this succinctly I am indebted to the admirable simplicity of Mark W. Roche's "Greatness and Limits of Hegel's Theory of Tragedy."

11. *PoH*, p. 22. See also *CT*, pp. 218–19.

12. Mulhall, *Stanley Cavell*, pp. 61–62. The third chapter of Mulhall's book—"Politics: The Social Contract" (pp. 55–68), is an informative discussion of this topic.

13. See the introduction, esp. sec. III.

14. Hammer, *Stanley Cavell*, p. 131.

15. See, for instance, *CoR*, p. 27. There is, however, a writer within the purview of Cavell's writings on literature who highlights more obviously than Ibsen the problem of how one withdraws one's consent to the social contract, and that is the Thoreau of *Civil Disobedience*. To summarize Cavell's views on the matter, "It is unclear how [withdrawal] is to be effected. This is in fact one of the standing mysteries of any theory of the social contract—how consent is shown, and therefore when and how its withdrawal can be shown." See *SoW*, p. 83.

16. On Cavell's reading of *A Doll's House*, the issue is not primarily one of Nora's withdrawing consent from the polis, but of her sense that the injustice of the polis compromises, corrupts, and pains her. See *CHU*, p. 112.

17. Mulhall, *Stanley Cavell*, p. 61.

18. Hammer, *Stanley Cavell*, p. 131.

19. It may be either of passing interest or of deeper significance that the Catch-22 clause, like the social contract, cannot be proven to exist, and many characters in the novel end up taking the view that it does not. Their disbelief does not exempt them, however, from its power over them.

20. Cavell cites *The Lady Eve*, *Bringing Up Baby*, *The Awful Truth*, *The Philadelphia Story*, *It Happened One Night*, *Adam's Rib*, and *His Girl Friday* as representative of the comedy of remarriage and *Stella Dallas*, *Gaslight*, *Letter from an Unknown Woman*, and *Now, Voyager* as representative of melodramas of the unknown woman.

21. On this point, see Rhu, *Stanley Cavell's American Dream*, pp. 29, 58.

22. Hard as this may be for unhappily married couples to imagine, everyday domestic strife can be viewed as analogous to political dissidence, in that, conducted in the right spirit, both are arguments about how to improve the current arrangement for living together.

23. Rhu, *Stanley Cavell's American Dream*, pp. 58, 116. See also pp. 29 and 58–59.

24. The extent of this degree is a matter for the next section of this chapter.

25. Divorce, however, is only dictatorial if it is unilateral, involving one party imposing its will on the other party and curtailing any attempt its partner might make to further the conversation of marriage. In *Pursuits of Happiness*, the marriages Cavell discusses are not like this: both parties initially feel that their conversation of marriage has ended by mutual agreement (or, better, by

mutual disagreement). They do not involve the asymmetry of *A Doll's House*, in which the Helmers' marriage is terminated by Nora despite Torvald's protests.

26. See also the last sentence of his essay on Ibsen in *Cities of Words*: "Nora's climactic declaration of Helmer's inability to provide an education for her as her proof that they are not in a state of marriage is an idea I am not sure I would have come to in defining the comedies of remarriage without Ibsen's example" (*CoW*, p. 264).

27. This conclusion is at stark variance with Cavell's view of Nora's descendants—the "unknown women" of Hollywood melodrama. For Cavell, their repudiation of marriage on grounds that it fails to adequately acknowledge them, and hence compromises them, is the equivalent of the individual's exercising the right, in a democracy, to assert idiosyncrasy and nonconformity against the tyranny of the majority. In other words, Nora's descendants are, for Cavell, rebuking a conversation they find stifling, which is tantamount to bettering the conversation. Whereas on my reading, Nora wishes to bring the whole non-conversation to the inglorious end it richly deserves.

28. A fair criticism to make of Cavell's writings on Ibsen would be the disproportionate emphasis he places on the play's climactic scene, not unlike that he places on the "hinge paragraph" of Poe's "The Imp of the Perverse," as discussed in the previous chapter.

29. Moi, *Henrik Ibsen and the Birth of Modernism*, pp. 232–33.

30. Moi, *Henrik Ibsen and the Birth of Modernism*, pp. 232, 247.

31. Moi, *Henrik Ibsen and the Birth of Modernism*, p. 240.

32. It is noteworthy that Cavell's discussion of Ibsen incorporates a discussion of promises that explores "why it is that promising has a relation to contracts and the law" (*CHU*, p. 115) and considers the idea that promising grounds political institutions.

33. The clearest articulation of this position is the essay "Must We Mean What We Say?," esp. pp. 21–23. For example, "The normativeness . . . which is certainly present, does not lie in the ordinary language philosopher's assertions *about* ordinary language use; what is normative is exactly ordinary use itself." *MWM*, p. 21.

34. Mulhall, *Stanley Cavell*, pp. 64–65.

35. Mulhall, *Stanley Cavell*, p. 65.

36. See Wittgenstein, *Philosophical Investigations*, §§217 and 124, respectively.

37. Both Cavell and Moi comment on the symbolism of this change, though they differ slightly in the significance they attach to it.

38. I prefer to call it a dialogue rather than a conversation, as later in this chapter I take issue with Cavell's usage of the term *conversation*.

39. Mulhall, introduction to *Cavell Reader*, p. 10.

40. Lyotard, *Differend*, p. 13.

41. Lyotard, *Differend*, p. xi.

42. Lyotard, *Differend*, p. xi.

43. Lyotard, *Differend*, p. 83.

44. I am aware that this description amounts to a serious simplification of Lyotard's *Differend*, and in particular that it omits any reference to the importance of Wittgenstein, to what Lyotard regards as the impossibility of translating between language games, and his related assertion that prescriptive statements cannot be grounded in descriptive statements. I have omitted these because, firstly, I have elsewhere demonstrated that Lyotard's arguments are flawed on these points and that his reading of Wittgenstein is based on a misunderstanding (see Rudrum, "Ethics, Justice, Translation"); secondly, there is an important debate to be had between Lyotard and Cavell on these issues, since Cavell's essay "Must We Mean What We Say?," which predates Lyotard's writings on the differend, demonstrates briefly and succinctly that the opposition

between descriptive statements and prescriptive statements is a false one, and so Lyotard's analogy between the differend and the impossibility of deriving prescriptives from descriptives is therefore equally false; and thirdly, though raising either (or both) of these intricate and compelling debates would inevitably require further discussion of Lyotard's notion of the differend, none of the matters involved is of moment in a discussion of Ibsen.

45. "I don't know much about the law, but I'm quite certain that it must say somewhere that things like that are allowed," she says (*ADH*, p. 176).

46. Rancière, *Disagreement*, p. 55.

47. Rancière, *Disagreement*, pp. xi–xii.

48. Rancière, *Disagreement*, p. x.

49. Rancière, *Disagreement*, p. xi.

50. Rancière, *Disagreement*, p. xi.

51. Rancière, *Disagreement*, p. 50.

52. Rancière, *Disagreement*, p. xii.

53. I am aware, once again, that I am oversimplifying Rancière by omitting key concepts like the "distribution of the sensible" and the "police order," but once again these do not pertain to the discussion of Ibsen, and, to hijack a phrase Cavell borrows from Emerson, we cannot spend the day in explanation.

54. Rancière, *Disagreement*, p. xi.

55. Wittgenstein, *Philosophical Investigations*, §241.

56. Lyotard, *Differend*, p. 10.

Chapter 7: Tragedy's Tragedies

1. For a critique of Cavell's parable of the Southern yokel, see Bristol, *Big-Time Shakespeare*, pp. 198–99.

2. Rather than resort to such extreme measures, it might be more diverting to allow such a situation to play itself out. If nothing else, it would demonstrate the full extent of the yokel's helplessness. As Cavell has it, "The little joke on the yokel is familiar enough of its kind. The big joke, and not just on the yokel, is his idea that *if* the thing were in fact happening he would be able to stop it, be equal to his chivalry. It is fun to contemplate his choices. Will he reason with Othello? (After Iago has destroyed his reason.) Tell him the truth? (Which the person who loves him has been doing over and over.) Threaten him, cross swords with him? (That, one would like to see.)—There is nothing and we know there is nothing we can do" (*MWM*, p. 330).

3. We may applaud his actions but perhaps not his motivation. I have described his behavior as "attempting to save a young lady from murder," whereas Cavell calls it attempting "to save Desdemona from the black man" (*MWM*, p. 327), which suggests that the yokel acts out of racism rather than gallantry.

4. On this point, Cavell quotes Nietzsche's *Birth of Tragedy*: "An audience of spectators, such as we know it, was unknown to the Greeks." See *MWM*, p. 157.

5. Cavell's rather more rhetorical response is to ask: "How might I forget this? . . . What am I to remember, and what good would it do if I did? . . . How do I remember something there is no obvious way for me to forget?" *MWM*, pp. 318–19.

6. Cavell often asks what kind of entity a (Shakespearean) fictional character might be. For a discussion of his treatment of the characters in Shakespeare, see chapter 2.

7. For Cavell's reading of the question "How can we know the dancer from the dance?" with which Yeats ends his poem "Among School Children," see *TOS*, pp. 45–47.

8. I suspect that these observations may well be indebted to J. L. Austin's work on pretending. For Cavell's discussion of these, see Cavell, *Pitch of Philosophy*, pp. 91–93.

9. Wittgenstein, *Philosophical Investigations*, §371.

10. Wittgenstein, *Philosophical Investigations*, §373.

11. For an early and concise account of Cavellian skepticism, see Eldridge, "Continuing Task." More recently and more expansively, see Hammer, *Stanley Cavell*.

12. Cavell's notion of acknowledgment has attracted an amount of philosophical critique, something he is well aware of. He clarifies his view of it by stating that acknowledgment "forms a key to the way I see both the problematic of skepticism and that of tragedy. This idea has been criticized on the ground, roughly, that in offering an alternative to the human goal of knowing, either it gives up the claim of philosophy to reason or else it is subject to the same doubts that knowing itself is. . . . But I do not propose the idea of acknowledging as an alternative to knowing but rather as an interpretation of it . . . as if what stands in the way of further knowledge is knowledge itself, as it stands, as it conceives itself" (*IQO*, p. 8).

13. For a useful discussion of these three aspects of Cavell's philosophy, their interrelatedness, and their differences, see Hammer, *Stanley Cavell*, ch. 5, "Ethics and Politics."

14. Cavell's engagement with Levinas is articulated in his essay "What is the Scandal of Skepticism?" (*PDAT*, pp. 132–54). The best discussion of the relationship between Cavell's and Levinas's philosophies is Standish, "Education for Grown-Ups." An earlier effort, partially outdated because it predated Cavell's own essay on Levinas, is Newton, *Narrative Ethics*. Probably the best of the many publications relating Levinas's thought to literature include Eaglestone, *Ethical Criticism*; and Robbins, *Altered Readings*.

15. For those not familiar with Levinas's somewhat esoteric terminology, he uses two different words to designate otherness—*autre* and *autrui*—sometimes capitalising the *a* of each word, sometimes not. It has been said that he therefore uses four different terms for different kinds of otherness, though his notorious inconsistency in this area often makes it hard to be certain what distinction he thinks he is making. This has created many difficulties for Anglophone Levinas scholars, for whom the only obvious word with which to render these terms is *other*. A convention has arisen among Levinas scholars that in English this word should be capitalized when used to designate the otherness of another human being, such as is involved in the experience of the face of the Other. This convention is by no means universally followed, however, and creates a variety of problems of its own (for details of which see the admirably succinct discussion in the preface to Peperzak, Critchley, and Bernasconi, *Emmanuel Levinas*, esp. pp. xiv–xv). Nevertheless, I follow it here, in order to highlight the specificity of this term within, and its central importance to, Levinas's broader philosophical project. Hereafter, when the word *other* is capitalized, it is to be understood in the sense given to it in Levinas scholarship.

16. Levinas, *Totality and Infinity*, p. 215.

17. See Levinas, *Difficult Freedom*; and Levinas, *Totality and Infinity*, p. 262.

18. Robbins, *Altered Readings*, pp. 67–68.

19. For a clearer sketch of why Cavell doesn't agree that the idea of God is necessary to ground ethics or otherness, see *PDAT*, p. 151.

20. For a discussion of the affinities between skepticism and narcissism, see *CoR*, p. 463.

21. Fischer, *Stanley Cavell and Literary Skepticism*, p. 97.

22. Mulhall, *Stanley Cavell*, p. 200.

23. Fischer, *Stanley Cavell and Literary Skepticism*, p. 96.

24. Mulhall, *Stanley Cavell*, p. 200.

25. Fischer, *Stanley Cavell and Literary Skepticism*. p. 86.

26. Wheeler, "Acknowledging Shakespeare," p. 159.

27. Hammer, *Stanley Cavell*, p. 91.

28. Fischer, *Stanley Cavell and Literary Skepticism*, p. 96.

29. Mulhall, *Stanley Cavell*, pp. 198–99.

30. Wittgenstein, *Culture and Value*, p. 12.

31. Cavell gives a great deal of consideration to this mistaken view in order to locate exactly where its mistake lies. It seems to lie in a tension between understanding a tragic plot as motivated by contingency and understanding it as motivated by necessity:

> [Tragedy] need not have happened. So a radical contingency haunts every story of tragedy. . . . Of course if Othello had not met Iago, if Lear had not developed his plan of division, if Macbeth had not listened to his wife . . . But could these contingencies have been prevented? If one is assured they could have been, one is forgetting who these characters are. . . . So a radical necessity haunts every story of tragedy. It is the enveloping of contingency and necessity by one another, the entropy of their mixture, which produces events we call tragic. (*MWM*, p. 341)

While the idea of such a nexus is appealing, "no one *knows* that [a tragedy] could have been prevented because no one knows what would have prevented it" (*MWM*, p. 341). Consequently, "the death which ends a tragedy strikes one as inexplicable: necessary, but we do not know why; avoidable, but we do not know how; wrapped in meaning, but the meaning has not come out, and so wrapped in mystery. This is clearest in the case of Lear, where critics differ over whether he dies from grief or (illusory) joy" (*MWM*, p. 341).

32. And for Wittgenstein. He immediately goes on to disavow his observation by saying, "But surely that is a one-sided view of tragedy, to think of it merely as showing that an encounter can decide one's whole life." *Culture and Value*, p. 12.

33. Nietzsche, *Untimely Meditations*, p. 213.

34. See Agamben, "What is the Contemporary?," p. 52. See also Agamben's *Time That Remains* for a comparison between Agamben's idea of the contemporary and Walter Benjamin's notion of *Jetztzeit*.

35. See Agamben, "What is the Contemporary?," p. 40. The quotation is from Barthes's lectures at the College de France.

36. Agamben, *Time That Remains*, p. 76.

37. Agamben, *Time That Remains*, p. 77.

38. Agamben, *Time That Remains*, p. 69, 74–75.

39. T. S. Eliot, "Burnt Norton," lines 4–5.

40. Mulhall, *Stanley Cavell*, p. 198.

41. Agamben, *Time That Remains*, p. 64.

42. Agamben, *Time That Remains*, p. 62.

43. Agamben, *Time That Remains*, pp. 64, 68.

44. Agamben, *Time That Remains*, p. 68.

45. Agamben, "What is the Contemporary?," p. 51.

46. Agamben, "What is the Contemporary?," pp. 51–52.

47. Agamben, "What is the Contemporary?," p. 53.

48. Agamben, "What is the Contemporary?," p. 75.

49. Mulhall claims that the essay is "the most important of these readings," while Rhu asserts that "in an especially telling way, Stanley Cavell's essay on *The Winter's Tale* demonstrates the unusual power and influence of his work in Shakespeare studies." Mulhall, *Stanley Cavell*, p. 201; Rhu, *Stanley Cavell's American Dream*, p. 136.

50. Mulhall, *Stanley Cavell*, p. 201.

51. See also Rhu, *Stanley Cavell's American Dream*, p. 155: "Saint Paul . . . is far more than the nominal prototype of Paulina in *The Winter's Tale*."

52. Rhu, *Stanley Cavell's American Dream*, p. 153.

53. Mulhall, *Stanley Cavell*, p. 202.

54. See *DK*, p. 193. Perhaps some answer to these questions is hinted at in the opening scene, which ends with a description of Mamillius overlooked in Cavell's reading. We are told that he is a child who "makes old hearts fresh: they that went on crutches ere he was born, desire yet their life to see him a man." Camillo is challenged on this by Archidamus—"Would they else be content to die?"—but he does not treat the question as facetious, nor does he admit to any hyperbole in his description of Mamillius: "Yes; if there were no other excuse why they should desire to live." Archidamus gets the last word: "If the king had no son, they would desire to live on crutches till he had one" (1.1.42–49). If Mamillius sounds almost like a messianic figure here—restoring faith, hope, and even life in old hearts—it needs to be pointed out that at the end of the play the king has no son nor any prospect of one (other than a son-in-law), and the older generation would thus seemingly lack such a reason to live. Is the loss of Mamillius's childhood designed to throw into relief the mourned-for eternal boyhood that Polyxenes recalls? Or is his premature death a way of ensuring that the eternal summer of *his* boyhood does not fade?

55. One possibility that might be explored here is that Leontes rejects the newborn Perdita because "she is something before her time deliver'd" (2.2.26).

56. Since the tragic part of the play begins with Hermione obliging Leontes's request to entreat from Polyxenes "the borrow of a week" (1.2.39), is it possible to see Leontes as living on borrowed time?

57. See "Shakespeare and Rohmer: Two Tales of Winter," in *CoW*, pp. 421–43.

58. Agamben, *Time That Remains*, p. 70.

59. Agamben, *Time That Remains*, p. 76.

60. Agamben, *Time That Remains*, p. 75.

61. Agamben, *Time That Remains*, pp. 77–78.

62. Agamben, *Time That Remains*, pp. 67–68.

63. Agamben, *Time That Remains*, pp. 82–83.

64. Rhu, *Stanley Cavell's American Dream*, p. 202.

Conclusion: Just an Ordinary American Tragedy

1. See chapter 2.

2. Miller, "Tragedy and the Common Man," p. 3.

3. Miller, "Tragedy and the Common Man," p. 4.

4. It may be significant to the discussion to follow that the terrain over which a key battle in this war of succession was fought was America.

5. Miller, "Tragedy and the Common Man," pp. 3–4.

6. Miller, "Tragedy and the Common Man," p. 3.

7. Miller, "Tragedy and the Common Man," pp. 3–4.

8. Miller, "*Salesman* Has a Birthday," p. 13.

9. Miller, "*Salesman* Has a Birthday," p. 15.

10. Miller, "Nature of Tragedy," p. 9.

11. Miller, "On Social Plays," p. 51.

12. See Miller, "On Social Plays," esp. pp. 51–56. There is also, of course, a passing resemblance to Nietzsche's *Birth of Tragedy* in this view.

13. Miller, "On Social Plays," pp. 55–56.
14. Miller, "On Social Plays," p. 58.
15. Miller, "Tragedy and the Common Man," p. 6.
16. Miller, "Tragedy and the Common Man," p. 6.
17. Miller, *Death of a Salesman*, p. 98 (hereafter *DoS*).
18. One of several possible reasons why Coriolanus does not attain the status of the tragic is because it is nearly impossible to pity him. This might seem to chime with Biff's warning to Willy, but unlike Coriolanus, Willy does seem to have aroused an immense amount of pity from audiences. This underlines my suggestion that Biff's comments (and Charley's) are there to raise questions about the play, not to pass definitive judgments on it.
19. Miller, "Introduction to the *Collected Plays*," p. 144.
20. Miller, "Morality and Modern Drama," pp. 203, 199.
21. Miller, "Morality and Modern Drama," p. 199.
22. See, e.g., *MWM*, pp. 12–16.
23. See Brandom, *Rorty and his Critics*, p. 90. Rorty offers a rather different reading of Cavell in his review of *The Claim of Reason*. See Rorty, "Cavell on Skepticism." For Cavell's response to Rorty's comments, see Goodman, *Contending with Stanley Cavell*, pp. 158–62. For a position offering a certain rapprochement between Cavell's thought and the pragmatist tradition behind Rorty, see Goodman, "Cavell and American Philosophy." For Cavell's comments on it, see Goodman, *Contending with Stanley Cavell*, pp. 170–72. For a more orthodox sketch of the fraught relationship between Cavell's philosophy and American pragmatism, see Eldridge, "Cavell on American Philosophy."
24. Laugier, "Rethinking the Ordinary," p. 82.
25. Laugier, "Rethinking the Ordinary," p. 91.
26. Miller, "Morality and Modern Drama," p. 203.
27. Miller, "Introduction to the *Collected Plays*," p. 118.
28. Miller, "Morality and Modern Drama," p. 198.
29. Miller, "Introduction to the *Collected Plays*," p. 148.
30. Miller, "Introduction to the *Collected Plays*," p. 150.
31. "It is necessary, if one is to reflect reality, not only to depict why a man does what he does, or why he nearly didn't do it, but why he cannot simply walk away and say to hell with it." Miller, "Introduction to the *Collected Plays*," p. 117.
32. Miller, "*Salesman* Has a Birthday," p. 14.
33. Miller, "Tragedy and the Common Man," p. 5.
34. My intuition about the similarities between Lear and Willy Loman was strengthened when I was told that Miller was said to have kept a copy of *King Lear* by his bedside for many years and that the actor who first played Loman (Lee J. Cobb) was likened by reviewers to an American Lear. I am grateful to Joshua Polster for this information (personal communication). See also n. 37 below.
35. Miller, "Introduction to the *Collected Plays*," p. 147.
36. Miller, "Introduction to the *Collected Plays*," p. 147.
37. It strikes me as highly relevant here that in 1939—at the very start of his career and ten years before the success of *Death of a Salesman*—Miller wrote a radio play entitled *William Ireland's Confession* about William Henry Ireland, the man who wrote and forged a happy ending to *King Lear* that was accepted as authentic for some time.
38. Of the many discussions of the role of *America* in Cavell's thought, see esp. Conant, "Cavell and the Concept of America"; Critchley, "Cavell's 'Romanticism' and Cavell's Romanticism";

Eldridge, "Cavell on American Philosophy"; Goodman, "Cavell and American Philosophy"; and Rhu, *Stanley Cavell's American Dream*.

39. Charley seems to confirm this diagnosis when he says, posthumously, of Willy: "He was a happy man with a batch of cement" (*DoS*, p. 138).

40. A fascinating comparison for which there is no space here would be between Biff's voyage of discovery, in which he sets out from the East Coast to find himself in finding America, and Henry James's voyage of discovery in *The American Scene*, in which he returns to the East Coast of America to find himself by revisiting the scene of his past. For Cavell's discussion of James's journey, see "Henry James Returns to America and to Shakespeare," in *PDAT*, pp. 83–110.

41. Laugier, "Rethinking the Ordinary," p. 84.

42. There is a very close link indeed between what Cavell thinks of as "Emersonian" and what he calls "American." As Simon Critchley has it, "The name 'Emerson' has a privileged status in Cavell's discourse. But it has to be associated with another name, a name to which it is intimately linked, a name which functions like 'Germanien' for Heidegger, like 'Auschwitz' for Adorno, and like 'Israel' for Levinas. That name is 'America.'" Critchley, "Cavell's 'Romanticism' and Cavell's Romanticism," p. 42.

43. Toward the end of the play, Willy discusses the option of suicide with his brother. Since this scene cannot have taken place in the past, it has to be asked to what extent Ben's scenes involve Willy reliving his past or hallucinating that past.

44. Willy explicitly relates his experience of his self as "temporary" to the absence of his father. This would make for an interesting comparison with Cavell's interest in "tales in which one parent is notably and suspiciously absent, a mother in *Lear* and *The Tempest*, a father in *Hamlet* and *Coriolanus*" (*DK*, p. 17). And, extending the discussion to Biff's relationship with Willy, it would connect with his interest in tales of absent sons and their lost boyhoods—Wordsworth's *Prelude* and "Intimations" Ode, Shakespeare's *Winter's Tale*, and most relevantly here, Emerson's "Experience."

45. Critchley, "Cavell's 'Romanticism' and Cavell's Romanticism," p. 45.

46. Critchley, "Cavell's 'Romanticism' and Cavell's Romanticism," p. 47.

47. Critchley, "Cavell's 'Romanticism' and Cavell's Romanticism," p. 43.

48. Desmond, "Second *Primavera*," p. 148.

49. Critchley, "Cavell's 'Romanticism' and Cavell's Romanticism," p. 45.

50. Miller, "Introduction to the *Collected Plays*," p. 116.

51. Miller, "Introduction to the *Collected Plays*," pp. 138–39.

52. For this suggestion (which, as it happens, I find highly problematic), see *DK*, pp. 15–16.

53. I say "according to most readings" because I am wholeheartedly sympathetic to Russell B. Goodman's efforts to demonstrate that certain ways of picturing pragmatism and certain strains of pragmatist thought are in no way at odds with the principle of perfectionism, and closer in many ways to Cavell's thought than Cavell himself seems to realize.

54. Critchley, "Cavell's 'Romanticism' and Cavell's Romanticism," p. 46. See also, in this connection, *TNYUA*, pp. 7–8.

55. "Men built like we are should be working out in the open," he says. *DoS*, p. 23.

56. Mulhall, introduction to *Cavell Reader*, pp. 10–11.

57. If we take the central insight of pragmatism to be that the ordinary world is the way it ordinarily is because it is as we have made it, and that therefore our world is produced by our ordinary practices (or, in a Rortean formulation, that our world simply *is* our ordinary practices), then pragmatism exposes the condition of the ordinary as made by us, which in turn makes it available for us to acknowledge as something to be made anew and made differently. Thus, a certain level of pragmatism is a precondition for perfectionism's quest for a new ordinary. According to this view,

there is a certain continuity between pragmatism and perfectionism, and the gulf between Rorty and Cavell is not quite as broad as Cavell is often wont to make out. It is for this reason that I resist certain characterizations of Rortean pragmatism as politically conservative, but that, alas, is a subject for a chapter in its own right, and in a book of a rather different nature from this one.

58. Miller, "Morality and Modern Drama," p. 195.

59. Miller, "Nature of Tragedy," pp. 10, 11.

60. Miller, "Tragedy and the Common Man," p. 7.

61. Miller, "Tragedy and the Common Man," pp. 6–7.

62. Miller, "Tragedy and the Common Man," p. 5.

63. This claim needs immediate qualification: it is not a claim that the drama is entirely specific or unique to America. Miller maintains, "I didn't write *Death of a Salesman* to announce some new American man, or an old American man." Miller, "Morality and Modern Drama," p. 199. Instead, he is at pains to insist that his play's themes are more universal. "When the play opened in New York," he recalls, "it was taken for granted that its hero, the Salesman, and the story itself, were so American as to be quite strange if not incomprehensible to people of other nations; in some countries there is, for instance, no word that really conveys the idea of the salesman in our sense." However, a reaction of "instantaneous familiarity" greeted the play wherever it went, for example, "in Catholic Spain, where feudalism is still not a closed era; among fishermen in Norway at the edge of the Arctic Circle; in Rome, Athens, Tokyo." Miller, "1956 and All This," pp. 92–93. So to claim, as I have, that *Death of a Salesman* shows us an ordinary American tragedy is not to emphasize the specificity of its American themes over and above its recounting of the ordinary.

64. Miller, "1956 and All This," pp. 108–9.

65. Wittgenstein, *Philosophical Investigations*, §599.

66. Cavell, "Interview with Stanley Cavell," pp. 53–54.

67. Cavell, "Interview with Stanley Cavell," p. 49.

Bibliography

Adorno, Theodor. "Trying to Understand *Endgame*." In *Notes to Literature*, translated by Shierry Weber Nicholsen, pp. 241–76. New York: Columbia University Press, 1991.

Agamben, Giorgio. *The Time That Remains: A Commentary on the Letter to the Romans*. Stanford, CA: Stanford University Press, 2005.

———. "What Is the Contemporary?" In *What Is an Apparatus? and Other Essays*, translated by David Kishik and Stefan Pedatella, pp. 39–54. Stanford, CA: Stanford University Press, 2009.

Austin, J. L. *How To Do Things With Words*. Edited by J. O. Urmson and Marina Sbisà. 2nd ed. Oxford: Oxford University Press, 1962.

———. *Philosophical Papers*. Edited by J. O. Urmson and G. J. Warnock. 3rd ed. Oxford: Oxford University Press, 1979.

Badiou, Alain. *On Beckett*. Edited and translated by Nina Power and Alberto Toscano. Manchester: Clinamen, 2003.

Bakhtin, Mikhail. *Problems of Dostoevsky's Poetics*. Edited and translated by Caryl Emerson. Introduction by Wayne C. Booth. Minneapolis: University of Minnesota Press, 1984.

Bates, Stanley. "Stanley Cavell and Ethics." In Eldridge, *Stanley Cavell*, pp. 15–47.

Beckett, Samuel. *Endgame*. In *Complete Dramatic Works*, pp. 89–134. London: Faber, 1986.

Bell, Millicent. *Shakespeare's Tragic Skepticism*. New Haven, CT: Yale University Press, 2002.

Bernstein, J. M. "Aesthetics, Modernism, Literature: Cavell's Transformations of Philosophy." In Eldridge, *Stanley Cavell*, pp. 107–42.

———. "Philosophy's Refuge: Adorno in Beckett." In *Philosophers' Poets*, edited by David Wood, pp. 177–91. London: Routledge, 1990.

Blanchot, Maurice. "Where Now? Who Now?" In *Samuel Beckett*, edited by J. Birkett and K. Ince, translated by Richard Howard, pp. 93–98. London: Longman, 2000.

Bloom, Harold. *How To Read and Why*. London: Fourth Estate, 2000.

———. *The Western Canon: The Books and School of the Ages*. Basingstoke, UK: Macmillan 1995.

Bradshaw, Graham. *Shakespeare's Scepticism*. Ithaca, NY: Cornell University Press, 1987.

Brandom, Robert B., ed. *Rorty and His Critics*. Oxford: Blackwell, 2000.

Bristol, Michael. *Big-Time Shakespeare*. London: Routledge, 1996.

Bruns, Gerald L. "Stanley Cavell's Shakespeare." *Critical Inquiry* 16, no. 3 (Spring 1990): 612–32.

Cascardi, A. J. "'Disowning Knowledge': Cavell on Shakespeare." In Eldridge, *Stanley Cavell*, 190–205.

Cavell, Stanley. *Cities of Words: Pedagogical Letters on a Register of the Moral Life*. Cambridge, MA: Belknap Press of Harvard University Press, 2004.

———. *The Claim of Reason: Wittgenstein, Skepticism, Morality, and Tragedy*. New ed. Oxford: Oxford University Press, 1999.

———. *Conditions Handsome and Unhandsome: The Constitution of Emersonian Perfectionism*. Chicago: University of Chicago Press, 1991.

———. *Contesting Tears: The Hollywood Melodrama of the Unknown Woman*. Chicago: University of Chicago Press, 1990.

———. *Disowning Knowledge in Seven Plays of Shakespeare*. Updated ed. Cambridge: Cambridge University Press, 2003.

———. Foreword to *Philosophical Shakespeares*, edited by John Joughin, pp. x–xiv. London: Routledge, 2000.

———. *In Quest of the Ordinary: Lines of Skepticism and Romanticism*. Chicago: University of Chicago Press, 1988.

———. "An Interview with Stanley Cavell." With James Conant. In Fleming and Payne, *Senses of Stanley Cavell*, pp. 21–72.

———. "The *Investigations*' Everyday Aesthetics of Itself." In *The Cavell Reader*, edited by Stephen Mulhall, pp. 369–89. Oxford: Blackwell, 1996.

———. *Must We Mean What We Say? A Book of Essays*. New ed. Cambridge: Cambridge University Press, 2001.

———. *Philosophical Passages: Wittgenstein, Emerson, Austin, Derrida*. Oxford: Blackwell, 1995.

———. *Philosophy the Day after Tomorrow*. Cambridge, MA: Belknap Press of Harvard University Press, 2005.

———. *A Pitch of Philosophy: Autobiographical Exercises*. Cambridge, MA: Harvard University Press, 1994.

———. *Pursuits of Happiness: The Hollywood Comedy of Remarriage*. Cambridge, MA: Harvard University Press, 1981.

———. *The Senses of Walden*. Expanded ed. Chicago: University of Chicago Press, 1992.

———. *Themes Out of School: Effects and Causes*. Chicago: University of Chicago Press, 1984.

———. *This New Yet Unapproachable America: Lectures after Emerson after Wittgenstein*. Albuquerque, NM: Living Batch, 1989.

Conant, James. "Cavell and the Concept of America." In Goodman, *Contending with Stanley Cavell*, pp. 55–81.

Critchley, Simon. "Cavell's 'Romanticism' and Cavell's Romanticism." In Goodman, *Contending with Stanley Cavell*, pp. 37–54.

———. "Know Happiness—On Beckett." In *Very Little . . . Almost Nothing: Death, Philosophy, Literature*, pp. 141–80. London: Routledge, 1997.

Davis, Colin. *Critical Excess: Overreading in Derrida, Deleuze, Levinas, Žižek and Cavell*. Stanford, CA: Stanford University Press, 2010.

Deleuze, Gilles. *Gilles Deleuze: Essays Critical and Clinical*. Translated by Daniel W. Smith and Michael A. Greco. London: Verso, 1998.

———. "He Stuttered." In *Gilles Deleuze and the Theatre of Philosophy*, edited by Constantin V. Boundas and Dorothea Olkowski, translated by Constantin V. Boundas, pp. 23–29. London: Routledge, 1994.

de Man, Paul. *Allegories of Reading: Figural Language in Rousseau, Nietzsche, Rilke and Proust*. New Haven, CT: Yale University Press, 1979.

Desmond, William. "A Second *Primavera*: Cavell, German Philosophy, and Romanticism." In Eldridge, *Stanley Cavell*, 143–71.

Eaglestone, Robert. *Ethical Criticism: Reading After Levinas*. Edinburgh: Edinburgh University Press, 1997.

Eldridge, Richard. "Cavell on American Philosophy and the Idea of America." In Eldridge, *Stanley Cavell*, pp. 172–89.

———. "'A Continuing Task': Cavell and the Truth of Skepticism." In Fleming and Payne, *Senses of Stanley Cavell*, pp. 73–89.

———. "Introduction: Between Acknowledgement and Avoidance." In Eldridge, *Stanley Cavell*, pp. 1–14.

———, ed. *Stanley Cavell*. Cambridge: Cambridge University Press, 2003.

Emerson, Ralph Waldo. *Selected Writings*. Edited by Brooks Atkinson. New York: Random House Modern Library, 1968.

Esterhammer, Angela. *The Romantic Performative: Language and Action in British and German Romanticism*. Stanford, CA: Stanford University Press, 2000.

Fischer, Michael. *Stanley Cavell and Literary Skepticism*. Chicago: University of Chicago Press, 1989.

Fleming, Richard. "A Literary Understanding of Philosophy: Remarks on the Spirit of Cavell's *The Claim of Reason*." In Fleming and Payne, *Senses of Stanley Cavell*, pp. 284–310.

Fleming, Richard, and Michael Payne, eds. *The Senses of Stanley Cavell*. Lewisburg, PA: Bucknell University Press, 1989.

Foucault, Michel. "What Is an Author?" In *The Foucault Reader*, edited by Paul Rabinow, pp. 101–20. London: Penguin, 1991.

Goodman, Russell B. "Cavell and American Philosophy." In Eldridge, *Stanley Cavell*, pp. 100–117.

———, ed. *Contending with Stanley Cavell*. Oxford: Oxford University Press, 2005.

Hammer, Espen. *Stanley Cavell: Skepticisim, Subjectivity, and the Ordinary*. Cambridge: Polity, 2002.

Ibsen, Henrik. *A Doll's House*. In *The League of Youth; A Doll's House; The Lady from the Sea*, translated by Peter Watts, pp. 145–232. London: Penguin, 1965.

Iser, Wolfgang. *The Implied Reader: Patterns of Prose Communication from Bunyan to Beckett*. Baltimore: Johns Hopkins University Press, 1974.

Kaplan, E. Ann. Review of *Contesting Tears*, by Stanley Cavell. *Film Quarterly* 52, no. 1 (1998): 77–81.

Kenny, Anthony. Review of *The Claim of Reason*, by Stanley Cavell. *Times Literary Supplement*, 18 April 1980.

Lane, Richard, ed. *Beckett and Philosophy*. London: Palgrave, 2002.

Laugier, Sandra. "Rethinking the Ordinary: Austin *after* Cavell." In Goodman, *Contending with Stanley Cavell*, pp. 82–99.

Levinas, Emmanuel. *Difficult Freedom: Essays on Judaism*. Translated by Sean Hand. Baltimore: Johns Hopkins University Press, 1990.

———. *Totality and Infinity: An Essay on Exteriority*. Translated by Alphonso Lingis. Pittsburgh: Duquesne University Press, 1969.

Lyotard, Jean-François. *The Differend: Phrases in Dispute*. Translated by Georges Van Den Abbeele. Minneapolis: University of Minnesota Press, 1988.

Melville, Stephen. "Oblique and Ordinary: Cavell's Engagements of Emerson." *American Literary History* 5, no. 1 (1993): 172–92.

Miller, Arthur. *Death of a Salesman*. Harmondsworth, UK: Penguin, 1976.

———. "Introduction to the *Collected Plays*." In Miller, *Theatre Essays of Arthur Miller*, pp. 113–70.

———. "Morality and Modern Drama: Interview by Phillip Gelb." In Miller, *Theatre Essays of Arthur Miller*, pp. 195–214.

———. "The Nature of Tragedy." In Miller, *Theatre Essays of Arthur Miller*, pp. 8–11.

———. "1956 and All This." In Miller, *Theatre Essays of Arthur Miller*, pp. 86–109.

———. "On Social Plays." In Miller, *Theatre Essays of Arthur Miller*, pp. 51–68.

———. "The *Salesman* Has a Birthday." In Miller, *Theatre Essays of Arthur Miller*, pp. 12–15.

———. *The Theatre Essays of Arthur Miller*. Edited by Robert A. Martin. London: Methuen, 1994.

———. "Tragedy and the Common Man." In Miller, *Theatre Essays of Arthur Miller*, pp. 3–7.

Moi, Toril. *Henrik Ibsen and the Birth of Modernism: Art, Theater, Philosophy*. Oxford: Oxford University Press, 2006.

Mulhall, Stephen. Introduction to *The Cavell Reader*, edited by Stephen Mulhall, pp. 1–21. Oxford: Blackwell, 1996.

———. "On Refusing to Begin." In Goodman, *Contending with Stanley Cavell*, pp. 22–36.

———. *Stanley Cavell: Philosophy's Recounting of the Ordinary*. Oxford: Clarendon, 1999.

Muller, John P., and William J. Richardson, eds. *The Purloined Poe: Lacan, Derrida, and Psychoanalytic Reading*. Baltimore: Johns Hopkins University Press, 1988.

Newton, Adam Zachary. *Narrative Ethics*. Cambridge, MA: Harvard University Press, 1995.

Nietzsche, Friedrich. *Untimely Meditations*. Translated by R. J. Hollingdale. Cambridge: Cambridge University Press, 1983.

Noggle, James. "The Wittgensteinian Sublime." *New Literary History* 27, no. 4 (1996): 605–19.

Norris, Andrew, ed. *The Claim to Community: Essays on Stanley Cavell and Political Philosophy*. Stanford, CA: Stanford University Press, 2006.

Nussbaum, Martha. "Narrative Emotions: Beckett's Genealogy of Love." In *Love's Knowledge*, pp. 286–313. Oxford: Oxford University Press, 1990.

Ogden, Benjamin H. "What Philosophy Can't Say About Literature: Stanley Cavell and *Endgame*." *Philosophy and Literature* 33, no. 1 (2009): 126–38.

Payne, Michael, and Richard Fleming. "A Conversation with Stanley Cavell on Philosophy and Literature." In Fleming and Payne, *Senses of Stanley Cavell*, 311–21.

Peperzak, Adriaan T., Simon Critchley, and Robert Bernasconi, eds. *Emmanuel Levinas: Basic Philosophical Writings*. Bloomington: Indiana University Press, 1996.

Perloff, Marjorie. "Witt-Watt: The Language of Resistance / The Resistance of Language." In *Wittgenstein's Ladder: Poetic Language and the Strangeness of the Ordinary*, pp. 115–43. Chicago: University of Chicago Press, 1996.

Poe, Edgar Allan. *Selected Tales*. Edited by David van Leer. Oxford: World's Classics, 1998.

Rancière, Jacques. *Disagreement: Politics and Philosophy*. Translated by Julie Rose. Minneapolis: University of Minnesota Press, 1999.

Rhu, Lawrence F. *Stanley Cavell's American Dream: Shakespeare, Philosophy, and Hollywood Movies*. New York: Fordham University Press, 2006.

Robbins, Jill. *Altered Readings: Levinas and Literature*. Chicago: University of Chicago Press, 1999.

Roche, Mark W. "The Greatness and Limits of Hegel's Theory of Tragedy." In *A Companion to Tragedy*, edited by Rebecca Bushnell, pp. 51–67. Oxford: Blackwell, 2005.

Rorty, Richard. "Cavell on Skepticism." In Goodman, *Contending with Stanley Cavell*, pp. 10–21.

Rudrum, David. "Ethics, Justice, Translation: Lyotard on Wittgenstein." In *Translating Identity and the Identity of Translation*, edited by Madalena Gonzales and Francine Tolron, pp. 132–40. Cambridge: Cambridge Scholars Press, 2006.

———, ed. *Literature and Philosophy: A Guide to Contemporary Debates*. Basingstoke, UK: Palgrave-Macmillan, 2006.

Shakespeare, William. *The Complete Works*. Edited by Stanley W. Wells and Gary Taylor. Oxford: Oxford University Press, 2005.

Standish, Paul. "Education for Grown-Ups, a Religion for Adults: Scepticism and Alterity in Cavell and Levinas." *Ethics and Education* 2, no. 1 (2007): 73–91.

Stewart, Garrett. "The Avoidance of Stanley Cavell." In Goodman, *Contending with Stanley Cavell*, pp. 140–56.

Thoreau, Henry David. *Walden*. Edited by Stephen Fender. Oxford: World's Classics, 1999.

Tubridy, Derval. "The Absence of Origin: Beckett and Contemporary French Philosophy." In Rudrum, *Literature and Philosophy*, pp. 24–36.

Wheeler, Richard P. "Acknowledging Shakespeare: Cavell and the Claim of the Human." In Fleming and Payne, *Senses of Stanley Cavell*, 132–60.

Wimsatt, W. K., and Monroe C. Beardsley. "The Affective Fallacy." In *Twentieth Century Literary Criticism: A Reader*, edited by David Lodge, pp. 345–58. London: Longman, 1972.

———. "The Intentional Fallacy." In *Twentieth Century Literary Criticism: A Reader*, edited by David Lodge, pp. 333–45. London: Longman, 1972.

Wittgenstein, Ludwig. *Culture and Value*. Edited by G. H. von Wright in collaboration with Heikki Nyman. Translated by Peter Winch. Oxford: Basil Blackwell, 1980.

———. *Philosophical Investigations*. Translated by G. E. M. Anscombe. 2nd ed. Oxford: Basil Blackwell, 1958.

———. *Tractatus Logico-Philosophicus*. Translated by D. F. Pears and B. F. McGuiness. Introduction by Bertrand Russell. London: Routledge, 2001.

———. *Zettel*. Edited by G. E. M. Anscombe and G. H. von Wright. Translated by G. E. M. Anscombe. 2nd ed. Oxford: Basil Blackwell, 1981.

Wordsworth, William. Preface to *Lyrical Ballads*. In *The Prose Works of William Wordsworth*, edited by W. J. B. Owen and Jane Worthington Smyser, 1:118–59. Oxford: Clarendon, 1974.

———. *Poetical Works*. Edited by Thomas Hutchinson. London: Oxford University Press, 1971.

Index